Heritage
&Horizon

THE
BAPTIST
STORY
IN
CANADA

Dedication

*To Rose, whose uncommon understanding and
untiring patience over more than forty-five years —
particularly during the long period of research and
writing — made the work possible*

Heritage
&*Horizon*

THE
BAPTIST
STORY
IN
CANADA

Harry A. Renfree

Canadian
Baptist
Federation

Fédération
Baptiste
Canadienne

7185 Millcreek Drive
Mississauga, Ontario L5N 5R4

Canadian Cataloguing in Publication Data
Renfree, Harry A.
  Heritage and horizon

Bibliography: p.
Includes index.
ISBN 0-921796-00-5

1. Baptists – Canada – History. I. Canadian
Baptist Federation. II. Title.

BX6251.R46 1988   286'.171   C88-095226-1

COVER PHOTOS. Front: *Joseph Dimock*, Maritime "father" of the Baptist Church, from *History of the Baptists of the Maritime Provinces* by Edward Manning Saunders (Halifax: Press of John Burgoyne, Granville Street, 1902). Portrait a tribute to Joseph Dimock by the Chester church and its pastor, the Rev. R. Osgood Morse, M.A.; *Shoal Lake Baptist Church*, Man., Canadian Baptist Archives; *Mme Henrietta Feller*, Canadian Baptist Archives; *The Serving Seven* — top from left: Maria Armstrong, William Armstrong; second row, from left: Rufus and Mary Sanford, George Churchill; bottom, from left: Flora Eaton, Matilda Faulkner. **Back:** *Henry Alline on horseback*. Detail from Eva Scott's painting, hanging at Acadia Divinity College, Wolfville, N.S.; *Rev. John Kolesnikoff* (Russian Baptist pastor) with two "Macedonians" on Niagara Street, Toronto, Canadian Baptist Archives; *Band at Blind River Baptist Church, Ontario*, Canadian Baptist Archives; *Thomas Todhunter Shields* (photo portrait), Canadian Baptist Archives; *Watson Kirkconnell*, president of Acadia University, 1948–1964 (painted portrait), Acadia University Archives.

Text and Cover Design: Jack Steiner Graphic Design

Printed and bound in Canada
10 9 8 7 6 5 4 3 2 1

CONTENTS

FOREWORD

In this age of hi-tech, impersonal living, our individual identities are in danger of being submerged and our collective past is easily forgotten. History is therefore more important now than it has been in any previous time. It is a corrective that insists we are not defined as a number in a data bank, but as people who have lived in relation to time and circumstances. Our roots lie not in a code but in interactions with other people and in the flow of daily events.

Canadian Baptists have eagerly awaited the day that someone would produce a comprehensive, candid and faithful report of who we are and what major events helped shape our identity. This book can only strengthen Canadian Baptist relationships, as it brings to mind our common or similar beginnings.

The author of this history, Dr. Harry A. Renfree, has done us an immense service by giving us a history worth reflecting upon and one which ought to spur us on to glorify God in His church's mission. Well qualified to share his gifts as writer and interpreter, Dr. Renfree is a Canadian Baptist who has given lifelong leadership in the cause of Christ in this country.

My hope is that readers of this book will come to understand how Canadian Baptists have sought to serve Christ throughout their history and right up to the present day. May God's leading in this historic endeavour cause us to grieve over the errors of the past, to rejoice in the grace of God that has marked our joyful times and to firmly resolve to go forth in this day in our land to honour the Baptist name through true humility and servanthood.

R. C. Coffin
General Secretary–Treasurer
Canadian Baptist Federation

PREFACE

In a CBC radio interview, American author Maya Angelou remarked that "no one can know where he is going unless he knows where he's been." This volume is a modest attempt to provide one avenue for Canadian Baptists and their friends to find out "where they've been" — to trace a few sources, not simply for the sake of the exercise but to open new vistas on the future, from heritage to horizon.

Most of us are so busy with living in this frantic era that reflections about the past have been infrequent. Yet a subtle change is discernible. The subject of "roots" has become a media favourite, and the designers and marketers of geneological tables are doing a booming business. Popular in malls are the booths that offer portraits taken in "gay nineties" attire, and in many metropolitan areas across the land celebrations give residents and visitors an annual opportunity to re-live the days of yore in style.

Modern foundation-shaking is creating a particular nostalgia for that which once was. This phenomenon has not bypassed the Christian community. The Word of the Lord recognizes the human tendency to commemorate past events and encourages it. After Joshua led the ancient Israelites safely across the Jordan River into the Promised Land, he erected a cairn of twelve large stones, one for each tribe, to mark the place and the passage so that later generations would ask their meaning. They did and they do.

For much of the twentieth century, voices in Baptist leadership in Canada have been expressing both the hope and the expectation that someone would take up the task of recording the Canadian Baptist story. Except for limited monographs this has not happened, the reasons for this omission being many and varied.

A number of good regional records do exist. That of George E. Levy reflects upon the life of the denomination in the Maritime provinces before 1946, with works by Edward M. Saunders, Ingraham E. Bill and J. M. Cramp covering only earlier periods. In the West, Margaret

E. Thompson's monumental chronicle is dated 1974 and that of Joseph E. Harris two years later, while C. C. McLaurin's was completed half a century ago.

Apart from Stuart Ivison and Fred Rosser's history—a classic dealing with mid-Canada "beginnings" up to 1820—no overall view of Baptist endeavours in the central provinces has been undertaken—that is, until this very year. Murray J. S. Ford of McMaster Divinity College has just completed a long-awaited history of efforts in the two provinces of Ontario and Quebec, commissioned by the Convention of that name. So the time was ripe for an all-Canadian history, but no one was coming forward to write it. I have attempted this task in the hope that it will give readers a sense of how our past has shaped the Baptist denomination of today and how it may affect the future.

Many thousands of "new" Baptists have joined the ranks in Canada in recent years and they, together with those whose roots are deeper, may well experience moments of justifiable pride—as well as chagrin—in this story. There are high points, low points and many humanly ordinary.

In Canada nearly two and a half centuries of development are involved, internationally almost four. It was early in the 1600s that John Smyth and Thomas Helwys led their little band of persecuted English Separatists to Holland, where, convinced of the scriptural requirement and privilege of believer's Baptism, they re-established as the church that became the Baptist trailblazer.

After part of the Amsterdam congregation under Thomas Helwys moved back to the British Isles, a number of Baptist churches soon resulted. From them a few individual Baptists joined the freedom migration across the Atlantic to the present-day United States, where their movement was destined to grow vigorously, becoming almost dominant in the South. More than a century after these North American beginnings, the movement proceeded north from New England, first to Nova Scotia, then to Upper and Lower Canada (now Ontario and Quebec). The first churches in the West were established much later.

Expansions near and far have resulted in a total overall baptized membership of some 35,000,000 in the Baptist World Alliance. Baptists are now recognized as the largest Free Church body in the world—a statistic of no little encouragement to Canadian Baptists, who by themselves are a more limited, albeit healthy, minority in the general population. Their particular story is worth telling.

For helping me in this attempt to tell the tale, sincere gratitude is expressed to Dr. George A. Baxter of Regina, chairman of the former All-Canada Baptist Publications, who encouraged and, through his committee, endorsed the undertaking, and to the Canadian Baptist Federation for continuing that support to the publication stage. To Dr. J. K. Zeman of Acadia Divinity College appreciation is extended both for wise counsel and for generous hospitality, and to a New Brunswick friend, who characteristically wishes to remain anonymous, for giving seed money toward initial travel and research expenses. The Historical Committee of the United Baptist Convention of the Atlantic Provinces is also thankfully included for support in this regard.

A particular debt is owed Kathryn Dean for perceptive copy editing. Her meticulous and painstaking scrutiny of the manuscript and her skilful emendations have made an invaluable contribution to the work.

Invaluable assistance in research was lavishly provided both by Mrs. Patricia Townsend, Acadia University Archivist, and Miss Judith Colwell, Archivist of the Canadian Baptist Archives, McMaster Divinity College. The arduous task of typing the manuscript was shared by Mrs. Kay Kaine of Calgary and Mrs. Doris Kroeger of Victoria. Genuine thanks to all of these . . . and to many others who helped along the way.

This work, then, is offered with the hope and prayer that a glimpse of the past will cast its glow on the present and beyond to the greater glory of the future. In the time-tested expression of the One who prepared us to pray: "Thy kingdom come. Thy will be done in earth, as it is in heaven."

Harry A. Renfree
Victoria, British Columbia
May 1988

PART I

In the Beginning

I T WAS THE LATE 1700S. THE FULL religious liberty that had been granted the New England Planters when they moved to Nova Scotia was rudely snatched away with the coming of the Loyalists — who were arriving in greater numbers than the settlers who had arrived before the American Revolution. Soon a little Loyalist oligarchy had taken the reins of government, particularly in the recently formed province of New Brunswick. Favouring an established Church of England, they did not put great store by religious liberty for others.

At that time, "dissenters" (those dissenting from the Church of England), including Baptists, had to obtain a government licence in order to preach. However, the ruling was not about to stop young Edward Manning, who was to become one of the "fathers" of the Baptist cause in the Maritimes and indeed in Canada. Licence or no licence, God had called him and he was going to proclaim the Good News.

On one occasion Manning was preaching up the St. John River at Fredericton in the homes of Christians. Word soon reached the authorities and they directed a magistrate to have him arrested. A man of some integrity, the good Judge Allen decided to hear the preacher for himself. When he arrived at the house where the meetings were being held, the place was jammed: some listeners were even outside. In order to be heard, Manning was standing in the doorway, and the judge, unknown to the preacher, found a spot outside, near to the door.

Manning announced his text as James 5, the latter half of the ninth verse, which in the King James Version reads: "Behold, the judge standeth before the door." History doesn't record what Magistrate Allen thought of Manning's unwitting choice of a text — but he is reported to have said: "God forbid that I should lay violent hands upon that young man: I wish there were many more like him."

Manning continued to preach.

CHAPTER 1

Roots

*"The Magistrate is . . . to leave Christian religion free to
every man's conscience."*
—JOHN SMYTH

Liberated, but compelled by the Word of God; delivered, but constrained by the Lord Christ; priestless, but with every believer a priest; independent, but interdependent; freemen, but duty-bound both to God and to Caesar — such are the Baptists, who compose the world's largest Free Church fellowship and give leadership to the modern Believers' Church movement.[1] Canadian Baptists are among that company.

Some would venture to assert that it all began back in the days of the earthly ministry of Jesus, for Baptists profess to be New Testament Christians. That claim, however, properly belongs to the whole Church of Christ. Specific Baptist beginnings were in early seventeenth century Europe, although it may be suggested that there were in earlier times, even in the Dark Ages, small groups of like-minded believers. Such were the Waldenses, who appeared in France in the late twelfth century, spreading to Germany, Italy, Spain and Bohemia, and the English Lollards of John Wycliffe two centuries later, both pointing the way back to early Christianity.

The Anabaptists, the "radicals" of the Reformation, are in this spiritual succession. Dissatisfied with the limited changes which in their view Martin Luther and Huldreich Zwingli had supported, they demanded more severe surgery. The Lutherans had found it necessary to reject only those characteristics of Roman Catholicism that were specifically forbidden in scripture. The Reformed Churches took an additional step by retaining just those principles for which there was scriptural justification. The Anabaptists were disposed to abandon all that was not distinctly presented in the New Testament.

A number who had come to these convictions approached Zwingli, whose work was centred in the Swiss canton of Zurich and who of all the Reformation leaders was perhaps the most kindred in spirit. But even he was not prepared to go that far nor to cut the ties with a state that favoured his endeavours. Thus, early in the sixteenth century, Conrad Grebel, who had been a good friend and co-worker, and Felix Manz parted company with him, forming a group that became known as the Swiss Brethren. Their denial of infant baptism brought down the wrath of the Zurich church-state officials and Grebel and Manz were tried and sentenced to prison for life. While both managed to escape, Manz was recaptured and executed by drowning, a sadistic satire on the baptismal rite. A similar fate befell Balthasar Hubmaier, a priest of Waldshut who had been won to the cause, his death differing only in its mode—burning. The Protestant world was not ready for a thoroughgoing restitution of New Testament Christianity.

Yet the movement of the Anabaptists, or "re-baptizers," as their enemies disdainfully called them, did not easily die. It spread widely throughout Europe, but it never became a cohesive force, because of the spontaneous nature of its varied sources and the excesses of some of its proponents.[2] Modern-day Mennonites are the prominent inheritors of the Anabaptist tradition, issuing from the leadership of Menno Simons, a priest from West Friesland in the present-day Netherlands. Renouncing his Roman Catholic orders, he was baptized as a believer in about 1536, becoming an itinerant preacher and leader of the Anabaptists in northern Germany and Holland. Close to Baptists in doctrine and adjacent in polity, Mennonites have common cause with them in a number of areas of church life.

Freedom's Price

The movement termed Baptist has been described as an end-product of the Protestant Reformation,[3] the restoration of New Testament Christianity carried to its logical conclusion. Both the British Isles and continental Europe were involved in its birth.

While the Reformation was in full swing on the Continent, Henry VIII occupied the British throne and, determined to rid himself of papal jurisdiction, directed Parliament to make him head of the Church of England. He instituted few doctrinal changes, however, and there were many both within the state church and outside it who were dissatisfied with such a limited reform. When young Edward VI ascended the throne on his father's death in 1547, more significant changes began to occur, only to be rudely halted just six years later with Edward's early decease. His sister Mary came to the throne and reinstated the Roman Catholic as the national church and her cruel persecutions caused many hundreds of religious leaders to flee to the Continent, earning the queen the epithet "Bloody Mary."

John Smyth, Pathfinder

Happily for the Reformers, Mary's reign was also brief, her sister Elizabeth taking the Crown in 1558. Again the Protestant cause gained ascendancy and, what is significant from a Baptist point of view, many of the exiles returned, greatly influenced by their experiences with the European

Reformers. These were to form the nucleus of the emerging Puritan party, who wished to renew the Church of England from within. Neither Queen nor hierarchy were open to the desired reforms, however, and among the Puritans there appeared Separatists, who concluded that it was impossible to bring about the needed correctives within the established church structure.

Among these was John Smyth. It has been said that in his own life he epitomized the steps of the English Reformation, beginning as a son of the Church of England under orders of that church, and then progressively becoming Puritan, Separatist and Baptist.[4] He was the pathfinder.

A graduate of Cambridge, John Smyth was undoubtedly influenced by one of his tutors, the Puritan and later Separatist, Francis Johnson. Following his ordination, Smyth became lecturer to the city of Lincoln, an envied position from which he was ousted within two years for, it was said, bringing personalities into his preaching. Returning to his home town of Gainsborough, Smyth was asked to minister to the little Separatist congregation there. By 1608, however, continuing persecution of Separatists under James I, who had come to the throne in 1605 on the death of Elizabeth, had become intolerable, and Smyth sought freedom. Assisted by another Separatist, Thomas Helwys, he led his little congregation to Amsterdam, where they re-established themselves.

In Amsterdam, Smyth's church was not far away from another expatriate Separatist church, where his old Cambridge tutor, Francis Johnson, was pastor. It would seem that Smyth and Johnson had serious discussions about the nature of the church, and that these were so decisive for Smyth that he came to the view: "Infants are not to be baptized."[5] The year after his arrival in Holland, Smyth had come to a major decision on the matter. Striving to fashion a New Testament Church, he baptized himself, then Helwys and other members of the congregation.

So there was constituted in Amsterdam, Holland, in 1609, with membership composed of English exiles, what may be said to be the founding church of the Baptists. John Smyth was pastor, Thomas Helwys the associate.

General and Particular Baptists

In 1612, Helwys and a handful of the Amsterdam congregation, convinced that they ought not to have fled persecution, decided to return to England. At Spitalfield on the edge of London they immediately re-formed as the first Baptist church on British soil. Smyth and the others remained in Holland, but Smyth was stricken with tuberculosis and died the same year before reaching the age of forty-five.

The theological views of these first Baptists were predominantly those of Dutch theologian Jacobus Arminius, who stressed the individual's freedom to choose, general atonement (that is, Christ died for all, not just the "elect") and the possibility of falling from grace. Their congregations, which spread across southern England, became known as General Baptist churches. Later, in the fourth decade of the seventeenth century, other Baptist churches developed, more Calvinistic in doctrine, supporting limited, or particular, atonement. These came to be known as Particular Baptists, and the two strains advanced side by side until 1891 when they merged, continuing to the present under the aegis of the Baptist Union of Great Britain and Ireland.

A Martyr to Freedom

Immediately after returning to England, Thomas Helwys sounded the clarion call for the religious liberty that has become a distinctive mark of Baptists through the succeeding centuries. His book *A Short Declaration of the Mystery of Iniquity* expanded on concepts earlier enunciated by Smyth. "Our lord the king," he wrote, "is but an earthly king, and he hath no authority as a king but in earthly causes, and if the king's people be obedient and true subjects, obeying all human laws made by the king, our lord the king can require no more: for men's religion to God is betwixt God and themselves; the king shall not answer for it, neither may the king judge between God and man."[6]

W. K. Jordan, the well-known British historian, says of his contribution:

> Helwys gave to religious toleration the finest and fullest defense which it had ever received in England. Not only was he one of the first men in England to conclude that persecution even of the most serious spiritual error was in itself iniquitous, but he was the founder in England of a sect which was never to depart widely from the principles which he had enunciated. He gave the magistrate the fullest authority in civil matters, but declared that so far as the Church was concerned he had no greater power than any other layman.[7]

The eminent American church historian, Kenneth Scott Latourette, echoes this tribute in his monumental seven-volume work, *A History of the Expansion of Christianity.*[8]

Helwys had spelled out all too clearly the principle of religious liberty and its corollary, the separation of church and state. The royal government quickly accepted the challenge and thrust Helwys into prison, where he died, a martyr to the cause of freedom.

Pilgrims and Strangers

It was this vision of freedom which summoned the Separatists and Puritans and then the first Baptists to the shores of North America. For his own reasons, James I encouraged the aspiration. Earlier, at a conference involving both Church of England and non-conformist ministers, the king had remarked to the bishops: "If once you were out and they in, I know not what would become of my supremacy, for No Bishop, No King." His decision was harshly unequivocal: "I will make them conform themselves, or else I will harry them out of the land, or else do worse."[9] He did just that, exiling and imprisoning the non-conformists, and his son, Charles I, carried on the tradition, aided and abetted by the latter's adviser, Archbishop Laud.

At the same time that John Smyth was establishing his congregation in Amsterdam, another congregation, from Scrooby, England, had also moved to Holland, settling in Leyden, The group had enjoyed close fellowship with his own Gainsborough congregation. Choosing not to return to live in England, many of them decided instead to go to the New World and on September 6, 1620, they joined other English emigrants to set sail for North America on the now legendary *Mayflower.* They settled on Cape Cod in what is now the state of Massachusetts. Such was the beginning of Plymouth Colony, which complemented the earlier Brittish settlement in Virginia. The first Baptists were yet to arrive.

A New Establishment

While it is likely that John Smyth had considerable influence on the Pilgrim Fathers [10] through John Robinson, it is also evident that the Pilgrims' Separatism had been modified by the time they set out, without Robinson, for the New World.[11] There the hardships and dangers of an untamed land and the arrival of ever-increasing numbers of settlers, many of them Puritan, tended to move them closer to their more dominant brethren.

Large numbers of Puritans made new homes around Massachusetts Bay in 1629 and 1630 and apparently intended to retain some Church of England connections. Instead they shifted in the direction of their Separatist kinsmen when they immediately inducted two of their own pastors by the laying on of hands, rather than waiting for a bishop to appoint a minister. They also tended toward a more self-governing polity. It has, indeed, been suggested that they went farther than they had initially meant to go, for without admitting their separation from the Church of England Establishment, they began referring to their churches as congregations and became known as Congregationalists.[12]

Out of these developments there emerged a peculiarly New England denomination, neither Separatist nor Anglican, but with some of the features of each. The Congregational Church of early New England, while supporting autonomy of the local church, became a virtual Establishment, and was referred to as the Church of the Standing Order, a situation which they had fled England to disclaim. The difference: they were now the Established, envisaging a Holy Commonwealth in New England as Calvin had in Geneva and Zwingli in Zurich. Unfortunately, those who had demanded tolerance became intolerant themselves.

"Whipped, Fyned and Banished"

As early as May 1631, the general court of Massachusetts Bay voted that in future "noe man shelbe admitted to the freedome of this body polliticks,

6

but such as are members of some of the churches within the lymitts of the same" — meaning, of course, Congregational churches, for at that time at Massachusetts Bay there were no others.[13] William Blackstone, a Puritan clergyman whose settlement on the shores of Massachusetts Bay, soon to be called Boston, had predated the arrival of the main body of Puritans in 1629–30 by six or seven years, was not thrilled with the "New England Way," as this church-state synthesis came to be called. He moved away, giving as his reasons: "I came from England because I did not like the lord-bishops; but I can't join with you, because I would not be under lord-brethren."[14]

Philip Ratcliffe was less favoured in the means of his departure. "For uttering mallitious & scandallous speeches against the government & the church of Salem," he was on June 14, 1631, sentenced to be "whipped, have his ears cut off, fyned 40ᵗ, & banished out of the lymitts of this jurisdiction."[15] There was more than a little truth in Artemus Ward's tongue-in-cheek remark that the Puritans came to America "to worship God according to their own consciences, and to prevent other people from worshipping him according to theirn."[16]

Pride and Prejudice

It was into this inhospitable environment that the initial handful of Baptists came, soon to be led by a man whose background bears more than a little resemblance to that of the pastor of the founding Baptist church in Europe, John Smyth. Like Smyth, Roger Williams was a Cambridge graduate, trained for the ministry of the Church of England. His Puritan views, further diluted with Separatist tendencies, made the outlook for him in Archbishop Laud's England most unpromising, so he emigrated.

Providence Founded

Arriving at Boston in 1631, Williams was welcomed as "a godly minister," but was soon at odds with the leaders of the theocracy. Declining the position of teacher in the Boston church because it had not at that time unequivocally separated from the Church of England, he served in Plymouth, where he found a more receptive climate for his ideas. After two years, he moved to Salem, but his ministry there was destined to come to a quick end. Summoned before the general court in Boston because of his sentiments concerning the separation of church and state and his support of Indian land claims, he was ordered to "departe out of this jurisdiction within six weekes" for having "broached & dyvulged dyvers news & dangerous opinions, against the aucthoritie of magistrates. . . ." That was in the fall of 1634 and, relenting just a little, the court permitted him to stay in Salem until the spring if he remained inactive. For Williams this was hardly possible and he was soon very much in evidence again, expressing his views. The magistrate then decided to act immediately, planning to put him on the first ship back to England.

Before that decision was carried out, however, Williams heard of it and though it was mid-winter, fled to the south with a few companions until they reached Naragansett Bay. There, in an action most unusual for the times, he *purchased* land from the Indians and "founded Providence as 'a shelter for persons distressed in conscience.'" Later the settlement was to be "united with other settlements as the colony of Rhode Island on the basis of complete religious liberty and full civil democracy."[17]

Roger Williams then took another step similar to one taken by John Smyth. Through his own study of the scriptures, and undoubtedly influenced by some English Baptists who arrived in Providence seeking sanctuary, he moved beyond the Separatist to the Baptist position. With no minister at hand, Williams was baptized by Ezekiel Holliman, who had been a member of his Salem church. Williams then baptized ten others, and thereupon founded at Providence in 1639 the first Baptist church in North America.

Infant Baptism Only

Later a church was formed at Newport, Rhode Island, under Dr. John Clarke, a British physician, its records as a Baptist church going back to 1648. Further expansion was not rapid, since apart from the Rhode Island Colony, the climate of New England was anything but conducive to this (so-termed) radical faith. Indeed, to ensure their continuing control, as well as to provide for the support of their ministry, as early as 1638 the Massachusetts authorities enacted an edict proclaiming that "every inhabitant who should not voluntarily contribute to all charges, both in church and Commonwealth proportionately, according to his ability, should be compelled thereto by assessment"—a return to English ecclesiastical law that was in force long before the Reformation.[18] Baptists in New England were not to be fully exempt from this religious tax for well over a century.

Even more specifically, the general court of Massachusetts decreed in 1644 that anyone opposing the baptism of infants would be sentenced to banishment, for the denial of the efficacy of that rite threatened the very fabric of the church-state relationship in the Holy Commonwealth. The listing of an infant's baptism in the church records also marked the recognition of a new citizen in the state and was a sign of deference to the state's authority. The same year, Thomas Painter of Hingham was publicly whipped for refusing to have his child baptized, and later Henry Dunster, the able president of Harvard, the colony's first university, was forced from his position for espousing believer's baptism.

While visiting in Lynn, Massachusetts, in 1651, Dr. John Clarke, the physician who was the founding pastor of the Newport church in Rhode Island, Obadiah Holmes, later to be his successor, and John Crandal held a meeting in the home of an aged friend who was unable to travel the great distance to attend church in Rhode Island. Two constables interrupted the service to arrest the visiting Baptists. After being imprisoned at Boston for two weeks, they were brought into court. Holmes and Clarke were fined thirty and twenty pounds, respectively, and Crandal five; the lash was the penalty for defaulting. Each refused to pay. Without his consent, some of Clarke's friends paid his fine, and Crandal was ordered to appear before the next court. Holmes paid a much greater price. Imprisoned for another two months, he was then given thirty stripes "in such an unmerciful manner, that in many days, if not some weeks, could take no rest but as he lay upon his knees and elbows. . . ."[19] At the trial Governor Endicott exclaimed: "You have denied 'Infants Baptism', and deserve death," adding that he "would not have such trash brought into his jurisdiction."[20]

Once again, "just as the blood of the early Christian martyrs was the seed of the Church, so the blood of Obadiah Holmes served to fertilize New England soil for the raising up of other Baptists."[21] Although growth was not striking during the remaining years of the seventeenth century, there being a total of but ten Baptist churches in New England by 1700, a small sturdy plant had been rooted and the new century witnessed major development.

Elsewhere, too, the movement was spreading, initially in Pennsylvania and New Jersey, where religious liberty provided more welcome surroundings. By 1707 a Philadelphia Baptist Association of five churches had been formed, followed by endeavours in the South. Soon after the mid-eighteenth century enough churches had been founded that associations were set up in South and North Carolina and eastern Virginia. All pre-dated the first New England association, which, significantly, was formed in Rhode Island in 1767.*

The Great Awakening

As Baptist churches extended south and west, in the northeast important developments were taking place which had major implications for what is now the nation of Canada and in particular for Canadian Baptists. Beginning in the 1720s, New England and some of the other Thirteen Colonies became the setting for a sequence of revivals which have become known as the Great Awakening. As Latourette records, Christianity in North America experienced phenomenal expansion because of the Awakening, and revival became a major characteristic in the spread of the Christian faith in the latter part of the colonial period and right into the nineteenth century. Influenced by the Pietist and Moravian revival in

---

*The Baptist association was (and still is today) the connectional body of churches nearest to the local church. Conventions and Unions are made up of associations, and the local church enters a Convention/Union by way of an association. Societies, which may or may not have spun off from associations, were generally composed of individual dues-paying members, while associations were usually made up of church-appointed representatives.

Europe and the Evangelical awakening of the Wesleys and Whitefield in Britain, the movement still had a strong North American flavour.[22]

Edwards and Whitefield

The conditions for revival were optimal. The Puritan-to-Congregational dream of a Holy Commonwealth had dimmed with the passing of a full century; the state-church ties were slipping. In order to retain even a semblance of the old unity, the authorities had adopted the Half-way Covenant in 1662, which gave those baptized as infants membership in the church — and thus full civil rights — although they were purportedly not allowed to take communion unless they showed evidence of regeneration. In practice, this soon resulted in keeping from the Lord's table only those whose lives were disreputable, all in all providing occasion for general spiritual laxity. Formality and deadness characterized many of the churches.

A Dutch Reformed pastor, Theodorus Frelinghuysen, is generally credited with lighting the first revival fire in New Jersey, beginning in the Raritan Valley. Contact with Frelinghuysen sparked similar results through the youthful Gilbert Tennent, a Presbyterian minister in the town of New Brunswick, also in New Jersey. Then, in 1734, a separate revival broke out in Northampton, Massachusetts, through the preaching of the renowned Jonathan Edwards, a Congregationalist. These were complemented by no fewer than seven visits by George Whitefield of England, a powerful evangelist who added mightily to the impact. Whitefield preached to thousands, from New England in the North to Georgia in the South in an early outreach by the new Methodist movement.

New Light

The Great Awakening was transdenominational both in its leadership and in its impact. The still meagre numbers of Baptists did not actually play a major role in the Awakening, but they benefited greatly from it. "In the term of two or three years thirty or forty thousand souls were born into the family of heaven in New England," wrote Trumbull in his *History of Connecticut*.[23] In addition, hosts of churchgoers experienced deep renewal.

Those so greatly impressed and changed by the revivals came to believe that theirs was a "new light" experience through the Holy Spirit, and the designation "New Lights" began to be applied to them, as opposed to their fellows, who supported a continuance of the Standing Order — the "Old Lights." The latter were critical of the emotionalism and deplored the excesses of the sweeping evangelistic outreach. Tensions developed in the churches, sometimes resulting in division, particularly as the New Lights showed that they were determined to return to strict New Testament principles, including the admission to membership only of those who were regenerated.

Such determination tended to move numbers of the New Light Congregationalists to the Baptist position, and in at least nineteen instances, whole congregations adopted Baptist principles.[24] Mainly through such accessions, between 1740 and 1775 twenty-two new Baptist churches were formed in Massachusetts alone. Nine years later the total number of Baptist churches there was seventy-three, with membership over three thousand.[25]

The congregations coming out of the Awakening were largely Separate Baptists, at first keeping themselves apart from the earlier Regular churches, whom they also criticized for laxness in the standards of church membership. They also carried over the New Light emphasis on personal inspiration through the Holy Spirit, and thus viewed with suspicion any broader church authority, associational or other.[26] Both the Separate and the Regular Baptists expanded south in mission work, where eventually they joined to become a powerful, expanding force on the frontier. But the Baptists had yet to go north, to a land with which they were still linked, but from which they would soon be parted politically.

Up to this point, their story has been the quest for freedom of conscience — religious liberty, it has been called — the right of every human being to worship (or not to worship) God as he or she desires, without either direction or hindrance from any authority other than God Himself. Such conditions, they averred, would prevail only in a free church within a free state or, put negatively, through the separation of church and state.

In 1872 the United States Congress placed a memorial of Roger Williams in the National Capitol, Washington. On that occasion Senator Anthony, representing Congress, said of him: "Roger Williams did not merely lay the foundation of religious freedom, he constructed the whole edifice, in all its impregnable strength, and in all its imperishable beauty. . . . He did not enquire if his name would survive a generation. In his vision of the future, he saw mankind emancipated from the thralldom of priestcraft, from the blindness of bigotry, from the cruelties of intolerance."[27]

The fullness of such a vision had not been realized, even by 1760, in many of the British colonies of North America. The charter given to the Massachusetts Bay Colony in 1691 provided only for religious tolerance, not freedom. The basic resolution of the long struggle did not come until the enactment of the American Constitution and the Bill of Rights following the American Revolution. In this process New England and Virginia Baptists played a significant role, the latter exacting a promise of backing from the first president himself, George Washington.[28]

Meanwhile, the vision had drawn some of them to Nova Scotia.

CHAPTER 2

An Inviting Climate

"I have a message from God to deliver, and I am in haste to deliver it."
— *EBENEZER MOULTON*

In 1760 the British Colony of Nova Scotia was in traumatic transition. That year also marked the arrival of the Reverend Ebenezer Moulton, "the ubiquitous Baptist evangelist from South Brimfield,"[1] Massachusetts. Although the long battles between Britain and France for control of the northern half of North America had halted with the capitulation of Louisbourg, Quebec and Montreal, the Treaty of Paris was not to be signed by the two powers until 1763. Moulton's countrymen were to be the wave of the future, emigrants from the British colonies to the south still being rare.

The End of an Era

Although the colony of Nova Scotia had been legally British since 1713, it was almost the middle of the century before Britain began to colonize it or prepare for its defence. But when the powerful fortress of Louisbourg was restored to France in 1748, the British decided to fortify the magnificent harbour at Chibucto. So it was that Halifax was founded in 1749, under Colonel Edward Cornwallis, who was appointed first governor of Nova Scotia.

Stalemate Halted

British sovereignty in the area was by no means assured, however, as 13,000 French-speaking Acadians still lived there. The British had been trying to deal with this perceived threat to their sovereignty ever since the signing of the Treaty of Utrecht, about forty years earlier, which declared that "the subjects of the said King [of France] may have liberty to remove themselves within a year to any other place, as they shall think fit . . . ."[2] Few had left, and in the intervening years the British vacillated as to whether they should compel the Acadians to take the oath of allegiance. Finally, Nova Scotia's second governor, Charles Lawrence, took action, deciding with his council in 1755 that the Acadians must give absolute allegiance to Britain or leave immediately. Many refused, and so in that same year, the British expelled seven thousand French colonists from the shores of the Bay of Fundy.

From the vantage point of centuries later, the action appears to have been unduly harsh and cruel. It was; those were harsh, cruel days, when an English scalp was worth a hundred livres. It is something of a commentary on the times that France made no protest over the deportation, obviously judging that Great Britain was justified in an action affecting subjects under British jurisdiction.[3]

The outbreak of the Seven Years War in Europe in 1756, with Britain and France again on opposing sides, once more had repercussions on North America, this time major ones. Montcalm, the recently arrived commander in New France had early victories in what is now central Canada, but the British had built up strong naval and troop contingents. Louisbourg was captured for the second time in 1758 and, with it, the Isles Royale and St. Jean (Cape Breton and Prince Edward Island, respectively). The fall of that stronghold opened the way to the fortress of Quebec and to Montreal, and these fell in succession in 1759 and 1760, bringing an effective end to French sovereignty in North America.

Of Plans and Planters

With the loss of the deported Acadians, Governor Lawrence was faced with the need for large numbers of settlers especially in western Nova Scotia. A good number of German Protestants had already been persuaded to cross the Atlantic to the colony in the early 1750s, settling along the Atlantic shore, where many became fishermen.[4] The major need, however, was for farmers to work the abandoned Acadian lands. The availability of these homesteads was advertised in the Thirteen Colonies, attracting considerable interest.

Nova Scotia had long been viewed as a possible area for New England expansion, but up to this point the idea had not been feasible, since the French fortress of Louisbourg was there and the best farm lands were occupied by the Acadians. With the changed situation, emigration became attractive to the British colonists to the south. Members of the Standing Order and their more Separatist countrymen, however, were somewhat reluctant to move. Neither liked the overarching Anglican power in the colony—the former because they would have to forfeit their own prerogatives, the latter because they would hardly trade limited shackles for ones even more oppressive. So, before agreeing to hazard their future in yet another frontier territory, the New Englanders demanded democratic rights not then granted in Nova Scotia.

To satisfy them, the British government in 1758 directed a recalcitrant governor to summon an elected assembly, this becoming the first such representative body in Canada.[5] The next year, Lawrence issued a proclamation which became known as the Charter of Nova Scotia, ensuring that "Protestants dissenting from the Church of England . . . shall have free liberty of conscience, and may erect and build meeting houses for public worship, and may choose and elect Ministers for the carrying on of Divine Service and administration of the sacrament . . . and all such Dissenters shall be excused from any rates or taxes to be made or levied for the support of the established Church of England."[6]

The reaction was swift, and it is estimated that as many as eighteen hundred "Planters" (farmers) reached Nova Scotia before the end of 1760, a total of between five and six thousand over the next few years.[7] Many were Congregationalists — both "New Light" and "Old Light"; others were Baptists. The latter, especially, were attracted by the promise of full religious liberty in the Charter.

Of those times, Arthur R. M. Lower, distinguished Canadian historian and scholar, writes: "These New Englanders, from the newer towns, had been washed by the wave of religious revivalism then sweeping the back country from Massachusetts to Georgia. . . . In New England, the more fervent areas became Baptist. It was this denomination that overtook the settlers in Nova Scotia. Today, the Annapolis Valley is one of the strongholds of the Baptist church. . . . When asked about their origins, it must not be suggested that they are 'Loyalist'; they are of an older breed: 'pre-Loyalist', they will proudly say."[8]

Trailblazer

It was with the vanguard of the Planters — these pre-Loyalists — that Ebenezer Moulton came. His is the double distinction of being the first Baptist minister to settle and serve in Canada, and to have planted the first indigenous church of the denomination in the land.

Connecticut-born Moulton had dissent in his veins. According to Isaac Backus, pioneer American historian, one of his forebears had been a member of the first house of representatives in Boston in 1634, who had become "a sufferer from the ruling party three years after."[9] In 1736 Ebenezer Moulton, together with ten others, petitioned the authorities in Massachusetts colony for exemption from parish religious taxes on the grounds that they were Baptist. Five years later he was ordained as pastor of the Brimfield church in southwestern Massachusetts, the church that had been established the very month he had led the protest against the payment of parish rates.[10] He was to be a fellow sufferer for his faith more than a century after his forefather, Robert Moulton, for in 1749 he was seized at Sturbridge as a "vagabond" and thrown into prison for baptizing over sixty persons there, including the pastor of the Separate church.[11]

Obviously an effective evangelist, Moulton, like so many of his times travelled widely in sharing the gospel. On one of those itineraries, he ministered in the parish of Titicut, having such an influence on the parish's Congregational minister — the same Isaac Backus mentioned above — that Backus reconsidered his own theological position and became a Baptist. This decision was to have far-reaching implications, for Backus became the recognized and honoured historian of New England Baptists, and compaigned for religous liberty during the American Revolution.[12]

Moulton's decision to emigrate to Nova Scotia was not without its difficulties. Hampered by the early Baptist antipathy to a "hireling ministry," like so many others he had to find paying work in addition to that of his Brimfield pastorate. Becoming a merchant, he enjoyed considerable success for a period, especially during the early part of the Seven Years War. Seemingly generous to a fault, he subscribed out of his profits a major portion of the funds needed to build a new Brimfield meeting house.

Moulton's fortunes changed, however, as many others scrambled to reap the benefits of the war economy. With greatly expanded competition and the recession which followed, he found himself incapable of discharging all his liabilities — at a time when there were no bankruptcy statutes to protect the insolvent. His northward move may well have been expedited in the hope of finding a more secure financial climate. In any event, after about a decade of significant service in Nova Scotia, he was able to go back to his homeland with the approval of his creditors, where "he was esteemed among his own people, until he died there in 1783."[13]

Upon arriving in Nova Scotia in 1760 Moulton first settled in Chebogue, near Yarmouth, where he was given a magistrate's commission and appointed to assign lands to the new immigrants.[14] He soon seized every available opportunity to preach the gospel, his prime calling, and is known to have held services frequently at Chebogue, Yarmouth and Barrington. But it was in the Annapolis Valley that he made his most enduring contribution.

The year that Moulton arrived also witnessed the influx of the largest single group of New England settlers: twenty-two ships bearing Planters and their families from towns in Eastern Connecticut docked at Horton landing (now Wolfville) to take up abandoned Acadian farms.[15] It was among these and later arrivals that the evangelist found his opportunity.

There are indications that Moulton might have visited and preached in Horton in 1763 or earlier, but it is certain that he was ministering there in 1765 when he founded a church. A letter from "the Baptist church of Christ" in Horton, dated October 27, 1771, to Elder John Davis of Boston reads in part:

> ... although some of us were members of an Imbodied Church in New England yet we were several years in these parts without the "Dispensation of the Gospel among us, until Divine Providence order'd that Elder Moulton should visit us in the year 1765 who tarried with us some time During which time it pleased the Lord in a very Wonderfull and powerfull Manner Convincing and Converting many souls as we trust and Believe to the true Faith in Jesus Christ; After which & during the stay of the said Moulton with us we thought it our duty to Join ourselves in Solemn Convenant. And accord-

ingly those who were not Baptized in New England were here Baptized and did sign Covenant together — Hence we call ourselves the Baptis Church of Christ in Horton in Kings County — Some time the latter part of the year 1767 it pleased the Lord to Remove from us said Elder Moulton and we were for a short time Destitute of an underShepherd — Soon after which it was the Divine Pleasure to favour us with a Visitation of Elder Joseph Reed from Cumberland, who administered the Gospell with us untill Death Removed him from this life in October 1770. Since which time we have Continued assembling ourselves together and Indeavour through Divine assistance to keep the worship of God according to the best Gifts bestow'd on us — But at present we have no minister among us. . . .

The writers go on to ask Elder Davis if he knows of a possible pastor and, if so, to "ingage him to come among us."[16]

Among the obvious facts confirmed by this letter are the effectiveness of Ebenezer Moulton as an evangelist in Horton in 1765. Many were converted and several baptized; a Baptist church was established, likely the same year, Moulton remaining as pastor until late 1767. It is also evident that the church continued for at least six years, probably longer, and formed the nucleus of a renewed church in 1778 — the Horton, now Wolfville, Baptist Church, which has had an unbroken history from that date to the present. In its initial formulation this church was the first indigenous Baptist church in Canada; in its renewal, the oldest continuing church.

A Flickering Flame

Horton is termed the first "indigenous" church, for another congregation has a slightly earlier, though more unusual, claim. It was in 1763 that thirteen members of three New England churches — Second Swansey, Rehoboth and Providence — formed themselves into a church in Swansey, Massachusetts. One of their number, the Reverend Nathan Mason, was pastor. As a group they sailed to the head of the Bay of Fundy and settled in "the Township of SacVill,"[17] then in Nova Scotia, now in New Brunswick, near the present Middle Sackville. The little company remained there until 1771 when the church dissolved and most of the members returned to Massachusetts where they re-formed again in present-day Cheshire.[18] A number of converts were won during their Sackville area stay, but no record remains of them after the dissolution of the church. Some undoubtedly joined the New Light congregation formed by Henry Alline about a decade later.

The Six-Principle Congregation

As in Great Britain, early Baptists in the colonies were divided into two basic groupings, distinguished by differences in doctrines concerning the sovereignty of God and the free will of man. The Regular, or Particular, Baptists placed major emphasis on the position held by Calvin — that is,

God's sovereignty. His "election" of the called, His irresistible grace and the perseverence of the chosen. Others were more inclined to Arminian views—those which stressed the individual's freedom to choose, general atonement and the possibility of falling from grace. In the New England Colonies, the Arminian group called themselves General Six-Principle churches, as they emphasized six principles described in Hebrews 6:1 and 2: repentance from dead works, faith toward God, baptism, the laying on of hands, the resurrection of the dead and eternal judgment. Nathan Mason and his Sackville congregation were of the Six-Principle, Arminian persuasion, as was the church by which they were commissioned before leaving Massachusetts, Second Baptist of Swansey.[19]

The "Separate" Congregation

Many of the Baptists in New England who were the products of the Great Awakening were more moderately Calvinistic than their earlier Particular/ Regular brethren, but were not of the Six-Principle strain. For a time, a number of them went under the name Separate Baptists. A church of that strain, according to the available evidence, grew up in Sackville alongside Nathan Mason's Six-Principle congregation. It developed out of a revival in the township beginning in 1766, and one of its converts was Joseph Reed, who became pastor of the Horton church after Ebenezer Moulton left.

Elder Joseph Winsor, pastor of the Separate Baptist Church of Gloucester, Rhode Island, visited Sackville in 1767 for nearly eight weeks, writing to Isaac Backus in September 17 of that year that "the Lord hath been pleased to remarkably visit that town by converting Grace and there is a church gathered there since I went down of thirty-seven members." Winsor also noted that the church had issued a call to Nathan Round of Rehoboth, Massachusetts, also a Separate Baptist, to become their pastor.[20] Round had been duly ordained by the Separate Baptist Church of Gloucester "to go labor in Nova Scotia with the people who went from these parts to settle there."[21] The Horton letter of 1771 confirms the presence of this second Sackville church and the arrival of Round as their pastor, noting: "There is also a Baptis Church in the Town of Sackville in Cumberland County under the care of Elder Nathan Round, who have been Regularly Imbodied for this several years past."[22]

When Elder Round left Sackville sometime between 1771 and 1777,[23] the church, like the Six-Principle church at Sackville, passed out of existence. Joseph Crandall, who visited the town at the turn of the century, later wrote of the experience: "I found a people who received me with open hearts and hands. There were many 'New Lights' but I think there is only one in the whole Parish who had been immersed."[24]

At Horton, following the death in 1770 of their second pastor, Elder Joseph Reed, the Baptist church carried on pastorless for an unknown period. Kirkconnell conjectures that in "a time-honoured North American back country practice of the time" services were carried on by the deacons for several years.[25] In any event, Moulton's converts were interested enough to recovenant the church in 1778, giving it an unbroken history to the present and earning it the distinction of being "the grandmother of Canadian Baptist churches."[26]

A Composite Congregation

The 1771 Horton letter to Elder Davis of Boston also noted that there were "a Considerable Number of Baptist in the Town of Newport in this County under the pastoral care of Elder Shubael Dimock."[27] It was not until 1799 that a fully Baptist church was to be established at Newport, near Windsor, but services of a mixed congregation were held there from the early 1760s until 1776, when a church was formed, still involving both Baptists and Congregationalists.

The pioneer leaders at Newport were Shubael Dimock and his son Daniel. A native of Mansfield, Connecticut, Shubael was stirred by the Great Awakening in New England and was drawn to the Separatists among the Congregational churches. Under persecution, he moved his family to Nova Scotia in the early wave of Planter migration. Daniel, then twenty-four, had become convinced of believer's baptism, but in deference to his father had not yet followed through on his decision.

Daniel Dimock's reluctance faded with the arrival of John Sutton, who baptized him during his stay in Newport. Sutton, a Baptist minister from Cape May, New Jersey, visited the area in 1763, accompanied by James Manning, the first president of the Baptist Rhode Island College —now Brown University.[28] Manning soon returned, but Sutton stayed in the vicinity of Newport for a while, at some point being joined by his brother James, also a Baptist minister. The movements of the Sutton brothers in Nova Scotia are not well documented, but there is some evidence that they returned for a second visit in the mid-1700s.[29] John Payzant, a contemporary, alludes to them briefly in his journal, in writing of a number of New England ministers who visited the colony in the early 1760s. Payzant's terse reference also includes an obvious mention of Ebenzer Moulton, whose name he misspells: "One E. Morton came to Horton preached the Gospel Some experienced under his preaching. Likewise John Sutton and his brother James preached at Newport and Falmouth, but they did not stay long in the province."[30]

By 1775 Shubael Dimock had become convinced of the Baptist position on believer's baptism and was that year immersed by his son Daniel. The two men carried on an effective lay ministry at Newport for many years, usually taking turns preaching. Daniel's eldest son, Joseph, born in Newport, was to become one of the true "fathers" of the Baptist denomination of the eastern seaboard.

Men like Ebenezer Moulton, Nathan Mason, and Shubael and Daniel Dimock were pioneers in planting Baptist churches in the Maritimes. As John Smyth had been drawn to Holland and Roger Williams had been attracted to North America, Moulton and the other Planters came to the Maritimes with the hope of finding religious freedom. Although most of the new arrivals were Congregationalists, both Old Light and New Light, it was the Baptists who, in Lower's previously recorded words, "overtook the settlers in Nova Scotia."

The story of that overtaking follows.

CHAPTER 3

The Nova Scotia Awakening and the Awakener

*"The Baptist Tabernacle is not always a graceful structure but at least we
say this of it, that the twin pillars are evangelism and liberty."*
— *H. WHEELER ROBINSON*

If religious liberty was the promise that attracted the first Baptists to
Canada's east coast, it was concern for the souls of men that soon moved
them out from their new pioneer homesteads to tramp through the
backwoods of the Maritimes. The liberty wherewith Christ has made men
free was a treasure not only to be cherished but to be shared. They were
soon about the sharing.

It was not an impressive base from which to begin. Once the two
Sackville churches disappeared in the early 1770s, no Baptist work was
visible there again for a quarter-century. Both Ebenezer Moulton and
Nathan Mason, the only ordained ministers at the time, returned to
Massachusetts: Moulton to Brimfield, where he remained until his death
in 1783, and Mason to Lanesborough (his name is found listed in the
"Annual Register of the Baptist denomination in North America" as late
as 1790 as pastor of the Lanesborough church).[1] To complicate matters
further, there were already serious political stirrings in New England
which would soon push deeply held loyalties to the severest test.

Reconstitution

When the decision was made to recovenant Horton Baptist Church in
1778, the ten participants were unable to call on any neighbouring Baptist
minister to assist — there was none. So, demonstrating the tenor of the
times, they invited Henry Alline, New Light evangelist of Newport-
Falmouth to help them in the service and in the ordination of the man
they had chosen as their pastor. That decision was a harbinger of good
things for the Baptists. Although he never became a Baptist, Alline, in
the fullsome phrasing of nineteenth-century Maritime Baptist historian,
I. E. Bill, "was to the Baptists of these Provinces what John the Baptist
was in his day to the coming Kingdom of Christ."[2]

Writing of the occasion of his *Life and Journal*, Henry Alline himself
recorded: "Being requested, I attended a meeting of some Baptists in

Horton, to advise about gathering a church there." After indicating his view of the unimportance of the mode of baptism, he then expressed some disapproval as to their choice of a pastor. "They gathered in church order, and made choice of one N. Person, (who was not endowed with a great gift in the Word) for their elder; intending to put him forward, until God gave them some better one, or brought him out more in the liberty of the gospel; after which he was ordained."[3] The next year the Baptist church at Horton repaid the favour, sharing with the New Light Congregational church at Cornwallis and the mixed-membership church at Newport-Falmouth in Alline's ordination. Ironically, the preacher was the Reverend Nicholas Pierson — the very same "N. Person" whom Alline had so faintly praised in his journal.

Nicholas Pierson was an English Baptist shoemaker and lay preacher who had emigrated to the colony. The Horton church obviously felt he was the best equipped among them or the most available for the pastoral task. During one year of Pierson's leadership, ten members were added to the church by baptism, including Thomas Handley Chipman, later to become one of the "fathers" of the denomination in the Maritimes. Pierson remained as pastor until 1791.

The Horton church also held meetings at Cornwallis and sometimes at Newport and Wilmot. When the Newport church was constituted in 1776, involving people from both Newport and neighbouring Falmouth, its membership was still mixed—both Baptists and Congregationalists— "part being Pado and part being anti-Pado" (paedobaptist and anti-paedobaptist or pro- and anti-infant baptism), as John Payzant, Alline's brother-in-law and co-worker, records in his journal.[4] Alline, who participated in the event, also recorded it in his own journal. Under date of September 27, 1776, he wrote: "The church was gathered both of Baptists and Congregationals: for we did not think that such small non-essentials as water Baptism, were sufficient to break any fellowship . . . ."[5]

Agony to Ecstasy

Henry Alline, whose ministry was to be so significant for the Baptists, was born, as he records in his journal, on June 14, 1748, in Newport, Rhode Island, of parents who had been reared in Boston.[6] When he was twelve, he moved with his family to Falmouth, Nova Scotia, part of the large group of Planters. Even at that time, Alline, brought up in a Congregational home, had deep spiritual reflections, most of a disquieting nature. He had, he reported, "something of the theory of religion, but it did not satisfy me; I was much afraid of being called away by death."[7] God ultimately reached his continually tortured soul — but not until he was nearly twenty-seven — when he was soundly converted, "now filled with immortal love, soaring on the wings of faith, freed from the chains of death and darkness, and crying out my Lord and my God"[8]—a pilgrimage from agony to ecstasy. During that all too brief pilgrimage, Alline remained within the Congregational fold, never becoming a Baptist. Yet he was destined to have a major influence on the Baptist cause.

The Nova Scotia Whitefield

Henry Alline had become a "New Light" Christian and almost simultaneously he felt a call to the ministry. But he lacked the necessary education for Congregational pastors, and since there were no training institutions in the pioneer territory, he made the best possible choice: to travel to New England to secure it. But that was 1775, and when he reached the Bay of Fundy port of embarkation to secure passage to Boston, he learned that the vessel had not yet arrived and later that it never would arrive, for it had been overtaken by an American privateer.[9] In his own laconic phrasing, "It was about the time that war broke out between Old and New-England."[10] He was prevented from making the voyage.

Early in 1776, with opportunities for formal education closed to him, Henry Alline "came out and spoke by way of exhortation,"[11] beginning a life of strenuous itinerant evangelism. Though lasting less than eight years—he died at the age of thirty-five—his Nova Scotia ministry sparked such a parallel to the Great Awakening in New England that he is remembered as "the Nova Scotia Whitefield."

In 1783 he pushed into New England, where his diary ends on November 17 of that year. Stricken by a serious lung condition—"consumption" it was called in those days—his body broken by his travels, Alline died at the home of one David McClure in North Hampton, New Hampshire, on February 2, 1784. Writing to Alline's father, McClure noted that "the effects which he has left are principally a horse and sleigh, his apparel and about twelve dollars in money," added the hope "that it might afford you unspeakable satisfaction that you have been blessed with such a son."[12]

Offered Meaning

It is exhausting even to read the list of all the places Alline visited. His journal records the names of approximately fifty to which he travelled several times, as well as "many settlements." He journeyed on horseback and snowshoes through dense, virgin forest, and sometimes travelled by coastal schooner or small boat. Everywhere he went revival followed: hosts were converted, large numbers restored.

Henry Alline was a fervent preacher, whose main concern was the souls of men. In a frontier setting, where life was always hard and often dull, he offered meaning, and did so dramatically. He had a fine voice for speaking and singing, talents which served him well in his evangelistic travels. He was a poet and hymn writer, producing nearly five hundred hymns, many of which he used in his revival services. He has been criticized for founding but few churches in the vast territory he visited, but it is clear that his great talent lay in evangelism. Then, too, he had little regard for church structure, "the anti-traditionalist spurning all formal religion and presenting a religion of power."[13]

He did, however, give leadership in the establishment of the Newport church with its mixed membership of Baptists and Congregationalists, and in similar churches at Annapolis Royal and at Maugerville in present-day New Brunswick. He instituted New Light work at Cornwallis and at Sackville, at Chebogue, Liverpool and Amherst, the last said to contain a somewhat different "mixed" membership of New Lights and Methodists.[14] And he also participated in the re-formation of the Horton Baptist Church.

Equally enduring was the mark he left on a number of young men who were later to become the "fathers" of the Baptist denomination in Canada. Notable among them were Thomas Handley Chipman, Theodore Seth Harding and James and Edward Manning. Of these all except T. S. Harding began his ministry as a New Light preacher, only to become a convinced Baptist before the turn of the century. One biographer writes of Alline: "It was in our great formative period, and he, more than any other man, molded the moral life of the people of these provinces."[15] Alline was indeed a father of fathers.

Resistance, and Other Roots

The work of Henry Alline was inevitably destined to stir up the animosity of mainline churches, even in a frontier situation, for he ran roughshod over their cherished dreams . . . and sometimes their congregations. Their ministers, some of them university trained, did not take kindly to the perceived threat of an unlettered interloper — and no denomination completely escaped Alline's evangelism.

While Roman Catholic priests had long been at work among the Acadians, the Church of England had provided early services to the British. Following the Treaty of Utrecht, missionaries of the Anglican SPG — Society for the Propagation of the Gospel — not only attended to the spiritual needs of the troops, but also worked in the communities near the forts. With the founding of Halifax, two ministers of the SPG accompanied the settlers there; earlier two others had been sent to the new German, French and English colonists living around Lunenburg. By Alline's time men were serving at Halifax, Cornwallis, Windsor and Cumberland and itinerant missionaries were travelling extensively throughout the province.[16]

Most of the early Presbyterians in Nova Scotia were Scottish and Irish immigrants, the first to serve them being the Reverend James Lyon of New Jersey, who established himself in Colchester County in 1764. He was followed two years later by the Reverend James Murdock from Ireland, who first ministered at Halifax and later moved to Horton. In the beginning, the Scottish colonists lived mostly in Pictou County and on Cape Breton, but small groups also settled at several points on Prince

Edward Island. Soon afterwards settlers appeared in Shelburne and in the region around Truro.[17]

The beginning of Methodism in Canada may be traced to a spontaneous revival in Cumberland county, which began with the Alline-like conversion of William Black, then nineteen, at a house prayer meeting. Those involved were Anglicans and remained so for a period, as the followers of John Wesley had not yet parted from the Established Church of England. When Alline visited the area, the revival was in progress, and this visit resulted in the formation of the church where Methodists and New Lights worshipped together.[18] Black later became the pioneer Methodist evangelist, preaching effectively and extensively throughout the whole Atlantic territory.

"Such Miserable Jargon"

To those of the Church of England, Alline was a "strolling evangelist,"[19] an opponent of the Establishment and of all the forms and ceremonies they held so dear. He was accused in 1777 by two of the Presbyterian ministers of preaching without authority and later, as he records, "In answer to a request, I met a number of bigoted Presbyterians and mountain-men to reason on points of doctrine and principles we differed in."[20] William Black soon broke with him after sending a copy of Alline's writings to John Wesley. In his reply to Black, Wesley disparagingly said of Alline: "He is very far from being a man of sound understanding; but he has been dabbling in mystical writers, in matters which are too high for him, and above his comprehension. I dare not waste my time on such miserable jargon."[21]

Beyond all of these was the determined resistance of Henry Alline's own Congregationalists — the continuing Old Light faction who were no more approving of what they saw to be excesses in New Light evangelism in Nova Scotia than they had been of the Great Awakening in the Thirteen Colonies. They had been the Establishment in New England, and if they could not receive preferential treatment in their new homeland, they at least expected no such disturbances as they had had to bear during the earlier revivals. Their Harvard-educated ministers were scandalized by the effervescent preaching and disorderly style of the New Light meetings. And there is no doubt that they had cause to fret, for Alline's movement was the beginning of the end for them.

Commenting on the reaction of Nova Scotia's Congregational churches John Payzant writes in his journal: "The Standing Ministers were doing all that lay'd in their power to prevent the work of God, they Said that a number of upstarts had invaded the ministry, men who had no classical education. But the more they exclaimed against them, the more they lost hearers. A number of them where (were) obliged to (leave) the country and others to abdicate their places. P. Philps of Cornwallis, I. Cheevers of Liverpool, Morse of Gra (n) ville, J. Murdock of Horton, J.

Scott of Yarmouth, who wrote against Mr. Alline, and his work which determined his dismission and final removal in 1782."[22]

Revolution

While the Awakening was having such an impact on the religious life of Nova Scotia in the 1770s and early 1780s, another much broader international movement came to a head. As Payzant puts it, apparently with no partisan overtones, "a Glorious work was in the land, which begun about the commencement of the American War"[23]—the Revolution that changed the face of a continent.

The conflict had long been brewing—a clash between rigid authoritarianism and the demand for political freedom, all the more bitter as it was a struggle between parent and child. With its imperial policy, Britain continued to view the colonies as producers of raw materials, and as captive markets for British manufactured goods. Manufacturing in the colonies was, of course, frowned upon if it competed with British goods. In addition, following the Seven Years War, Great Britain had been faced with an enormous debt and had sought to levy taxes on its colonists to help repay it. The motherland also eyed with no little disfavour the huge contraband trade from New England ports upon which no duty was paid. Britain imposed a stamp tax and later a duty on tea, which resulted in the famous Boston Tea Party and other skirmishes. Finally, the American colonists formed the Continental Congress of the American colonies, which broke off all commercial relations with Britain, and on April 18, 1775, the shots that started the American Revolution were fired at Lexington. It was to be more than six years before the fighting ended and two more before the peace was finally signed—another Treaty of Paris, 1783.

The concerns of the colonists went beyond the fiscal to the religious, back to the principles that had drawn their forebears to North America in the first place. A case in point was the reaction of the first Continental Congress to the passage of the Quebec Act, which, they felt, indulged Britain's new French-speaking subjects to the north. The Congress issued an "Address to the people of Great Britain," which roundly criticized Parliament for giving support to the Roman Catholicism which they said was "fraught with sanguinary and impious tenets" and responsible for "impiety, bigotry, persecution, murder and rebellion to every part of the world."[24] From the point of view of possible Quebec support of the Revolution, this proved to be a costly position to take.

Nova Scotia Yankees

Thirteen colonies along the Atlantic seaboard began the American Revolution. A fourteenth, Nova Scotia, did not join them. Considering the makeup of the province's population at that time, the decision was notable and surely unexpected. A census taken in 1767 showed that Nova Scotia (which then included New Brunswick and Prince Edward Island) had a total of 13,374 people, 6,913 of them New Englanders. This represented just over half the population, and nearly all that had been in their new home fifteen years or less. By 1770 it was estimated that three-quarters of the population of Nova Scotia had come from New England.

The Time of Decision

After the imposition of the Stamp Tax, which had led to open defiance in New England, there were merely two mild protests in Nova Scotia. The men of Liverpool burned some stamps, and an effigy of the stamp-master was hung on the gallows of Halifax's Citadel Hill. Tea was boycotted in a limited way, and one case of arson took place in the navy yard, but until the conflict began in 1775 there was little evidence that Nova Scotians would join their neighbours in combat. Indeed, the assembly of that year made a patriotic declaration of attachment to the motherland.[25] They just did not believe that their confreres in the other colonies seriously wanted to break away.

But with the declaration of war, the moment of decision came. Halifax, with its leadership of British gentry, was secure enough in the motherland camp, as were the Scots of Pictou County and the recently arrived York-shiremen in Cumberland county, although New Englanders in both Pictou and Cumberland posed some problems.The main uncertainty, however, centred on the other "Nova Scotia Yankees" who dominated so many of the townships. Considering the changed circumstances, they could not be expected to remain unconcerned. Wisely, it would seem, they demanded neutral status, insisting that they would not serve in the forces against the Americans. The men of Yarmouth put it this way:

> We do all of us profess to be true Friends & Loyal Subjects to George our King. We were almost all of us born in New England, we have Fathers, Brothers & Sisters in that Country, divided between natural affection to our nearest relatives, and Good Faith and Friendship to our King and Country, we want to know if we may be permitted at this time to live in a peaceable State, as we look on that to be the only situation in which we with our Wives and Children, can be in any tolerable degree safe.[26]

Almost immediately after the onset of war, American forces attacked Canada (what is now Ontario and Quebec), and came close to gaining victory. Lacking the necessary support of a navy, however, they were unable to make similar forays in strength into Nova Scotia and had to confine themselves to privateer raids along the coast. These wreaked considerable hardship on the inhabitants, but resulted in turning a good deal of the sympathy of the people away from the revolution.

Early in the conflict British General Gage had requisitioned most of the regular troops stationed in Nova Scotia for the defence of Boston, then turned to the Planters to provide supplies for him. The great majority did deliver such provisions, to the annoyance of some of their number. There were, indeed, many instances of disaffection and some of open rebellion, but during the course of the war, the allegiance of the Nova Scotians increased.

Alline Not Swayed

A number of historians, including Maurice Armstrong and George W. Rawlyk, believe that Henry Alline had a great influence in the decision of the erstwhile New Englanders to remain loyal to the Crown. The Awakening then sweeping the province placed an emphasis on the spiritual and eternal, which may well have dimmed the more mundane aspects of colonial life—even thoughts of rebellion. Writes Rawlick: "Alline had intuitively realized that most Nova Scotians, during the American Revolution, were acutely troubled and disoriented and were desperately searching for some meaning in life and for meaningful relationships. And Alline saw that the New Birth provided both."[27]

If his writings are considered conclusive evidence, Alline himself appears not to have been swayed one way or the other. The fighting did interrupt his educational plans and he does mention in his journal two occasions on which he was captured and held temporarily by American privateers who had sent raiding parties ashore. But he makes no observations about the meaning or progress of the conflict.

The same is true of his brother-in-law John Payzant. For them and the other New Light leaders, the prevailing demand of the times was heavenly rather than earthly, a need for changed men rather than altered political allegiance. The call of the kingdom of God was so all-consuming that the choice between the Georges (George III of England and George Washington of the Americans) seemed almost immaterial.

In 1783, a new nation, the United States of America, was established in the southern half of the continent. There was as yet no nation to the north, but colonies existed on the Atlantic coast and in the centre, which, together with the great Northwest, were destined to become the Dominion of Canada. If Nova Scotia had become the fourteenth American state, commanding the Gulf of St. Lawrence, it would have doomed Canada in 1812 if not in 1783. Instead, there remained a solid British bastion on the Atlantic coast of North America.[28]

The Loyalists Move North

The former New Englanders of Nova Scotia who remained loyal to Great Britain paid a heavy price both economically and emotionally. That price was soon to rise even higher for many. Their cherished liberties were about to be threatened, not because of any adverse activities on the part of the new Americans but because of an influx of fellow supporters of the Crown who were forced out of their New England homes by the victors.

The coming of these Loyalists was destined to change the political and religious climate for over half a century.

The New Majority

The citizens of the Thirteen Colonies who continued their attachment to the motherland during the Revolution had to endure harsh treatment at the hands of the insurgents. Historian Arnold Toynbee sees this harshness in the handling of noncombatants as perhaps history's first example of "total war," a "totalitarianism [by which] these United Empire Loyalists were expelled bag and baggage — men, women and children — from their homes after the war was over." This was in marked contrast he says, to Britain's treatment of the conquered French Canadians in Quebec.[29]

At about the time when Henry Alline died and the revival fires of the Nova Scotia Awakening were continuing to spread, the Loyalists began pouring across the new border — twenty-five thousand of them within a few months. Almost overnight the newcomers became the majority of the population, and the monumental task of settling them was undertaken. Three thousand began a new city at the mouth of the St. John River in 1783. They named it Parrtown, in honour of governor John Parr; later it was to be renamed Saint John. Many others settled up-river. Another three thousand landed at Annapolis Royal, creating on acute housing crisis.[30] So they spread throughout the land, the sufferings they had endured convincing them to battle fiercely for their rights in the face of any real or perceived republicanism around them.

An almost immediate political shift occured in the province. Prince Edward Island had been given its own administration in 1769, and the Loyalists settling in western Nova Scotia saw advantages for themselves in a similar move. So, with the approval of the British government, Nova Scotia was cut across the Isthmus of Chignecto, and New Brunswick was formed in 1784. Similarly, Cape Breton was divided off and given its own lieutenant governor and council, although it was reunited with Nova Scotia in 1820.

The sudden arrival of the Loyalist flood was hardly an unmitigated blessing for the pre-Loyalist Planters, and especially for the growing coterie of Baptists among them, since the loyalists adhered to the Church of England. As the new arrivals tried to establish the Anglican as the state church, the Planters suffered for many decades the loss of some of the cherished rights and liberties that had first led them northward, claims that had been assured in Lord Cornwallis's Charter of Nova Scotia.

Meanwhile, although Henry Alline's New Lights and their Baptist comrades had repressed any revolutionary tendencies they may have had, the Old Light Congregational ministers did not follow suit. Their educational and cultural ties with New England were so strong that they felt compelled to support the movement for independence, and when Nova Scotia failed to head in that direction, they had no choice but to leave. One knowledgeable Maritime historian declares that "it is doubtful if a

Congregational clergyman remained here after the outbreak of hostilities, while some who left had been dangerously outspoken in their public utterances."[31] So the two movements, one spiritual, the other political — the Nova Scotia Awakening and the Revolution — nearly brought the Congregational churches to a standstill in the colony, and the way was paved for significant Baptist development before the end of the century.

CHAPTER 4

The Days of the Fathers

"The flame that . . . set the Valley meadows on fire . . . "
— WATSON KIRKCONNELL

The legacy left by Henry Alline was far greater than the horse and sleigh, the rough clothing and the slim twelve dollars he had in his pocket when he died in New Hampshire. The "Nova Scotia Whitefield" had so stirred the pioneer settlements spiritually that the influence of his fiery evangelism would long remain and provide the basis upon which the Baptists were to build and to flourish.

Alline was not only indifferent about the subjects and mode of baptism and about the forms of church order, but also held some theological concepts that were subject to question. While he lived, however, he was able by the force of his personality and earnest consecration to keep in fellowship the hybrid assemblies that grew up in the wake of his revivals. With his death a process of change began, resulting not in the dampening of the revival fires but in a redirection. Over the next twenty-five years, the great majority of these loosely knit congregations with little order became well established, interdependent churches with firm theological views. Their story is singularly linked to a group of pastors who, with little if any formal education and convinced only of the call of God and the approbation of their fellows, gave striking leadership in those important, formative days. They were, as they have been historically termed, the "fathers" of the Baptist denomination in British North America. To include them all in any detail would stretch too far the limits of this volume — but a representative number will be described.

T. S. Harding, Burton and George

The only church that was completely Baptist in 1784, the year Alline died, was the one at Horton. For two years after its recovenanting in 1778 the Horton church practised strict, or close, communion, limiting the Lord's table to those who had been immersed. When the New Light Congregationalists of Cornwallis sought fellowship with the Horton church, it initially demurred, to the annoyance of its neighbours. The

Congregational church minutes are explicit: "The Congregational Church of Christ, January 31st, 1779, in Cornwallis requested Sisterly Fellowship and Communion with the Baptist Church in Horton and Cornwallis, but was by said Baptist church denied and refused."[1] The next year the Baptists relented, voting that "the Congregational brethren who are sound in the faith be invited to sit down with us at the Lord's table occasionally, and that the mode of baptism is no bar to communion."[2] It was a step towards friendship, but one that caused difficulties down the road.

Nicholas Pierson remained pastor until he retired in 1791. For four years the Horton church was without regular leadership, but was served occasionally by lay preacher Peter Martin. Then, in 1795, the church invited twenty-two-year-old Theodore Seth Harding for a six-month period. He stayed sixty years.

A Brilliant Star

T. S. Harding's pilgrimage was unique among the fathers. Born in Barrington, Nova Scotia, in 1773, of Planter stock, he was strongly influenced as a boy of eight by Henry Alline, who, learning from his widowed mother of the loss of her husband, placed his hand on the lad's head and prayed: "May God be a father to this boy."[3] Harding ascribed his actual conversion to the ministry of Freeborn Garrison, a Methodist missionary, and at the age of twenty, Harding began preaching, having been granted a licence by the Methodists. Because of Calvinistic views received from his Presbyterian mother and other tendencies seen by the Methodist as New Light, questions arose concerning him and Harding reluctantly withdrew from that body.

Invited to speak at Horton, Harding began to examine his beliefs about baptism. Convinced, he travelled to Halifax, where he was immersed by the Reverend John Burton, the only active Baptist minister in Nova Scotia at the time. That was May 31, 1795. A week later Harding was invited for his six-month trial period, after which a call was issued to him. He was ordained in July the next year, confirming a relationship that was preserved until his death in 1855 at the age of eighty-two.

Theodore Seth Harding's unusually long ministry at Horton was also memorable. At a memorial service following Harding's death, historian I. E. Bill spoke of him as "a brilliant star in this bright constellation; in pulpit eloquence he exceeded them all. . . . When this departed Father commenced his great work as a Baptist, in 1796, his was the only Baptist Church in these Provinces, except the small Church in Halifax . . . now in 1855 . . . the denomination numbers two hundred Churches."[5]

An Opportunity in Halifax

The capital city of Nova Scotia, Halifax, had been a stronghold of the established church since its founding, and it was not until 1795 that the Baptists were able to establish a church there. The Reverend John Burton, the only minister engaged in the Baptist cause in Nova Scotia in 1795 and the one to whom T. S. Harding went for baptism that year had landed in the capital three years earlier from England. He was thirty-two. A native of Durham county with an Anglican background, he obtained a licence as a Dissenting minister in his homeland and carried on a travelling evangelistic ministry there until he decided to emigrate to North America. He had intended to go to the United States, but on disembarking at Halifax he discovered an opportunity to preach in a hall owned by a Methodist layman and decided to stay there. Late in the summer of 1793, Burton did go to the United States for a ten-month period, and while he was there he became a convinced Baptist. He was baptized in Knowlton, New Jersey, and ordained a month later.

When he returned to Halifax, he found only one person of Baptist persuasion — his wife, who during his absence had come to the same conclusion. His earlier friends were decidedly cooler towards him, but that year he baptized seven converts, including his wife, and the next year, ten, at which point a close communion Baptist church was organized.

Historian I. E. Bill, who knew him in later years, describes with deep feeling Burton's concern for the large number of blacks who had settled around Halifax after the American Revolution and who "were in a state of moral barbarism." "In the spirit of the good Samaritan," he says, Burton "poured the oil of consolation into the lacerated and bleeding souls of these suffering sons and daughters of an enslaved race. He was emphatically an apostle to the coloured people. They received and loved him as such." Bill indicated that Burton's influence was such that a number of successive provincial governors "were very much disposed to give the general management of these people principally into his hands."[6]

Born a Slave

Another pioneer Baptist preacher had tried to initiate work in Halifax earlier — in the 1780s — but, as he later reported, "as no way was open to me to preach to my own colour, I got leave to go to Shelburne (150 miles, or more I suppose, by sea,) in the suite of General Patterson, leaving my wife and children, for a little while, behind."[7]

David George was born a slave in Virginia about 1742. Converted through the witness of a fellow slave, he began to preach among his own people. He was illiterate, but by dint of his own efforts, the use of a spelling book and assistance from some white children, he learned to read the Bible and continued preaching.

When the British were forced to evacuate Charleston during the American Revolution, David George was given the opportunity, along with a few other blacks, to sail with fellow Loyalists to Halifax. He was received well by General Patterson and later befriended by Governor Parr. Beginning services in the open woods in Shelburne — no houses were as yet erected—George preached effectively among his own people. Gradually, his open-air meetings attracted some whites, although his reception from the main body of settlers was hostile. Soon he baptized four of his own race and, along with his wife and himself, they formed a Baptist church. Not long afterwards, there were fifty members and a simple meeting house had been erected.

A recently arrived British Baptist couple, William Taylor and his wife, supported the new church, and in this way David George, his family and his congregation were able to eke out a precarious existence. But when he dared to baptize Deborah Holmes, a white woman of Jones' Harbour, her relatives "were very angry, raised a mob, and endeavoured to hinder their being baptized."[8] Subsequently George's home and those of several black church members were overturned and smashed by a gang of disbanded soldiers, and George was beaten and hounded into a swamp. So fierce was the opposition that the family had to move temporarily to nearby Birchtown.

David George soon returned to Shelburne, however, and there was "a considerable revival of religion."[9] He also preached to white settlers at Ragged Island (Lockeport) at their request. He then travelled much farther, conducting evangelistic meetings among his own race in Saint John, New Brunswick, and in Preston on the outskirts of Halifax.

When the British government offered them an opportunity to settle in a recently established colony in Sierra Leone, Africa, many of the Nova Scotia blacks, including David George and "almost all the Baptists,"[10] sensed an opening for a new life free of harassment. They accepted and set sail about 1793.

The work at Shelburne was temporarily at an end, although the few, scattered Baptists who remained formed the nucleus of a renewed church some years later under the guidance of the Reverend John Burton. The meeting house lot and the rest of George's land—about half an acre in all—were sold to a local merchant for £7. Yet an unusally fine and lasting contribution had been made, a spendid legacy left, and the power of God had been demonstrated in the life of a solitary man severely handicapped by birth and by worldly circumstances.

T. H. Chipman and the Manning Brothers

While in 1795 there were only two churches left in Nova Scotia bearing the name Baptist, there were to be major additions within the next five years and a veritable explosion within two decades. The sources of this expansion lay in earlier years, however. From the outset at least some people of the Baptist persuasion attended the New Light church at Annapolis Royal founded by Henry Alline in 1780. This impulse towards an increasingly baptistic position in the church was accelerated with the appointment of Thomas Handley Chipman as the first pastor.

Avowed Baptist Principles

Born in Rhode Island in 1756, Chipman was brought by his family to Cornwallis during the Planter emigration, and in his early twenties was converted under the influence of Henry Alline's preaching. Convinced that believer's baptism was the proper scriptural practice, he was immersed by Nicholas Pierson at Horton and was among the group of ten who joined that church in 1778. Encouraged by both Pierson and Alline, who recognized his obvious gifts, Chipman began to preach almost immediately, and was called to the new Annapolis Royal church. He was set apart to the ministry there in 1782 under Alline's direction[11] — the second Baptist minister to be ordained in Nova Scotia, following Horton pastor Pierson.

Although he ministered to a mixed-membership church, Chipman continued to adhere to his avowed Baptist principles, and during a period of changing allegiances, remained in Annapolis Royal for thirty years — just half the length of T.S. Harding's service at Horton, but lengthy by almost any standard. He was an effective preacher, for "a revival of religion attended his settlement in this place"[12] — a work which continued to grow until a second pastorate was established to the west along the Annapolis Basin at Lower Granville. Like his contemporaries, Chipman travelled widely on evangelistic missions, in addition to carrying out his local responsibilities.

The Changing Pattern

The first New Light church that Henry Alline had founded at the beginning of his whirlwind ministry was at Cornwallis, opening just three months before the Baptist church at Horton was re-established. The evangelist was ordained by the Cornwallis church and had a close relationship with the congregation during his lifetime. John Payzant, who had married Alline's sister, became pastor before Alline's death, serving until he moved to Liverpool, where he remained, like Alline, a lifelong New Light, generally tolerant but somewhat critical of his Baptist coworkers.

Payzant's successor at Cornwallis, Edward Manning, had been greatly influenced by Alline when he was a boy, but it was during revival services in his home town conducted by Payzant that both he and his older brother James made personal decisions. "When I came to Falmouth," writes Payzant in his journal, "there were many who came out in religion, [including] James and Edward Manning, who afterwards became preachers. . . ."[13]

The two had been born into an Irish Roman Catholic family that had emigrated to Nova Scotia, settling at Falmouth. Edward's conversion occurred in 1789 "when an indescribable glory appeared in everything,"[14] and he joined the Cornwallis New Light Church. Almost immediately he felt the call of God and began an itinerant ministry. Ordained in 1795, he became minister at Cornwallis the same year. His ordination certificate, which was in the possession of historian J. M. Cramp, describes his church as "the Church of Christ (consisting of Baptists and Congregationalists) in Cornwallis"[15] — an early sign of mixed-membership congregations.

Edward Manning was soon to influence the changing pattern in a conspicuous way. An observer at a baptismal service conducted by Thomas Handley Chipman in 1797, Manning later wrote about the experience: "I was then and there brought to bow to the authority of the God-man, our Law-giver and King. I was quite overcome. I could trifle no longer with my convictions, but told my brother James, on whose opinion I leaned, that those who had brought their children to be sprinkled must take them away, for that I should never sprinkle another, old or young, as long as I lived."[16] Manning recorded that soon afterwards he himself was baptized by Chipman, adding this note about his congregation: "The brethren were kind, and concluded to leave me to baptize in my own way, and still continue me as their pastor."[17] He stayed there for more than fifty years.

Predictably, John Payzant was of a different mind. "Ed Manning," he wrote in his journal, "was Minister of the Church of Cornwallis, and that was a Congregational. Mr. Chipman advised Ed Manning to have them made into an open Communion, than [then] to give them an other turn and make them close communion Baptist. It appeared that he intended to carry all by force."[18] But Payzant vainly tried to stem the rising tide among the churches.

I. E. Bill, who knew a number of the fathers, says of Edward Manning that he "may be regarded as the leader of the hosts of his day . . . one of the few men born to rule."[19]

Although he was older by two years, Edward's brother James was often overshadowed by the younger man's strong preaching and striking personality. Edward readily admitted his reliance on James's advice, however. Perhaps because of the influence of his neighbouring pastor at Annapolis Royal, James Manning seems to have come conclusively to the Baptist position soon after arriving in Lower Granville in 1796. He was baptized that year by Chipman, a year before his brother. He became the first regular minister at the Lower Granville, or Second Annapolis, Church on the Annapolis Basin and remained there for twenty-two years until his untimely death at fifty-five.

Harris Harding, Dimock, Crandall and Towner

Until the late 1700s, the Congregational church was predominant in Yarmouth, where the pioneer Ebenezer Moulton had originally settled. The Baptist presence was barely felt, if at all, and Henry Alline's ministry there was strongly opposed by the Reverend Jonathan Scott, minister of the Congregational church at nearby Chebogue. Then, in 1790, a New

Light church of combined Congregationalist and Baptist membership was formed, mostly as a result of the efforts of Harris Harding.

No relation to Theodore Seth Harding, Harris was born in Horton. While he was still a young child, his Anglican parents moved to Connecticut, where young Harris received a much better education than he could have obtained in the Nova Scotia of those days. He also experienced at least one memorable encounter as a youth in the New England of revolutionary times. While employed by the rebellious colonists in transporting goods by ship from New York to Boston, he was arrested by the British, taken aboard a man-of-war and held for several weeks before being released.[20]

When he was twenty-two Harding returned with his family to Horton and had been up to that point "a stranger to experimental religion."[21] He became a schoolmaster in Cornwallis and while there was converted under the preaching of John Payzant. Abandoning his occupation as a teacher, he went from meeting to meeting among both New Lights and Methodists, "exhorting sinners to turn to the Lord,"[22] and doing so with considerable success.

His early preaching took place mainly in nearby Kings and Hants counties, but he soon launched out on wider evangelistic travels, visiting many communities on Nova Scotia's south shore, as well as Yarmouth and Onslow. At a New Light church that John Payzant had organized in 1792 in Onslow, near Truro, Harding was ordained as pastor two years later. But Yarmouth was to be the scene of his greatest labours. While still pastor at Onslow, Harding held services at Yarmouth, finally settling there and serving for fifty-seven years until his death in 1854 at the age of ninety-two.

A Profound Change

Sixty miles along the south shore west from Halifax was Chester, where the first church had been established in 1788. Although the church was Congregational in name, with the Reverend John Seecombe as founding pastor, a number of Baptists were also there. Like his fellow Congregational ministers of the Standing Order, Seecombe favoured the American cause during the Revolution and, according to the minutes of the governor's council, was charged before the council with "preaching a Sermon tending to promote Sedition and Rebellion," and with "praying for the Success of the Rebels."[23] He was placed under a £500 good behaviour bond and allowed his liberty.

When Joseph Dimock succeeded Seecombe in 1793, a profound change came to the Chester church. Dimock, who had been born in Newport in 1768, was the eldest of Newport lay preacher Daniel Dimock's eleven children and a grandson of Shubael, who had brought the family to Nova Scotia from Connecticut in 1759.

Joseph Dimock's educational opportunities, like those of his contemporaries in eighteenth century Nova Scotia, were limited, but he was eternally grateful for the advantages he perceived around him. Writing many years later in his diary when he had just passed his eighty-sixth birthday, he records:

> My Father, a Baptist preacher who taught me the need of a Saviour & how undone I must be without him—gave me a common Education though small, beyond my Associates in the village where I lived—implanted in my Nature a thirst for Education so that I do not remember to have ever been so taken up with any pastime but I would willingly leave it for a Book . . . My parents taught me to read my Bible Daily . . . but every week if no more, I was taught to repeat the Assemblies catechism [i.e., of the Congregationalists] except one answer the last half blotted out so that it read thus Baptism is not to be administered to any untill they profess their Faith in Christ and obedience to him. . . .[24]

Neither the biblical teaching nor the Baptist emphasis were lost on young Joseph. Converted at seventeen in 1785, he was baptized by Nicholas Pierson and joined the Horton church two years later. By 1790 the call to preach had become incessant and he, like his fellow preachers, began a travelling ministry until called to Chester.

John Payzant felt that Dimock's move to Chester indicated that he favoured the New Lights. In his journal Payzant records: "Dimock had joined the Horton Close communion Church, and thought it his duty to leave them and join with more free Christians, as Mr. Chipman had done. The Church of Chester was a free Church that is they might be Baptised eather by sprinkling or diping as the candidate desired."[25] "Leaving," however, was hardly in the Reverend Joseph Dimock's mind, for, like T. H. Chipman, he remained a convinced Baptist and was to be one of the small group who had a vision of a strong body of Baptist churches in the future.

"There must have been a striking contrast between the rather youthful strippling 'with his five smooth stones from the brook' and his predecessor, the aged, erudite, well-to-do-preacher, three times and more the age of his successor. The latter, dedicated as he was, had little more than the rudiments of book learning."[26] So writes Maritime historian, George Levy, of Joseph Dimock's initial impact upon Chester. Yet, except for a two-year absence preaching in New England between 1796 and 1798 (while he still retained his position at Chester), he served the church continuously until his death in 1846—a pastorate of fifty-three years.

Talking about Their Souls

For many years after Nathan Mason's departure from Sackville, there was no Baptist or Congregational church. Christians did meet there in fellowship, however, as Henry Alline recorded in his journal after visiting in 1781: "The church now began to gather together in Gospel followship, without any bars or separation about sects or denominations, but whoever loved and sought Christ and belonged to Him were fully received into communion."[27]

Joseph Crandall, another "father" of the Maritime churches, who left a brief "New Brunswick Baptist History" in his own unusually attractive handwriting, records that he was born in Rhode Island and emigrated with his parents to Nova Scotia "about a year before the Revolution." When he was thirteen, his mother, who had a strong spiritual influence on his life, passed away. Soon afterwards there came two visitors to their home in Chester, who "talked of a strange man who was preaching in Windsor and adjoining places; he preached in the night and people were becoming crazy and talked about their souls." This was Henry Alline, of course, as he adds, "My father had heard this man preach and as he happened to be there at the time he explained to the stranger that this preacher Henry Alline was a 'New Light' and that the New Lights were people of God for they were Christians, and that none could go to Heaven unless they were converted."[28]

Later Crandall moved to Liverpool, where he became a fisherman. His life in that community was in his own words, "exceedingly sinful." Then at "a meeting of Christians from different parts of the country" at Onslow he was converted under the preaching of Joseph Dimock and Harris Harding. Having by that time returned to live in Chester, he was baptized by Dimock in 1795, uniting with that church.[29]

Like the other fathers, Crandall heard the call to the ministry almost immediately and, encouraged by Harris Harding and John Payzant, he began to work in his own area, gradually moving into parts of New Brunswick, including Sackville. In describing the New Brunswick part of his travels, Crandall specifically mentions the contribution of "Brothers Christian and Henry Steeves [who] held meetings and exhorted the people"[30] — two patriarchs of a long line that has made a remarkable impact on Canadian Baptist life.

In response to an urgent appeal from the Sackville area, the churches of Chester, Horton and Cornwallis sent representatives to form a church there and ordain Joseph Crandall as their pastor. As a result, writes Crandall, "a church was organized on gospel grounds, with the exception that unimmersed Christians might commune."[31] William Chipman, who with pastor Edward Manning, made up the Cornwallis section of the examining council for the ordination, recorded his impressions of the service. He writes: "A host of people were in attendance and thirteen were added to the church before we left the place."[32]

So it was that after an absence of some thirty years there was a Baptist church in Sackville.

A Loyalist Warden

Unlike its surrounding areas, the county of Digby, Nova Scotia, seems to have been virtually untouched by the evangelical cause until the mid-

1790s. If it had been reached in any way, it was certainly unmoved, for "at that time there was not a dissenting meeting-house in the County."[33] The man who first made inroads in Digby differed in some respects from most of the other Baptist fathers. He was a Loyalist, and Episcopalian and in his forties when he was called to the ministry.

Enoch Towner was born in Newbury, Connecticut, in 1755, and during the American Revolution he served as a sergeant in the British forces. Emigrating with other Loyalists at the end of the war, Towner settled in Granville township, where he became warden of the Anglican church in Digby.

During revival services in Lower Granville conducted by James Manning and Joseph Dimock, Towner, dissatisfied with his earlier spiritual experience, "after a lengthy period of deep heart-searching came to a clear consciousness of sins forgiven."[34] Baptized by the Annapolis Royal pastor, T. H. Chipman, Towner became an active Christian in the district surrounding his home, and it was soon discovered that he had preaching talent. When the Lower Granville Church was formed, he placed his membership there, and was about the same time commended to the ministry.

Towner did not begin by going over ground already covered by the others. Instead he moved over into Digby county in 1797 when "there was probably not a Baptist in it."[35] Facing severe opposition, he succeeded in winning a number of converts scattered throughout the county.

By 1779 such interest had been aroused that the new converts sent seven of their number to seek counsel from James Manning, the Lower Granville pastor, as to whether they should form a church. They were formally organized — becoming the Sissiboo (now Weymouth) church, the centre for the Baptist witness in the whole county. The same year, at a meeting of the fathers in Lower Granville, Enoch Towner was ordained, and with a circuit covering the whole area, he served the Sissiboo congregation for seven years.

The fathers of the Canadian Baptists were an unusual order of men. In nearly every instance their experience of conversion was climactic, emanating from a deep conviction of sin. Their call to the ministry was equally striking, leaving them in little doubt as to the will of God for their lives. With only a few exceptions, they started out on their task with pitifully meagre educational qualifications. However, their experiences led them to rich appreciation of educational opportunities, which they helped to make available for those who followed. They were a band of completely committed men, unmindful of hardships and unconcerned about creature comforts. God used them in a remarkable way.

In one sense, as rugged individualists, they typified their developing churches; in another, as devoted associates, they burned their brand on their emerging denomination.

CHAPTER 5

Origins in the Canadas

"What are the prospects?" "As bright as the promises of God."
—*ADONIRAM JUDSON*

As the churches on the eastern seabord developed and struggled to discover their identity as Baptists, events were also shaping important opportunities in the region that was destined to become the provinces of Ontario and Quebec. As in the east, the movement had its sources in New England — but it appeared in the Canadas about thirty years later than in Nova Scotia, by which time the new United States of America had been formed.

Political events inevitably left their mark on the religious.

The Secular Milieu

The French dream of Empire lay shattered with the signing of the 1763 peace treaty that ended the Seven Years War between France and Great Britain. France had been ousted from most of North America, and the whole continent seemed to be within Britain's grasp in that decade of the 1760s. Such was not to be, of course, but at least the northern half, the part Voltaire mistakenly dubbed "a few acres of snow,"[1] remained within the British orbit.

The Old Custom of Paris

Out of the conquered territory belonging to France, Britain fashioned the province of Quebec, initially confined by boundaries drawn along the watershed of the Allegheny Mountains on the east and a little beyond the Ottawa River on the west. Toward what was then French Canada, the British showed a generosity that was unusual for the times. No landholders were expelled, as had happened in Nova Scotia, and Governor James Murray was sympathetic in his treatment of the new subjects of King George III. However, as Canadian historian Donald Creighton writes:

> English common law could only have been imposed by brute force in a province where land had been granted 'en fief et signeurie', and where every

40

will and contract had been drawn up and executed in terms of the old Custom of Paris. English representative political institutions would have been almost equally difficult to establish without either disenfranchising the largest part of the population or altering—or evading—the antiquated laws by which Protestant Great Britain still sought to prevent Roman Catholics from taking part in municipal or national government.[2]

Britain's New England colonists would have disagreed violently with this assessment. As mentioned in Chapter 3, Britain's decision under the Quebec Act of 1774 to permit the French to retain their language and their civil law, with Roman Catholics guaranteed freedom of worship — "the Magna Carta of cultural liberty to the Canadians"[3]—became one of the major irritants provoking the American Revolution.

The citizens of the increasingly restive Thirteen Colonies were thus in something of a quandary, for despite this stance, the rebellious colonists hoped to gain French Canadian support in their fight with Britain. In an open letter their Continental Congress appealed to the Canadians to join them in the struggle,[4] and early in 1775 it sent agents to Quebec to enlist their backing.

The Defence of the Country

Roman Catholic Bishop Briand of Quebec, who had been consecrated to his office in France while Britain turned a blind eye, soon repaid the favour, indicating that the French Canadians should support their recent conquerors rather than the rebellious Americans. "Perform with joy everything asked of you by a benevolent Governor." Briand wrote in a directive, adding: "You are not required to carry the war into the distant provinces; you are only asked to strike a blow to repel the enemy."[5]

While the inhabitants were not quite as positive in their response as the leaders had requested, "a few hundred Canadian recruits" being drawn to the rebel camp,[6] several companies of militia did join ranks with the British in defence of the colony. When the Americans invaded Canada in 1775, forces under General Richard Montgomery quickly captured Montreal. Benedict Arnold was not successful at Quebec, however, even when joined by Montgomery, who was killed by the defenders. The next year the Americans had to retreat from Montreal and return home following the arrival of British naval and troop reinforcements.

Loyalist Influx

Following the signing of the peace treaty with France twenty years earlier, Great Britain had hoped that a host of Anglo-Saxon and Celtic settlers would be attracted to the conquered Quebec soil, but it was only in the aftermath of further war — this time with the Thirteen Colonies — that significant immigration occurred.

The first to come were the United Empire Loyalists. They settled in two main areas. The first put down roots along the upper St. Lawrence in the newly surveyed townships between the last French communities and the Bay of Quinte on the northern shore of Lake Ontario. A much smaller group established themselves in what are now the Eastern Townships of Quebec. A second large body proceeded along the Niagara River into the Niagara Peninsula and along the shore of Lake Ontario toward what is now Hamilton and along the north shore of Lake Erie.[7] The Loyalists were soon followed by many other Americans interested in the two-hundred-acre land grant made available to new immigrants. The virgin wilderness was giving way to the axe and plough as the new settlers pushed westward.

As in the Maritimes, where Loyalist pressure resulted in the division of Nova Scotia and the formation of New Brunswick, similar influences brought about the separation of Quebec into two provinces, Upper and Lower Canada, regions covering about the same area as the Ontario and Quebec of today. The Constitution Act of 1791 which effected this division made provision for an elected assembly in each province, together with a legislative council that had to approve all assembly action.

The Religious Setting

The Constitution Act also set aside about one-seventh of all Crown lands for the support of "a Protestant Clergy" and approved the founding of rectories for the Church of England[8] — measures which subsequently produced one of the most serious struggles based on a religious question in Canada's history. And Baptists were to play a significant role in the final setlement of the issue.

The Church of England

As in Nova Scotia, the British government undoubtedly favoured an "established" Anglican church in the Canadas, although the prerogatives granted to the Roman Catholic church in the region of Lower Canada under the Quebec Act and the Constitution Act effectively blunted the full institution of the Church of England there. The factors that ultimately produced a similar result in Upper Canada were more varied, influenced both by the frontier and the heterogeneous nature of the virtually new population.

The period of the American Revolution was particularly trying for the Church of England. Without bishops in the Thirteen Colonies, the clergy were seriously divided over the issue of independence, and many returned to England. While a good number of its people were Loyalists and eventually fled to Canada, the majority of the laity were on the revolutionary side, as were many of its leaders, for two-thirds of those who signed the Declaration of Independence were counted in its membership.[9]

Convinced that the American experience without bishops had been detrimental to their cause, the Anglican Loyalists were committed to ensure that such appointments were made in Canada. Charles Inglis, who had been rector of Trinity Church in New York City, was thus named

Bishop of Nova Scotia in 1787, his initial diocese spreading far beyond that province to include Quebec, Newfoundland and Bermuda. Among the early accomplishments of the new bishop was his acquisition of a former Jesuit chapel in Montreal, which he renamed Christ Church, forerunner of today's cathedral in that city.

Among the Anglican clergymen who arrived with the Loyalists was Jacob Mountain, who came in 1793. He was consecrated in England as Inglis had been and arrived as Bishop of Quebec, his principal sphere of labour being in then-developing Upper Canada. At the end of his long episcopate in 1825, the number of clergy under his jurisdiction had grown from nine to sixty.[10]

The Presbyterians and Methodists

While Lower Canada remained predominantly Roman Catholic, Upper Canada developed "a religious mosaic" as had Nova Scotia. The Anglicans and Presbyterians prospered, particularly in the few towns that had grown up before 1812, while the Methodists and Baptists proved to be more effective in the rural areas.[11]

The first Presbyterian witness in the Canadas came with the soldiers of the Fraser Highlanders who were part of Wolfe's army, together with some Scottish merchants and a number from New England. The first congregation, in Quebec Town, was drawn together by the Reverend George Henry, an army chaplain. A second congregation was gathered in Montreal in 1786. By 1793 there were three churches, whose ministers formed a presbytery that year; it did not survive, but was reconstituted as the Presbytery of Montreal ten years later.

Quebec Town was also the scene of Methodist beginnings — through a supply officer of the 44th Regiment stationed there in 1780. James Tuffy, who had been one of John Wesley's helpers in England, undertook some lay preaching and direction of Methodist "class-meetings." In 1802 in Montreal a "society" of seven founded the historic St. James Methodist Church, sometimes called "the cathedral of Methodism" in Canada.

However, early Methodism in the Canadas was to receive its main impulse from the recently formed United States. As the new settlers poured into Canada, Methodist circuit riders followed — no fewer than seventy-six missionaries being sent in a twenty-two-year period after 1790. So massive and effective was this leadership and so suited was the Methodist polity to that Canadian frontier situation that, as one interchurch historian concludes, "it was not long before Methodism became a dominant force in religious appeal and political influence."[12]

The Lutherans

Among the Loyalist refugees who escaped the persecution of their erstwhile neighbours was a body of German Lutherans, some of them "Hessian mercenaries adrift from their regiments." The original German settlement was in Stormount County near present-day Ottawa, adjacent to the expanding Presbyterians, who found on their other side their compatriots, the Highland Roman Catholics.[13] A number of Lutheran congregations were formed, which kept their ties to the United States.

A Hole in the Ice

It was against this background, secular and religious, that the initial Baptist thrust into Lower and Upper Canada was made—and made into a rugged hinterland area of but slim population. According to a historical review in the Toronto *Globe* of July 1, 1867—Confederation Day—it was not until 1782 that the population of what was to become Upper Canada reached 10,000 inhabitants. The Lower Canadian segment, which had been settled earlier and had a much higher birthrate, recorded 113,000 a year later.[14] Both were soon to expand rapidly.

As on the Atlantic coast, Baptist work in the Canadas began among settlers who had formerly lived in the Thirteen Colonies. But the churches in what are now Ontario and Quebec also grew as a result of missionary outreach from the United States. The Nova Scotia work, by contrast, was largely indigenous.

An indication of the growing health of the Baptist movement in the new United States of America was the fact that at least six Baptist missionary bodies were involved in this northern outreach. Four of these agencies played a prominent role in early Baptist life in central Canada for about two decades: Woodstock, New York, Shaftsbury and Massachusetts. About twenty-five missionaries were sent altogether.

Caldwell's Manor

While most of the missionary activity occurred after 1800, occasional trips into the Canadas had been made in the previous decade, one of them resulting in the formation of the first Baptist church in the two provinces. It was in 1793 that two missionaries of the Woodstock Association of Vermont, John Hebbard and Arial Kendrick, crossed the border into Lower Canada after a visit to Fairfax, Vermont, where evangelist Elisha Andrews was holding services in the Baptist church.

Crossing to the northern tip of Lake Champlain, the travelling missionaries came upon the community of Caldwell's Manor, where a number of former Americans, mostly from Connecticut, had settled. The settlement was located on a large tract of land, the old seigneury of Foucault, which had been purchased by a Sir John Caldwell.

It is not likely that there were many Baptists at Caldwell's Manor before Hebbard and Kendrick arrived. In fact, there were very few Baptists among any of the Loyalists. The Baptists in the Thirteen Colonies were by and large supportive of the revolutionary cause.

When the two missionaries held services at Caldwell's Manor, a number of people were converted, but Hebbard and Kendrick did not baptize them or form a church at that time. Nevertheless, a good foundation had been laid, for the next year the people of the village requested that a minister be sent to visit and to baptize a number of candidates.

The call reached Elisha Andrews in Fairfax and in an account of his visit written for the *Christian Watchman*, he records the response:

> As I was the only Baptist minister in the region except Elder Call, and he was an aged man, and ten miles further off, there could be no doubt with respect to the path of duty. A friend of mine volunteered to take me down in his sleigh. We started Monday morning and proceeded to Highgate, (Vt.); here we put up in the house of a German by the name of Wagoner. In the morning we followed his direction; crossed the Missique Bay and arrived at the Manor in season to appoint a meeting in the evening. We put up with Dr. Cune, a Baptist from Rhode Island. In the morning we crossed over to the West side of the manor about eight miles, into the neighbourhood where the revival had been most powerful. Soon after we arrived the house was filled with people and I preached to them; and again in the evening. The next morning we met at 9 o'clock in the morning and spent the whole day examining candidates for baptism; we heard and received thirty of all ages from 10 to 50 years. . . . The next day we repaired to the Lake, cut a hole in the ice, and fifteen of those happy and devoted disciples were in the name of Father, Son and Holy Ghost, immersed agreeably to the command of the divine Savior. The baptism of the remaining fifteen was deferred until the next Monday, it being their choice to have it performed in the vicinity where they resided.[15]

Andrews spent the ensuing week preaching and visiting among the people of Caldwell's Manor before returning to Fairfax. A month later he came back to the manor, bringing with him representatives of the Fairfax church to assist in establishing and recognizing a new church. Thus, in 1794, "The Baptist Church of Christ in Caldwell's Manor" was founded — the first of the denomination in central Canada.

Hallowell

One of the next churches to be founded was established in Upper Canada in 1795 — at Hallowell on West Lake in the Bay of Quinte area of Lake Ontario. On this occasion the formation was not sponsored missionary work, but rather through the efforts of a licensed minister who had come as a prospective settler. David Benedict, pioneer American Baptist historian, whose work was published in 1848, quotes the Reverend George J. Ryerse of Woodhouse, U.C. (Upper Canada):

> In June of 1794, elder Reuben Crandall, then a licentiate, settled in Hallowell on the northern side of Lake Ontario, now in Prince Edward Co.; a religious reformation followed his labors, and the year after a church was gathered by his instrumentality. This was the first reformation in this part of the country.[16]

Ryerse, who provided much of the central Canadian material for Benedict's early "North American" review, was the Baptist cousin of the better-known Methodist Ryersons, the difference in name having apparently come about through a mistake in spelling in a military record of one branch of the family.[17] Ryerse was acquainted with Elder Crandall, the Hallowell church's founder, who gave him first-hand information about its origins.[18]

Reuben Crandall was born in northeast Duchess county, New York, where a Baptist church had existed since 1751. One of the many descendants of Elder John Crandall of Rhode Island, he is presumed to have been licensed by the Northeast church before he moved to Upper Canada.

Thurlow

Probably less than a year after the church at Hallowell was organized in 1795, another immigrant Baptist elder, Asa Turner, gave leadership in gathering a congregation in Thurlow township north of Prince Edward township. Turner, who had been ordained in the United States, was among a group of American newcomers who settled near the Moira River in 1789 when they were unable to secure waterfront land in Prince Edward.

Turner was the first ordained Baptist minister to settle in Upper Canada and, according to missionary Joseph Cornell who visited him about seven years after the Thurlow church's founding, his work had proved to be strong and lasting. Wrote Cornell: "His labours have been remarkably blessed this year past. . . . He has baptized upwards of twenty in a short time past, who appear to be disciples, well instructed in the doctrine of the kingdom of God."[19]

Beamsville

A second region in Upper Canada—farther west—also lays claim to an early church. Variously named Thirty Mile Creek, Clinton and Beamsville, this community in the Niagara area is believed to have had a Baptist church at least by 1796, perhaps before.[20] The initial Clinton church was evidently Arminian in doctrine and may well have been of the same Six-Principle stamp as the first little church in Sackville (in what is now New Brunswick) which had been transferred from New England. Lemuel Covell, a missionary of the Shaftsbury Association, visited the district in 1803, and reported: "We found no place of the Baptist order, though there were a number of brethren in several places. There had been a Baptist church at Thirty Mile Creek, near 50 miles from Queenston, but they have pretty much lost their visibility, although a number of members still reside there."[21]

Missionary Asahel Morse, also of the Shaftsbury Association, visited the area four years later. He was more definite but less charitable:

> I had been informed that there was a Baptist Church in this place; I found indeed a number of baptized professors but no church I could fellowship. They were in part, destitute of articles of faith and practice, and of a regular church convenant; without discipline, and in a situation where they could

not minister it. They had been imposed upon by an imposter by the name of Tims, who called himself a Baptist minister, but of Arminian principles. He formed them into something called a church, without order, union, or government. . . .[22]

Morse's view that there was "no church [he] could fellowship" may well indicate that the church was still functioning, albeit rather lamely. His problem, an inability to associate, would of course have resulted from his strict Calvinism, which would hardly allow him to tolerate the group's Arminianism. Although belittled by Morse, former pastor Tims is charged only with such Arminianism and a failure to introduce proper church order in his congregation. Even if this was true, it hardly gives justification for the label "imposter."

Spin-offs

Meanwhile, activities in Caldwell's Manor had accelerated. Soon after it was established, the church licensed William Marsh, Jr., one of its members, to preach for them. Marsh, a native of Shaftsbury, Vermont, was the son of a magistrate who was killed during the American Revolution while serving in the British forces. Persecuted for their Loyalist stand, the family fled to Lower Canada about 1783.

In 1796 the Caldwell's Manor church called a council to examine Marsh for ordination. Two Vermont churches, at Fairfax and Cambridge, responded, and Marsh was ordained, the first Baptist in the Canadas to be set apart in that way. Marsh then demonstrated his pastoral gifts and missionary zeal by initiating churches the next year at Sutton Flats, Stanstead and Hatley in the Eastern townships, just north of the American border. The members of the Caldwell's Manor church soon relocated on new government-granted lands in nearby Eaton township. This Eaton congregation later became the Sawyerville church and thus may be said to have had a continuing life since its founding at the Manor in 1794.[23]

Abbott's Corner

Marsh began the linked Stanstead-Hatley work with the help of American missionary Jedediah Hibbard, who had settled at Abbott's Corner in the nearby township of St. Amand. In this co-operative venture, both men displayed the barrier-breaking power of the grace of God, for in direct contrast to the Loyalist sympathies of Marsh, Hibbard had served in the American revolutionary army and was pro-American in outlook.

Hibbard himself was responsible for founding a new church at Abbott's Corner by 1799, where he remained for ten years until his death.

Cramahe and Haldimand

Elder Reuben Crandall, who had led in establishing a new church at Hallowell, Prince Edward township, in 1795, moved on the next year to the adjacent Cramahe township. Elder Joseph Winn took his place as pastor at Hallowell. A Loyalist, Winn had been born in Duchess county, New York, as had Crandall. He had served in the British forces during the Revolution and, coming to Upper Canada, had settled near Hallowell and may well have assisted Crandall in the church's formation. An island in West Lake still bears the Winn name.

Winn was obviously an effective workman. American missionary Joseph Cornell, reporting in the *Massachusetts Baptist Missionary Magazine* of 1803 on a visit he had made to Upper Canada, wrote of Winn that he "is now favoured with a glorious revival of religion among his people."[24] Similarly, missionary Timothy Sheppard, who made two tours into Upper Canada in 1817 and 1818, recorded after the second visit that "there has been baptized, on profession of faith, since my last winter's tour nearly four hundred persons. Elder Joseph Winn has baptized one hundred and twelve. . . ."[25]

On moving to Cramahe, Reuben Crandall promptly arranged services for the township and adjacent Haldimand, and a church organization soon followed. The still-preserved Haldimand minute book is precise. Under date of June 23, 1798, it records:

> Brethren and sisters assembled for the purpose of obtaining fellowship with sister churches, and entered into solemn covenant with each other before God, to walk together in love and fear of God, Christ strengthening them; and to watch over each other for good, and to be for God and no other; to maintain family and public worship on the Lord's Day; to attend conference every two weeks to set in order the things that are wanting in the church of Christ.[26]

Strong roots were developing.

By 1800 there were thus some eight Baptist churches in the two Canadas, divided into three clusters: in the east, Caldwell's Manor, Sutton Flats, Stanstead-Hatley and Abbott's Corner; in the centre, Hallowell, Thurlow and Cramahe-Haldimand; in the west, Clinton/Beamsville.

All ministers and congregations were new Canadians and, particularly in Upper Canada, the frontier to which they came was rough and demanding. There were no ready-made farms as there had been for some three decades before in Nova Scotia. None of the congregations included "Pre-Loyalists" with Baptist roots in New England — it was too late for that. Indeed, few of them would be able to add "U.E." to their family names, for most of the Baptists of the Thirteen Colonies supported the cause of independence and remained. Added to the limited number of such Loyalists who came were numbers who, attracted by the offer of homestead land, saw new opportunities for themselves and their families.

Indeed, on that rude frontier, there were a scant few Baptists, just enough to spark and fan the revivals that did occur. Undeterred by small numbers, the earliest missionaries and the homesteading pastors proceeded to enlist the settlers . . . by the way of the Cross.

PART II

Of Principles and Practices

O N PROUD DISPLAY IN THE McPHAIL Memorial Baptist Church in Canada's capital are two ancient and worn stirrups, the long-time possession of one whose name the church bears.

Not the legacy of a legendary range rider or horseman of the law, the stirrups (which are not even a matched pair) did support the feet of a devoted pastor — "the Elijah of the Ottawa Valley" — as he spent uncounted hours in the saddle of his faithful grey, Prince, travelling from colonial settlement to settlement sharing the Good News.

One of the stories issuing from the period tells of a particularly black and stormy night when, his eyes unable to pierce the inky blackness, Daniel McPhail had to depend entirely upon his horse to find the path. Finally, coming to a familiar bridge across the river, Prince carefully carried him over and home. Not until the next day was it discovered that, apart from a bare few planks, the bridge had been washed away. Instinctively, the trusty animal had picked his precarious way to safety. As one discerning observer has commented: "Perhaps his master's Master was guiding Prince."

McPhail's legacy includes two men whom he baptized (on the same day it is believed) in the waters of the Castor River: Alexander McDonald and John McLaurin. The first became the pioneer Baptist missionary to western Canada, the second a pioneer missionary to India.

CHAPTER 6

A Developing Awareness

"The Holy Scriptures, viz, the Originals, Hebrew and Greek, are given by Divine inspiration, and in their first donation were without error, most perfect, and therefore Canonical."
—JOHN SMYTH

In any short list of basic Baptist principles, one certain to be at or very near the top will be the centrality of the scriptures. As one more recent statement puts it: "More than any, Baptists have been known as 'people of the Book.' This Bible is the guide-book, the complete creed, the authoritative, self-sufficient rule of faith and practice. Hence, what Baptists believe about life and death, beginning and ending, time and eternity, meaning and purpose, are found in the Scriptures."[1]

A Logical Progression

It was probably this view of scripture that played the greatest part in prompting the New Light ministers and their Maritime congregations to move to the Baptist position and link with the Baptists as the eighteenth century was drawing to a close. Many years before in New England, a number of prophetic voices had pondered a similar possibility, given the advance of Puritanism, with its goal of a biblical order in church and community. David Benedict, one of the early American Baptist historians, recorded that this view was held by Episcopal Bishop Sanderson, among others. "The Rev. Archbishop Whitgift, and the learned Hooker, men of great judgment and famous in their times," said the Bishop, did long since foresee, and declare their fear, that if Puritanism should prevail among us, it would soon draw Anabaptism after it."[2]

Sanderson was, of course, alluding to the Baptists, whom he called Anabaptists or "re-baptizers," and the prophecy, which pre-eminently proved to be accurate in the new United States, was in no small measure also fulfilled on Canada's eastern seaboard. By 1800 the Baptists to the south, had "emerged from relative obscurity to become the largest denomination in America."[3] Although the achievement was never to be quite as thoroughgoing on Canada's Atlantic coast except in New Brunswick, the total Maritimes region was much more hospitable to the Baptist cause from the outset than either central or western Canada, where conditions appeared to favour the Methodists with their superior central planning and more disciplined methods.

"A Rage for Dipping"

As has been intimated earlier, the Pre-Loyalists who, upon the invitation of the Nova Scotia colonial government, had taken over the vacant Acadian farmlands, were largely Congregationalists of the Standing Order. Although that peculiarly American brand of Puritanism never did have in Nova Scotia the massive impact upon community life that it did in New England, its religious status was significant. With the spread of spiritual lethargy, however, the New Light faction became dominant and this, coupled with the departure of most of the Congregational ministers to support the American side during the Revolution, dealt a near-fatal blow to the mainline Congregational cause.

The New Lights were the next to face disruption. In what Bishop Charles Inglis somewhat contemptuously termed "a rage for dipping," there was a widespread movement toward the Baptists. In the instance of one church — at Waterborough on the St. John River — Elder Elijah Estabrooks led his whole New Light congregation to the baptismal waters.

Signs of the Times

Joseph Crandall, who had been baptized as a believer after his conversion, was conducting evangelistic services up-river after previously preaching at Waterborough and called in again on his return journey. He writes of the experience:

> We landed at Brother Marster's and soon the boats came loaded with anxious enquirers asking about the reformation up the river; for they had heard about such numbers being immersed that many of them had been led to read their Bibles and were prepared to yield obedience to the Lord's commands. In that house, an hour or two after my arrival, the Lord's work commenced and a number rejoiced in the Lord. It was wonderful to see the aged, the middle-aged and the youths relating in the language of Holy Scripture what the Lord had done for their souls. Elijah Estabrooks, a holy man of God, their leader, led the way and the whole society followed in the holy ordinance of immersion.[4]

Such were the signs of the times. As Anglican author Arthur W. H. Eaton writes: "By 1800 all the New Light ministers in Nova Scotia except Rev. John Payzant at Liverpool had been immersed, and on the 23rd and 24th of June of that year a 'Baptist Association' was formed."[5]

The First Association

The Nova Scotia Awakening sparked by Henry Alline continued apace after his death but, as so often occurs in human history, the removal of the leader altered the scene and the movement began to display abberations. While he was with them, Henry Alline was able to keep his followers on a reasonably even keel, but when the influence of his magnetic personality was removed, excesses developed in some quarters. A kind of antinomianism reared its head, extending even to immorality. Recurring from time to time since the sixteenth century, this doctrinal deviation suggests that the Christian, freed of guilt, unfettered by the Law and resting safe in "eternal security" may wander from the pathway with some impunity. According to this view, there is a dichotomy between spirit and flesh, and all wrongdoing may conveniently be blamed on the latter. It was a perverted Calvinism, which threatened the widespread spiritual quickening. Added to these moral dangers were the "revelations" of self-appointed prophets who declared themselves to be the recipients of special and personal inner visions which should be accepted as superseding even the scriptures.

A number of the pastors, deeply concerned about the deteriorating situation and the lack of order in the churches, decided to meet to discuss the state of affairs. Gathering in 1797 in Cornwallis, they issued the following circular letter to the churches: "We take this method of acquainting you that we, John Payzant of Liverpool, Thomas Handley Chipman of Annapolis, James and Edward Manning of Cornwallis, have met on the 12th July, 1797, and being agreed together in our minds to walk together in fellowship as ministers of Jesus Christ, have agreed to hold a yearly conference to know our minds and the state of the different churches standing in connexion, by their delegates being sent by them."[6]

Combatting a Dangerous Tendency

The first meeting of such a "conference" was held at Cornwallis on June 15, 1798. Harris Harding, as yet not a Baptist, sought membership in the group, but first had to acknowledge—and sign—that he had himself erred in supporting the "New Dispensationers," as those who treated indifferently the moral law were termed. The minutes of the conference contained the statement that, "The ministers discoursed largely on the necessity of order and discipline in the churches, and continued until midnight in observing the dangerous tendency of erroneous principles and practices, and lamenting the unhappy consequences in our churches."[7]

It was at this conference that Edward Manning witnessed Thomas Handley Chipman conduct a believer's baptism with a number of candidates. Deeply impressed, he vowed: "I will never sprinkle another person old or young as long as I live."[8] He didn't, and was soon himself immersed.

By the next meeting, which took place in June 1799 at Horton, the little body had become "The Baptist and Congregational Association," and Edward Manning was named to make ready a plan of association to be placed before the session scheduled for the same month the following year. A later commentator described the crowd as it would have looked:

Seven plain, farmer-like looking men are assembled, and they have come from New Brunswick as well as Nova Scotia. They are all comparatively young in years, and younger still in their experience of ecclesiastical affairs. And not more than one, if even one, has ever attended an Association in his life. They have met in a small, old-looking meeting-house . . . used occasionally as a court-house, a false floor being spread over the gallery for that purpose, where the Judge's bench, Jury box, &c. &c. occupied a temporary locality above the pulpit, during the process of civil trials; then to be removed to make place for the worshippers. It is to be regretted that there are not notes of that meeting. . . . There were present Edward Manning, James Manning, T. S. Harding, Joseph Dimock, Elijah Easterbrooks, Thomas H. Chipman, and John Burton.[9]

It is curious that the name of John Payzant is not included in the 1799 list, for he had apparently not then severed connections with the others. He was to be present at the next year's founding session according to the Reverend William Chipman who was there,[10] although again his name does not appear. Two important names do emerge at the preparatory meeting—those of Baptist ministers John Burton and T. S. Harding.

Changeover Complete

Thus it was on June 23 and 24, 1800, the way prepared, that the first Baptist association convened in what is now Canada. The location was at Lower Granville, where James Manning was pastor of the Second Annapolis church. Nine churches were represented, one of them Sackville in New Brunswick, the rest in Nova Scotia. All the churches sent their pastors—except Newport, which was represented by a layman. First and Second Annapolis each sent a lay "messenger."*

Edward Manning, who had been asked to plan for the meeting, had obviously done his work well, fashioning the design after that of a New England association: the Danbury Association. The inauguration was consummated when the name chosen by the new body was the Nova Scotia Baptist Association; the word "Congregational," which had been included the previous year, was dropped.

The changeover was complete. As Arthur R. M. Lower has written of

---

*The following are the names of the delegates who attended the historic meeting:

Church	Minister	Messenger
Horton	T. S. Harding	
Cornwallis	Edward Manning	
Newport		George Dimock
First Annapolis	T. H. Chipman	Abner Hall
Second Annapolis	James Manning	Timothy Rice
Digby	Enoch Towner	
Yarmouth	Harris Harding	
Chester	Joseph Dimock	
Sackville	Joseph Crandall	

the chain of events, "While all came [to Nova Scotia] as nominal Congregationalists, they were simple people and the heady appeals of the 'New Lights' under such preachers as Henry Alline reduced stiff New England Congregationalism into something warmer and cruder, whence in turn it swung around into a little more stability in that successful frontier denomination, the Baptist."[11]

The one sad figure on the occasion was that of John Payzant, who, although he was present and indeed preached the Sunday sermon before the opening Monday session, could not abide the decision to become thoroughly Baptist. It would have meant his own immersion and for that, unlike all the others, he was not prepared. Although he never did become a Baptist, Payzant remained on generally friendly terms with his erstwhile co-workers, even inviting them to occupy his pulpit when they visited Liverpool.

The name of the Reverend John Burton of Halifax is also prominently missing from the list of registrants at the 1800 conference. This may be explained by the decision of the Halifax church to practise close communion, restricting the Lord's table to baptized believers. Such a practice was not adopted initially by the churches of the association, but was to become a subject of no little contention in years to come.

Principles of Association

Official minutes of the association were apparently not printed until the year 1810. Only a brief review of one year, 1802, has been discovered — in the handwriting of Edward Manning. Happily a copy of the Preamble, Principles and Rules of the founding association of 1800 were preserved.

Pointing to the experience of associations in England and the United States, the founders anticipated the benefits that should be expected — "maintaining more effectively the faith . . .—obtaining advice and counsel in cases of doubt and difficulty, and assistance in distress—and in general being better able to promote the cause of God." While disclaiming any "coercive right," and recognizing the independence of the local church, the association did require a church to apply for admission, "setting forth their faith and order . . . and willingness to conform to the rules of the associated body."[12] It was expected that the churches would send regular reports of their statistics and activities, and they could be dropped for failure to do so or to send messengers or financial support for a three-year period. This balance between the independent/interdependent has always proved a delicate one for Baptists over the years, the recognized solution being that the situation is seldom either/or but both/and.

As many Baptist connectional bodies have done historically, the new association at the very outset adopted a well-defined Confession of Faith — that prepared by British Baptists in 1687 and accepted by the Philadelphia Association in 1742. In North America, it is generally known as the Philadelphia Confession.

In the Canadas

Just two years after the formation of the initial association on the east coast, there was a similar, although considerably smaller, development in the Canadas. Quite localized, it was not an impressive company — consisting of just three struggling little churches — but it proved to be the first brave effort in a more than eighty-five-year endeavour to establish an effective and continuing regional body in central Canada.

The Thurlow Association

The three churches, grouped near the Bay of Quinte area on the north shore of Lake Ontario, were those at Cramahe-Haldimand, where Reuben Crandall served; Hallowell, whose minister at the time was Joseph Winn; and Thurlow which was under the pastoral care of Asa Turner. Such a partnership had been the goal of the Haldimand church since its inception: the members of that church had characterized themselves in their convenant as "brethren and sisters assembled for the purpose of obtaining fellowship with sister churches."[13] And within five years — in 1802 — their dream, however limited, had been fulfilled.

While records are scant, some information about the new Thurlow Association can be found in letters written by itinerant American missionaries. In 1803, after his second tour into Upper Canada, Joseph Cornell made these observations in the *Massachusetts Baptist Missionary Magazine* of that year: "The few churches of our denomination in the Province have formed an Assocation, with whom we now met, and assisted in accommodating some differences of opinion among them. I believe it would have given all our brethren a new spring of soul, to have seen the assembly crowded till the house would hold no more, and a number out in the weather."

Here Cornell mentions that he and "Brother Roots" had preached at the associational gathering. Peter P. Roots, like Cornell a missionary of the Massachusetts Baptist Missionary Society, was also on an Upper Canada tour at the time. Cornell continues:

> O my soul! never forget this day of God's power in blessing the labours of us his unworthy servants in this remote wilderness. The whole of this meeting was attended with good order, and our encouragement was great, for pools of water have broken out in the desert, and it begins to look like a garden.
>
> Elder Winn, one of the ministers present, lives at West Lake . . . Elder Turner lives at Moyers' Creek . . . Elder Crandall has had a comfortable season this past year. . . . They all complain of living at such a distance from their brethren.[14]

Like Paul and Barnabas

Both Cornell and Roots met again with the Thurlow Association the next year, Roots reporting that "this infant association was involved in some difficulties, but happily all subsided, and it was a time of love, joy, and peace."[15] An extract from the minutes of that meeting, together with a letter from the association to the Massachusetts Society appeared in the society's journal. The two missionaries who sent it may well have found the writing slightly embarrassing: they were major subjects in the letter and, as moderator and clerk for the occasion, had to sign and dispatch it . . . and also request financial aid. The letter also expressed the "unfeigned thanks" of the association to the society for sending the two missionaries, whose coming was "like Paul and Barnabas visiting the churches," and who the year before had restored harmony in the face of some difficulties.[16]

Ties with the United States

The churches in Lower Canada also had their early associational ties with the United States. Situated as they were in the Eastern Townships, close to the American border, they had good opportunity for a fraternal relationship with the association in nearby Vermont. The minutes of the Richmond Baptist Association of that state, 1805–10, show that there were churches at Hatley and Stanstead, Stanbridge, St. Armand and Sutton in Lower Canada in 1805.[17]

The churches of the western cluster in Upper Canada also looked to the south for fellowship at first, served as they were so frequently by American missionaries. The Charlotteville church, for instance, which was organized in 1804 by missionaries Obed Warren and Lemuel Covell, applied the same year for membership in the Shaftsbury Association of New York, Vermont and Massachusetts.

An Immediate Threat

At its very inception in 1800, the Baptist Association of Nova Scotia and New Brunswick (the name soon taken in recognition of growth in the latter province) learned of a serious challenge to another cherished Baptist principle, that of religious liberty. Prompt action was taken. Enoch Towner, minister of the Digby church, had just been charged with the "offence" of performing a marriage by licence. By law only Church of England clergymen were permitted to do this, the others being allowed to officiate only after the publication of banns. The penalty was £50, a large sum in those times.

Towner, having married a couple by licence a year earlier, had indeed performed a second such marriage just nine days before the association convened. This time the Anglican rector of Digby informed Bishop Inglis in Halifax and the bishop laid a complaint before the authorities. Towner was summoned for trial in the capital.

By the following resolution the association moved to Towner's defence: "That whereas brother Enoch Towner is prosecuted for the solemnization of the banns of matrimony, which affects the whole body, we agree to recommend to our churches to contribute towards defraying the expenses of the said suit; and further agree that brother Chipman, brother Dimock and brother Edward Manning should accompany him and advise and assist in said business."[18]

Victory for Religious Freedom

In a celebrated trial, with Attorney-General Richard Uniake prosecuting, judgment was given in favour of the defendant on the basis that the Church of England had not been formally established in Nova Scotia by special act of the provincial legislature. The defendant, the judgment continued, was a regularly ordained pastor of a church body loyal to the Crown and a verdict in favour of the plaintiff might well lead to serious consequences as those adversely affected would unite in opposition, even at the risk of their lives.[19] It was a significant victory for religious freedom, although the statue under which Towner was originally prosecuted was not removed until 1834.

James Innis, a New Brunswick Baptist minister, did not fare as well, paying a very high price for his daring. Charged with the same so-called offence in that province some time later, Innis was not only fined £50 but imprisoned for a year. Justice for non-conformists in the early 1800s in the Maritimes was neither even-handed nor fair.

A Special Pardon

Nor was the situation any better in rapidly developing Upper Canada. Even in 1820 the position was intolerable, the penalties substantially more severe. In the same year that he founded the Hallowell and Cramahe-Haldimand churches, Reuben Crandall was arrested for conducting marriages in contravention of the statutes. His "crime" consisted of performing marriage beyond the limits of his authorized area—although he did so unwittingly. The attorney general in this instance also sought to bring the full force of the law to bear on the culprit, and the judge had no option but to sentence Crandall to the mandatory punishment — fourteen years' banishment. The prosecutor objected strongly when the judge, supported by the jury, sent Crandall to the lieutenant-governor with a plea and recommendation for a special pardon. It is relieving to record that the pardon was granted and Crandall freed.[20]

Once full religious liberty was lost on the Atlantic seabord it was difficult to regain. In the Canadas it developed only slowly.

It was in the last years of the eighteenth century that Baptist self-awareness really began to develop in British North America. Obviously this did not happen overnight, although, particularly on the east coast, the culminating achievement was seen in 1800 when Canada's first Baptist association convened. And it happened because of a thoroughgoing emphasis on the complete acceptance of scripture.

Significantly, that awareness showed itself not in what some have perceived to be a Baptist proclivity for overmuch independence, but rather in an authentic demonstration of mutual reliance and co-operative effort — the formation of associations. The little Haldimand church in Upper Canada set the tone, expressing in its covenant the goal of "obtaining fellowship with sister churches."

While many of the Baptist churches in the Maritimes developed from elements within Congregational churches that already existed, a good number of the churches in the Canadas were planted by American missionaries. Because of that American presence, the early affiliations in the Canadas were naturally cross-border. The exception, of course, was the tiny Thurlow Association, but even in that situation there was obvious dependence on the journeying missionaries and their supporting societies.

War and changing patterns of immigration were to affect the picture in the Canada, while to the east the subject of the ordinances was exercising the new association.

CHAPTER 7

Frontiers of Faith and Order

*"If the word of truth be preached among you, the worship of God preserved in
its purity, and the ordinances of Christ observed according to their primitive
simplicity, God will dwell in you."*
—ANDREW FULLER

Baptists are probably most distinguished from other historically mainline
Protestant denominations by their beliefs about the very nature of the
church. The New Testament clearly teaches, Baptists hold, that the
church is constituted exclusively of believers, individuals who have personally accepted Jesus Christ as Saviour and Lord and have been reborn
through the Holy Spirit. Hence, the church does not include potential
believers or believers-by-proxy, whether or not they were born within a
"convenant" or were involuntarily baptized. As in the New Testament,
the church is a believers' church, and each must decide for himself or
herself to enter into the kingdom and the church through faith. Concerns
of faith and order in the church are thus of vital importance and the
principles may be drawn solely from the scriptures.

The Ordinances

The ordinances of the church—baptism and the Lord's supper—are for
believer participation, and the forefathers sought to be carefully scriptural
in their practice on that point. While available early records are fragmentary, it is evident that the new Baptist Association of Nova Scotia and
New Brunswick immediately wrestled with problems concerning the
ordinances.

Edward Manning did leave a brief handwritten account of the association meeting of 1802 held in Cornwallis, in which he indicates that a
major item of business on that occasion concerned the conduct of baptism. The reference is succinct: "Agreed that the ordinance of Baptism
should not be administered to any but those that join the churches,
except in places where they cannot be blessed with such a privilege."[1]
Baptism and church membership were thus viewed as taking place concurrently. Just as baptism was the earmark of entry into the universal
church, so it signified admission into the local church, the local being an
essential "outcrop" of the universal. To separate baptism from church

membership created an artificial situation, dangerous not only to the emerging churches, but also to the new believer, who would be left without responsibility or the support of a caring fellowship. Then, too, unattached Christians were not found in the New Testament; all were linked in a fellowship.

Serious Difficulties

The subject of communion, the Lord's supper, next became a focus of weighty discussion among the churches of the association. As mentioned earlier, the Horton Baptist Church had declined the offer of the Cornwallis New Light congregation in 1779, when it had sought "Sisterly Fellowship and Communion" with them. The next year Horton unbent, permitting the Cornwallis friends "to sit down with us at the Lord's table occasionally . . . [with] the mode of baptism [being] no bar to communion."[2] How frequent or variable "occasional" was deemed to be is not clear, but the practice of the Horton church, which later became an early model for the other burgeoning Baptist churches (except the ones at Halifax and Ragged Island) was, de facto, open communion.

In the circumstances that surrounded the new Baptist development, this practice was destined to cause serious difficulties. A number of the delegates present at the association meetings of 1805 were called as a council to meet with representatives of the Cornwallis (now Baptist) church over the issue. Since Edward Manning's own immersion, nearly all who were subsequently converted under his ministry had been similarly baptized. Yet there remained within the Cornwallis membership a good number of Congregationalists, and Manning wanted his church to become completely Baptistic in practice as well as in name.

At Considerable Cost

After serious deliberation the council was unable to come to a resolution of the question, and the issue must have remained undecided for another three years, since the Cornwallis church applied to the association again at that time for a decision on the communion matter. The final judgment did not come easily, but the advice then given the Cornwallis church was to move to "close" (or "closed") Communion.

By the time the association gathered in 1809, opinions had shifted so significantly that only one delegate supported open communion, and a resolution was passed, "to withdraw fellowship from all churches who admit unbaptized persons to what is called occasional communion, and to consider themselves a Regular close-communion Baptist Association."[3]

The decision was made at considerable cost. Of the eighteen churches then in the association, four withdrew, including Yarmouth and Chester, which were founding members. Chester returned within two years, but greatly reduced in size; Yarmouth remained apart for nearly two decades.

From the vantage point of nearly two centuries later, it may well be argued that the forefathers were shortsighted in demanding a limited

Lord's table, for no major Baptist group in Canada today practises close communion, holding instead that the requirements are between the participant and his or her Master. The action taken at that time, however, may well have been vital to saving the infant Baptist body from the gradual dilution and decline that would have resulted from persisting "mixed" membership and lack of common purpose.

The resolution also opened the way for two other fellowships to join: those at Halifax and Ragged Island, which had held to close communion from their inception. They immediately became part of the association.

The communion question was to become even more acute in the Canadas. Over a long period of time it was one of the major factors obstructing any wider union of the churches and restraining the development of Christian higher education.

Developing Faith and Order

At the 1810 annual meeting held in Sackville, New Brunswick, two fraternal messengers were welcomed from the Lincoln Association of Maine: Elder Daniel Merrill who preached the opening sermon and Elder H. Hale. Writing in the *American Baptist Magazine* on his return, Merrill paid significant tribute to the development of the ten-year-old body:

> It was very pleasing to me to behold my beloved brethren in Nova Scotia and New Brunswick, who have so lately emerged into gospel liberty, so expert in discipline, so determined in Christian order and Communion, and so marshalled in battle array. They appear, in a very good degree, like veterans, while they are, in age, but very children. . . . They can count nearly forty (churches) and some of them are large and flourishing.[4]

Continuing Revival and Co-operative Ordination

Merrill also related that in just one county, Annapolis, he believed that between two and three hundred had been baptized during the year — one of the signs that revival fires continued to burn brightly in the eastern provinces. Historian George A. Rawlyk calls the period "the Great Reformation," the culmination of what was effectively a Second Great Awakening in Nova Scotia. Within one three-month span some 150 were converted in the Yarmouth-Argyle area and during another several-month period Enoch Towner of Digby baptized more than 100. Joseph Dimock of Chester immersed over 40 in the months of October and November 1807.[5]

The 1814 assembly grappled with yet another ordinances question — whether or not a minister might baptize anyone without the permission of his church. They decided that the church's permission would be required unless a pastor was ministering in some distant place where there was no organized church.

Although Ministerial ordination among Baptists had always been primarily the responsibility of the local church, in previous meetings of the Nova Scotia and New Brunswick Association, and again later, a number of ordinations were carried out by the association itself. In 1814 a procedure was followed that suggested the pattern for the current practice of Canadian Baptists, which might be described as co-operative ordination. The association, responding to a request from a local church, advised them to call a council of representatives of sister churches to examine the candidate. The council's recommendation would then be passed on to the applying church for action. On future occasions the association or Convention/Union were asked to name the council. While this decision displayed a clear recognition of the local church's primacy in ordination, it also indicated that action should be taken in co-operation with member churches of the general body.

Mission

While by 1814 the Nova Scotia and New Brunswick churches had made great strides in developing order and discipline, the association meeting of that year, which was held in Chester, Nova Scotia, was to be even more momentous. Two decisions were made at that meeting which proved to be milestones in the story of the denomination in Canada. Their significance can hardly be overstated:

> Voted, that brethren Joseph Crandal and Samuel Bancroft visit the . . . [non-Christian] inhabitants [east of Chester], and that each of them receive five shillings per day, during three months . . .
>
> and
>
> A contribution was made for the poor Heathen, to be sent to the Treasurer of the Auxiliary Bible Society at Halifax, and forwarded by that Society. Amount received £8,13s[6]

American Elder Daniel Merrill's assessment of the growing stature of Maritime Baptists had not been overstated. With just fourteen years' experience, the association had officially established a home missions enterprise and had begun plans for work in overseas missions.

Interdependence

The local churches and their pastors had certainly undertaken a good deal of outreach in their own areas even before the 1814 Chester decisions. Because pastors were still itinerant to a great extent, their influence spread over a wide area. This no doubt had much to do with the establishment of many of the forty churches that Merrill had noticed.

The association's 1814 decision to launch a home missions project in no way reflected adversely upon the efforts of the churches but was, in fact, made at the request of the Chester congregation. It was a dramatic move in the developing Baptist interdependence, a recognition that a good number of tasks are better accomplished co-operatively.

A Bright Star

Pioneer Baptist historian I. E. Bill, writing just over sixty years after the event, pointed to the second Chester decision as "the commencement of our Foreign Missionary Enterprise,"[7] an enterprise that remains a bright star in the Canadian Baptist constellation.

The next year the home missions venture was regularly established when it was "voted that the Association is considered as a Missionary Society, and with them is left the whole management of the Mission business."[8] On the occasion of a "missionary sermon" from Elder Edmund J. Reis at that meeting, an offering of £29.13s was received for the home missions outreach. No time limit was set on the commission of Joseph Crandall and his new co-worker, James Munroe. The place of mission was shifted "to the Eastward of Halifax," and the stated remuneration set at "one dollar per day," (dollars and cents were beginning to replace British currency by that time).

The "missionary society" into which the association resolved itself for the purpose of home missions work was but the association "wearing another hat." Societies later to be established in the Canadas were different, being patterned after those instituted by the Baptists of the northern United States. The Maritime model was composed of messengers or delegates of the churches who were ultimately responsible to the churches. The membership of societies in the Canadas was to be made up of interested but self-appointed individuals who subscribed financially to the particular society but bore no responsibility to a local church or the association. This difference proved to have a major effect on the rate at which the denomination advanced in the two regions.

Outreach in the Canadas

The American Missionaries, whose work was so vital in establishing the Baptist witness in Upper and Lower Canada, were as concerned as the Maritime leaders about setting up adequate bases of faith and order in the fledgling churches. Matters like correctness of doctrine, the ordinances, membership requirements and ordination were given primary consideration. The intellectually and spiritually well-equipped missionaries had a vision for these churches that held very close to scripture. During the first decade of the nineteenth century, no fewer than twenty-three missionaries from south of the border undertook a total of thirty-four tours in various parts of Upper and Lower Canada.

Of Men and Movements

As a result of these many missionary thrusts and the complementary efforts of some dozen known ordained and lay pastors of the region, during that first decade at least ten new churches were added to the earlier eight. These were at Charlotteville (Vittoria), Markham, Townsend (Boston), Niagara (Queenston), Oxford, Stephentown, Percy, Rawdon, Ameliasburg and Sidney.[9] During this period the church of Clinton was also reconstituted.

Titus Finch . . . Charlotteville

The name of Titus Finch is closely linked with the founding of the first Baptist church in Charlotteville in 1803 — the first in the Long Point district on Lake Erie. Originally a lay preacher, Finch was living and serving in Charlotteville when Shaftsbury Association missionaries Obed Warren and Lemuel Covell visited there that year, "baptized 30 persons and gave them fellowship as a church."[10] Indeed, Finch himself was one of the candidates, Covell later writing that "when we arrived there, brother Finch had never been baptized"[11] — an omission which the missionary soon rectified.[12]

Titus Finch is believed to have come from New York state, where at the time of the Revolution he joined a British regiment, was captured and spent two years as a prisoner of war. Upon discharge, along with other soldiers of his regiment, he settled on a land grant along a tributary of the St. John River in New Brunswick, where, it is conjectured, his inclination toward the Baptist position may well have been formed or strengthened during revival services conducted by Edward Manning in that area in 1793. Earlier family influences may also have played a part, as the Finch name was well-known in New England Baptist circles.

Finch moved to Upper Canada in 1799, resettling at Long Point, where he soon began to hold services among the other homesteaders. Peter Fairchild of nearby Townsend frequently assisted him, and their efforts resulted in the thirty candidates who were baptized and formed into a church by missionary Covell in 1803. Concerning this church, early historian David Benedict was to say: "The Charlotteville church became a distinguished nursery of sister communities in after years. The First Townsend was set off in 1805, then in succession went out from this prolific mother: Oxford, Baham, Walahide, Wolsingham, Walpole, Middleton and Second Charlotteville; they had all been branches of the parent stock."[13]

Peter Fairchild . . . Townsend

In addition to his 1803 visit to Upper Canada, Lemuel Covell made trips in 1805 and 1806. During the 1805 trip, a lay preacher named Peter Fairchild also played a leading role in the founding of the Townsend church. Like Titus Finch, Fairchild was a New York native, who had migrated to Upper Canada in 1793. Although he settled at Townsend, Fairchild initially joined the church at Charlotteville about sixteen miles away, and helped Finch in his ministry there. With the arrival of a number of Baptist settlers at Townsend, Fairchild began work in his home community, starting to conduct services there in 1804.

The next year Covell came to help form the Townsend congregation into a church and installed Fairchild as pastor, although he was not to be ordained until the following year, in 1806. Fairchild was the pastor at Townsend until 1818. Unfortunately, his tenure was brought to a somewhat inglorious conclusion. In 1818 he remarried after his first wife's death, with the result that the church withdrew fellowship from their minister "for marrying an unbelieving character and justifying himself to our dissatisfaction."[14] Even the "U.E." which he bore after his name as a recognized Loyalist did nothing to validate his action in the eyes of his congregation. The code of Christian ethics was high — at least for ministers.

Elijah Bentley . . . Markham

A third lay minister to have major responsibility for establishing a church in that decade — at Markham north of present-day Toronto — was Elijah Bentley. Like Fairchild, Bentley came to Upper Canada with other members of his well-known Baptist family, in the wave of American immigration after the Revolution. Bentley was instrumental in instituting the church in 1803, the same year that the church at Charlotteville was founded. Markham was to become the fourth church in the little Thurlow Association the next year.

Unlike Finch and Fairchild, Bentley allowed his sympathies to remain with his homeland, for in 1813, during the War of 1812, he was "convicted by a jury of using seditious language in a sermon preached in Markham township on May 2nd,"[15] which resulted in a six-month jail sentence. This was a blow that not only silenced Elijah Bentley, but apparently submerged the little Markham church for nearly twenty-five years.

Elkanah Holmes . . . Queenston

The name of Elkanah Holmes is prominently associated with the organization of a church at Queenston in the Niagara Peninsula in 1808. Born in Massachusetts and ordained about 1773, Holmes served as a chaplain to a New Jersey regiment during the Revolution and later held pastorates in Connecticut and New York. The first moderator of the New York Baptist Association, which he helped to initiate, Holmes volunteered for missionary work in the western part of the state, particularly among the Indians of the Six Nations, a chief of whom had invited him.

In 1801 Holmes joined the missionary staff of the Baptist/Presbyterian New York Missionary Society and was sent to work among the Indians near Fort Niagara and Buffalo Creek, where his effective work impressed the legendary Mohawk chief, Joseph Brant. After the New York Baptists withdrew to form their own society, they were joined by the Massachusetts Baptist Missionary Society, which continued to support Holmes and his Indian work.

By 1807 Holmes had expanded his horizons to include a new venture among the settlers across the border at Queenston, where, with the assistance of Shaftsbury Association missionary Nathaniel Kendrick, he was instrumental in forming a church the same year. Queenston joined the New York Association in 1810. While Holmes had been made pastor of the new church, his boundless energy could hardly be contained within a single cause and like so many of his fellow ministers, he moved out to other scattered congregations, including the rejuvenated Clinton.

War again became a divisive force weakening the infant Baptist endeavour. Like Bentley, Holmes favoured the American cause in the conflict of 1812. Indeed, he had been party to a New York Association letter of 1800 which held "with what gratitude should we behold with increasing lustre, the goodness and wisdom of God in our separation from the British Empire."[16] Completely pro-American, Holmes even entertained invading American officers in his home. When the U.S. forces had to retreat, they took Holmes along, but he was captured by the British. He was rescued, then captured again, but finally escaped and reached safety in the United States, remaining there until his death. Holmes' Queenston church was dealt a heavy blow by the war, and it was not long before "its membership in the New York Association ceased, and evidently the church became dormant for a time,"[17] likely until the early 1830s.

Oxford

The first Baptist church in Oxford county was established largely as a result of the efforts of Peter Fairchild, then pastor at Townsend. Shortly after the turn of the century, Shaftsbury Association missionaries had begun making periodic calls to the region: Obed Warren and Lemuel Covell in 1803, David Irish in 1806 and Asahel Morse in 1807; but it was Fairchild whose two visits in 1808 led to the church's founding, first as a branch of the Townsend church.

During Fairchild's second trip to Oxford, when he was accompanied by yet another Shaftsbury missionary, Nathaniel Kendrick, the Oxford Baptists decided to seek recognition by the Shaftsbury Association as an extension of Townsend. In just a year, congregational growth was such that they were encouraged to request recognition on their own. Thus the First Regular Baptist Church of Oxford was officially established in 1809, and was received into the Shaftsbury Association in 1811.

Stephens and Derbyshire . . . Stephentown

In eastern Upper Canada more churches were also being established. In the township of Bastard, Leeds County, at a settlement called Stephentown (which was named after Abel Stephens, U.E., a Baptist preacher and colonizer), a church developed very early in the century. Stephens, apparently an ordained minister, and lay-preacher Daniel Derbyshire laid the foundation for the church, which was actually formed in 1803 during the first of two trips that Joseph Cornell of the Massachusetts Missionary Society made to Upper Canada. After his visit Cornell made this observation in the *Massachusetts Baptist Missionary Magazine*: "Their hearts were so cemented together in Stephentown, that after passing an examination of their faith and practice, they formed themselves into a church, consisting of fourteen members. We met the Lord's day after, and it would have given pleasure to our churches in general, to have seen the assembly meeting, when they had come through water up to their sleigh boxes."[18]

The kind of commitment Cornell saw at Stephentown augured well for the future. When he made his second tour the next year, accompanied by another missionary, Peter P. Roots, they "got to see the little vine planted last year in Stephentown," he wrote, adding that they "found the church met together waiting for our advice and assistance in the ordination of brother Derbyshire."[19]

A day for the examination and ordination was set, the resulting scene being reminiscent in at least one respect of that described in Mark 2:4, where the crowd listening to Jesus was so large that the palsied man had to be lowered through the roof. "With a view to accommodate [the crowd]," wrote Roots of the Stephentown ceremony, "the upper floors of the house were broken up."[20] It proved to be a unique occasion: a double ordination. Not only was Derbyshire set apart to the ministry, but so was Abel Stephens. "The legality of a former ordination" was in some question, Cornell wrote, adding that "we thought it advisable to ordain him again to put an end to all doubts."[21]

A newcomer, Jesse Brown, became pastor in Stephentown in 1809 under somewhat unusual conditions. Minutes of the church dated February 25 of that year indicate that after "a brief relation of his life and experience"[22] Brown was called to be pastor of the church. Less confidence was suggested in both Brown's and his wife's membership qualifications, however, probably since they could not supply letters of dismission or transfer from their previous church. The same minutes noted that "for the obtaining of other credentials it was thought proper not to join in convenant bonds at this time." Happily, the next month's minutes were reassuring, as "Brother Brown and sister Brown came forward and joined the church, having letters from other churches."[23]

The Stephentown account once again indicates that faith and order concerns were of major importance in the frontier churches. Obvious care was taken in assessing both the fitness of prospective members and the qualifications of those seeking ordination as pastors. The American missionary leaders were most careful to ensure a maturing of the spiritual community.

Although documentation is scanty, it is known that at least four other churches were established in Upper Canada—at Percy, Rawdon, Sidney and Ameliasburg—in the period between the turn of the century and the onset of war in 1812.

Clinton/Beamsville Renewal

The first congregation at Clinton, or Beamsville, in the Niagara Peninsula, does not appear to have lasted beyond the tenure of founding Pastor

Tims. As already noted, however, Asahel Morse did discover "a number of baptized professors" when he passed that way in 1807. Some of these were obviously interested in a renewal of the church, for Morse wrote in his journal: "As I proposed visiting them on my return I advised them to call a council from the churches of Townsend and Charlotteville; and for those who could fellowship with each other and agree in sentiment and practice according to the Baptist order, to offer themselves to the council, and if they could gain fellowship, to be united into a Baptist church."[24]

Morse's advice as to renewal "according to the Baptist order" was obviously acceptable, for when he did return he was able to give leadership in the formation of the council, involving representatives of the Charlotteville and Townsend churches. The council "found nine men and eleven women, who appeared to be pious people, and could fellowship with each other in sentiment and practice." Unfortunately — once more indicating the care with which membership was handled — "a number more offered themselves, but were rejected on account of irregular walk [with God]."[25] With the approval of the council, the acceptable twenty revived the work at Clinton and re-established the church.

Lower Canada

In Lower Canada the missionary influx was not as extensive or perhaps as effective during the early period of the nineteenth century. To the settlements in the Eastern Townships the Shaftsbury Association sent three missionaries, and the Massachusetts Baptist Missionary Society sent four.

Two Shaftsbury elders, Jonathon Finch and Calvin Chamberlain, included Lower Canada in their itineraries — Finch in successive years 1807 to 1809, and Chamberlain in 1808. Cyrus Andrews served in the Townships in 1810. A number of other American missionaries visited Lower Canada during the first years of the nineteenth century, but the last visit seems to have taken place around 1811. While in Upper Canada a more limited but still appreciable Baptist missionary effort from the south was to be resumed at the end of the War of 1812, there was no similar restoration of activity in the lower province.

The missionaries to Upper and Lower Canada not only planted churches and gave competent guidance to a dedicated coterie of local pastors who laboured well on the scene. They also planted ideas, solid spiritual concepts, which were yet to make for strong congregations of God's people. They also emphasized the significance of faith and order in the frontier churches, providing the sinews for the strong body still to emerge.

CHAPTER 8

Hiatus and Hope

"None but changed men can change the world."
— EMLYN DAVIES

The War of 1812 is said to have been "one of the massive foundation stones of modern Canada."[1] The combat pitted the United States against her former motherland, Great Britain, with the continent of North America as the battleground.

Reasons for the hostilities may be traced to frictions both on this continent and abroad. Among the irritations, there was major annoyance in the West over the opposing interests of the American frontier settlers and the British colonial fur traders with their Indian allies. Many in the American central region were also casting expansionist eyes on the fertile timbered lands of the Canada, already settled by many of their erstwhile countrymen.

The Canadas Invaded

Overseas, Britain was locked in a fight to the finish with Napoleon, with only her navy standing between the Emperor and the accomplishment of his dream of world domination. In her extremity, Britain took actions which greatly angered the Americans. Responding to Napoleon's 1806 Berlin Decree, which called for the blockade of the British Isles, Britain invoked her own orders-in-council the next year to institute a counter-blockade of the European continent.

This action cut off lucrative U.S. trade with Europe, to the exasperation of those American leaders who favoured war and who were also especially incensed by the British practice of stopping and searching American ships on the high seas. This was done, it was charged, not only to remove British naval deserters, but frequently to press U.S. citizens into British naval service.

The United States declared war on June 19, 1812, and immediately invaded the Canadas. With Britain's hands completely tied in Europe, and having the confident expectation of a warm welcome from their former countrymen in the still sparsely populated Canadas, it is little wonder that the Americans expected an easy conquest. Authorities have estimated that of Upper Canada's population, said to be no more than 136,000 in 1812, one-fifth were of Old Country origin, one-fifth Loyalist and three-fifths "ordinary Americans."[2]

But the vast majority of ordinary Americans had become Canadians in outlook by then and generally proved faithful to their adopted land, as did those of French lineage in Lower Canada. In campaigns over three years the invaders were repulsed. Then, when large numbers of battle-experienced British regulars arrived in 1814 after the defeat of Napoleon, the aggression came to an end and peace was restored — a cherished peace which has remained unbroken for nearly two centuries.

New England Disagrees

It is interesting that almost no reference to the conflict is made in the Nova Scotia and New Brunswick associational documents. There is just one allusion in the 1813 minutes in the suggestion to the churches concerning the usual annual day of prayer and fasting, that God "would be graciously pleased to remove the dreadful calamities of War . . . [and] to establish Peace among all nations."[3] Little else may be gleaned regarding the War of 1812 — a conflict which A. R. M. Lower views as definitive for the future of Canada: "It is possible that there would have been a Canadian Nation without the War of 1812, but it would have been a less self-conscious one, one less securely based emotionally, one whose continued existence would have been less certain."[4]

The seemingly limited concern of east coast Baptists in the hostilities may well have issued from the lack of any military operations on their soil. Indeed, the neighbouring New England states did not agree with the war party in their nation and strongly opposed the conflict, fearing the disruption of trade with Britain far more than the interruption of trade with continental Europe. Except for the forcing of American prize ships into Halifax harbour, a limited foray into Maine by the troops of Nova Scotia Lieutenant-Governor Sherbrooke (who held the town of Castine for some months), and the dispatch of a New Brunswick regiment to the Canadas, the hostilities hardly touched the Maritime region. As Lower describes it: "New Brunswick and Maine came as close to being neutral in this strange war as two official combatants could be. Communication does not seem to have been interrupted and there was no suspicion of hostilities on the border."[5]

Baptists and the War of 1812

In the Canadas, where the defensive war was largely fought, the effects were predictably far more distressing. Pillage and destruction followed in the wake of successive American attacks and withdrawals, and casualties were high. For the struggling Baptist cause the consequences were devastating, at least temporarily.

As seen in the previous chapter, a number of the slim band of

American-born pastors preaching in the Canadas were less content in their allegiance to their recently embraced country than were most of their parishioners. At least two of them were vocal and active in support of the "enemy " cause. The results of such divided loyalties submerged a few churches and weakened others.

Even more debilitating was the loss of the able leadership of the American Baptist missionaries, none of whom was able to continue the vital work. The missionaries had been true "fathers in God" to the small, scattered settlements — preaching, teaching, conducting the ordinances, handling ordinations, organizing, even settling disputes. Then, on returning home after each trip, they had raised funds to support the tiny congregations.

Except for the Reverend Barnabas Perkins, who participated in the ordination service at Hatley in 1811, and Elder Cyrus Andrews who, according to the minutes of the Shaftsbury Association, was in the province of Upper Canada in 1812,[6] no American Baptist missionary seems to have crossed the border for nearly five years after 1810.

During the war years, the onus of leadership in Upper Canada fell upon the three pioneer Loyalist pastors — Joseph Winn, Titus Finch and Peter Fairchild — with Reuben Crandall going on itinerating missions. Two of them, Winn and Finch, were, like the Apostle Paul, "tent-maker ministers," at least during that period. Winn used his team of horses to haul supplies for the defending forces, while Finch farmed and also operated a mill near Port Dover on Lake Erie. During the course of the war Finch's mill was razed and burned by the invaders.

If anyone had taken a poll on the future of the Baptist cause in Upper Canada at that time, the opinion registered would have been close to "without hope." Events seemed to be conspiring to snuff out the churches altogether. Yet there was a sense, as the great Apostle long before had forecast, in which great purposes would not be thwarted.[7] Because the churches were deprived of outside leadership, they were forced to discover resources closer to home. This would have happened in due time, of course, but the war hastened the process and may well have made for earlier maturity of the local churches.

The Aftermath

At the end of the war, missionaries were able to travel north of the border once again, but they did not come in as vast numbers as before 1812, nor did they make the same impact. Lower Canada appears to have been bypassed completely.

The Hamilton Baptist Missionary Society of central New York State dispatched Nathan Baker, Timothy Sheppard and John Upfold. According to his own account, Baker's itinerary of 1816 was lengthy, covering an area extending from near Lake Huron to the west end of Lake Ontario. En route, he reported: "[I] went past the battleground at Chippewa . . .

passed on to Bridgewater, viewing the places where the dead were buried or burnt . . . from thence passed through the village of St. David, had an extensive view of the ravages of war."[8]

A New Vision of Hope

While the limited number of American missionaries were helping plant the seed, the local pastors were reaping the harvest—and it was a bountiful one. The hiatus of the period of war and suffering had given way to a new vision of hope. One missionary, Timothy Sheppard, reported that he found nine Baptist ministers and thirteen churches in the upper province. The numbers were about to expand considerably.

The last of the trio of Hamilton Society missionaries to work in Upper Canada was a transplanted Englishman, John Upfold, who toured twice in 1816, the first time spending a brief period around Clinton, the second time covering Kingston, the "Bay of Quinty," York (Toronto), Yonge Street (extending north of Toronto), and the Niagara region.[9] Upfold apparently liked what he saw in Upper Canada, for the same year he accepted the call of the Clinton church, remaining for nine years before he returned to the United States.[10]

Developing Churchmanship

With four Upper Canadian churches holding tenuous links—Charlotteville, Clinton, Townsend and Oxford—the Shaftsbury Association, which had already contributed so much to Baptist life north of the border in the first decade of the century, was most anxious to start its mission work again. Again three missionaries were involved: Stephen Olmstead, Cyrus Andrews and Charles Lahatt.

Olmstead and Andrews worked in the Niagara Peninsula area in 1815, the Shaftsbury Missionary Committee reporting the next year a most encouraging itinerary that would "stimulate them to further exertions."[11] Both missionaries were in Clinton in September 1815 to serve on a council called to consider the ordination of Samuel Burdick. Unfortunately for the candidate, the council concluded "that his opportunity of acquaintance with the Scriptures and with Human Nature in general have not been sufficient to warrant us proceeding with his ordination at this time,"[12] and Burdick's ministry seems to have come to an abrupt end. The influence of the missionaries remained potent in matters of faith and order, continuing to ensure the development of a sturdy churchmanship.

A New Accent

With the exception of a Scottish elder named Carson at Augusta and the English American John Upfold at Clinton, Baptist ministerial leadership in both Canadas until 1816 was almost exclusively American or former American. That year the situation was to change with the emigration of a band of Baptists from Perthshire, Scotland to the Ottawa Valley, whose type of piety and polity stemmed from the Haldane revivals in the Highlands of Scotland.[13] Their arrival was to have a lasting effect upon Baptist work in that region.

Speaking the Gaelic

The Haldane revivals were sparked by two brothers of that name, Robert and James, who had, under the influence of the widespread renewal movement of their day, given up their professional occupations and sold their not inconsiderable possessions to engage in the winning of Scotland. In addition to conducting extensive evangelistic campaigns in Great Britain and on the Continent, the Haldanes established a ministerial and lay institute — called the Literary and Theological Institution — in their homeland. A host of Christian workers was trained there, many of whom came to North America. Initially Presbyterian, the Haldanes had come to the principle and practice of believer's baptism by 1808 and their more than thirty affiliated congregations then added a stable, warmly evangelical tone to Scottish Baptist life.[14]

The Haldane converts who came to Canada during and after 1816 first put down their roots in Lochiel Township, which had initially been settled by some of their Scottish compatriots as early as 1794. Unlike the Americans, who placed considerable emphasis on interdependence and the importance of careful ordinance and ordination procedures, the new Scots obviously felt themselves to be fairly self-sufficient. They established a church almost immediately, in the summer of 1817, and appointed two preaching elders and an equal number of deacons from among their number to lead the congregation. Again, unlike the Americans, they initially held to open communion, a practice which was to become the focus of long and divisive debate, restraining Baptist progress for many decades in the Canadas.

An Educated Ministry

Unfortunately for the new congregation, the two elders whom they had named came to a parting of the ways over a doctrinal dispute, and in 1821 the Breadalbane church divided in support of the different positions of the elders. This situation was corrected after five years when the two factions reunited, but it was not until 1830 that they were able to obtain a trained, ordained pastor.

Meanwhile, another Scot, John Edwards, a shipwright, emigrated to Upper Canada, finally settling at Clarence on the Ottawa River in 1822. More open than his fellow Baptists at Breadalbane, Edwards had more appreciation for an educated ministry. Returning for a visit to his homeland in 1829, he prevailed upon two able Scottish ministers, William Fraser of Inverness and John Gilmour of Aberdeen, to move to the Canadas. Fraser was called to the Breadalbane church, while Gilmour accepted the invitation of a group of Baptists to establish a church at Montreal. The Montreal church was founded in 1830. More Scottish churches were soon established at Thurso (east of present day Ottawa), St. Andrews (just north of Cornwall), Dalesville (Chatham) and Bytown (Ottawa).

Gilmour has been described as "a man of excellent culture and judgment, and truly apostolic spirit, who was to be instrumental in lifting the denomination to a higher plane." Fraser, "the ablest controversialist among his brethren," who had studied at the Haldanes' Institute, "did more than any other man for many years to give tone to the religious life and theological thinking of the Baptists of Eastern Ontario."[15] John Edwards, the man responsible for their enlistment, was later ordained himself, and went on to serve the Baptist cause with distinction.

Another Affluent

Another tributary of the Baptist stream at that time came through black Baptists from the United States, whose contribution in central Canada has been enduring, though their numbers have been small.

Most of those who settled early in the Canadas were runaway slaves, the earliest probably arriving in the Niagara district in the 1780s. Although it had been initially possible for southern slaveholders to pursue and recapture escapees even into the Canadas, in 1793 Lieutenant Governor George Simcoe introduced a bill banning slavery in British North America. By 1820 there were black settlements at Wilberforce (north of Peterborough), Dawn (Dresden), Chatham and Buxton.[16]

Unfortunately, a warm welcome was not always assured in those times even north of the border, so the newcomers were inclined to form their own churches, the earliest appearing to have been at Colchester on Lake Erie south of Windsor in 1821.[17]

Twelve former slaves, who began to meet for prayer on the shores of Toronto Bay, were organized into a congregation by Elder Washington Christian, a native of Virginia. This became Toronto's First Baptist Church in 1826, preceding by three years the congregation that became Jarvis Street Baptist.

Other black Baptist churches later grew up at Amherstburg, St. Thomas, Sandwich, Chatham, London and Shrewsbury.[18] While the churches of black membership continued to be in Upper and Lower Canada, even more widespread development was slowed by the proclamation of the Emancipation Decree by President Lincoln in 1863, and the Thirteenth Amendment to the United States Constitution passed soon afterwards. Slavery had been completely abolished and many blacks went back to the United States.

Failure to Unite

While these developments were occurring, the churches were struggling to reach out to new areas. This new activity had become especially important since missionary assistance from the south had wound down. The progress of the movement, however, was to be painfully slow.

Graphic Difference

One well-informed observer commented less than a century after the period that with respect to home missions "during the first half of the [nineteenth] century there was little or no attempt at organized effort. . . . For nearly forty years there was no general co-operation among the churches, no serious effort at field supervision, no resolute attempt at establishing strong churches in the larger centres of population."[19]

It is obvious that distance, lack of communication, inadequate transportation, overemphasis on local autonomy, differences of background and theological expression, together with the number and variety of continued transborder links conspired to impede concerted progress. The Methodists, with their well-formulated and centralized polity, proved to be better prepared for the task in the Canadas, as they were to be later on the western plains. Apart from their work in the Maritimes, Baptists were slow to seize opportunities for church planting.

In the United States, on the other hand, Baptists became the largest Protestant denomination, with the Southern Baptist Convention even now retaining the status of the nation's largest. It is impossible to know exactly why the situations in the two countries were so different. However, faster frontier development and bursting population growth in the United States were certainly major factors. So was the American form of democratic government, which at the time offered a great deal more freedom of action, highly suited to the Baptist outlook, than did the colonial and "Family Compact" rule in British North America. There were other elements, too.

In the Canadas there were obvious dissimilarities between the longer-settled former Americans and the newer British immigrants. "The tradition of professional ministry among British Canadian Baptists," writes historian Mary Bulmer Hill, "militated strongly against the preacher-farmer lay ministry of American Baptists," which was a characteristic leading to the rapid Baptist advance in the United States. She adds: "Because the British Baptists succeeded in developing a professional clergy in the Canadian Baptist Church,* the center of power shifted to them."[24] The American Baptists, both northern and southern, also developed a "professional" ministry, of course, but later, when the frontier had been conquered and the denomination was well-rooted.

The Canadian Ethos

When the question of open or close communion emerged in the Canadas, it led to more bitter dispute than in the Atlantic region and prevented

---

*Mary Bulmer Hill uses the term *Baptist Church* rather than *denomination*, which Baptists usually prefer, applying the word *church* only in a local or universal sense.

any union of Baptist forces in the Canadas until the middle of the nine-teenth century. Indeed, no lasting union was achieved until almost the last decade of the century. The pattern of agency organization also had a singular influence on this lack of development.

Churches in the Canadas formed societies, rather than Conventions or Unions and this tended to discourage large-scale co-operation. As described in the previous chapter, the true society was founded on the basis of personal, rather than representative, membership, a grouping of dues-paying, self-appointed persons linked by a common interest. Such societies did not tend to draw local churches together as more repre-sentative bodies would likely have done. In this emphasis the Baptists in the Canadas were understandably patterning their agencies after those of their mentors and friends of the northern states, who themselves have not historically enjoyed the great growth of Baptists in the south, who favoured the Convention, church-responsible concept.

The whole ethos of the Canadian scene, that which distinguishes the inhabitants of the northern half of this continent from those to the south, began to take shape very early, influencing the Baptist cause as it did every other. As Canadian author S. D. Clark points out, even then there were significant differences in the social, political and religious milieux: "The radical departures from accepted practice which were characteristic of the thinking and behaviour of American frontier populations in political organization, justice, family life, cultural relationships and religious orga-nization were less evident in the Canadian frontier population. The con-servatism of the country as a whole acted as a powerful force in checking innovations."[21] And Baptists have consistently been at their best as innovators.

Tentative Steps

Despite these obvious infirmities, a number of local pastors and the churches they served did join hands in more geographically restricted fellowship. As has been seen in Chapter 6, as early as 1802 the three churches of Cramahe-Haldimand, Hallowell and Thurlow formed the Thurlow Association, which met regularly for some years and grew mod-erately in the process.

The Release of American Ties

Churches in the Niagara Peninsula–Lake Erie region, all initially con-nected with U.S. associations, began fraternal realtionships on a loosely organized basis by 1810, becoming known as the Clinton Conference. By 1816 the Conference had become almost an association — still with strong American imput. With missionary Stephen Olmstead as modera-tor, the Conference was convened that year at Townsend, and Clinton (Beamsville), Charlotteville and Oxford, were represented, as well as the host church. It was a good deal more than a fellowship gathering, for during the three days of meetings, the representatives discussed such weighty subjects as doctrine, discipline and missions,[22] indicating their increasingly wide-ranging concerns.

The three churches of the original Thurlow Association were subsequently joined by a number of others, including Markham, Stephentown and Townsend, the last retaining at the time its formal connection with the Shaftsbury Association and a loose link with the Clinton Conference. Talbot Street (later Aylmer) near London, Ontario, which had been founded in 1816 through the efforts of Titus Finch and Reuben Crandall after Stephen Olmstead's visit the previous year, entered the Association in 1818. In 1819, a significant year in early associational development, the name was changed from Thurlow to the Haldimand Association, a renewal which continued, with the churches east of Kingston later "hiving off" to form with others with Johnstown Association.

The Scottish churches of the Ottawa Valley came together with Montreal to establish the Ottawa Association in 1836. This development had taken nearly twenty years.

A Token Effort

Although the associations grew slowly, a number of established churches engaged in outreach and personal missionary efforts. However, this work was never carried out on a denominational scale. As historian G. Gerald Harrop has written, "Although the proliferation of churches would seem to indicate a great deal of missionary activity on an individual and congregational basis, there were no attempts to form larger unions for missionary purposes before 1833."[23]

What might be viewed as at least a token effort in that direction had been made by the Clinton Conference in 1816 in forming "the Upper Canada Domestic Missionary Society for the sending of the gospel among the destitute of this Province and parts adjacent."[24] While the vision was obviously shared by a few, either the means or the will or both were lacking. As E. R. Fitch concedes: ". . .there appear to be no further records regarding this Society, [so] it is probable that it never did any real missionary work."[25]

About the same time, as the *Western New York Baptist Missionary Magazine* reported, missionary Timothy Sheppard, in visiting Hallowell and East and West Lakes had "spent some time in starting a Missionary Society to be known by the name of the Baptist Missionary Society in Upper Canada."[26] Once again, this seemingly splendid objective of 1817 apparently failed, probably because it was too far ranging to be carried out with the very limited resources available.

Even the attempt of 1833 proved to be abortive. That year the Eastern, Western and Haldimand Associations formed The Baptist Missionary Convention of Upper Canada "to reach the destitute of this Province." Despite its "convention" designation, the new organization was really a society, membership being on a personal basis with the payment of one dollar per year in dues. Ambitious plans included the purchase of a printing press and the publishing of a religious paper, but again the dream was dimmed by harsh reality, for the body "for want of concert and energy, soon became extinct."[27] Significant unity proved to be most elusive.

CHAPTER 9

Coming of Age

*"As Baptists we cherish three great ideas — Truth, Freedom, Unity;
and we rank them in that order."*
— GEORGE W. TRUETT

In retrospect it might well be said that the 1821 division of the Baptist Association of Nova Scotia and New Brunswick was a mistake. Hindsight allows us to see that it might have been better if that body had become a Convention or Union, with participating associations in each province. That was to happen twenty-five years later, but in the intervening years developments occurred in each province that would have been better handled in concert.

The Association Divides

By 1815, the association of Nova Scotia and New Brunswick, which was the only assembly beyond the local church, had in effect become the denomination, the voice of the Maritime churches. Its work had become too great to handle, and it was thought that two could probably share the burden more capably and at closer range than one.

Female Mite Societies

The problem — and it was a good one — was growth. In just ten years, from 1810 to 1820, the number of churches in the association had doubled as had the number of ministers. Acting also as a missionary society, the association was sending out full- and part-time domestic missionaries throughout Nova Scotia and New Brunswick. "Female Mite Societies" — forerunners of the woman's missionary societies — were beginning to appear on the horizon, the first to show in the associational records of 1818 being Saint John.[1] (The societies derived their name from the two "mites" offered by the poor widow, as described in Luke 21:2.) By the next association meeting there were seven. In further missionary outreach, it had been decided "to request Brother Burton of Halifax, to accept a Mission among the People of Colour, at Preston and Hammonds Plains for six weeks,"[2] his effective work resulting in the formation of the church at Hammonds Plains.

The Best of Intentions

The initial movement toward the apparently practical — and amicable — division was seen at the 1817 association meeting in Fredericton, where it was voted that the churches "consider the wisdom of dividing into two Associations as proposed by the Upper Granville [Nova Scotia] Church."[3] No further action was taken until 1820, when separate committees were established to superintend missions in the respective provinces,[4] and the next year, this time "at the request of a number of brethren from New Brunswick," it was unanimously agreed "that this Association be divided, and that the line which separates New Brunswick from Nova Scotia, be the dividing line."[5] Nothing more was said, a remarkable paucity of words characterizing the records of those times.

As indicated, the move was made with the best of intentions and in utmost friendship. Each continued to send "messengers" to the other's gatherings. In 1821 there were seventeen churches in Nova Scotia, thirteen in New Brunswick, and an overall membership of 1,827.[6]

The following year, meeting separately for the first time, each association continued its policy of acting as a missionary society. As the "societies" were simply associations under another name, all the churches were involved rather than a self-selected, if concerned, group of individuals. This greatly buttressed Maritime Baptist work from the outset and became a major reason for the larger and continuing proportionate strength of Baptists on the east coast.

Prince Edward Island

While under French sovereignty, Prince Edward Island had been called Île St. Jean, the name being translated to The Island of St. John when Great Britain took over. It was finally given its current name in 1798, after Edward, Duke of Kent, the father of Queen Victoria.

After the deportation of the Island Acadians, the land languished for many decades, as the landlords who had received British grants, showed little interest in making them productive. Religious activity was at low ebb. Henry Alline, who visited there in 1795, found the Islanders "a very dark people and indeed most of them openly profane."[7]

By the opening of the nineteenth century, however, an influx of new settlers, mostly Scottish and Irish, joined the few Highland Scots, Loyalists and remaining Acadians. As in Upper Canada, there were a number of Baptists among the Scottish immigrants.

Unacceptable Views

Once again the Literary and Theological Institution of the brothers Robert and James Haldane was to be influential. John Scott of Perthshire, who had attended the Institution was among the newcomers, settling at North River in 1806 or 1807. Scott, "a deeply pious man, and much troubled by the prevailing spiritual desolation,"[8] began to hold services there as well as at West River, preaching in the Gaelic.

Alexander Crawford, another student of the Haldanes, first visited the Island in 1811 or 1812 after originally settling as a teacher and preacher in 1810 at Yarmouth, Nova Scotia, where he had discovered that some of his views were not acceptable to his brethren in that already strong Baptist centre. With an above-average education for the times, Crawford, according to Maritime church historian Robert Wilson, "found the emotionalism and lack of teaching to be foreign to his ideas," Wilson adding that "his relationship with [Yarmouth pastor] Harris Harding was somewhat cool."[9]

But Crawford was warmly welcomed by his countrymen in their new Island habitation, and he found them very receptive to his preaching. Through his efforts a church was formed in Three Rivers (Montague) in 1812—independent but holding to Baptist principles. After visiting the Island again in 1814 Crawford moved there permanently the following year. His work laid the foundations for the Scottish churches at East Point, Tryon and Bedeque. Because of personal convictions Crawford remained unordained throughout his ministry, which was cut short by his untimely death at the age of forty-two. Writing of him twenty years after his death, the Reverend Alexander McDonald held that "the Baptist cause on the Island owes its existence, under God, to his self-denying labours."[10]

Crawford and Scott had made a beginning when in 1825, at Crawford's invitation, the Nova Scotia Association sent its first missionary to Prince Edward Island. It was Charles Tupper, father of Sir Charles Tupper of later Canadian political fame. Tupper was to become one of the most respected ministers of his day. Although self-taught, it was said that he mastered over a dozen languages[11] and was an able preacher, teacher and writer. During his first visit, sometimes in company with Crawford, Tupper visited a number of centres, including Tryon, North River, Bedeque and Charlottetown.

A Shipwreck

The next year each association sent a missionary—Theodore S. Harding from Nova Scotia and Joseph Crandall from New Brunswick. Crandall preached at a number of places, including Bedeque, where Harding joined him, and together they "organized a Church under the gospel plan."[12] In the following year, 1827, that church became the Island's first to link up with the Nova Scotia Association. That year, after holding three previous missions on Prince Edward Island, Charles Tupper became pastor of the Bedeque-Tryon field.

Churches at St. Peter's Road and North River had been founded in 1830 as a result of the efforts of Nova Scotia missionary Samuel McCully. About the same time, one at Lot 49, forerunner of the church at Alexandra, was formed more dramatically—in the wake of a shipwreck. Benjamin Scott of Yarmouth, Nova Scotia, whose youth had been spent recklessly, had been soundly converted and there licensed to preach. On a voyage from Yarmouth to Port Hood, his ship foundered, but he managed to clamber safely ashore near Lot 49. Welcomed by the village, where he decided to stay, Scott offered to minister among his new-found friends. Soon, enough people were meeting to form a church and, aided by Hezekiah Hull of Guysborough who came for the occasion, Scott organized the church in 1831. The following year Scott was ordained during a visit by Edward Manning and T. S. Harding.

The Belfast/Uigg congregation grew up through the efforts of Alexander Crawford and, later, teacher-preacher Samuel McLeod, who had arrived with another group of Scottish Baptists in 1829. In 1833 McLeod also helped another teacher and preacher, John Shaw, formerly of the Scottish independent church, to organize the East Point congregation. It also had predominantly Scottish antecedents.

The New Epoch

1827, the year Bedeque joined the Nova Scotia Association, was especially notable for future Baptist development particularly on the Island. During that year a denominational magazine was launched and the first halting steps were taken toward setting up a pension-type fund for retired pastors and their widows. Interdenominational interest was aroused in the relationship between church and state, and the Granville Street Baptist Church of Halifax was founded. The formation of this church was to have a great effect on the whole denomination, especially in the field of education. In the description of two well-known historians, I. E. Bill and George E. Levy, east coast Baptists were on the threshold of a "New Epoch"[13] and 1827 was the portal year.

Adoniram Judson

The concept of the denominational journal was first discussed in 1825 when the Nova Scotia body voted to ask its New Brunswick counterpart to unite in the publication of a "Religious Periodical Magazine."[14] Volume 1, no. 1 of the *Baptist Missionary Magazine of Nova Scotia and New Brunswick* was issued in January 1827.

British North America's first Baptist paper, a quarterly, it was published under joint editorial direction until Charles Tupper was named editor in mid-1827. He remained in the post until he accepted the Bedeque-Tryon call in 1833. As its name indicates, the small pamphlet-sized paper focused on overseas missions, particularly the outreach of American Baptists, and home missions. The latter included mention of the contribution of American missionaries in the Maritimes. For many years before and after the War of 1812 there was a good deal of border crossing, a number of Maritime Baptist pastors holding meetings in New England and many more Americans assisting in the provinces. The rapport was complete, with messengers from Nova Scotia and New Brunswick attending various New England associations and vice versa.

Most of the interest in foreign missions at the time was focused on the "Burman" work of Adoniram Judson. Included in the first issue was an extract from a Judson letter. The July 1827 number made reference to the passing of the great pioneer American Baptist missionary, which had occurred in October of the previous year — the lag time being an indication of the slow-paced communication of the early nineteenth century.

Missing the Boat

Such writing helped to spark a widespread missionary interest very early among Maritime Baptists and in turn aided in the development of a surpassing consciousness of the denomination as an entity.

On the other hand, the first issue of Volume II, apparently unwittingly, points to a situation where the Baptists almost literally "missed the boat" to a mission field not too far distant. Under the heading "The State of Religion in Newfoundland," referring to information obtained from a Congregational minister in St. John's, an unnamed reporter described the scene: "Little has been done about their moral necessities . . . very many of the settlements have languished in almost total neglect. . . ." The writer added that the future of some 90,000 scattered inhabitants was somewhat more hopeful in this "most neglected of British colonies," and he commended the work of the Episcopal and Wesleyan missionaries, "who for many years, and almost alone, laboured among the benighted inhabitants of this island."[15] But the Maritime Baptists of the time apparently paid little attention to the ramifications of the report. Not until 127 years later — in 1955 — would Baptist work be undertaken in Newfoundland.

Publication of the *Baptist Missionary Magazine* was continued without interruption for ten years, although financial troubles surfaced with depressing regularity! However, it was the desire for a more adequate and more frequently published paper that eventually brought about change. The Nova Scotia Association meeting of 1836 voted to begin producing a weekly "Religious Newspaper" in conjunction with New Brunswick "provided a sufficient support can be secured."[16] The association minutes of the sister province the following year record a motion respecting the *Christian Messenger* to "adopt it as the organ of the Baptist denomination in this province."[17]

An Influential Association

During the 1827 meeting the whole question of ministerial stipend was also examined. The associational letter from that meeting urged that the pastoral leader was "worthy of his hire" and should not have to earn his livelihood in whole or in part through secular pursuits.[18] The letter of

1831 centred on the importance of a solid, well-rounded education for the ministry.[19]

More evidence of denominational maturing lies in the 1827 associational appointment of a committee "to meet and confer with a Committee appointed by the Presbyterian Synod for Civil Purposes."[20] The decision was consistent with the historic Baptist stand on religious liberty, the emphasis on a free church in a free state. For the obvious growth in so many areas of Maritime Baptist life the official scribe gave much credit to the association, from which, he wrote, "as far as human agency is concerned, has proceeded the rapid increase of our churches."[21]

Undeniably, the Maritime associations very early became influential in the life of the rapidly increasing number of churches. They regularly employed home missionaries in outreach for shorter and longer periods. Sunday schools were promoted, temperance societies supported. Considerable discipline was exercised—even to the extent of voting, as the New Brunswick Association did soon after its formation, to withhold fellowship from any church that did not strictly observe "the Rules of Church discipline prescribed and enjoined by the word of God."[22] The same association later urged its churches "not to receive any Minister, who is not in fellowship with some Calvinistic Baptist Church or Association."[23]

Revival

It might have been expected that these movements toward a more settled and organized type of ministry would tend to dampen the fires of evangelism that had burned brightly as the churches became increasingly Baptistic. True, the excesses that had characterized some of the late-eighteenth-century practices of Alline's followers gradually faded and worship took on a more rational form.

Concern for those outside the fold did not diminish, however. The April 1828, edition of the *Baptist Missionary Magazine* contained an account of a significant revival in Moncton, while the Nova Scotia Association report of the next year noted that 151 had been baptized at Nictaux, with Wilmot sharing "largely in the Outpouring of the Holy Spirit, during the period of the late Revival, in the Western parts of the Province," having eighty baptisms. Resulting from the same outpouring, two new churches were formed when groups "hived off" from Nictaux— forty-three to form the Aylesford church, thirty-seven to begin that of New Albany.[24] Historian John H. Moir calls the three decades before Canada's Confederation "the golden age of Baptist missions, [years] which were to make the Baptist fellowship the most dynamic religious force in the Maritimes" during the period.[25]

Visions Abroad

Interest in overseas missions first took visible shape with the 1814 offering "for the poor heathen" taken by the Baptist Association of Nova Scotia and New Brunswick. Then during the winter of 1827 the Saint John church formed itself into a missionary society to give aid to the American Baptist Mission in Burma. The same year the Female Mite Societies of Sackville, New Brunswick, and Amherst, Nova Scotia, decided to give part of their receipts to overseas missions. In 1828 a missionary society was formed at Salisbury, New Brunswick, to support the overseas efforts of both the American and the British boards.

At the Nova Scotia Association meeting of 1830, E. A. Crawley, "a seer of God's purposes . . . [in an] impassioned address, said that young men would go from Horton Academy to the foreign field."[26] A tract was prepared for distribution among the churches. Fanned by the *Baptist Missionary Magazine* and the *Christian Messenger* and increasingly encouraged by the Female Mite Societies, a deep concern for the souls of those in distant lands gradually developed into a strong cause.

Some Suitable Person

In 1837 the New Brunswick Association decided that "the attention of the churches should be directed to the subject of Foreign Missions and that they should begin to enquire, 'what God requires of them in reference to Heathen nations'."[27] The next year Nova Scotia echoed the call in their June meeting. "Having taken into consideration the lamentable condition of the heathen world" and the imperative duty to send the Word of Life, they proposed to their sister association the formation of a "United Society for the Maintenance of Foreign Missions."[28] Taking a further step, they urged that attention be given "to the adequate education of some one suitable person as a Missionary in some foreign field so soon as one possessed of suitable character shall be found. . . ."[29]

The New Brunswick Association met just two weeks later and concurred immediately on both counts, naming representatives to meet with those of the Nova Scotia Association.[30] Events continued to move rapidly, and by 1839 "a young brother had presented himself as a candidate."[31] Arrangements were soon made for Richard E. Burpee to attend the newly founded "Queen's College" (later Acadia College) at Horton, each association bearing half his expenses. Then, even as arrangements were underway for Burpee's training, a two-person committee, one from each association, was to make inquiries "with regard to the most eligible field of labour for our missionaries" (the vision already included "another missionary to accompany Bro. R. E. Burpee").[32]

Among the Karens

Richard Burpee was a New Brunswick native who entered the ministry after carrying on a thriving business in Fredericton and studying at the Fredericton Seminary. Ordained in 1837, he was pastor of the St. Patrick's, New Brunswick, church when the opportunity for overseas service beckoned. He had long yearned for it. Recognizing the importance of adequate training, he readily entered Acadia's degree program, graduating in 1844 in the first class to include theological students.[33]

Burpee and his wife, the daughter of Dr. Lewis Johnstone of Horton, visited among the churches and then sailed from Halifax for Boston en route to Burma on April 20, 1845. They were the first Protestant missionaries to go overseas from British North America. With support from the two Maritime associations, the Burpees began working under the aegis of the American Baptist Missionary Union among the Karens, then a primitive people in the hilly jungle area of Burma. (The work had been pioneered by Adoniram and Ann Judson.)

It might be noted that from the very outset the Baptists were pledged to provide the support their missionaries required on the field, never expecting them to be responsible personally for raising the necessary funding. The original motion called for the formation of a United Society indicated that it would be for the "maintenance" of foreign missions. Even more specific was a resolution of the 1844 Nova Scotia Association meeting. Recognizing that "immediately on sending abroad a Missionary, the Board will be called upon to enter into strict business engagements," the decision was made to form a "system which may, with the Divine blessing, ensure a regular income."[34] The missionary task was viewed as corporate: those sending were responsible for providing for both spiritual and temporal support under God.

The Burpees' stay in Burma was to last no more than five years. Early in his service he began to develop "symptoms of pulmonary disease," which eventually forced his return home. I. E. Bill tells of meeting him in London on his way back "broken down by disease, and in search of restoration."[35] Such a restoration was not to be granted, however, and Richard Burpee died early in 1853 — the first of a long line of missionary volunteers who would give all for their Master and for needy humankind. Others would soon take up the torch that Burpee had given up.

Forming the Convention

All of these exciting developments increased the need for greater synthesis and denominational cohesiveness, as did two other major movements within the churches: Sunday schools and temperance societies.

Once the Sunday school movement took hold in a major way in the United States after the War of 1812, it began to influence churches in British North America — particularly in the Maritimes. It was in neighbouring New England that the movement had begun.

Sabbath School Union

According to Edward M. Saunders, "Sabbath schools" as they were then called, flourished in the Maritimes between 1820 and 1840. The church at Chester, for example, had a school of one hundred at that earlier date, and Saint John recorded a large school in 1831.[36] Lunenburg reported to the Nova Scotia Association in 1834 that there were three Sunday schools, with some two hundred scholars.[37]

In 1836 the New Brunswick Association voted "to prepare a Catechism for the use of the children in the Sabbath schools and families belonging to the Baptist Denomination,"[38] and a year later the sister association resolved to establish a Sabbath school union[37] to promote the growth of schools in every church. By 1840 plans had been consummated for the founding of the Nova Scotia and New Brunswick Sabbath School Union, which stretched beyond the two associations to "embrace persons of all denominations who conform to the . . . principles."[40]

The Temperance movement was an interdenominational phenomenon, as it originated in a community-wide concern. Again the initial influence came from the United States, particularly through the leadership of pulpit giants like Lyman Beecher, whose temperance sermons Edward Manning used extensively.[41] Drunkenness had reached almost epidemic proportions on both sides of the border, even extending into the church. The situation was so bad, writes George E. Levy that "it had been said that half the people in Halifax sold, and the other bought intoxicants."[42]

Temperance Societies

The Nova Scotia Association minutes of 1835, for example, include a plaintive description of a situation which seems to have made it impossible for one church to continue paying the minister's stipend.

> This [First Clements] Church as well as some others has . . . been called to pass through deep trials, in endeavouring to suppress the evils of intemperance among their members . . . to preserve peace and union in their body, and to keep up the exercise of discipline, in dealing with offenders; they have consequently been compelled to withdraw fellowship from several of their number. They are now so weak as to pecuniary means that they are unable to support their Pastor, and he has been by mutual consent released from his Pastoral charge.[43]

Nor was First Clements alone in facing such problems. The churches took action on several fronts. Bear River, Nova Scotia, appears to have been the first to form an organization — a "Total Abstinence Society" — in 1828, followed the next year by Wilmot, a Temperance society cofounded by I. E. Bill and Methodist S. V. Bayard. Saunders says that the temperance campaign was carried forward on the revival flood that swept through the province, adding that by 1831 it was reported that such societies were found in nearly every Baptist church and in other denominations.[44] There was also a strong response from the New Brunswick churches.

The 1830 Nova Scotia associational letter made a forceful case for total abstinence,[48] and it was recommended before the association two years later that the cause of temperance be raised before the provincial legislature.[46] While commending the churches for strong support of the Temperance movement in 1836, the association expressed the fear "that the zeal in this good work may abate too soon," suggesting that letters from the churches revealed the problem was far from coming to an end.[47]

These multifaceted advances highlighted the need for closer co-operation among Baptists of the three provinces and particularly for greater integration of supporting fund-raising efforts. While the various Baptist agencies had been formed directly by the associations and, by and large, had the same membership as the associations themselves, they all laid claim to the same central treasury, which could not meet all the demands for funds.

An Enlightened Principle

To remedy this problem, the Nova Scotia Association was first to act, forming itself in 1842 into "the Associated Society of Baptists in Nova Scotia." Its purpose was to further "the cause of Education, Foreign and Domestic Missions, Sabbath Schools, and [to] support superannuated Ministers and their families."[47] Parallel "union societies" were to be formed in each church. The next year, with Alexander Sawers of Halifax named central secretary, the associated society recommended that all contributions be sent to a single location and there divided proportionately to fund the several activities. If they wished, contributors could also direct their gifts to specific areas. This was the embryonic form of what would later become known as a "denominational fund." In 1845 the New Brunswick Association took similar action in founding "the General Society of the Baptist Denomination in New Brunswick" and asking each church to constitute a local union society.

Usefully Unite

Even while this consolidation was taking place in each association, seeds were being sown that would soon result in wider regional union and the formation of the first bona fide Convention* of Baptists in British North America. The mutual interest in education, the combined support of the Burpees and the common concerns of Sunday schools and temperance made such a merger most advantageous.

In 1844 the Nova Scotia Association decided that their messenger to

---

*The word "convention" came into use in Canada by way of the Baptists of the United States (while the alternate term "union" was derived from the British). It basically signifies the act of coming together. Baptists on both sides of the border have increasingly used it to denote those who have come together, acted together and continue to act together as a unit, so that "convention" has become the name of the acting body, as well as its meetings.

As an option, some Conventions and Unions use the term "Assembly" for their annual meetings, so that the combination "Union Assembly" or even "Convention Assembly" may appear. The Canadian Baptist Federation uses Assembly for its triennial gatherings, and the Baptist World Alliance employs "Congress" for its meetings held at five-year intervals.

New Brunswick should "express to that body the earnest desire of this Association for increased intercourse and union," specifically suggesting that they might "usefully unite their efforts in the cause of education."[47] Interestingly, the action was taken against the background of a committee report which assessed the concern of many of the churches that the association itself should be divided for more effectiveness. Thus there was a dual movement—both for general unity and for greater decentralization of the intermediate units.

The Nova Scotia messenger was Charles Tupper, who was a strong supporter of union. His presentation found an attentive hearing and immediate backing. Holding in abeyance their own plans for associational division, the New Brunswick body appointed members to a joint committee "for the purpose of consulting upon the expediency of forming a convention of both Provinces."[50]

By the next year the committee was in full operation, empowered to draft a constitution and meanwhile to act as an executive committee to carry out mutually agreed upon objectives.[50] In the summer of 1846, both associations approved the report of the joint committee and on September 21 of that year, with the meeting in Saint John, New Brunswick, the inaugural session of the Baptist Convention of Nova Scotia, New Brunswick and Prince Edward Island was held in First Baptist Church, now Germain Street.

A Co-ordinating Convention

The original constitution was framed in basic terms, the major objects being "to advance the interest of the Baptist Denomination, and the cause of God, generally," and "to maintain the religious and charitable Institutions hereinafter mentioned."[52] In order to bring together the various activities of the denomination, a widely representative body of delegates was initially authorized — from the associations, local churches, union societies and a number of supporting individual members. At the outset, the union societies were used as collecting agencies for the Convention, their receipts being sent to one of the two provincial secretaries of the Convention.

With the leadership of the associations so entrenched in the life of denomination, the new Convention did not attempt a rapid takeover of functions. Instead, it viewed its early task as one of co-ordination. At the founding meeting, overseas missions, Bible distribution and the fund for superannuated ministers were the only areas taken over by the Convention. The next year, with the concurrence of the associations, education and domestic, or home, missions were added to its list of responsiblities, and the Convention soon assumed the more significant role. Its importance was heightened by the fact that the associations began to take decentralizing steps. By action of the New Brunswick Association in 1847, that body divided into two, the Eastern and the Western,[53] while Nova

Scotia took similar action three years later, dividing three ways into Western, Central and Eastern associations.[54]

At the establishment of the Convention in 1846, Nova Scotia and P.E.I. churches numbered 100, with 9,271 members. New Brunswick recorded 69 churches and 4,906 members—a total of 169 churches and 14,177 members.

Even as these unifying developments were taking place a number of voices were calling for even wider co-operation—to include the Baptists in all of British North America. As early as 1840, the New Brunswick Association appointed a committee "to open a Correspondence with the Baptist Denomination in the Provinces of the Canadas,"[55] which represented at least a tentative demonstration of interest in a national fellowship.

The Goal a Century Away

Although Baptists in the Canadas were not close to unity themselves, a letter from that region was read at the 1846 Nova Scotia Association— the meeting at which final arrangements were made for the formation of the Convention — "expressing the desirableness of a closer Union between all the Baptists of British North America being effected and manifested."[56] The letter, written from Montreal, was from the Canada Baptist Union, which had been set up three years before in one of several attempts to bring Baptists of the central region together. As one commentator writes, "the strong men of the denomination were at its head, and yet the churches refused to follow."[57]

The letter indicated that J. M. Cramp, then president of the Baptist College at Montreal, would travel to the Maritimes and represent the Canada Baptist Union, and the association named a committee to meet with the visitor and report to the assembly. While he was in the Maritimes, Cramp also addressed the association, presenting "the claims of the Swiss Mission, at Grand Ligne in Canada . . . part of his object in visiting this country."[58] After sitting down with the emissary, the committee reported that it was "highly desirable to form a closer Union between the Baptists of British North America," and suggested correspondence concerning annual statistical reporting, interchange of delegates and co-operation in missionary enterprise—"especially with regard to the French population of the Provinces."

Although this was the beginning of a strong Maritime interest in the Grande Ligne Mission, it is apparent that conditions conspired against the pursuit of any national partnership at that time. The subject did appear on the Convention agenda in 1847, when a committee report was heard and received with considerable interest,[60] but the goal was not to be reached for another century.

CHAPTER 10

Growing Pains

"Isolation is weakness and slavery: fraternal unity is strength and liberty."
—J. H. RUSHBROOKE

Baptist unity in the Canadas was achieved much later than in the Maritimes, and after a tortuous journey. Some responsibility for the slow movement toward union must, of course, be borne by the leaders and members of the frontier churches. Yet there was a sense in which, as bodies of Christians so often do, they reflected at least some of the characteristics of the surrounding secular society and the divided land which was still a colonial satellite of Great Britian. That land, as Canadian historian Donald Creighton describes it, was suffering from "growing pains."[1] So were the Baptists.

Changing Patterns

Up to the War of 1812 the population of the Canadas had been made up of the original French homesteaders and their descendants in Lower Canada, and English-speaking colonists. The first English-speaking settlers had come from the Thirteen Colonies and later ones had come as Loyalists or as emigrants from the new United States. Few had arrived directly from the United Kingdom.

By the early 1820s, with a hiatus in the Napoleonic Wars in Europe, immigration patterns changed dramatically, and over the next thirty years waves of British people came in tens of thousands to the Canadas, particularly to the upper province, and to the Maritimes. In the twenty-five years from 1825 to 1850, New Brunswick's population expanded from 74,000 to 194,000, and Nova Scotia's, from 104,000 to 277,000—both increases of over 160 percent. In the same quarter-century however, Upper Canada's population simply surged ahead, jumping from 158,000 to 791,000, a phenomenal 400 percent.[2]

Forces of Reform Loosed

Such an influx of generally impoverished newcomers was bound to cause a great deal of social dislocation and religious tumult, particularly in a colonial milieu with "Family Compact" governments comfortably ensconced in the seats of authority. Agitation soon appeared on the political scene. Deprived of any measure of democratic or even responsible government, numbers of the colonists, both old and new, were attracted to the insurrectionary notions of Louis-Joseph Papineau in Lower Canada and William Lyon Mackenzie in Upper Canada. Poorly planned "rebellions" occurred in 1837 in both the Canadas; both were crushed with dispatch by the British redcoats and the Canadian militia.

Lingering skirmishes took place along the boundary as Americans unofficially came to the support of the revolt, but their several raids were repulsed, and the most recent armed conflict on the continent soon ceased. As Creighton writes: "In effect, the Rebellions of 1837 were the armed attempts of a small minority to pressure the Canadians to alter the course of their history and to accept the American Revolution which their fathers and grandfathers had rejected sixty years before."[3]

Although the resisters had surrendered their arms, the forces for reform had been loosed, and increasing demands arose for greater civil and religious liberty. Over the next decades the British authorities gradually complied, moving toward responsible government.

A Mixed Review

A first-hand, though impressionistic, account of the status of Baptist endeavour in the Canadas in the 1830s has been left by F. A. Cox, who visited the region at that time. Cox and J. Hoby, English Baptist ministers, were sent by their countrymen "principally to obtain information respecting their kindred community beyond the Atlantic."[4] After attending the Eighth Triennial Assembly of the denomination in the United States in 1835, Cox travelled north of the border while his colleague visited the American West.

Cox's was a mixed review. In the upper province, he reported, there were "between sixty and seventy churches, and forty ministers, many of them very dependent in circumstances, and unlearned men . . . . Both in the Upper and Lower provinces, [he added] there is a great deficiency in Sunday schools; and in the former, a considerable division of sentiment, some tending to arminianism, and others to antinomianism."[5]

The "antinomianism" to which, in Cox's view, a number tended, would undoubtedly be a reflection of the loose moral practices of the spreading frontier, which some might self-justify in their hyper-Calvinism, while the "arminianism" would likely refer to the tenets of the Free Baptists, of whom more will be said in a later chapter.

Around Toronto the visitor found "six places of public worship," (including all denominations), adding that "the state of religion, I am apprehensive, is not at present very thriving."[6] On the other hand, in Niagara he discovered a small Baptist church which was part of an association of nineteen others, and that association had sanctioned and sustained missionary tract, Sunday school and educational societies."[7]

He vividly described his visits to Breadalbane, near Ottawa, where he "enjoyed the fairest possible opportunity of witnessing the influence of religion on unsophisticated minds," and at Fort Covrington, where he saw "the third scene of a remarkable revival of religion, which it had been my object to visit."[8]

The "revival of religion" which Cox had observed was a major factor in the growth of the Ottawa Valley churches and the founding of the association of the name in 1836. Indeed, according to one of Cox's contemporaries: "The great revivals in Breadalbane, Dalesville, and Montreal from 1834 to 1836 . . . were of such a powerful and radical nature that they determined the general type of religious work done subsequently among the Baptists of the Ottawa Valley."[9]

The Most Effective Means

By this time the several associations, geographically circumscribed as they were, had become increasingly influential units in Baptist life beyond the local church—for many decades, in fact, they were the only significant units. A number of wider groupings were attempted, but all were to die stillborn or in early childhood. The frontier churches in the Canadas seemed loath to share important responsibilities even if it was necessary for the greater good. For half a century the association remained, except for American and some British input, the most effective means of extension.

The Association at Work

From the available records it is apparent that the time for fellowship and inspiration loomed large in the planning of the early associational gatherings. At least for the first half of the nineteenth century, Baptists were predominantly a rural people and, since opportunities of meeting with those "of like mind" were rare on the rugged frontier, they were deeply cherished.

Yet the Lord's business was carefully executed. The association members' diligence, honed by precept and example, was at least in part a legacy of the itinerant missionaries of the first decades of the century, strengthened by initial membership in their American associations.

Tramp Preachers

Outside the Ottawa Valley, the constitutions of the associations were, for the most part, patterned after those of their American counterparts. The Johnstown Association constitution, for example, reflected the well-known American articles, which called for a composition "of Delegates from Regular Baptist churches agreeing in their faith . . . who shall convene in the manner specified."[10] While the association claimed no authority over the autonomous churches, it did affirm the "power of withdrawing from any church proved to be corrupt."[11]

From the outset the associations were involved in the ordination process, Ivison and Rosser stating that no minister was to be so set apart by a local church "without the presence and participation of some ordained missionary or representive of an Association."[12] The associations were equally concerned about travelling ministerial imposters and "tramp preachers," Haldimand recommending to its churches that such be required to produce adequate testimonials.[13]

One of the main objectives in the founding of the Ottawa Association was to "aid, in every possible way, to supply the vacant churches with Pastors."[14] The 1830 circular letter of the Western Association carried a poignant plea on behalf of the pastors. "Our ministers," they wrote, "are unable to support themselves and families."[15] Even sixteen years later, in reporting that the American Baptist Home Mission Society had surveyed the state of the churches in "that part of Western Canada [Ontario] which lies between the Niagara and Detroit Rivers, Lake Ontario and Lake Huron," the minutes of the same association recorded that there were only about half as many ordained men as there were churches and "two-thirds of these depend chiefly on farming or other labour for their support,"[16] By mid-century, reasoning that "whereas the churches in Canada are unable to pay such a salary to their ministers as will enable them to leave their families with any means of support when they are dead," the Grand River Association laid plans to set up a £100 life insurance policy for each pastor.[17]

Hiving Off

Although efforts were spasmodic, unco-ordinated and lacking in adequate funding, the various associations tried to stimulate outreach, initially through "part-time" missionaries and encouragement of the churches. But some of the most effective early missionary advances were taken by the churches themselves. At times they dismissed a number of their own members to form the nucleus of churches in nearby communities. This "hiving-off" occurred in Charlotteville in 1828 when thirty-one members of that church were released to form a church at Walsingham (now Port Rowan).[18] Four years later Charlotteville repeated the farsighted process when thirteen of its members, seven by letter from other churches and two who were baptized that day "joined to establish the Stony Creek Church."[19] By the forties at least two associations, the Eastern and Ottawa, had widened the vision to include Native peoples, and a church was organized among the Tuscaroras.[20]

Occasionally, the associations were called upon to adjudicate disputes between churches. A letter from the clerk of the Louth church in Lincoln county, dated June 2, 1839, indicated that "Elder Curry's membership" had been returned to the Grantham church "according to the decision of the Committee appointed by the Association last year."[21] Later the Haldimand Association was faced with a delicate situation involving a difficulty between the white and black churches in Niagara, which was settled in favour of the former. The decision was softened, however, by "a faithful and affectionate remonstrance" and a committee was appointed to meet with the church deemed erring.[22]

Support of the Reformers

As in the Maritimes, the associations in the Canadas—the united province of Canada after 1840—frequently urged their members to abstain from alcoholic beverages completely.[23] Similarly, the formation of Sunday schools was consistently advocated to meet the needs of the young. Like the associations to the east, they deplored the refusal of the British and Foreign Bible Society to translate the scriptures concerning baptism objectively and finally turned their support to the American Bible Society.[24]

The associations also vigorously defended Baptist conduct during the short-lived rebellions of 1837. Because of their continuing American ties, their love of liberty, their objections to Anglican dominance and their general support of the Reform cause, Baptists as a whole were suspect by those in authority. Yet there was no evidence to warrant such apprehension. Although most Baptists could be counted among the strong supporters of the Reform party, there is little doubt that they decried the Rebellion itself.

There is good evidence, writes W. G. Pitman, which "gives reason to believe that although the Baptists were decidely liberal in their leanings, they were for the most part as surely constitutional in their opposition [to the rebellion]."[25] The June 1838 circular letter of the Upper Canada Eastern Association clearly identifies that stand. "Since last we met the scourge of evil warfare has made its appearance in the land and has been withdrawn, God in his mercy having scattered the people who delight in war."[26]

In 1837 the Ottawa Association acknowledged a debt of gratitude to Great Britain for "the civil and religious liberty we enjoy,"[27] and in 1842 it established a committee "for the purpose of preparing a loyal address to his Excellency the Governor General."[28]

Attempts at Denominational Structure

Yet there was no significant vehicle beyond the limited associational boundaries to give focus to these wide interests and to draw Baptists in the Canadas into a denominational whole. Unity did not elude them for want of trying, however.

As has been described in Chapter 8, two token efforts undertaken before 1833 proved to be abortive. That year the Eastern, Western and Haldimand associations jointly tried to widen their scope with the founding of the Baptist Missionary Convention of Upper Canada—not truly a "convention" despite its label, but rather a society made up of dues-paying members. In reality a home or domestic missionary society aiming "to reach the destitute," the small company also ambitiously planned for a religious journal and printing press, all to little avail, this being but the first of at least five societies between 1833 and 1851 which were in G. Gerald Harrop's phrase, "untimely born" and due to collapse.[29]

With the failure of the Baptist Missionary Convention of Upper Canada, its embryonic missionary work was carried on by the Eastern Association. In 1836, still hoping to fashion some instrument even of limited co-operation, two of the associations in the previous grouping—the Eastern and the Western — agreed to try again after the latter appointed a committee to confer "on measures to form ourselves into the Upper Canada Baptist Missionary Society."[30]

Appeal to Britain

The new body chose two immediate objectives: the establishment of a training centre for ministers and the launching of a religious journal. Deacon Jacob Beam offered a large farm property in Beamsville on which the training centre could be built, but there remained the task of raising the necessary funding for building and operation.

Despite the continuing American connections and the fact that there were seven pastors in Upper Canada at the time supported at least in part by the American Baptist Home Missionary Society,[31] the new society decided to make its financial appeal to Great Britain, sending Elder William Rees across the Atlantic to make the approach. This decision may have been influenced by the fact that there was a growing number of British immigrants swelling the population by then or there may have been a feeling that they had been to the American well too frequently. In any event, to England Rees went, only to make a disconcerting discovery: he was second in line; John Gilmour had already been there on a similar mission for the Ottawa Association, and Rees could only glean from a field already harvested. The imperturbable British strongly — and wisely —urged that the two, east and west, should "combine for the accomplishment of the commendable project."[32] The later vain attempt to combine the Upper Canada Baptist Missionary Society with that of the Ottawa Association in the project would be but the prelude to a chorus of failures in unity efforts.

Establishing a journal was at least temporarily more promising. For nearly two years from July 1836, the *Upper Canada Baptist Missionary Magazine* was produced bimonthly from Toronto which was then incorporated as a city of over 9,000. The paper was edited by J. E. Maxwell, a missionary of the society, and was given limited support over its brief life by four associations. The May 1837 issue expressed something of the unrealized yearning for greater Baptist unity: ". . . in our opinion the spread of truth, and consequently the dearest interest of the church and the world, and the glory of God, would be greatly promoted, could all Baptists be brought to unite their efforts."[33]

While this confined effort of just two associations to do some co-operative work was limping along, a similar but somewhat more successful outreach was in the making. At its well-organized founding in 1836, the Ottawa Association, in addition to providing assistance to the churches to secure pastors, constitutionally aimed to promote missionary outreach and "to sustain a Seminary for the education of young men . . . [for] the ministry."[34]

Powerful Letter

It was to secure support for these causes that John Gilmour preceded William Rees to the United Kingdom. Gilmour had long been interested in the promotion of domestic missions and education on an inter-church basis, records of the interdenominational Canada Education and Home Missionary Society indicating that he was its secretary in 1831.[35] Now he had the opportunity to participate in a fully Baptist mission.

Even before Gilmour sailed, arrangements had been made to open an academy in Montreal the following year, with Newton Bosworth, an English Baptist minister who had emigrated to the Canadas in 1834,[36] as interim teacher. The Ottawa Association were showing that they meant business.

In a powerful letter to the *London Baptist Magazine* Gilmour described the dismaying religious scene in the Canadas under the vast surge of new British population and appealed: "Will you not help your expatriated friends and relatives?" They would and did. Gilmour's appeal was two fold: for education and for missions. "We propose," he wrote, "the education of twenty students, and to aid in the support of ten missionaries, with a sum not exceeding £760 per annum."[37] With gifts from his native Scotland and from England, Gilmour arrived home with nearly £1,600. More than that, the Baptist Canadian Missionary Society had been formed at a meeting held in the City of London Tavern to continue the support.

In order to provide a suitable working arrangement with the new society, the association, which had postponed its 1837 meeting to await Gilmour's return, immediately proposed another society — the Canada Baptist Missionary Society — again composed of individual subscribers. Those initial subscribers added another £20 to Gilmour's receipts on the spot.

Yet all the while John Gilmour was unaware that William Rees would be following him on a similar errand to Great Britain. Such was the state of communications and Baptist interrelationships in 1836 and 1837.

With the hope of creating a wider interest in the plans of the Ottawa Association through its new society, Gilmour embarked on a visit among the churches, only then learning that the Upper Canada Baptist Missionary Society had been formed the previous year for the same purposes. Obviously a positive thinker, he saw it "a token for good that the two Societies should have been formed about the same time, and in the same denomination."[38] To assess the possibilities of co-operating in education,

Gilmour called at Rees' home in Brantford, but Rees was away and communication lapsed again.

The Upper Canada Baptist Missionary Society did make a serious effort to join forces with the Canada Baptist Missionary Society later the same year. In fact, it was decided that the two Canadian societies should meet, as they did at Haldimand in 1837 to consider an appropriate site for the college.[39] Deacon Beam's repeated offer of a farm property at Beamsville did not prove to be acceptable, but it was agreed that a two-year interim location in Montreal would be satisfactory, pending decision on a final situation. Unfortunately, as historian W. G. Pitman suggests, the site was not seriously reconsidered as Baptists to the west gradually lost interest and Ottawa Valley and Montreal Baptists assumed total leadership.[40] Yet, while it was obviously unwise to remain in Montreal without further consultation, a meeting of the Long Point Association in mid-1842 still recommended to the churches the support of the Baptist College there — "at least till one is erected in the upper part of the Province."[41]

No Sense of Destiny

While these developments were occurring, the Canada Baptist Missionary Society, as the arm of the Ottawa Association, had moved rapidly into the field of publication. Even as the first regular meeting of the society was to be held in June of 1837, the initial issue of the *Canada Baptist Magazine and Missionary Register* appeared. In its twelve-year lifespan, the *Register* had a great impact on the religious and secular scenes in the province of Canada. It was a strong champion, for instance, of the "voluntary" principle in church-state relations and gave dynamic leadership in two historic contests in that arena: the clergy reserves and the university question. Historian A. H. Newman pays high tribute to the magazine:

> From the beginning this Baptist Press kept its readers informed on the missionary movements of the world . . . . The editors never lost an opportunity to express their horror of slavery or to encourage those who were labouring for its abolishment. Its readers were kept thoroughly abreast of secular movements as well as religious. It is doubtful whether any Canadian publication equalled the Montreal Register while Cramp [the second editor] was at the helm, and whether the Baptists of Canada ever had a better paper.[42]

The Canada Baptist Missionary Society also gave serious attention to home missions opportunities, although the results hardly matched the hopes for ten missionaries expressed in Gilmour's effective letter to the *London Baptist Magazine*. The September 1837 issue of the *Montreal Register* included a report of the society indicating that the parallel British Society had been asked to send six missionaries to the Canadas.[43] Even this more modest number seems not to have been attained, an 1840 report of the Canadian Society denoting that three missionaries were being supported: William Fraser, who itinerated along the Ottawa River; Daniel McPhail, pastor of the Osgood church of sixty members; and John McEwen, working in the "Indian Lands."[44]

The actual planting of a church among Indians of the Six Nations may be attributed to Elder John Miner who, while a member of the Dundas church, visited the reserve in 1841. Moving the same year to Jerseyville, the church nearest the reserve, Miner began work among the Tuscaroras after a group of the Native people personally sought such a mission. At the end of just one year Miner was able to report that "the gospel was preached among them and many gladly received the Word and were baptized both men and women. Since last spring, when this work commenced, upwards of a hundred have been hopefully gathered into a church, and, that too, in the face of priestly intimidation and strenuous efforts to deter them from following their Christian convictions."[45]

A "Round House" Baptist chapel in Tuscarora township—octagonal outside and round inside—was completed early in 1843, the year Elder W.H. Landon took over the work from Miner. Landon had been appointed by the Eastern Association as a kind of mission superintendent to oversee the Indian work, and when no one was found to replace Miner, who had accepted a call elsewhere, Landon undertook the task himself. Soon living on the reserve, Landon was assisted by recently arrived English lay pastor, B.W. Carryer who succeeded him in 1846.

None of these early missionaries mastered the native language, and they had to preach and otherwise communicate through an interpreter. Commenting on this continuing mission effort, one commentator laments "a problem which has ever since beset our Baptist work." The problem: "that of securing a leadership for, and called specifically to this distinctive type of mission [i.e., to Native peoples]."[46]

Giving evidence of at least limited co-operation at the time among Baptists of the eastern and western parts of the central region, funding for the Tuscarora Mission was provided by the London Baptist Missionary Society, with an annual grant of some £121, enabling Landon "to give his undivided attention" to the work.

In 1840, after the famous Durham Report, the Union Act was passed, declaring the merger of Upper and Lower Canada and the formation of one province of Canada (Canada West and Canada East). According to historian Donald Creighton, the most important function of the Durham Report "was to help British North Americans to recover their belief in their own chosen destiny."[48] Such a sense of destiny was yet to be granted the Baptists of the merged province of Canada, however. This was particularly true in the sphere of education, where Dr. Benjamin Davies, first principal of the Montreal College that had been started in 1838, deplored publicly the failure of Baptists to support the institution: "It was anticipated from the spirit displayed by our brethren from Upper Canada at the meeting in Haldimand . . . that some important assistance could be expected from that Province. As yet the expectation has not been realized, and we have only to rely on the steady liberal support of the Ottawa Association and friends of the Society in Montreal."[49] The wider support never did materialize. The "growing pains" had not yet eased.

CHAPTER 11

Discord and Concord

*"Freedom of conscience, unlimited freedom of mind,
was from the first the trophy of the Baptists."*
—GEORGE BANCROFT

There are few disagreements as painful as those concerning tenets of faith. Conversely, there are few undertakings which can bring greater satisfaction than the wholehearted support of mutually accepted principles. The Baptists of the province of Canada were involved in both during the 1840s—the end result being no little confusion and the continuation of their considerable growing pains.

Discord about the Communion

Undoubtedly one of the most contentious religious issues of the nineteenth century for British North American Baptists centred on the ordinances, specifically the Lord's supper. Was the Lord's table to be open to all confessing Christians, whether or not they have been baptized as believers — open communion — or should the local church confine the privilege to those who had witnessed to their personal faith in Christ in the baptismal waters—close, or strict, communion?

Taking Up the Cudgels

It should be noted immediately that the debate was not over open membership, according to which a church could permit any and all professing Christians, regardless of their age at the time of baptism or christening, to full status as members. While G. Gerald Harrop suggests that two of the Scottish Ottawa Valley churches founded prior to 1840 allowed open membership as well as communion,[1] J. U. MacIntosh could find no record of a church in the province of Canada that would permit an unimmersed person to join.[2]

Unlike the Canadians, the Maritime Baptists faced the communion question from the very time that their association was formed in 1800. As most members of the association had come from the New Light Congregationalism of Henry Alline, they initially embraced the open position. "They were much pleased with it at first," writes pioneer American historian David Benedict, "they were all new lights together in the good cause." Then he adds with obvious approval: "The practice was laid aside, not by any sudden revolution or conventional rules, but it died away by slow degrees, as one church and minister after another found themselves embarrassed, beyond endurance, by the inconsistencies, inconveniences and collisions in which it involved them."[3]

The change, by which practically all became close, or strict, communionists within a couple of decades undoubtedly made for a stronger denominational consciousness and growth at the crucial period.

Deep Divergence

Most of the early Baptists of central Canada were, except for some Free Baptists,* immigrant American Baptists, made in the Calvinist mould and strongly supportive of close communion. This 1799 statement of the Hatley church is typical: "We believe we have no right to a visible standing in the Church, nor to communicate at the Lord's Table till we have been baptized upon a profession of faith in the name of the Father, the Son and Holy Ghost."[4]

There were obvious exceptions, or course, a major one in Upper Canada to be found in the district around London, which had been influenced by the Freewill Baptists. That situation caused some heart-burning as early as 1837 when the close communion Eastern and Western Associations met with the more open London churches in the hope of bringing them into the Upper Canada Baptist Missionary Society. Almost successful in the discussion phase, the conference was at the end frustrated by a small group of rigid strict communionists, the final resolution being "[for the sake of peace] to proceed no further on the subject at present."[5]

At first the leaders of the Canada Baptist Missionary Society to the east sought to sidestep the issue, although John Gilmour strongly favoured the open position, as did Davies and the other English ministers in the area. But the issue would not go away.

So in the western part of the joined province, the strongest voices called for continued strict communion, while to the east the churches of the Ottawa Association and its parallel society were divided. Widest was the divergence between the western churches and the Montreal College, together with the English ministers of the area. The dispute became increasingly sharp after 1840, dying down only after the formation of the Convention nearly fifty years later.

Feelings at the time were so strained that on occasion some refused visiting brethren a hearing in their assemblies. In his personal diary, the Reverend Newton Bosworth, one of the leading English-reared ministers,

---

*The term "Free Baptists" covers a number of different groups, including the Free Communion and the Freewill Baptists.

tells of a painful visit on June 9, 1843: "Went with Mr. Burtch and the above [Dr. Davies, Messrs.-Winterbottom, Girdwood and Landon] to the Long Point and Western Association. Disagreeable meeting — as much as last year. 2 or 3 hours occupied in debating whether we should be invited, as visiting brethren, to take seats during the meeting. Negatived by a large majority! No hope of coalition."[6]

Principles were strongly held and fiercely defended on the frontier in the 1840s.

Concord: The Separation of Church and State

There was one issue on which Baptists, if they had opportunity to speak, spoke with one voice. And though they were weakened by their inability to unite they made such a contribution in the province of Canada that the whole nation became their beneficiary. The issue was that of the separation of church and state. Baptists, who so dearly prize religious liberty, have always held to the separation of the two — that the church should be free in a state which is free, each supreme in its own realm under God.

Canada Baptist Union

At least three aspects of the church-state relationship became troublesome in the first half of the nineteenth century and came into focus in the thirties and forties. There was the Church of England's attempt to claim the same privilege of Establishment it had enjoyed in England — acting as a partner with the state. Stemming from that position were the problems of the clergy reserves and the founding of a provincial university. Largely in an effort to face these difficulties, a further unit of attempted co-operation was set up in 1843, the Canada Baptist Union.

While the Union did not consist merely of members who paid dues, it did lack the authority of a body inaugurated on a representative basis. It was simply a group of leading Baptists from various associations and societies in the province of Canada, including close and open communionists. It allowed Baptists to meet together and to sound one voice in facing the issues of the day. Since it appeared that the associations were unable to manage such an alliance, the Union was trying to offer a representative future, inviting each association and church to send delegates and including "every approved Baptist minister in the Province."[7]

Because of lack of trust, however, the Union did not gain the hoped-for support from the associations or the churches (the executive committee reporting in 1845 that only one association had even forwarded its requested minutes)[8] and gradually it faded from the scene. But while it existed it provided, together with the *Montreal Register*, a powerful mode for expressing Baptist opinion to both government and the community. It also defended religious liberties.

Bishop Strachan

And religious liberties were indeed being threatened at the time. Much of the trouble was connected with John Strachan, Archdeacon of York, later Bishop of Toronto, who had come to the Canadas in 1799 as a Scottish Presbyterian schoolmaster. Within four years he had taken up Anglican orders and had opened a "school for the sons of gentlemen" at Cornwall. By 1812 he was rector of York.

From the first, Strachan strongly supported the concept of Church Establishment in Upper Canada, which had initially been promoted by Governor Simcoe. Throughout his ministry, aided by a number of his former students who had themselves become "gentlemen" and members of the governing caste, Strachan constantly advanced this view, strengthened by his later position on the executive and legislative councils of Upper Canada.

Although, the Anglican church did have immediate access to the heights of power and although many of the educated were counted among its members, it did not have the numbers, ranking behind both the Methodists and Baptists.[9] Then, as Canadian historian A. R. M. Lower describes it, "Strachan's furious blast against Methodists and republicans"[10] in a sermon at the funeral of Bishop Jacob Mountain did not win many friends and actually drew young Egerton Ryerson into the public fray as a Methodist champion. He proved to be more than Strachan's match and made a unique contribution to the country, particularly in the field of education. In the end, an established church was never actually instituted.

Strachan's presumptuous reference to other Protestant bodies as "Dissenters" drew a protest from the *Montreal Register* of April 28, 1842, denying that the term had any basis in law or in fact and pointing out that there was no established church in the land. The Canada Baptist Union in 1844 sent a petition to the legislature, which began: ". . . the denomination of Christians called Baptists has ever been foremost in maintaining the principle that man, not being responsible to man for his belief, civil governments have no right to distinguish between religious sects by giving one a privilege or imposing on another a disability . . . ."[11]

"The church-state question," write Canadian historians John S. Moir and Robert E. Saunders, "entered politics mainly on two issues: the Clergy Reserves and education."[12] These formed the basis of the "disability" felt by the Union.

The Clergy Reserves and the University Question

The debate over the clergy reserves "disordered public life in Upper Canada for sixty years"[13] and was said by William Lyon Mackenzie to be the most important single cause of the Rebellion of 1837.[14] The bone of contention was that the government had reserved under the Constitution Act of 1791 approximately a seventh of the land for "the support of a Protestant clergy." This phrase was "interpreted by authority to mean the Anglican ministers without question and ministers of the Church of Scotland grudgingly."[15]

Led by Strachan, the clergy of the Church of England assumed that they were to be the sole possessors of the bounty until the Church of Scotland ministers in 1819 also laid claim, suggesting that as theirs was an established (in Scotland) and Protestant church, they were entitled to a share. That claim was upheld by the legal officers of the British Crown, all others being excluded.

Little was actually realized from the vast grant until 1824 when the government formed the Canada Company to invest in the public lands of Upper Canada and "the Clergy Reserves ceased to be merely a grievance in principle and became a grievance in fact as well."[16] The situation was further inflamed when authorization was given by a departing governor for the public funding of forty-six Anglican rectories.

At this point even the legislature began to stir. Measures were introduced in 1834 to provide for the sale of the clergy reserves, with the proceeds to be used for education, but the legislative council, which held veto power, refused to pass them. Later the legislative assembly tried again, but it was rebuffed once more. However, by 1840, after the joining of the two Canadas, the Imperial Act was passed to ensure that proceeds from the sale of the clergy lands would be divided among the Protestant denominations.

The Baptist Solution

"Thus," says W. L. Morton, "the principle of state religion was preserved, while that of an exclusive establishment was abandoned." However, he quickly adds: "This plural establishment was to prove little more acceptable than the old dual one. The 'voluntary principle' of some denominations and many individuals was to keep alive the demand that the Reserves be secularized."[17]

Baptists put up the strongest defence of the voluntary principle — "a principle," says historian Donald Creighton, "which always had the endorsement of the Baptists and increasingly won approval from the Methodists and members of the Free Church."[18] Through the pages of the *Montreal Register* of January 1845, the Baptist call was renewed "that the Clergy Reserves may be sold as soon as possible and the proceeds of the sales appropriated to General Education on liberal principles."[19] Three years later a surplus in the clergy reserve fund was temptingly offered to all Protestants. Some succumbed, but though badly in need of finances themselves, the Baptists spoke through a motion of the Canada Baptist Union the next year, saying "that measures be taken to devote the portion which might be supposed to fall to the share of the Baptists to the Provincial Normal School."[20]

The issue was finally put to rest in 1854 when the clergy reserves were "secularized." With continuing provision being made for clergymen then depending on the revenue, the remaining proceeds were given to cities and counties according to population. The voluntary principle had triumphed.

King's College Controversy

The other church-state issue of the hour — the university question and public education in general — provoked vigorous, though not so pro-longed, debate. And it was resolved in a similar way.

Once again Bishop Strachan was deeply involved. In 1826 he sent a letter to Lieutenant-Governor Maitland expressing his hopes for a university that would allow youth growing up in the colony to complete their education "under teachers of approved ability and tried attachment to the Parent State and Established Church."[21] Commissioned to go the next year to England to seek a royal charter for such a university, Strachan not only achieved his goal, but also secured a grant of Crown lands to support his project.

However, the ensuing controversy prevented the realization of his ambition until 1843 when King's College, ostensibly a provincial insti-tution, was opened in Toronto with Strachan as president. Meanwhile, the Anglicans had established Upper Canada College, a preparatory school, the Methodists Victoria University and the Presbyterians Queen's University.

In the intense struggle to prevent King's College from becoming the state university, Baptists played a prominent role, particularly in the 1840s. While minor amendments had been made to the original charter, it still appeared that the college was essentially an Anglican institution. Commenting on the laying of the cornerstone of the college, a writer in the *Montreal Register* expressed the fear that the institution was still "the engine of High Churchism."[22] A *Register* issue that appeared later the same year reported that Baptists had joined with Methodists, Presbyter-ians and Congregationalists in Montreal to protest "the exclusive and arrogant policy which threatens to turn the National Colleges in Toronto and Montreal into Espiscopalian monopolies"[23] — for a similar situation existed in what was previously Lower Canada. Baptists were by no means objecting to sectarian colleges — they had one themselves — but only to the state aid given them.

When the Canada Baptist Union drew up a petition to the legislative assembly at its first annual meeting in 1844, the university question and the clergy reserves were given equal emphasis. The Union held

that the great principles of Religious Liberty which they [the Baptists] thus hold have been grievously violated in the manner in which the Episcopalian sect of Christians have been allowed to divert a large portion of the funds set apart for the education of the youth of this Province, from their original purpose, and to obtain an undue influence in the distribution of the benefits and management of the affairs of the University of King's College at Toronto.[24]

The new Union also prepared a draft petition for use by the individual churches, setting forth the Baptist voluntarist position that only state universities should receive state endowments and that religious bodies should provide their own funding, theological training being their responsibility.

After a number of fruitless attempts by the legislature to settle the matter, it remained for Robert Baldwin, "that devout low-church Anglican," as Canadian historian W. L. Morton describes him, to be the "principal architect" of the resolution. He continues: ". . . though a pupil of John Strachan [Baldwin] had defied the Compact and undone much of the work of his former tutor and present father in God, the Bishop of Toronto. Baldwin thought that Strachan had placed the Anglican Church in an invidious and impossible position by his attempts to maintain the whole apparatus of establishment."[25]

Thus, the provincial University of Toronto was formed in 1849, secular in character and supported by the endowment first provided for King's College—"the fulfillment of all the dreams of the Baptists."[26] Those hopes included the establishment of a Baptist Theological Seminary, attached to the university and funded by the denomination.

Inefficiency of Commons Schools

In the broader educational field and more particularly in the limited number of public schools, Anglican domination was also evident in the earlier decades of the nineteenth century. But the reaction to the situation was somewhat slower than in the case of the university. Reflecting the then typical Baptist mistrust of public education, the columns of the *Montreal Register* of January 19, 1843, carried these sentiments: "While we very much need education, and while it has very much to correct among us, we must be careful that, in its introduction we do no harm . . . . There is great prejudice among many, both of our ministers and people against education."[27]

Led by recent British arrivals, however, the Baptists soon demonstrated strong opposition to sectarian religious teaching in the classroom, the *Montreal Register* charging the Church of England with aiming to increase its membership and strength through such instruction.[28] The Canada Baptist Union also complained of the inefficiency of the common schools due to "the small number of competent teachers and the want of uniformity of system."[29] Resistance to the use of public funds for separate schools was consistently voiced.

When the Methodist Egerton Ryerson was appointed superintendent of education, he first received Baptist support, but lost it when his School Act of 1846 gave extensive authority to his own office, the *Register* calling his action "Prussianism."[30] "As a result of Baptist agitation," writes A. J. McLaughlin, "Canada's foremost educationalist of the nineteenth century was prevented, by people who believed in the democratic principle, from laying a faulty foundation for future building." The "Great Charter" of 1850, McLaughlin adds, was much more democratic and became "the foundation upon which all educational programs in Ontario have been built."[31]

Public Victory ... Private Defeat

It is lamentable that neither the Canada Baptist Union nor the *Montreal Register* were long to enjoy or even to view the fruits of their splendid labours. Nor indeed was the Canada Baptist College. As already indicated, the *Register* folded in 1849, swamped by an avalanche of debt. A similar financial situation crushed the college in the same year. Although the Union did not suddenly expire, it dwindled away over the next decade, decimated in membership and almost completely lacking in influence among Baptists, but remaining a small voice for those espousing open communion.

Pressure on the Canada Baptist Union

As mentioned in an earlier chapter, the Union, envisaging a much wider alliance of Baptists, first wrote to their co-workers in Nova Scotia and New Brunswick, then in 1846 sent an emissary in the person of Dr. J. M. Cramp, who was president of Canada Baptist College at the time. The reaction was so favourable, it seems, that the executive committee exulted in reporting to the next year's meeting of the Union that "the union between the Baptists of the Provinces . . . is satisfactorily effected." The statement was quite premature. Nearly a century passed before union took place.

It is obvious that in spite of its able leadership, the Canada Baptist Union was unable to carry its own constituency, for in 1848 the attendance at the annual meeting totalled only fourteen. Yet those fourteen bravely, almost defiantly, considered and acted upon such weighty matters as slavery, the clergy reserves, public schools and the university question.[32]

The chief pressure on the Union — beyond even its precarious financial situation — was the continually nagging communion question, which was not to be fully resolved until the late eighties. As early as 1844, numbers in the western part of the province had signalled their intentions to split off over the issue.

By the mid-forties the western associations had become restive and, as one church historian has described it, "the unity displayed in the late 1830s was fast disappearing."[33] It was in the years 1843 and 1844 that the Long Point and Eastern associations refused to seat the Montreal delegation, including Principal Davies and the Reverend Newton Bosworth.

A Thundering Response

All this was but the prelude to the 1848 formation of the Regular Baptist Missionary Union of Canada by five of the western Associations: Haldimand, Eastern, Western, Grand River and Johnstown. The new Union's objectives were both aspiring and comprehensive, including the support of missions (home and overseas), the promotion of Sunday schools, the establishment of a literature depot, the defence of religious liberty and advocacy of the voluntary principle, together with the publication of a denominational paper.

The paper was already being produced when the Union first met in September. The *Evangelical Pioneer*, new and privately backed, had gone to press, its second issue of June 3, 1848, thundering out a response to leaders of the faltering Canada Baptist Missionary Society, who had defended the position of open communion. "Regarding the position and prospects of your Society in this region," it said, ". . . we cannot in any way recognize it," adding prophetically, "You will find that, when they proclaim the union of the Baptists in Canada, they will, at the same time, combine to declare non-intercourse with the Canada Baptist Missionary Society."[34]

At its founding, the Regular Union took over the *Evangelical Pioneer*, but the paper fared little better than its predecessors, succumbing finally to mounting debt. The Union itself, though started with such high hopes, was able to gain the support of less than a quarter of its churches and soon became yet another in the lengthening series of disappointments.

This last failed Union prided itself on its "Regular" status and thus would have had no cause to quarrel over the communion question. Underlying all, lack of trust seemed to be a major difficulty. A comment in the *Montreal Register* in 1843 suggested that even the associations were suspect, the writer holding that

> We do not object to what are called Associations provided they are designed simply to bring the churches into intimacy and sympathy. . . . There is, however, some danger lest these unions should become legislative . . . . When we hear of conventions among the Baptists, it reminds us of convocations among the Episcopalians, and we feel a jealousy for our independence.[35]

The Baptists' continuing dilemma over the relative importance of independence and interdependence was never more clearly demonstrated than in Upper and Lower Canada in the first half of the 1800s. While in the Maritimes the problem was well on the way to being solved, the process was to take many more decades in the Canadas. The losses were significant, particularly for the yet-to-be settled western regions of British North America.

CHAPTER 12

A Yearning for Learning

"If I plough in the study, I shall reap in the pulpit."
— *EDWARD MANNING*

At the leading edge of the movements foreshadowing the "New Epoch" among Maritime Baptists in the mid-1820s and Baptists in the Canadas a decade later was the cause of education. This awakening occurred in the context of a larger intellectual renaissance in British North America after the War of 1812, inspired by new educational trends in Scotland and the United States.[1] At the forefront of that interest was training for the ministry.

Ever since the Alline days — and long before in New England — New Lights and Baptists had been suspicious of "anything scholastic as tending to repress the freedom and vigour of spontaneous religious expression."[2] A number of the leaders, however, such as Edward Manning, Theodore Seth Harding and Joseph Dimmock lamented their lack of academic and theological training — while they attempted "the work of preachers and pastors . . . not even knowing their own language, and shut out from all the ordinary resources of learning."[3]

Closed Doors

There was no school in the region open for the training of a Baptist minister in the Maritimes in the early nineteenth century, and opportunities in New England were distant and beyond the financial capacity of most. The Church of England's King's College, Windsor, which had been established in 1789, effectively barred "Dissenters" from enrolling. For a brief period after 1817 it appeared that the Presbyterian-sponsored Pictou Academy might be an option, but again distance from the centres of Baptist population and quarrels between parties within the Presbyterian church over control of the school turned off potential students. Finally, the realization of a good number of Baptist hopes was given timely impetus through the founding of a church in 1827.

Anglican Beginnings

The first important stirrings had occurred slightly earlier. It was 1824 when the Reverend Archibald McQueen sent a letter to Charles Tupper, proposing that a theological seminary be established in Saint John or Halifax to prepare "pious young men for the ministry."[4] Tupper passed the letter on to Edward Manning, expressing his support for the proposal, but while Manning agreed, four years elapsed before the matter appeared on the agenda of the Nova Scotia Association's annual meeting. A catalyst was needed.

It should not be surprising that the agency through which the proposal came to a head was an individual congregation, for therein lies the source of Baptist genius, the local church. The roots of the church in question were found, strangely enough, in St. Paul's Anglican Church, Halifax, then the religious and social centre of the capital. The story began in 1823.

That year John Inglis, rector of St. Paul's, was named bishop of the diocese, giving the parishioners the opportunity to petition the Society for the Propagation of the Gospel to have their very popular evangelical curate, James Thomas Twining, succeed him. The colonial secretary, Lord Bathurst, supported by the new bishop and claiming Crown privilege, denied Twining the rectorship and made another appointment. A considerable group left the church over the rebuff, and after first worshipping in a local hall, they began constructing a chapel on Halifax's Granville Street.

Later, when Twining became reconciled with Inglis, the majority of the breakaway group returned to St. Paul's, dissolving the newly formed congregation. About twenty declined to do so: James Johnstone, a lawyer, the leader of the group; his brother Lewis, a physician; J. W. Nutting, chief clerk of the Supreme Court; John Ferguson, a merchant and importer; and Edmund A. Crawley, a lawyer. These ultimately became the nucleus of a second Baptist church in the city.

Already influenced by Twining's strong evangelical preaching, John Ferguson had conversed with Edward Manning, a distant relative, and finally he was baptized at Cornwallis in 1825. When the chapel congregation disbanded, he persuaded his friends, who had previously interviewed Halifax Baptist pastor John Burton, to attend Burton's church.

Impact in Education

This they did for more than a year before purchasing the Granville Street building and returning to it. There, with the assistance of Professor Ira Chase of Newton Theological Seminary, Massachusetts, and Alexis Caswell, an instructor at Columbian College, Washington, they finally organized the Granville Street Baptist Church on September 27, 1827. Chase, who had been invited to preside at the dedication services was accompanied by Caswell, who was visiting New England at the time. The new church immediately called Caswell as pastor and so, in addition to leading the dedication exercises and conducting two baptismal services, Chase presided at Caswell's ordination.

The addition of the Granville Street Church, which was accepted into the Nova Scotia Association the next year, did not bring a large infusion of members. What it did bring was an unusually talented and well-educated little group of pacesetters to complement the strong and dedicated leadership of the rapidly growing denomination. They were to have a particular impact on the field of education.

Pacesetting

Although Alexis Caswell remained in Halifax for no more than a year, returning to take up a professorship at Brown University, where he later became president, he began to set the educational wheels in motion through a correspondence with Edward Manning.[5] Manning's interest in the possibility of a theological seminary was quickly revived, for he wrote immediately to Charles Tupper, suggesting that Tupper might communicate with the Baptists in England, telling of their dream and requesting financial assistance.[6]

As the plan evolved, however, the focus moved from a specifically theological seminary to "a seminary for education . . . [affording] the means of instruction in the usual branches of English literature and of scientific, classical and other studies which usually comprise the course of education at an Academy and College."[7]

Shortly before the 1828 annual meeting of the association, Caswell, together with Ferguson, Nutting and Crawley, met with Manning at Cornwallis and finalized plans for a presentation to the association. With interest throughout the constituency roused to a high pitch, the June 23rd association gathering was particularly well-attended — six women from Lunenburg country even walked some 120 kilometres to participate.

Unusual Move

Edmund Crawley, acting as spokesman for the sponsors, presented a prospectus outlining the educational objectives and plans, and calling for the establishment of the Nova Scotia Baptist Education Society to oversee the task. Overwhelming approval followed quickly.

In a move unusual for the times, administration was not confined solely to the sponsoring denomination. Others were allowed to participate as well although, for protection, more than half of the directors and members of the committee of management were to be members of churches connected with the association, and the Baptist members were to be entirely responsible for the theological department. It was also stipulated "that the Seminary be open to children and persons of any religious denomination."[8] Then, in an interesting clause that was perhaps more reflective of the times, there was a requirement that "diet and dress of the scholars . . . be of the plainest kind."[9] — certainly a worthy democ-ratizing provision and also financially necessary at that juncture.

The association-backed Education Society, with Edward Manning as president and Charles Tupper and J. W. Nutting as vice-presidents, chose Horton, now Wolfville, as the site for a new academy. By the spring of 1829, a farm had been purchased and space in the farmhouse refurbished as a classroom. Through the good offices of Chase and Caswell, Ashael Chapin, a graduate of Amherst College, Massachusetts, had been appointed the first principal, and Horton Academy opened its doors to about fifty students on May 1, 1829.

Approaching New Brunswick

So the new venture was successfully and enthusiastically launched. The only cloud on the otherwise clear horizon is reflected in this comment by historian Edward M. Saunders: "There is no reference to any attempt having been made to unite the Association of New Brunswick with that of Nova Scotia in founding the Academy."[10] Had that been attempted, the educational pathway might have been a good deal smoother for both associations, especially in its financial aspects.

Parallel Development

In 1833 New Brunswick faced a great deficiency in its ministerial ranks and encountered educational restrictions similar to those in Nova Scotia. The New Brunswick Association, "deeply impressed with the importance of having a suitable Seminary in this Province," voted "immediately [to] adopt some plan for the accomplishment of this desirable object" — that is to set up their own school. A large general committee was named to promote the objective, a smaller one to prepare a prospectus.

The next year it was reported that the Maugerville site first suggested for the school was unsuitable, and the committee of management of the recently formed Baptist Education Society of New Brunswick was directed to build at Fredericton.[12] The New Brunswick Baptist Seminary was opened with an enrolment of seventy students on January 4, 1836, the Reverend F. W. Myles being principal of the Male Department and his wife head of the Female Department.[13]

Overstretched Resources

By establishing a Female Department, Baptists were again pioneering. To be a leader in the cause of women's education in the 1830s was in itself unique. To serve both men and women on the same campus was unrivalled in British North America. As at Horton, classes were open, subject to no social or religious distinctions.

In 1827, the year before the decision was made to build Horton Academy, Baptist associational membership in Nova Scotia and New

Brunswick was too low to provide the necessary financial support. And the debt load increased as building expanded. Both associations therefore made a conscious decision to seek immediate government assistance, a choice which was to have important repercussions, particularly over a century and a quarter later in Nova Scotia. Pioneer Baptists in the Maritimes were not as adamant about the separation of church and state as were their counterparts in the province of Canada. From the first they were more than willing to accept, even to claim as do other religious bodies, government funding as a right in providing higher education for the community, as well as for their own sons and daughters. They were even prepared to allow the government "some supervisory power"[14] in academic institutional management if support was granted. From time to time they declined support, particularly for theological training, but even on this point, there has not always been consistency.

Application for assistance towards the necessary building and general objectives of the Horton Academy was made to the Nova Scotia house of assembly in 1829 and again in 1830 and 1831, but no aid was received until 1831, as the governor's legislative council vetoed the initial decision of the House. Viewing the disparity between the treatment meted out to the Establishment churches and the Baptists in Nova Scotia, historian Edward Saunders suggested that "King Charles reigned at Windsor, and Cromwell at Horton."[15] But "Cromwell" was not to be denied forever.

Two Baptist Schools

The 1835 New Brunswick Association was not far behind, quickly noting that "the very liberal grant made by the House of Assembly" of that province had also been rejected by the legislative council — grounds for complaint, it was felt, "especially when they recollect that liberal grants had been made by the Legislature of a Sister Colony in aid of a similar Institution"[16] (Horton, of course). The legislative council of New Brunswick then resisted positive action by the House for four further successive years until in 1840 a grant of £500 was made "without a dissenting voice in either branch."[17]

So by 1835, two Baptist schools were operating at the academy or high school level in the Maritime region. The one at Fredericton continued until 1871, although it was continually plagued by financial stresses. Horton Academy, on the other hand, had a long and honoured history until its closure in 1959. Both trained many successful and committed students, including ministers, and sparked a new denominational interest in higher education.

The Founding of Acadia

When the Nova Scotia Baptist Education Society and the Horton Academy were established, their founders had intended to expand beyond the secondary school stage to college. Pressure to do this increased as students graduated. If they wanted to pursue further studies, they were forced to look to the United States, and many did not return once their education was complete. The earlier scepticism of Baptists about the benefits of education had dwindled markedly, partly because no fewer than four waves of revival had swept the Academy and the town between 1829 and 1835,[18] paralleling similar movements throughout the province. There was therefore general support for extension, although the financial situation had deteriorated because the legislative council had again vetoed any grant in 1835.

This was when members of the Granville Street church of Halifax stepped in again to play a catalytic role. The first was the Reverend John Pryor, a former Anglican, who had been at King's College when the original Granville Street group broke off from St. Paul's. He had joined the seceding group, and afterwards gone to New England to study theology at Newton Theological Institution near Boston. In 1830 Pryor was persuaded to return to Nova Scotia to become principal of Horton Academy, although he was in the middle of his term. He stayed until 1838 and then resigned, despairing of any college development. He planned to take up his theological studies again but was destined at that time not to move far.

Dalhousie College

Meanwhile, another Granville Street member, Edmund A. Crawley, had come to the forefront. Immersed by Alexis Caswell in 1828, the former lawyer had gone to Brown University and Andover Theological Seminary soon afterwards to train for the Baptist ministry. After returning to Nova Scotia, Crawley acted as financial agent for the academy in the United States and England for a year and then became minister of his own Granville Street church, supplementing his pastoral work by giving private instruction in classics and other subjects in a room on the Dalhousie College premises in Halifax.[19]

Dalhousie, built in 1820, had been the dream of the British Earl of that name who was lieutenant-governor of Nova Scotia. Realizing how the Anglican exclusiveness at King's had proved detrimental to the colony, Lord Dalhousie, a Presbyterian, had resolved to establish the Halifax college on a non-sectarian basis. Financial backing for building was granted from what was known as the Castine Fund, an amount of some £10,750 collected by the British government in custom duties at the captured Maine port of Castine during the War of 1812 that had been turned over to Nova Scotia by a grateful motherland. With the governor's support, the legislature added further monies, and building began.

After Lord Dalhousie's departure to Upper Canada to become governor-general of the whole of British North America, interest in the institution languished, and regular classes did not begin until 1838. In that year the legislature decided to resuscitate Dalhousie College as a provincial institution, transferring for its support £200 of the £500 regularly granted to the Presbyterian Pictou Academy and drawing that academy's head, Dr. Thomas McCulloch, to Dalhousie as president. Baptists and other dissenting denominations were asked for co-operation, and the Baptists promised to offer theirs on condition that one of their number be named to the faculty.[20]

Shut Out

Concerning a Chair still to be filled, I. E. Bill writes, "Rev. Edmund A. Crawley, as a representative Baptist, whose sentiments at that time were in favour of one university for all the people, was induced to apply for appointment to the vacant Chair. In fact he was requested by one of the Trustees. . . . But to his utter surprise and mortification, his application was rejected. . . . Why? for the simple reason that those in charge felt themselves bound, as they said, to connect the college exclusively with the Kirk of Scotland."[21]

Shut out by both King's and Dalhousie, as well as the Anglican college at Fredericton, Baptists were driven back on their own resources. Meeting on November 15, 1838, the Nova Scotia Baptist Education Society resolved to establish a college-level insitution of their own.

John Pryor was once again prevented from continuing his theological training in the United States, as he was offered a professorship in classics and natural philosophy at the new college, where he, together with E. A. Crawley as professor of moral philosophy, logic, rhetoric and mathematics, made up the original faculty. They rotated in the position of president. Each had a Master of Arts degree. It was specified that "no restriction of a Denominational character shall be placed upon the appointment of the Professors or Officers or the matriculation or the graduation of Students."[22] A Presbyterian, Edward Blanchard was in fact named to succeed Pryor at the Academy and the two institutions would have a common administration.

"Joe" Howe

The new college opened on January 21, 1839, with twenty students. Application was immediately made to the legislature for a charter under the name "Queen's College," but the timing was not the best. Now that the Baptists had founded a third denominational college in a province of very limited population, many of the politicians had come to favour a single, non-sectarian institution. The Baptist response was, of course, that it was too late to do that, since they had been barred from the other two colleges, sealing the issue. The struggle thus inevitably took on political overtones.

Joseph Howe had recently entered the legislature as a member of the Reform party and had begun to make his presence felt. Most of the Baptists, coming from dissenting stock, favoured the Reform camp — except for the Halifax group who had come from the Establishment and were Tories. With Howe and other Reform leaders pushing for a single provincial university, the divided loyalties of most Baptists caused considerable strain. When the issue came to a head, however, there was no doubt that the greater loyalty of all Baptists was to the denomination, and this was ultimately demonstrated in the political arena.

A Reluctant Vote

The original application for a college charter was defeated in the house of assembly by one vote, although, apparently to ease the distress, £300 was granted to Horton Academy. In 1840, with strong support from the association and the churches, the measure passed, although the organizers were asked to change the name from Queen's to Acadia. Queen Victoria, to whom the matter had been addressed, would not allow her name to be used, as the favour, "might give serious anxiety and pain to other classes of Her Majesty's faithful subjects."[23]

Although Howe opposed the concept of denominational colleges, and said so during the debate, he reluctantly voted in favour both times the application was made. Up to that time he had apparently decided that he needed Baptist votes in order to stay in office to make his desired constitutional reeforms. But soon afterwards, he removed his token support, causing a conflagration in the political life of the province. The spark was an appeal for funds for the new college commensurate with those already regularly granted to King's and Dalhousie. On opposite sides were the Honourable Joseph Howe, now a member of Lieutenant-Governor Sir Collin Campbell's executive council, and the Honourable J. W. Johnstone, the Halifax Baptist and long-term council member. Both were in the newly formed coalition government, but Howe was from the Reform party and Johnstone was a Tory.

The original grant sought in 1841 was £500 per year for four years —this including the £300 already granted to Horton Academy. Howe was adamantly opposed, and so was accused by Professor E. A. Crawley of voting to give Acadia a charter only to destroy her.[24] A one-year grant passed, however, as a slightly smaller one did the next year, with Howe still vocally hostile.

Howe's antagonism was undoubtedly aggravated by the running dispute he was having at the time with James Nutting and John Ferguson, editors of the *Christian Messenger,* copies of which were printed from 1837 to 1840 on the presses of Howe's paper, the *Novascotian.* Continually in financial difficulties, the magazine, although legally the responsibility of the editors, was considered to be the denominational organ. At the end of 1840 Howe sent a bill totalling £800 and sought immediate payment from the editors, whom he had induced to sign personal notes. Payment was delayed partly because of questions about some of the charges. These were finally taken to arbitration, when the money was raised by the denominational leaders to pay the arbitrated amount. Meanwhile, Howe had used pages of his *Novascotian* to castigate the editors — so seriously that a special meeting of the association was called early in 1843. The editors were strongly upheld and utmost confidence expressed in them.[25]

A Major Election Issue

Against this background, Howe supported his colleague William Annand in the introduction of a series of resolutions into the House to the effect that "the policy heretofore pursued of chartering and endowing collegiate institutions of a sectarian or denominational character is unsound and ought to be abandoned."[26] Although the question did not come to a vote, procedural manoeuvering was required to avoid it, and the lines of battle were clearly drawn. The life of the new Acadia was at stake.

The matter became a major issue in the Nova Scotia election of 1843 and "for the time being, the subject of responsible and party government was thrown into the shade by the college question."[27] Baptist Attorney-General J. W. Johnstone resigned from the legislative council to contest a seat for the house of assembly in the Annapolis county riding against another Baptist, S. B. Chipman, who was with Howe in favouring a single state college. With strong Baptist support, Johnstone swept to victory, and although his Tory party secured only a limited majority, he was able to ensure the future of the denominational colleges. Howe resigned from the legislative council, not to return to office for more than four years. When in 1849 another move was made to abolish grants to all provincial colleges, he declined to support the action, remarking somewhat ruefully: "You cannot sweep them away. You may withdraw your public money, but there will be more socks and mittens knit on the hills of Wilmot, more tubs of butter made, more fat calves killed and more missionary travellers sent through the country and Acadia College will still stand on the hillside, in spite of the withdrawal of our grant."[28]

Despite the state aid, finances had continued to be in a precarious position for a number of years. In 1849, with arrears of £3,700, New Brunswick members of the Convention, which had been founded three years before, offered to assist in meeting the debt, provided that the Convention was allowed to control the administration of Acadia. This was accomplished in 1851, and renewed efforts were made to raise the necessary funds at home and abroad. Agents sent to England almost immediately ran into severe opposition because the college had accepted monies, as this was felt to be inconsistent with Baptist principles. Finally it was agreed that such grants should go only to the Academy. Then, under the leadership of the newly appointed president, J. M. Cramp, a large endowment was raised mostly through the Baptist churches. Financial independence was finally in sight.[29]

Public Education

The Baptists at Acadia made many enduring contributions to education in Nova Scotia, not least in the role they played in setting up the Free School System in the provinces of Nova Scotia. As early as 1832 the Nova

Scotia Baptist Education Society sought improvement in public prepar-
tory education, petitioning the legislature on the matter numerous times.
It was finally a government under the leadership of Charles Tupper, Jr.,
a former Horton Academy student, that introduced the measure. Nova
Scotia's first public education system had been set up, and its first superintendent was Theodore Harding Rand, an Acadia graduate of 1860.

The new system was so successful that a few years later T. H. Rand
was invited by the government of neighbouring New Brunswick to design
an Act instituting a similar system for that province. This he did — and
became the first superintendent at Fredericton as he had done previously
at Halifax.

Baptist Education in the Canadas

By the 1830s the Baptists of the Canadas, like their Maritime counterparts, had become aware of the need for higher education, especially for
ministers. It was this that had led to the formation of both the Upper
Canada Baptist Missionary Society and, to the east, the Ottawa Association. When John Gilmour was dispatched to Britain by the association
and William Rees by the society, although unknown to one another, the
Baptists were on the threshold of establishing their own institution of
higher education.

Canada Baptist College

Gilmour returned from Britain with considerable funds to set up a training
college, and he had also obtained the promise of financial support for a
principal to head it. Rees came back with little funding, but had been
advised that the two groups should co-operate in the project.

Canada Baptist College opened its doors in temporary quarters in
Montreal in 1838, and although other sites were considered—Brockville,
Bytown (Ottawa), Kingston and Toronto—a conference convened in Haldimand, that included Elder Rees, could reach no joint decision except
that the college continue to operate out of Montreal for a time. In the
same year the Reverend Benjamin Davies, who had a doctorate from the
University of Leipzig in Germany — the first Ph.D. on any Canadian
faculty[30] — arrived from Britain as principal, supported by the Baptist
Canadian Missionary Society, London.

Davies remained for six years, toiling "with intense zeal," although
"the number of students was disappointingly small, never exceeding sixteen, even after the larger building was entered."[31] There were a number
of problems. Looming large was the fact that the churches in the western
part of the Canadas distrusted Davies's and Gilmour's "open" stance on
the communion question. Location was seen as a further drawback:
Montreal was regarded as being too far from the centres of Baptist
population. European-style course offerings were also hardly appropriate
or appealing to the untempered ministerial trainees or their congrega-

tions in the frontier settlements of the 1830s and 40s. "In addition to Classical Literature, Philosophy, Theology and Ecclesiastical History, Davies's syllabus included Oriental Literature and "such linguistic skills as Greek, Hebrew, Latin, Aramaic, Syriac and German [but not French, and in Quebec!]."[32]

Dr. J. M. Cramp, also English-born, succeeded Davies in 1844 and almost immediately embarked on a major construction program, resulting in the erection of the "larger building" already mentioned, at a cost of $30,000, an astronomical figure for those times, particularly as only 10 percent of it had been subscribed when building began. The burden of this debt was never eased, and with financing complicated by a serious economic downturn in the country, the college foundered in 1849 — but not before giving the denomination a number of excellent future leaders.

Proposed Maclay College

Even before the failure of Canada Baptist College, Montreal, the churches of the western area had written it off and were again planning for their own institution at Toronto. A proposal was placed before the first annual meeting of the Regular Baptist Union in June 1849 to establish a theological school with short six-week terms, given twice a year if possible, and three, or at least two, professors teaching voluntarily. But "the modest scheme thus projected never took practical form."[33]

The effort was revived in 1852 when a new organization, the Regular Baptist Missionary Society of Canada, replaced the Union. After a number of halting steps, Dr. A. Maclay of Toronto was secured to promote the cause, which he did with vigor — and without pay. It appeared that his efforts were to be rewarded when the newly-formed Regular Baptist Theological Education Society of Canada proposed naming the school Maclay College, with Maclay himself as the first president. Maclay accepted the position but resigned when it became apparent that there would not be enough financial support. Finally, in 1856, the undertaking was discontinued.

The Educational Society did not disband, however, but appointed Canadian-born Robert Alexander Fyfe as its president, the man who was destined to head the Canadian Literary Institute, Woodstock, to be opened in 1860, and "the leader who was to succeed in putting Baptist educational work [in the Province of Canada] upon a lasting basis."[34] That narrative and the story of the consequent founding of Toronto Baptist College and McMaster University appear in a later chapter.

PART III

New Frontiers

IT WAS 1835 AND A FRENCH-speaking Swiss widow in her mid-thirties was facing a crucial decision. A few years before, her serene world had fallen apart as first her only child, a little daughter, and then her husband had been snatched away by death.

She had plunged into a life of service for God and the needy of her native Lausanne but, fulfilling as it was, there remained a conviction that God had something else for her. She couldn't shake it.

Two friends, her former pastor and his wife, had gone the year before to North America, where they had settled in Montreal to do missionary work among the French Canadians. A letter had just arrived from them begging for reinforcements. Dare she leave all and travel to an unknown, perhaps forbidding land to face resistance and persecution?

Despite the strong opposition of family and friends, the critical decision was finally made: she would go. Simultaneously God's hand was on another shoulder and in the end she didn't have to travel alone. A youthful teacher also responded, a young man who proved to be over many years a most valued associate.

Travel in the 1830s was hardly a joyous experience. The ship voyage to New York took over a month. As yet there were no rail lines to Montreal, so travel was again by boat, up the Hudson River through Lake Champlain to St. John's, Quebec.

She asked to be told when the American-Canadian border was reached, and at that point began a prayer . . . so that she might enter her sphere of labour on her knees. After landing at St. John's, with her first steps on Canadian soil, she slipped behind a pile of lumber to pray and commit her future to her Saviour.

A rough and fatiguing stage-coach run to La Prairie, Quebec, followed and once more a boat was taken — this time to Montreal and her waiting friends. Henrietta Feller had arrived — soon to inaugurate one of the most difficult and gripping chapters in Canadian Baptist history.

Hers is the story of the foundation of the Grande Ligne Mission . . . and it unfolds as it began, with commitment and prayer.

CHAPTER 13

The Other Line

"No frontiers . . . separate us in the fellowship of the Spirit."
—BAPTIST WORLD ALLIANCE EXECUTIVE, 1972

There are two strains in the Baptist heritage worldwide: the "particular" (or Regular) and the "general." The former have historically held closer to John Calvin's view that Christ's redemption was for the "elect" or the pre-chosen, while the latter tended to the position of another well-known theologian, Jacob Arminius, that redemption was general, for all. The first put greatest emphasis on the sovereignty of God, the second on man's free will. With time, of course, the two positions have converged, free will and predestination being two parts of a whole, neither of which is complete without the other.

But early proponents of the two principles held strong opinions, and in both Britain and the Americas the particular and the general developed side by side. However, in the United States and in British North America, the Calvinist, or Regular, Baptists soon became the more dominant group.

Canadian historian A. R. M. Lower maintains that in Upper Canada "there were no non-Calvinist Baptists" before 1820.[1] The same does not hold true for Lower Canada, however, where as early as 1802 the Freewill Baptists began work. The first congregations were in Hatley and Stanstead, two communities in the Eastern Townships where pioneering missions had been planted five years before by the Regular Calvinist Baptists through William Marsh, Jr.

But these were not the first Baptists of Arminian order to enter what is now Canada. Of the same persuasion were the General Six-Principle Baptists organized in Rhode Island in 1670, progenitors of the little company of temporary émigrés from Swansea, Massachusetts, who transferred as a church to Sackville, then Nova Scotia, in 1763. So perhaps was the original Arminian congregation at Clinton, Upper Canada, led by Pastor Tims, a group which Lower apparently missed in his count.

Origins

Benjamin Randall, founder of the Freewill body, came to his Arminian Baptist convictions by a somewhat circuitous route. A seaman and sailmaker as a youth in New Hampshire, he was shocked into responding to the claims of Christ on learning of the death in 1770 of evangelist George Whitefield, whose preaching had greatly impressed him. The next year Randall joined the Congregational church in New Castle, New Hampshire, where he had established a business, but that link was soon broken when he perceived moral laxity among the church's members and withdrew. When he and a number of supporters who had gathered around him began to study the scriptures and found no warrant for infant baptism, four of them, including Randall, asked for believer's baptism and joined the Regular Baptist church in Berwick, New Hampshire.[2]

Randall's pilgrimage was not over. He began to preach, and while on an itinerary through the eastern part of the state, was called to the pastorate of the Congregational church at New Durham. This he accepted on the understanding that he would be free to continue his travelling evangelistic ministry. As he did so, Randall came under increasing criticism from the then strict Calvinist Baptists of New Hampshire, Vermont and Maine for the Arminian views he espoused.

In 1780 Randall withdrew the membership that he had retained in the Regular Baptist church at Berwick, and united with the newly formed Arminian Crown Point Baptist church in Stafford, New Hampshire. Being ordained almost immediately by two Arminian Baptist churches, Randall proceeded to establish the church in New Durham to which the Freewill Baptists of North America trace their origins.

Fanning out from that New Hampshire centre, Randall was responsible for planting about fifteen new Freewill churches by 1782—a remarkable achievement in just two years. By 1910, when they united with the Northern Baptist Convention (now American Baptist Churches), the number had grown to over 1,500.[3]

The Free Baptists in the Canadas

It was an American Congregationalist, Avery Moulton, who first brought the Free Baptist line into the Canadas. Influenced by a Free Baptist revival just before emigrating to Stanstead in the Eastern Townships, he began holding services in nearby Hatley, in association with a Methodist[4] minister. After a few meetings, they decided to invite two New England Free Baptist ministers, Robertson Smith and Joseph Boody, to conduct further services, and this resulted in the forming of congregations in both Hatley and Stanstead, the first Freewill churches north of the border. Undoubtedly their founding retarded the development of the recently established Regular churches there.

Treason Charged

Moulton was baptized by Robertson Smith in 1803 and was ordained the next year as the Stanstead pastor. The only Freewill minister in the

Canadas at the time, he moved to Hatley in 1806 but included an itinerating ministry as well as a ministry in nearby settlements for many years.

During the War of 1812, because of his American connections and specifically because of a sermon he preached based on John 18:36 ("My kingdom is not of this world: if my kingdom were of this world, then would my servants fight. . . ." KJV), Avery Moulton was charged with treason. The authorities had apparently concluded that Moulton was encouraging Canadians not to fight the Americans. On the day of the trial, he held a baptismal service in front of the house where court was to convene, and later conducted his own defence at a hearing which was said almost to have turned into a revival meeting.[5] Moulton was acquitted, but the two churches had a difficult time during the period of hostilities because most of their members were American and they were close to the border and the war zone.

In 1818, four years after the war was over, Willard Bartlett, a Freewill minister, moved to Melbourne, Lower Canada, where he founded a church and remained for nearly forty years. Freewill churches followed at Compton (1819) and Durham (1821).

In 1832 the Freewill churches of Stanstead, Barnstead, Compton, Hatley and Durham, which were all part of the Wheelock Quarterly Meeting in the United States, were dismissed to become the Stanstead Quarterly Meeting — the quarterly meeting being analogous to the Regulars' association. Hatley came into the group in a weakened condition, the majority of its members having withdrawn five years earlier under the disaffecting influence of a false "Christian" minister who had joined the congregation.

A Little Sheep Stealing

The Free Communion Baptists were the first of the Free Baptists to emerge in Upper Canada. They differed from the Freewill mainly in their belief in the perseverance of the saints[6] — that is, that God would enable truly converted believers to complete their spiritual pilgrimages and finally arrive in heaven. This belief is based on Jesus' words recorded in John 10: 29: "No man is able to pluck them out of my Father's hand." On this point, they were, of course, in harmony with the Regulars. Thomas Tallman, who first introduced the Free Communion Baptists to the Canadas, had been a soldier in British General Burgoyne's army during the American Revolution, but afterwards had settled in New York state and there became a Free Communion Baptist minister. Once, when he was on a church-planting mission to Canada, Tallman was invited to preach in the London area, where revival followed. Elder Tallman proved to be effective and persuasive, and was apparently not too averse to a little "sheep-stealing", for the author notes that in the resulting formation of a church at Oxford (now Woodstock) in 1822, "The persons whose names constitute 'The First Free Communion Baptist Church in the Town of Oxford' had been members of the 'Close Communion Church in Oxford.'[7]

Expansion came almost immediately. The original minutes of the Free Communion Baptist Association of Upper Canada, held in 1825, indicate that letters were tabled from congregations at Blenheim (37 members) Southwold (15), Oxford, (79) and Norwich (15).[8] Others to link with the association and Conference (the Free Communion equivalent of a Convention) included Westminster, Windham, Waterford, Bayham, Zorra, Missouri and Hope—all in the Woodstock area.[9]

London Area Productive

Unlike the Free Communion and Regular Baptists, Freewill Baptist churches in the upper province were not established by American missionaries. It was Andrew Banghart who began the work—a pastor who was likely converted under the Free Communion Baptists in Westminster township, western Ontario, in the early 1820s. Almost as soon as he began to preach, he won nearly fifty of his neighbours. Seeking to unite with a compatible denomination, Banghart learned of the Freewill Baptists in New York state and, after a fruitless initial visit, later met with them at a quarterly meeting in Bethany, New York, where he was accepted, baptized and ordained.

Then the Americans became involved. Herman Jenkins, a New York Freewill minister, called upon Banghart in Westminster, where he found a church of twenty members. He went on to assist Banghart in establishing work at Dunwich and later Southwold, in Elgin country north of Lake Erie.

The area around London proved to be the most productive for the Free Baptist cause and one of the main agents for expansion was Thomas Huckins, a Freewill Baptist from the Maritimes. He moved first to Dunwich and then to London. Attending a yearly meeting in New York state in 1826, he asked for—and received—assistance to found a church in his adopted city, and within three years there were three Freewill and four Free Communion churches in the vicinity.

By 1837 the Free Communion Baptists were showing interest in discussing the possibility of amalgamation with the Regular Baptists. The discussions were obviously not successful, for no merger was accomplished during that year. Differences in theology and in polity were likely too pronounced at a time when the Regulars were beginning to sense their own identity.

There were never many Free Baptist members in the Canadas. At its peak in Canada West in 1859 the movement had just over twenty churches and slightly fewer than a thousand members.[10] Although the dwindling congregations were finally absorbed by the Regular Baptists, the Free Baptist influence was to be singularly powerful in moulding the thought and practice of the continuing denomination.

Maritime Launching

Nova Scotia

Free Baptists did not establish their first churches by the shores of the Atlantic for nearly two decades after they had begun work in Lower Canada, but at about the same time that they did in the upper province — the early 1820s. Despite their late start, they were able to benefit to some degree from the Alline legacy — especially the latent support in some quarters for open communion.

Elder Asa McGray could be considered the Free Baptists' founding "father" in the Maritimes. Born in 1780 in Yarmouth, Maine, McGray was first licensed to preach by the Methodists in 1813, being ordained by the Free Baptists the following year. After preaching for two years in his home state, while still plying his trade as a wheelwright, McGray moved to Windsor, Nova Scotia. He found the religious climate there somewhat cool for his position, and moved on to Cape Sable Island, where in 1821 he founded a church of nineteen members. The same year he "reorganized" the Regular Baptist church of nearby Barrington on the mainland, and a native of the town, Thomas Crowell, who had been converted under Henry Alline's preaching, was installed as pastor. With this reorganization, he was, of course, inducing the church to sever its Calvinist roots, which extended back to its founding in about 1800. Within five years the Barrington Freewill congregation had a membership of 130 and a number of other Freewill churches had been formed in the vicinity.[11]

Without an Equal

Another immigrant elder, Jacob Norton, arrived on the same Nova Scotia shore at about the same time. Although then not technically a Free Baptist, Norton had been ordained at the age of twenty-two in Swanville, Maine, by a group with similar views that called itself the Church of Christ. In 1819, apparently with assistance from McGray and Crowell, he formed a "Christian" — sometimes termed "Christian Baptist" — church at Argyle.

Also among the Free Baptist pioneers in Nova Scotia were Edward Reynolds and James Melvin, who blazed the trail in Queens County, and Charles Knowles, whom one historian has described as "probably without an equal as a public speaker in Western Nova Scotia."[12] Knowles founded churches in Kemptville, Chebogue, Session Hill and Pubnico.

With a number of autonomous churches thus springing up, McGray, Norton, Crowell, Reynolds and Knowles met in 1836 "to consider the propriety of uniting in one body."[13] McGray had drawn the little Freewill group into a Conference two years earlier, so a good start had been made. The merger took place in 1837, the united body taking the name Free Christian Baptist.

Personality Differences

The united Conference adopted the characteristic quarterly meeting plan of the New England Freewill Baptist movement. This involved regular assemblies every three months, one of these being the annual meeting. Business was also conducted at each of the quarterly sessions, however. This practice was a continuing feature of Free Baptist polity.

Unfortunately, deep personality differences between McGray and Norton caused an almost immediate rift. McGray and most of the members of the Cape Sable Island church withdrew and re-assumed the Freewill designation, joining the Farmington Quarterly Meeting in Maine in 1840. The state body sent assistance by way of a number of visiting missionaries and soon three churches—Cape Sable Island, Wood Harbour and Beaver River—were linked in the Barrington Quarterly Meeting and part of the Maine Central Yearly Meeting.

McGray's little free Baptist grouping reached a peak of but seven churches and just under five hundred members in the mid-1850s. Meanwhile, the Free Christian Baptist Conference, although suffering from the secession, expanded to thirteen churches by 1843 and to twenty-seven by 1867, the year the two bodies were finally reunited as the Free Baptist Conference of Nova Scotia.

New Brunswick

Although it began later, Free Baptist progress was both more rapid and more extensive in New Brunswick than in Nova Scotia. Maritime Baptist historian George Levy observes that their successes may help to account for the slower growth of the Calvinist Baptists in New Brunswick than in Nova Scotia at the time.[14]

Free Baptist development in the Maritimes, particularly in New Brunswick, did not take place on well-ordered lines. As in New England, there were continuing pockets of resistance to the hyper-Calvinism that increasingly characterized numbers of the Regular churches after the association adopted close communion. Edward Weyman, one of the Free Baptist pathfinders in New Brunswick, refers to the issue in one of his personal memoranda:

> Had the Baptist churches in the Province and their ministers stood where they began, free from the antinomian use of the doctrine of grace, we would not have been a distinct people . . . there would have been no necessity for our denominational existence. . . . To their teaching about election, predestination and a limited atonement, large numbers of their own churches were unreconciled, and the hearts by many people were closed against them.[15]

Around the little pockets of dissent there grew up, almost willy-nilly at first, a number of unconnected local congregations that were gradually drawn together by common interest and capable leadership.

New England Interest

Information about specific Free Baptist origins in the province is fragmentary. The Reverend Joseph McLeod, son of the Reverend Ezekiel McLeod, one of the dominant figures in early New Brunswick Free Baptist history, states simply that "When the Free Baptists of New Brunswick began to be, history does not say."[16] It is certain that a Conference of six churches, involving two ordained ministers, elders Samuel Nutt and Charles McMullin, and licentiate William Pennington, was organized at Wakefield, Carleton County in 1832. The six were Jacksontown, Bear Island, Little River, Lincoln, Upper Sussex and Wakefield.

The Freewill Baptists of New England had earlier noted some interest in their cause in New Brunswick, and in 1826 the denominational paper, the *Morning Star*, reported that "There are a number of preachers there, whose views of doctrine and discipline are similar to ours, and they wish to become acquainted with the Freewill Baptists of Maine."[17]

Yet it was not the Freewill Baptists, but the little Church of Christ group from which Jacob Norton had come to Nova Scotia, who seized the New Brunswick opportunity, for the body formed at Wakefield took the name of the New Brunswick Christian Conference. This designation, according to the younger McLeod was never quite satisfactory, for fifteen years later it was changed to Free Christian Baptist and very much later to Free Baptist General Conference.[18]

The First Moderator

The story of the Free Baptists of New Brunswick at this juncture is more an account of men than of movements. A number of pioneers — they, too, could be called fathers — were closely involved, including McMullin, Nutt and Pennington, who were present at the founding Conference.

Charles McMullin, born at Deer Island in the Bay of Fundy near Saint John, was ordained in Maine in 1829 by ministers of the Church of Christ. He began work in New Brunswick the next year and was responsible for establishing a good number of Free Baptist congregations in Victoria County, beginning with a church serving the two communities of Perth and Andover. It was McMullin who persuaded Samuel Nutt, a minister of the Church of Christ in Maine to make periodic visits to the Bear Island church and who recommended the forming and naming of the Conference, becoming its first moderator.

Licensed to preach by the Bear Island congregation when he attended the founding Conference, William Pennington was the first to be ordained by the New Brunswick Christian Conference. A native of Queensbury, York County, he effectively established some twenty churches and baptized more than one thousand converts.[19]

Samuel Hartt, born at Sheffield, Sunbury County, and Sussex-native Samuel Weyman, who was later to be a strong advocate of the union of all Baptists in the Maritimes, were also in that distinguished company.

Hartt was baptized in 1825 when he was twenty-six by an uncle, Lathrop Hammond, a Regular Baptist minister. While still unordained, he began preaching, but moved gradually away from his Calvinist position until in 1831 he was ordained by the Free Baptists. An effective evangelist and singer, "he probably did more to mould the religious beliefs of the people along the St. John River than any other man."[20] Born at the turn of the century, Weyman was ordained two years after Hartt. In contrast to his co-worker, Weyman's major gift lay in "the care of the churches."

The Towering Figure

Two British-born ministers also had a great impact on the Maritime Free Baptist movement: Robert Colpitts, who arrived in New Brunswick at age fourteen with his English parents, and Alexander Taylor, who came with his Scottish family at the age of six.

At the time that the first Free Baptist churches were being established in the East, Colpitts was considerably older than the other leaders. In his early thirties he began to preach independently around Moncton and later near Sussex and Norton. He was not baptized until 1830—at about sixty years of age—and was not ordained as a Free Baptist until two years later, serving effectively for a number of years.

Both of Alexander Taylor's parents, who had emigrated to Saint John, died when he was fourteen. Taylor was baptized in Maine at the age of twenty, and joined a Freewill church. Ordained in 1841, he served in that state until moving back to New Brunswick in 1853, where he served until his death in 1888. He was a strong preacher and church builder.

Undoubtedly "the towering figure"[21] among the New Brunswick Free Baptist ministers was Ezekiel McLeod who, like Weyman, was born in the Sussex district. Although said by his son to have been "thoughtful and studious . . . from his boyhood . . . [he was] impressed that he must some time preach the gospel."[22] He was thirty in 1842, when he publicly professed his faith. And it was six years later when, finally answering a call that "involved large financial sacrifices,"[23] Ezekiel McLeod was ordained, later becoming pastor of the Free Baptist Church in Saint John, Waterloo Street. From 1848 until his death in 1867 he ministered to the George Street Free Baptist Church in Fredericton.

McLeod was a man of immense energy, making a major contribution in many areas of Free Baptist life. In addition to his regular pastoral duties and other leadership responsibilities in the denomination, which demanded extensive travel, he was founding editor of the Free Baptist weekly, the *Religious Intelligencer*, which began publication in 1854 and which he edited for thirteen years until his passing.

Among Ezekiel McLeod's far-reaching contributions were his proposals for regularizing home missions work, the formation of Sunday schools and an increased emphasis on education. He also played a significant role in providing the denomination with an improved organizational pattern, including a treatise of faith.

Relations Warm

By 1847 the number of Free Baptist churches in New Brunswick had reached 40, with a membership of 2,000. The parallel Regular Baptist Association of New Brunswick then listed 73 churches and approximately 5,000 members. The Free Baptists were making a significant impact.

At the time, the small Nova Scotia Free Baptist Conference numbered only 17 congregations and 1,150 members. Its relations with the New Brunswick Conference had been consistently warm, and soon after the New Brunswick group took the name "Free Christian Baptist General Conference" in 1849, the two bodies decided to call themselves "one denomination." Each would retain its own government and send delegates to each other's yearly meetings. In addition, the *Religious Intelligencer* was adopted by the Nova Scotia Conference as its official organ. Full organic union, however, was not to occur for many years — and then in the context of the larger amalgamation of all Maritime Baptists.

The Free Baptist Legacy

While in the Maritimes the Free Baptists were never more numerous than the Regulars, and in the province of Canada they were a small group, they have had a great influence on succeeding generations of Baptists in this land.

From their inception the Free Baptists insisted more on interdependence than on independence. Quarterly or district meetings, together with yearly or conference meetings were always a feature of their organizational pattern. Benjamin Randall, who was a capable administrator, established the quarterly gatherings of nearby churches, the Conference soon becoming the co-ordinating body of the whole.

The larger assemblies of the Free Baptist Church also had more "teeth" than their Regular counterparts. A treatise drawn up by the Free Baptists of New Brunswick points to the greater authority exercised by the more general bodies—in contrast to the sometimes fierce local autonomy of the early Calvinist Baptists. "The church," the treatise declared, "is directly amenable to the District Meeting to which it belongs, and indirectly to the General Conference, for the general good of the denomination."[24]

Additional provisions enabled a district meeting, in the instance of a divided congregation, "to take charge of the church,"[25] and in cases of faulty doctrine or disloyalty to the denominational constitution, the district meeting could "acknowledge and sustain as the church those members who shall be found loyal to the denomination and . . . if deemed necessary . . . [to] have the power to reorganize such members into a church which shall bear the name and date of the original organization."[26] A church was "bound to recognize the doings of the General Conference and act on the same."[27] Ordinations were controlled by the Conference and all ordained ministers were required to attend every Conference meeting.

These positions, while not accepted *in toto* by Canadian Baptists at the close of the twentieth century, have greatly modified the extreme insistence on absolute local autonomy. There is much greater willingness to accept the guidance of the more general bodies.

Greatly modulated, too, is the hyper-Calvinism of the previous two centuries, together with the insistence on close communion, the latter having given way completely. The majority of present-day Canadian Baptists would probably be regarded as moderate Calvinists, although they would be somewhat unhappy with any label that might come between them and the Lord of the New Testament scriptures.

All these changes are part of the Free Baptist legacy.

CHAPTER 14

Sur la Grande Ligne

"No! You cannot kill the freedom of belief,
Or imprison Christ in jail!
The example of His Triumphs
Will live in hearts He's saved."
— GEORGI VINS

Contrary to the conventional wisdom, not all the original settlers of New France vested their spiritual allegiance in the state church of their motherland. Nor, indeed, did all their administrators. "For a time," writes Stuart Ivison, "there were as many Huguenots in positions of leadership in French North America as there were Catholics. . . ."[1]

Pierre du Gua, Sieur de Monts, was one of the best known. In 1603 he was granted the charter to monopolize the fur trade in France's North American territory by Henry IV, who had himself been reared as a Protestant but had expediently embraced the Roman Catholic faith to ease his path to the throne. De Monts was, in fact, the patron who sponsored Samuel de Champlain as he voyaged to the New World the next year, taking both a priest and a Protestant minister with him. After settling first on an island in the mouth of the St. Croix River in what is now New Brunswick, the explorers moved over to Port Royal, now Annapolis, in Nova Scotia.

Again under de Monts, Champlain sailed up the St. Lawrence in 1608 to explore and to colonize. That year he founded Quebec, and many Huguenot merchants and settlers emigrated to the new colony with the Roman Catholics. But that situation did not last long. The more tolerant Récollect Order that first dominated the scene in New France gave way to the more militant Jesuit and, under succeeding French administrations, Huguenot immigration was choked off and any budding Protestant endeavour smothered. It is doubtful that many of these early Huguenots survived as settlers of New France.[2]

That condition was to remain unchanged for most of two centuries. After the British conquest and the Treaty of Paris in 1763, the way was opened for Protestant churches to be established, but it was not until more modern times that this actually occurred. By 1807 a few missionaries of the American Methodist Episcopal church were at work among the French of the Ottawa Valley, and in 1815 Jean de Putron of the English Wesleyan Society arrived in Lower Canada from England, "to preach to the French emigrants and settlers, among whom the Lord has begun a good work of grace."[3] Then in 1830 a Quaker of Huguenot descent, Etienne Grellet, came to L'Acadie, a parish containing the village of Grande Ligne. Well received by the people in his evangelistic efforts, Grellet was made to feel quite unwelcome by the local curé and was soon forced to abandon his mission.

Swiss Source

Strangely enough, French-speaking Baptists in Quebec can trace their roots back to that pair of remarkable brothers, the Haldanes of the Scottish highlands. But their influence was far from direct. On one of his wide-ranging evangelistic missions, Robert Haldane preached at Lausanne, Switzerland, and among his converts were a number of the younger ministers and theological students of the Reformed church, which was dominant in that country at the time. It was during one of those periods of spiritual depression when that church "had sunk into a cold, formal state of evangelical torpor."[4]

Baptized by Gilmour

Henri Olivier, one of the younger ministers, was among those whose lives were forever altered by that encounter. Together with his wife, Olivier volunteered for missionary service among Canadian Indians under the auspices of the newly formed Lausanne Missionary Society. Denton and Gavin, two students of the Lausanne Institute, which had been founded by the Haldanes, volunteered to accompany them, and the group sailed for Montreal.

Although it had been their intention to minister among the Native peoples, the Oliviers immediately recognized the dire need among the French Canadians, whose language they spoke, and during the first year Henri preached in a gospel hall in Montreal and beyond to St. John's, Berthier and La Prairie. During that initial winter the Oliviers became convinced of believer's baptism and both were immersed by Montreal Baptist pastor, John Gilmour — after which they had to sever relations with the Missionary Society of Lausanne. The Oliviers were on their own, and became even more isolated when, the next spring, the students Denton and Gavin decided to travel west to undertake the Indian work. The Oliviers supported themselves by taking boarders and giving private lessons.[5]

Meanwhile, in Lausanne, a young widow, Henrietta Feller, who had also been converted under Haldane's preaching, had been urged by her good friends the Oliviers to join them in a mission to the spiritually destitute in French Canada. Born Henrietta Odin in Montagny near Lausanne in 1800, she was the daughter of a former officer in the French army who later became an educator and hospital administrator in Lausanne. Well educated, even as a young girl she took a deep interest in people, especially the suffering, and she often visited the wards of her father's hospital. At fifteen she joined the national Reformed church, not because of any personal conversion experience, but because "it seemed to be the right thing to do."[6]

In 1822 she became the wife of Louis Feller, a widower nearly twenty years her senior and the father of three children, the eldest fourteen. A baby girl, whom they named Elsie, was born into their home, and after M[me] Feller's conversion, soon to be followed by that of her husband, their happiness seemed to be complete. Then tragedy struck. One after the other, her three-year-old Elsie, her husband and her sister were taken away from her. A widow at twenty-seven, Henrietta Feller picked up the pieces by continuing her hospital visitation and looking to God for an answer as to her future.

Priestly Opposition

That answer came in the form of the Olivier's letter, in which they described the bleak spiritual conditions in Montreal and entreated her to come. Her response was not long delayed. In company with Louis Roussy, a young teacher who had trained at the Institute and had volunteered to join the mission, M[me] Feller sailed to New York, and after a long trip by boat and stagecoach, arrived in Montreal, where her friends the Oliviers were waiting. Shortly after she arrived, Henrietta wrote to friends at home saying, "You have no idea of the relief which a stranger feels in being kindly received."[7]

It was 1835 and the Oliviers began another winter's work, this time working side by side with M[me] Feller and Louis Roussy. They had been forced by priestly opposition to leave the gospel hall and had to hold their meetings in private homes. Results were slender and, to make matters worse, both the Oliviers became so ill that they had to return to Switzerland. Such a combination of circumstances might well have broken the spirit of a less committed person, but Henrietta Feller did not flinch. "Before I left Switzerland I foresaw what might befall," she wrote in a letter, adding, "I did not enter this career under any delusion. I sat down to count the cost. I had not overlooked the loneliness, the abandonment, the poverty, or even death in a hospital. I am conscious of no hesitation as to the course I should adopt. I came to this country to labour here for the advancement of the glorious Kingdom of Christ."[8]

In order to secure pupils for the small school she and M[me] Olivier had started, M[me] Feller visited house to house with Roussy, distributing scriptures and inviting parents to send their children to the school. At first the response was positive, but they soon had to discontinue when the Roman Catholic clergy forbade parents to allow their children to attend. Meanwhile, to bolster the school's finances, Roussy had accepted a teaching position at nearby L'Acadie, but that lasted a mere two months; he was dismissed for carrying on extracurricular evangelistic activities.

Two Garret Rooms

Hoping to find a more welcoming climate in a smaller town, Henrietta Feller and Louis Roussy began to concentrate their efforts on St. John's, where they were allowed to use the Methodist chapel and were also engaged in colportage — distributing tracts and selling Christian literature. Although they were not shunned in the rural areas surrounding St. John's, they were given a frigid — and sometimes violent — reception in the town. As one writer describes the situation: "M. Roussy was so maltreated that he had to desist from his labours. At one place he was beaten by a crowd of women who fell on him armed with sticks."[9]

Undaunted, M[me] Feller and Roussy moved on once more, this time to a village south of Montreal called Grande Ligne, so named because it was situated on "la grande ligne," the great line, or boundary, dividing two counties. The village gave the stouthearted newcomers a small toehold, as they had one personal connection there. While in L'Acadie, Roussy had been the means of the conversion of a Mme Lore, whose married daughter Mme Lévesque, lived in Grande Ligne. That good woman allowed Mme Feller to use two rooms in the attic of her unpretentious cabin.

In those two garret rooms in 1836 the Grande Ligne Mission was born — a work which has a long and honoured history now well into its second century. Many thousands of kilometres away from comfort and home, and knowing only her God and, happily, the language, Henrietta Feller, then in her mid-thirties, set to work with her young assistant, Louis Roussy.

One of the small rooms served as M[me] Feller's bedroom; the other was a combined kitchen, living room and schoolroom — for it all started as a school. While Roussy engaged in wide-ranging colportage in many of the surrounding villages, M[me] Feller taught some twenty children, mornings and afternoons, and conducted a daily 6:00 P.M. meeting for adults — a composite school and Bible class. By the end of January 1837, four converts had been baptized, and they became the nucleus of a Protestant church, to which seven more were added by baptism the following August.[10]

A Temporary Retreat

Yet the times did not lend themselves to successful missionary work. They were the days of the Rebellion of 1837, and insurrections were breaking out in both Upper and Lower Canada. Feelings ran particularly high in the lower province, and although the infant mission was in no way connected with political events, it received a good deal of the backlash. Canadian historian John S. Moir puts the persecution in perspective. Noting that since the British conquest the Roman Catholic church had remained loyal to the new authorities in times of crisis, he writes:

For several years before 1837 the violent French Canadian nationalists had been accusing their church of selling out to "les anglais". . . . South of Montreal, in the Saint Jean valley, the rebels threatened to take their revenge on the famous Grande Ligne mission, a French Protestant school operated by Henrietta Feller, a Swiss widow who was responsible for the conversion of several local Roman Catholics.[11]

M[me] Feller herself describes some of the terror they experienced as the "patriotes" attacked the mission and the new converts:

> The movements of the rebels always took place at night. They met in companies of one hundred, two hundred, and sometimes more. They were all masked, and were furnished with instruments of every kind imaginable, to get up a charivari. They went from house to house, mingling their infernal music, shouts and imprecations still more infernal. Those who did not come out immediately were pelted with stones and threatened with fire. Some houses were entirely destroyed, with their contents. . . . I could hardly believe that they were men. . . . On Saturday, Oct. 28th, a kind English friend, Mr. Richard McGuiness, came on horseback to warn us of the danger in which we were placed. Next day, Sunday, we held three meetings as usual. Our Canadians were in great distress. They saw clearly that it was our duty to leave, but they trembled at the thought of being forsaken at such a time.[12]

Leave they finally did, but they did not forsake their Canadians — they took them with them. Roussy, who had gone to Champlain in New York state to discover if anyone there could give them accommodation, returned with good news. M[me] Feller writes: "On Wednesday, Nov. 4th, we quitted Canada. Our company consisted of upwards of fifty persons, and we left behind thirteen others, who had not been able to complete their arrangements, but would follow us soon."[13]

In about two months the refugees came back — to ravaged crops, damaged and emptied homes, some of them razed to the ground. Yet the bane had turned to blessing. Not only did their neighbours show some grudging admiration, but a new wave of sympathy and support arose in the Canadas and abroad in Switzerland and the United States. And while they were in Champlain, the group had stayed with American friends of the new mission, which in itself attracted widened attention in New York and adjacent states.

Baptist Involvement

The Ottawa Association and its Canada Baptist Missionary Society had always taken a great interest in the Grande Ligne Mission — even to the extent of taking some of the credit for its founding. The *Montreal Register* of August 1838 reported that, "The mission to the French Canadians has occupied the anxious attention and unremitting care of your Committee. This mission was commenced by the Ottawa Baptist Association at the time of its establishment early in the year 1836, when Mr. Roussy was immediately engaged to preach the gospel to our Canadian neighbours."[14] Although Henrietta Feller would likely have questioned the association's claim of founding the mission, the article clearly shows that Baptists supported its outreach from the beginning.

Largely through the efforts of John Gilmour and with funds from the Canada Baptist Missionary Society, a small schoolhouse had been built by the fall of 1837 to replace the garret rooms.[15] This soon proved to be inadequate for the rapidly growing school and for meeting purposes, and again Gilmour and the Society helped the mission launch a financial drive for larger quarters. This time the Secretary of the Evangelical Foreign Missionary Society of New York also helped M[me] Feller obtain support in the United States. All these efforts bore fruit in 1840 when a two-and-a-half-storey stone building was completed. There was plenty of room now for pupils of the day school, for housing and training young men for ministry and for worship services. Situated on a farm property, it later became the site of Feller College.

The Most Brilliant Moment

Even before the stone building was erected, the growing group of believers decided to organize their congregation formally, electing their first deacons and adopting a constitution in September 1839.[16] The new Grande Ligne church, with Louis Roussy as pastor, was the first of a long line of distinguished churches and pastors who today make up L'Union des Églises Baptistes Françaises au Canada.

By 1840 the Grande Ligne Mission was on the threshold of major expansion. "In point of important conversions," wrote Théodore Lafleur in 1900, "it was perhaps the most brilliant moment in the history of the Mission."[17] Thirty converts were present at the opening of the new school and worship centre, and these were soon to be joined by the Reverend Léon Normandeau, Dr. C. H. O. Côté, Narcisse Cyr and Lafleur himself.

Normandeau, a priest who had been a professor at the Roman Catholic Seminary of Quebec, visited the mission at Grande Ligne in 1841, seeking to discuss some troubling personal and theological issues. He was destined to remain as convert, preacher and teacher. Dr. C. H. O. Côté came into the mission in a different way. An eminent physician, member of the legislative assembly, recognized orator and one of the major leaders of Louis Joseph Papineau's Patriotes in the Rebellion of 1837, he had fled to Vermont when the rebellion was put down. Learning of Côté's interest in spiritual matters, Louis Roussy crossed the border to visit him. Under Roussy's influence, Côté was converted and almost immediately began to preach the gospel, initially in New York state. When he was able to come back to the province of Canada, Côté became a devoted associate of Roussy and Mme Feller in the missionary outreach.

Narcisse Cyr and Théodore Lafleur were youthful residents of Napierville, Côté's home village, when they came to terms with Jesus Christ and joined the church at neighbouring Grande Ligne. Both became students of the school there, later travelling to Geneva to complete theological studies before returning to Canada and long service with the mission.

Léon Normandeau became a teacher at the school in Grande Ligne as well as a missionary, while Dr. Côté undertook extension work at Ste. Marie (Marieville), Roxton and St. Pie, mission stations that were developing into organized churches. A mission house was erected at St. Pie, which also served as a girls' school for about twenty students. The initial director was Sophie Jonte, who had taught with Mme Feller at the Grande Ligne school.

By 1844 the Grande Ligne Mission possessed a large mission house and seven mission stations — some south of the border. Connected with the mission were four ordained ministers including a recently arrived missionary from Europe named Wolff, seven teachers, two colporteurs, fifteen boys and seven girls in training for full-time service, as well as 150 pupils in the schools and nearly 200 converts.[18] Such was the astounding achievement completed in just eight years of arduous toil in the face of intense and sometimes violent opposition.

Le Semeur Canadien

In 1847 Henrietta Feller and Louis Roussy, both of whom had come from a Reformed church background in Switzerland and had consistently sought and secured interdenominational aid for the mission, became convinced of believer's baptism and were immersed by Dr. Côté. The next step was to be even more fateful. The Grande Ligne Mission officially became Baptist two years later, linking formally with the Canada Baptist Missionary Society, the mission arm of the Ottawa Association, which had been interested in its work from the start. Minutes of the mother church at Grande Ligne dated August 26, 1849, incorporate a revised constitution, indicating that the new name of the congregation was to be "The Baptist Evangelical Church of Grande Ligne."[19]

That year Narcisse Cyr returned from his studies in Geneva, was ordained and became co-pastor of the Grande Ligne church. When Théodore Lafleur returned the year after that, he was also ordained and named pastor of the St. Pie field, which included Roxton and Berea. In addition to pastoral duties, Lafleur assumed the principalship of the school for girls at St. Pie and Cyr and began publication of Le Semeur Canadien (the Canadian sower), the first Protestant journal of French Canada.

The St. Pie girl's school was destroyed by fire in 1854, but was soon rebuilt at a superior location in Longueuil. The same year four new parishes were established, and two decades after the mission's founding, the work extended over forty parishes or townships in the province of Canada and the northern parts of Vermont and New York state. The mission proclaimed the gospel through twenty preaching points, and converts numbered some 3,000. Of these, 700 were members,[20] many others obviously having found their spiritual homes in churches outside the mission.

Appeal to American Baptists

The move to explicit denominational affiliation had, of course, a number of implications for the mission. The Evangelical Foreign Missionary Society of New York, an interdenominational group, felt obliged to withdraw all assistance, as did supporters who believed in infant baptism. Not all the non-Baptists withdrew their aid, however, for Mme Feller had gained a host of friends on both sides of the border. She is known to have taken eight extended trips into the United States during her thirty-three-year missionary career, accompanied on occasion by Dr. Côté or Lafleur in efforts to secure financial help for the mission. Grande Ligne ladies' associations were formed in a number of large centres, including Boston, Philadelphia, New York, Brooklyn and Washington.[21]

Despite these efforts, writes Charles Foster, "the Mission was almost continuously financially embarrassed."[22] When the faltering Canada Baptist Missionary Society came to the point where it did not have enough resources to handle the added burden, an appeal was made once again, to Baptists south of the border. The response was generous, the American Baptist Home Missionary Society agreeing to provide the salaries of the ordained missionaries.

Again the Communion Question

However, a rider was attached to the agreement which put the Grande Ligne Mission in the midst of the most critical Baptist theological dispute of the times—the bitter debate over open and close communion. There must have been at least an implicit understanding that the mission would support the close position held by the American Baptists—and indeed by the vast majority of Baptists in the Province of Canada—for in 1854 six of the Grande Ligne pastors met to discuss the issue with two representatives of the American society, B. M. Hill and H. C. Fish. The six pastors, including Roussy, Normandeau, Cyr and Lafleur, signed a statement at that meeting regretting "the existence of any occasion for the practice of open communion," declaring that it was the aim of each of the ministers of the mission "to build up Regular Baptist churches so far as practicable."[23]

Obviously it was not always "practicable," for the vexing question did not go away. Narcisse Cyr precipitated something of a crisis in 1862 by resigning and sending a copy of his letter of resignation to the denominational paper, by then named *The Canadian Baptist*. In it he complained that the mission committee was "composed mostly of open communion Baptists," some of whom gave but lip service to the denomination "to which they profess to belong."[24] The claim appeared in the March 20 issue of that year, to which a response from Louis Roussy on behalf of the mission was published the next month. "All our churches," wrote Roussy, "are composed of members who are baptized believers," and he added that "none but Baptists can be elected as members of the committee of directors."[25]

The *Canadian Baptist* itself jumped into the fray in July with an editorial implying that the Grande Ligne Mission had not lived up fully to its agreement with the American Baptist Home Missionary Society and questioning the propriety of Regular Baptists providing any further support. Roussy responded immediately, holding that the missionaries were maintaining the spirit of their agreement,[27] a reply which was not acceptable to the editor of the journal.[28]

As the issue heated up, in mid-1863 the mission invited the Baptists of the western area of the province of Canada to send a delegation to discuss the problem. This they did, but the western representatives were apparently not satisfied with the missionaries' response, so they returned home with an adverse report. Official support was then cut off, and for a time the Regular Baptists bestowed their financial favours on Cyr and a few associates, who set up a French Regular Baptist Missionary Society. Cyr soon abandoned the new society, however, to assume the pastorate of the French Evangelical Society church in Philadelphia — a congregation which was not only open communion but open membership![29] The life of the French Regular Baptist Society was short, however, and gradually most of the Baptists renewed their support of the Grande Ligne mission. (Indeed, some of them had never taken it away.)

Finally, in 1888, the Grande Ligne Mission, which had been incorporated in 1855 as the Evangelical Society of La Grande Ligne, secured a new Act of Incorporation from the Quebec government, which formally and legally recognized Baptist direction, the Act providing that all directors must be members of a Regular Baptist church.[30]

"The Old Order Changeth"

The mission's difficulties with the Baptists were compounded by events south of the forty-ninth parallel. During the first half of the 1860s the Americans were fully engaged in the Civil War, with little time and fewer resources to share with their neighbours. The American Baptist Home Missionary Society, which had supported the Grande Ligne pastors with an annual contribution of almost $30,000 over some eleven years, would have been impelled to retrench even without the complications of the communion question.

Altogether, the mission suffered severe financial strain in the 1850s and 1860s. In 1867 "the funds were so low and the embarrassments so distressing"[31] that the school at Grande Ligne was closed for a period. And it was during this time that Henrietta Feller died.

In 1859 M[me] Feller was fifty-nine years old, and her failing health had become a matter of serious concern to her co-workers. That year she wintered in Florida but failed to regain her strength and was persuaded to go back to her native Switzerland for a time. She could not be kept from her cherished task, however, and returned to Canada in 1861 to take over her responsibilities again, carrying on until her death in 1868. In her final words she reiterated a lifelong concern for others, especially the young: "Go tell my boys to seek Jesus and to trust in Him."[32]

Five months later M[me] Feller's "boys" and the rest of her "Canadiens" erected a monument on her grave, with this inscription:

> A tribute of gratitude and love, presented by the French-Canadians to the memory of their dear benefactress, whose Christian devotedness procured to them the knowledge of the Gospel of Jesus Christ.[33]

So concluded the earthly pilgrimage, but not the impact, of one of the most eminent Canadian Baptists.

The Golden Age

Louis Roussy, who was considerably younger than M[me] Feller, continued in the active direction of the Grande Ligne Mission, worn by his labours but still occupying the president's chair in the year of his passing, 1881.[34] Like Henrietta Feller, he was sixty-eight when he died. His had been a remarkable ministry of devoted associate leadership.

In 1868 — the year after the nation's Confederation and just over three months after Mme Feller's death — nine organized churches of the mission founded the Union des Églises Baptistes de Langue Française "to cultivate the spirit of union and peace by mutual relationships . . . to progress in godliness and to cultivate, individually, the missionary spirit." "The missionaries had built well,"[35] writes Nelson Thomson, in an article on Witness in French Canada. The formation of the new Union was not only a sign of growing self-sufficiency but the harbinger of a day — still a century away — when the churches of the Grande Ligne Mission would become the completely indigenous fourth constituent Convention/Union of Federation Canadian Baptists.

The names of both founders were memorialized in structures which were to have a living presence and witness far beyond their immediate location. In 1876 the girls' school at Longueuil was shut down because of lack of response from the local townspeople and moved to Grande Ligne. The composite school, with its new girls' school wing, took the name Feller Institute. In 1883 a fine new church was built alongside the Institute and named the Roussy Memorial Church.

About the same time another building was constructed in Montreal to house what became L'Oratoire church. This work had begun under Narcisse Cyr in 1860, first as part of the English-speaking Baptist church on St. Helen Street. When Cyr left the little group to go to the United States two years later, Théodore Lafleur, who was then principal of the Longueuil school across the St. Lawrence, assumed the pastorate, in addition to his administrative and teaching duties. With the changes at

Longueuil and the rapid growth of the Montreal work, he confined his efforts to working with the congregation in 1877.[36] For over thirty years Lafleur was secretary of the Grande Ligne board, and was considered by many at the time to be "the most able speaker in French Protestantism."[37]

Slowdown

After Roussy died, work was carried on by a small army of pioneer missionaries in cities and towns of Quebec, and in 1885, the fiftieth anniversary of the arrival of Mme Feller and Louis Roussy in Canada, Théodore Lafleur notes that there was a "revival of great power." At the Jubilee celebration at the mission headquarters in Grande Ligne, forty were converted, thirty-six of whom were baptized.[38]

Yet the next period in the life of the mission never quite matched the golden age in accomplishments or vigour. Indeed, it was not to be until the mid-twentieth century when the impact of Quebec's "Quiet Revolution" was felt that work in French Canada would regain the momentum of the founding years.

There were reasons for this, of course, very good reasons. Religious persecution was still widespread and many converts were forced to emigrate. Quoting the Fortieth Annual Report of the Brooklyn, New York, Association in Aid of the Grande Ligne Mission, Nelson Thomson suggests that "the exceedingly slow progress in the number of churches is now easier to understand."[39] That the persecution was sometimes still overt is evident by a reaction in Hull when services were begun there in 1890. The first meeting was disturbed by a mob of about 2,000, armed with guns and stones. Despite the threatening atmosphere, the missionaries obtained a building and carried on for a number of months.[40] Similarly, at Quebec City, where work began as early as 1853 but faded in the face of strong opposition, missionary Adam Burwash managed to secure a hall and begin services again forty-one years later. But once more, the religious authorities and press "began co-ercive measures [and] a fanatical mob attacked with stones and other projectiles."[41]

Yet the missionaries persevered. When all but the most recently built wing of the Feller Institute burned to the ground in January of 1890, a considerably larger and more suitable replacement was completed by October of the same year. At Maskinongé two years later, work was underway among a group of erstwhile Roman Catholics who were displeased with the seemingly arbitrary decision of their ecclesiastical head to relocate their sanctuary. The same year a beginning was made at Sorel in face of distractions that made police protection necessary.[42] Missionary outreach was also undertaken in the Ottawa Valley and in the nearby lumber camps. As the new century dawned, much had been accomplished.

CHAPTER 15

In Demonstration of Unity I:
The Maritimes

"I do not know that I can say that I wish to be young again, but if I were . . . I should like to winter on this indented shore; and when I could not cross the coves and rivers in boats or on the ice, I would head them, and should not fear the storms whistling among the branches of the forest, while before me was a prospect of telling my fellow sinners the story of Calvary, or of comforting the dear saints of God."
— *JOSEPH DIMOCK*

It is perhaps significant that a Maritime Baptist was the first Canadian statesman to propose in legislative assembly the "political union of all the British North American provinces,"[1]—for an overriding sense of unity has consistently marked their outlook, especially since the formation of the Maritime Baptist Convention in 1846. And the Honourable James J. Johnstone, who presented the motion, was typically as interested in his Convention as he was in his country. One of the founders of the Granville Street (now First) Baptist Church of Halifax, where for many years he was Sunday school superintendent and invariably attended the mid-week prayer meeting, Johnstone served the Convention as its president on three separate occasions. A distinguished Nova Scotia barrister, he became attorney general in 1843 and then premier from 1857 to 1860, and was again elected premier in 1863. Later he was made a judge in equity and finally was appointed lieutenant-governor of Nova Scotia, although he died suddenly before he could take office. He was the same James Johnstone who resigned his seat in 1843 to fight an election on behalf of continued support for Acadia College.[2]

The political federation which was on many minds and which Johnstone articulated in 1854 came quickly, but not without anguish. The Union Act of 1840 which had merged Upper and Lower Canada into the Province of Canada had proved to be unworkable when it came into effect in 1841, "the public affairs of the Province [being] characterized by a permanent state of sectional conflict and a chronic condition of political instability."[3] Simply to divide the province again would be but a return to an equally unsatisfactory situation, so a full British North American federation of several provinces offered the greatest hope.

While the provinces on the eastern seaboard had been thinking more of Maritime union, they did respond (sometimes reluctantly) to the entreaties of the central region, and after conferences were held at Charlotte-town and Quebec City in 1864, Confederation became a reality on July 1, 1867. The founding provinces were Ontario, Quebec, Nova Scotia and New Brunswick. Prince Edward Island, which had hosted the first conference, demurred until 1873; Newfoundland, which had attended the second, remained outside Confederation for eighty-two more years.

A New Surge

While there was little unity among British North American Baptists at that time outside the provinces of Nova Scotia, New Brunswick and Prince Edward Island, in that region the denomination was a functioning whole, marked by steady growth. In the 1860–61 government census which, of course, went beyond membership to include denominational preference, 62,040 Baptists were recorded in Nova Scotia—second only to the Presbyterians among Protestants; New Brunswick had 57,730 Baptists — the largest Protestant body, a position consistently maintained in that province; and Prince Edward Island had 3,450.[4]

A Century of Revivals

Less than thirty-five years after the founding of the Maritime Baptist Convention in 1846, the number of churches more than doubled — to 350. While the general population during the period is estimated to have expanded by about 75 percent, Baptist membership multiplied by over 160 percent to more than 37,000.[5] In 1873 baptisms reached 3,021, almost one baptized convert for each ten members, the net increase in membership being nearly 8 percent in just twelve months.[6]

That year was obviously one of the periods of renewal—especially in Nova Scotia and Prince Edward Island, which had more than 2,500 of those baptisms. The Convention committee of that year, reporting on the state of the denomination, observed that "the conversions took place among persons of all ages, from the child of ten years to the old man of almost eighty," adding "that among the converts were many who had passed through previous revivals unmoved."[7]

Such waves of the Spirit were common in Maritime Baptist life throughout the nineteenth century. In 1848 a revival went through much of Nova Scotia, and the experience was not at all abnormal. "Baptist churches and Baptist ministers are the offspring of revivals," holds the eminent Maritime Baptist historian Edward Saunders, writing in 1902. Posing a series of questions about the force behind the growth of the churches, the enlistment of ministers, the establishment of educational institutions and the recruitment of missionaries for both home and overseas service, Saunders unhesitatingly responds to each: "Revivals, of course."[8] The Honourable James Johnstone himself was the product of one of those revivals.[9]

Democracy and Unity

A residue of the societal idea did surface from time to time — that organizations beyond the local church should be made up of dues-paying "interested" members rather than the church-named representatives who were sent as delegates to the associations. While east coast Baptists were never as wedded to the "society" concept as were their counterparts in the central region of British North America, a residue of the idea did come to the surface from time to time. Initially the Maritime Baptist Convention was something like a society, in that individual members could join it if they paid a specified fee. However, most of the delegates were chosen by the churches — the components of a true "Convention."

With the founding of the Convention, three subsidiary boards were formed to attend to specific tasks between annual meetings. There were a board of directors (similar to today's executive or council), a board of foreign missions and a board to control the Fund for Superannuated Ministers. This last indicated that measures were being taken to solve the long-standing problem of ministerial support, and this was an important sign of denominational maturing.

Those who were named to guide the affairs of the new Convention wanted to ensure its continuing unity and protect its democracy. Their prime objective was "to . . . carry out such measures as may, with the Divine blessing, tend to advance the interests of the Baptist Denomination, and the cause of God generally."[10] To do so meant at times curbing its ancillary boards of the all-too-human inclination toward "empire building," which would adversely affect the whole body.

The minutes of the 1856 annual meeting suggest that the Convention's foreign mission board was chided gently for "appropriating money without the concurrence of Convention" — the apparent misstep being the dispatch of an unauthorized grant of £100 to the English Baptist Missionary Society. In order to forestall any further such unapproved disposition, a resolution was passed that year, which enunciated a clear principle of board responsibility to the convention. The original constitution also contained a proviso regarding denominational support, which has stood the test of time. This allowed a donor "paying into the funds of the Convention more than the sum required to constitute membership, [to] be at liberty to direct the application of the surplus to the several objects contemplated . . . or to any one or more of them separately."[11] Such a principle allows for "designated giving," but assumes that such donations will be "over and above" the donor's support for the total program of the denomination.

Greater Responsibilities for the Convention

Initially, the newly launched Convention took on a co-ordinative role, rather than an all-encompassing directive function. It did not, however, rest on its oars. Early on, the Convention approached associations regarding educational and home or domestic missions concerns, seeking their views as to possible oversights on the part of the Convention.[12] By 1851 the Convention constitution was amended so that Acadia College and domestic missions fell within the jurisdiction of the three-province body.[13] The administration of the college proved to be easier than governing domestic missions.

Cheerfully Concurring

As outlined in Chapter 12, a movement to transfer control of Acadia to the Convention began in 1849. The Honourable James W. Johnstone once again played a prominent part. It was he who as chairman of a committee on education recommended that the Convention take control of Acadia and, to facilitate this, left to the Baptists in "each Province the support and duty of maintaining and managing such schools and academies as it now supports or may deem proper hereafter to establish."[14]

With the Nova Scotia Baptist Education Society, which had always operated both the academy and college "cheerfully concurring,"[15] the college, including its theological chair, came under the full control of the Convention, and the situation remained that way until the Nova Scotia government removed the Convention's control more than a century later. The society continued to manage the academy until 1865, when it was also transferred to the Convention.[16]

The Convention immediately encountered difficulties as it assumed Acadia's heavy debt. Further complications arose when the church-state issue surfaced as two representatives of the denomination, pastors I. E. Bill and John Francis, sought assistance in Britain. They discovered that a letter writer to the Baptist periodical there was stirring the waters by indicating that Maritime Baptist educational institutions were receiving government funds.[12] This was against the principles of British Baptists and, indeed, Baptists generally, as a violation of the precept of the separation of church and state. However, both Nova Scotia and New Brunswick Baptists had always accepted and even solicited such funds—on the rational basis that their schools were educating a cross-section of the community including many non-Baptists.

Implications for New Brunswick Seminary

After hearing the report of their returning representatives, the 1850 Convention decided that while grants would be accepted for Horton Academy, none would be accepted for Acadia College and its limited theological segment. This decision created a temporary crisis in the college but one which was eased when John Mockett Cramp, who has been called Acadia's "second founder," headed a campaign by which £10,000 was pledged by the end of 1852. Twenty churches subscribed more than half of the amount.[18]

The decision to transfer Acadia College to Convention supervision but to leave the two high-school level institutions, the New Brunswick Seminary and Horton Academy, in provincial Baptist hands had more serious implications, particularly financial, for the seminary. Baptist interest in both New Brunswick and Nova Scotia then tended to centre on Wolfville, for it was difficult to perceive the Horton Academy there as distinct from the college.

Both preparatory schools, and indeed the college, had been founded to provide educational opportunities for Baptist young people in the face of religious discrimination. The new provision for public education at least lessened the need for such schools, a view quite easily accepted by a financially strapped Education Society in New Brunswick. The resignation of Calvin Goodspeed, the principal, occurred the same year and in 1872 the seminary (as it was called) closed after service of over thirty-five years and the Fredericton property was sold.

Many New Brunswick Baptists were not completely satisfied with the closing, however, and in 1879 the Western Association officially expressed the hope that there might yet be an academy in their province like Horton, affiliated with Acadia. Two years later the report on education in the Eastern Association reflected a similar desire and the Southern echoed the call in 1882. That year the hope became reality and what some term a "revived" seminary was opened in temporary quarters in Saint John — ten years after its apparent demise.[19] While the length of the revived seminary's life was to be but half that of its predecessor, it was to become the first striking evidence of still greater unity among Baptists by the shores of the Atlantic.

Home Missions

The associations, which by 1851 numbered three in Nova Scotia and two in New Brunswick, favoured the formation of a unified home missions board of the Convention, but the process of effective consolidation in that department took a lot longer than in other facets of the association's work.

Although the original two-province association correlated the task of outreach, Nova Scotia had formed its own society in 1815, six years before the division of the association, and by 1818 had engaged four short-term missionaries, three for eight weeks and the other for six.[20] After the association divided into two, both the Nova Scotia and New Brunswick associations formed themselves into home missions societies. Up to the founding of the Convention they had been heavily involved in evangelism and extension (the planting of new churches), both in employing missionaries for periods of varying length and in supporting grassroots efforts by local pastors. Many pastors spent their holidays in outreach and evangelism — "a remarkable signal of commitment!"[21] one commentator remarked.

Under Convention Direction

After the division of the New Brunswick and Nova Scotia associations, no fewer than five supervisory agencies were set up in the field of domestic missions. The Convention attempted to solve this problem by organizing a single board, which included not just representatives but all the members of the existing associational committees. It was a valiant attempt, but the total democracy proved to be far too unwieldy, and for many years the concerns of Maritime missions continued to be the responsibility of the associations, either singly or in combination.

In 1853 the New Brunswick association decided to undertake the task jointly, as did the Central and Eastern associations of Nova Scotia four years later, the Western continuing on its own until joining the other two in 1872. Prince Edward Island, which had formed its own association in 1868, united with Nova Scotia in home missions work in 1874,[22] and five years later home missions finally came under Convention direction. By that time the number of home missionaries had reached forty-eight.[23]

Most analysts agreed that earlier united direction of Maritime missions outreach at home would have made for more ordered expansion. Yet it must be said that while it was perhaps not as "ordered," expansion throughout the region was extensive, given the largely rural population at the time and the difficulties of transportation and communication. A great deal of the evident progress no doubt resulted from the new decentralized, concentrated administration.

Acadians at Yarmouth and Digby

Although the associations retained most of the leadership in missions, the Convention played an important role in lifting sights beyond the customary concerns. It was a Convention committee on domestic missions which in 1849 "recommended favourable consideration . . . of the French and Indian Missions, as one object under the Domestic Missionary Boards of the Provinces."[24] Previously, Maritime Baptists had shown only spasmodic interest in either group.

Pastor Obed Chute from Wallace, Nova Scotia, who had worked briefly in 1849 among the French-speaking Acadians in New Brunswick, responded two years later to a request from the Nova Scotia Western Association to assess the situation in the township of Clare. The appraisal led him to a significant decision: to volunteer for full-time service. The mission board of the association then sent Chute to Grande Ligne to improve his facility in the language, and when in 1853 the association voted to "establish a mission among the Acadian French of this province,"[25] Chute became the first missionary. He worked in Yarmouth and Digby counties until he had to retire because of ill health in 1858.

Recommended by Henrietta Feller of Grande Ligne, Michael Normandy was appointed to succeed Chute, and work progressed at Tusket,

Saulnierville and St. Mary's. The "Acadian French Mission Church" was admitted to the association in 1870, and a small French school with Ellen Porter as teacher was established. Growth was very slow: converts numbered no more than two or three a year and the membership never quite reached fifty. In 1853 the association had transferred the supervision of the Acadian work to a French mission board formed that year, but in 1872 it returned the direction to its home missions board, combining English and French activities.[26] The integration of work with the two language groups at that stage was probably a step backwards. Experience certainly showed that French missions were more effective when administered by French-speaking people.

L. P. Rossier, a medical doctor whose father had been an instructor at Feller Institute, joined the staff briefly in 1879, and McMaster graduate F. E. Rouleau took over direction of the mission from Michael Normandy in 1885.[27] The work was phased out three years later, as the missionaries were unable to "succeed in making a permanent impression on the stubborn environment . . . . "[28]

"The Apostle to the Micmacs"

The story of the mission among the Native peoples of the Maritimes is that of a single, unusual man, who heroically bore a long-term burden. Historian John S. Moir calls it "one of the most remarkable chapters in Canadian church history."[29] Within the focus of the man's concern were the Micmacs, the regional Indians of Algonquin stock, and their neighbouring Mohawks and Maliseets.

This "Apostle to the Micmacs" was Silas Tertuis Rand, who had descended from a family of New England Planters. At twenty-three, a farmer-stonemason with meagre education, Rand presented himself at Horton Academy hoping to enroll. He stayed just four weeks, but in that short period discovered a love and facility for languages and for learning in general. Later, he did undertake some formal studies for a limited time, but "in his literary studies following the light of his own erratic genius,"[30] Rand never did graduate. He remained a lifelong student, finally to be granted honorary doctorates from three colleges: — Acadia, King's and Queen's.

In 1833, after his brief sojourn at Horton, Rand resumed his work as a stonemason and continued studying Latin, which he had begun at the academy. The next year his innate ability and obvious dedication were recognized and he was ordained as minister of the church in Parrsboro, Nova Scotia. In addition to his pastoral duties with that congregation, he began to study Greek and Hebrew on his own. Pastorates at Horton, Liverpool, Windsor and Charlottetown followed the one at Parrsboro. But it was when he was ministering in Charlottetown that he encountered a challenge that completely changed the direction of his life.

Associational Interest

In 1846, the year the Maritime Baptist Convention was founded, Professor Isaac Chipman of Acadia College suggested to the former stonemason that there were heathen in his own land as well as abroad and with his language ability, he could readily prepare himself to reach them. "I took hold of the idea," writes Rand, "and determined thenceforth to devote my life to the work of civilizing, educating and Christianizing the semi-savage Indians of the Maritime Provinces."[31] Still working as a pastor in Charlottetown, he spent the next two and a half years learning the Micmac language with the help of one Joseph Brooks, whose father, a sailor in the French navy, had been captured by the British and brought to Halifax. Joseph had married a Micmac woman and had lived among her people for a time.

In 1847 the Nova Scotia Association had taken note of Silas Rand's interest "in seeking the enlightenment and salvation of the Indians," and by the next year a special committee was appointed to supervise the work. Foreshadowing later interdenominational involvement in the mission, the committee extended thanks to "the religious community of Halifax . . . [and] those in other parts of the Province . . . and the friends in Prince Edward Island, who have contributed so essentially to the comfort and support of the missionary."[32]

Almost Alone

Meanwhile, Rand had begun to fashion his dream into reality, but not quite as the association had anticipated. Favouring wider participation, Rand formed the transdenominational Micmac Missionary Society late in 1850. Then, moving to Hantsport, Nova Scotia, which he used as his base for some thirty-five years, Rand crisscrossed the Maritime provinces, visiting the various tribal centres with only limited support from his society.

With strong and continual opposition from the Roman Catholic clergy who in the view of some observers had just "modified the mythology of the Micmacs,"[33] Rand, working almost alone, faced a mammoth task. After nearly twenty-five years he reluctantly reported that "but a small number have openly renounced their connection with the Romish church . . . [although] a widespread enquiry has been awakened among them."[34] Rand died in 1889, seeing little more evidence of results.

Ten years later, a well-known editor of another denomination lamented: "The Micmac Mission is now seemingly forgotten. It was never well organized, never adequately supported. Can it be revived? Where is Dr. Rand's successor? Would the Lord call any of our young, earnest and devoted Baptist brethren to this work, the new missionary ought to have at his back the whole influence, the spiritual and material resources of the denomination."[35]

But Silas Rand had not taken the Baptist denomination with him and the interest was not revived. Yet, besides the few converts, Rand left a number of magnificent and lasting memorials. He translated the New Testament, Genesis and the Psalms into the Micmac language and prepared a Micmac dictionary, which was later published by the Canadian government. A good number of poems also flowed from his pen. One, "The Dying Indian's Dream," speaks with sensitivity of the Native person's lot and infers the unusual love of one man who tried to better it.

A Black Legacy

David George was a pioneer black minister of the Maritimes who joined the 1,190 people of African descent who resettled in Sierre Leone, West Africa, in 1792. Writing about that decision, anthropologist and sociologist Savanah E. Williams says: "With him he carried a new religion that flourishes today, and in Nova Scotia a Baptist legacy was left with those who remained."[36]

John Burton, who arrived in Halifax the same year from England and soon became the founding pastor of the city's Granville Street church, continued that legacy among the colony's black citizens, giving counsel and support to many and integrating a good number into his congregation. One of those who joined (about 1816) was young Richard Preston, a former slave from Virginia.

Under Burton's tutelage Preston blossomed as a preacher-evangelist and before long his ordination was considered. Preston himself was hesitant because he had little education and experience, and arrangements were made with the West London Association of English Baptists for his training in England. After he finished his training in 1832, the newly established Cornwallis Street Baptist church, Halifax, requested that Preston be ordained. The ministers of the West London Association complied, and Preston returned to Halifax an ordained minister. He had brought with him donations from English benefactors to purchase property for the new congregation — said to be the first church with an all-black membership in any denomination in Canada.[37]

Under Preston's leadership black congregations were soon established at Dartmouth, Preston and Hammonds Plains. While still the Cornwallis pastor, Preston also travelled throughout the province, establishing new congregations under lay leadership. By 1853 he had gathered together the delegates of no fewer than twelve churches, and the African Baptist Association was organized. The first meeting was held the next year at Granville Mountain on the shore of the Bay of Fundy.

In the centennial year, one of the outstanding black leaders, William Oliver, wrote, "After one hundred years, there are twenty-two organized churches with a membership of 1,480 and approximately 10,000 adherents."[38]

While John Burton may be credited with both displaying his own deep concern and passing the torch on to Richard Preston, individual pastors and home missionaries also helped the struggling churches from time to time. However, the work among blacks in the Maritimes was undertaken mostly by blacks, and their churches were established from within.[39] Their continued growth in the face of extreme poverty, daunting obstacles and narrow prejudice doubtless resulted from their fine independence of spirit, convincing courage and deep dedication to the God who had led the exodus of an earlier people. No other minority group in North America has borne such fruit.

A New Overseas Wave

In May 1850 when Richard Burpee, broken in health, returned home with his wife from their mission field in Burma,[40] the search for a replacement began. Originally, the Maritime Baptist Convention had intended to enlist another missionary to work alongside the Burpees, but those and earlier plans came to naught.[41]

Twenty-eight Native Workers

A year after the Burpees' return, a name was placed before the annual Convention: that of Arthur R. R. Crawley, an Acadia graduate who was completing theological studies at Newton.[42] Crawley and his wife were readily accepted, and by the next summer Crawley had fulfilled his preparation requirements. Richard Burpee had hoped to go back to Burma, but it had become all too obvious that this would be impossible and the board hesitated about sending the Crawleys on their own. They were now reluctant to send just one couple, in view of the strain placed on the Burpees, who had worked on their own. Organizational difficulties also impeded progress. The Convention board was negotiating with the American Baptist Missionary Union at the time, attempting to co-operate with the Americans, but wanting to exercise a measure of direction over its own missionaries. The discussions had not proved fruitful and a hiatus developed.[43]

To overcome this impasse, Crawley and his wife, who was Burpee's wife's sister, decided to place themselves entirely at the service of the American Union, who promptly welcomed them, sending them out in 1853. Disappointed but not resentful, the Maritime board still arranged to give $600 a year towards Crawley's salary, this amount later being forwarded to him directly for the support of national workers. By 1869, no fewer than twenty-eight such workers were being backed financially by the board, churches, and individuals in the Maritimes provinces.[44]

The Golden Isle of the Sea

At the same time the board's attention was drawn to Australia, where shiploads of convicts from Britain had been sent as late as 1849.

In 1856, the Australian Mission Board, which had been appointed earlier, reported that Isaiah Wallace, a recent Acadia graduate and pastor, was ready to go to "the golden Isle of the Sea, to teach her perishing thousands the path that leads to heaven."[45] Accepted, Wallace was sent on a foray into the constituency to stimulate interest, but instead found opposition to the Convention's plans, and the project was dropped.[46] His aspirations "thus thwarted," Wallace himself writes, "I was compelled to abandon the Australian Mission and give myself with renewed vigour to the work of the Lord in my native land."[47] He became a powerful evangelist, home missionary and pastor.

"Dry" Period Ends

While strong support was continued for many national pastors in Burma, it seemed that during this interval every effort to send missionaries overseas was frustrated. Interest at home was keen and volunteers were not lacking. David Freeman, S. N. Bentley, Edward Anderson, J. F. Kempton and Bennet Chute offered their services, but for various reasons, including health, it was not possible to send any of them. Even Silas Rand, who became the Apostle to the Micmacs, was invited, and according to his diary had "partially consented," only to change his mind when "Mrs. Rand objected, and I gave it up."[48]

The "dry" period ended in 1867, the year of Confederation, when Miss Minnie DeWolfe volunteered before the Convention,[49] sailing early the following year for Burma. The Maritimes-American relationship was settled temporarily when the Convention board became an auxiliary of the American union, "but with the universal and deep conviction that we must contemplate an independent mission."[57] Minnie DeWolfe, who bears the distinction of being the first single woman missionary from any Canadian denomination to serve overseas,[51] was soon joined by William George and his wife, all expenses of the three, including initial salary, being borne by the Maritime Convention board.

First Women's Missionary Society

Another single woman, Hannah Maria Norris, was next to volunteer, and with her begins the graphic story of the UBWMU, the United Baptist Woman's Missionary Union. Minnie DeWolfe had gone to Burma in direct response to a Macedonian call from the women of that land: "Are there no female men who can come to teach us?"[52] and Maria Norris, a teacher at Acadia Seminary, responded to the same call. When it was discovered that the Convention's board did not have the funds to send her, she decided to go to Boston to offer her services to the American Baptists. But when she was on board ship in Halifax harbour ready to sail to Boston, Norris was dramatically persuaded to disembark and reapply to the Foreign Mission Board. This time she was accepted — but on the understanding that she secure financial support by organizing women's missionary aid societies throughout the Maritimes. She accepted the challenge.

After forming the first society in her home church at Canso on June 18, 1870, Maria Norris by phenomenal effort organized a total of thirty-two societies before she sailed for Burma just three months and three days later.[53] According to historian E. M. Saunders, it was "the calm, magnetic power of Miss Norris [that] aroused the women of the Baptist churches."[54]

The Spirit was moving. By 1873 two couples, two single women and a bachelor were ready to go overseas, and the Convention board's treasurer reported that some $10,000 was on hand to provide support.[55] These pioneering missionaries, who have become justly renowned as "the Serving Seven," included Flora Eaton, Maria Armstrong, Rufus and Mary Sanford, George and M. M. Churchill and William F. Armstrong (no relation to Maria). After a crowded commitment service at Windsor, Nova Scotia, on August 25, the seven sailed for New York just over a month later, arriving in Rangoon in early January 1874. There they were greeted by Maria Norris, who increased the numbers of the Serving Seven to eight when she became William Armstrong's bride before the month's end.

All-Canadian Mission

Now that the newcomers had arrived, the group began an earnest search for an area of service where their work might become independent of the American Baptists. Three alternatives presented themselves, including the possibility of serving in an untouched area of Burma or moving over to Siam to minister to the Karens there. Both would entail supervision by the American Baptists. The third option, the one finally chosen, was to relocate in India, where a contingent of Canadian missionaries sent by the Baptists of Ontario and Quebec had already settled in the Telegu country around the Bay of Bengal. These missionaries had in fact extended an invitation to the Maritimers to join them there in the formation of an all-Canadian mission. So at a special Convention at Amherst, Nova Scotia, in 1875, it was decided that the overseas work would be re-established in Cocanada (later called Kakinada) and that the eight-Maritime workers would serve alongside their co-workers from Ontario and Quebec. Each group retained its own autonomy, but there was a co-operative working arrangement and the forecast of even greater unity ahead.

CHAPTER 16

In Demonstration of Unity II: Ontario and Quebec

*"We are now outside the Garden of Eden,
and everything valuable must be effected by work."*
— *ROBERT ALEXANDER FYFE*

In the mid-nineteenth century the still-rugged conditions of the frontier land militated against any strong sense of unity among Baptist churches in what were to become Ontario and Quebec. Life on the primitive farms remained hard, transportation and communications elementary and income scant. Most Baptists were rural people at the time and, having no centralized authority like that of the Methodists, they struggled even as the nation struggled toward some resemblance of confederation. Since the demise of the *Montreal Register* in 1849 and the *Evangelical Pioneer* the following year, they were, to use a phrase employed at the time, altogether "ignorant of one another's movements."[1] Obviously, they recognized the problem.

Despite constant reversals, the Baptist churches had grown. Limited missionary assistance had been received from the United States and Great Britain, and the local churches, while struggling themselves, had undertaken a good deal of outreach to nearby areas—frequently supported by the associations. There have been various estimates of the total Baptist membership in the province of Canada in 1850, the most reliable placing the numbers at just under 10,000. 1851 census figures of the religious affiliation of Upper Canadians indicate 45,353 people of Baptist persuasion, or 4.8 percent of the total population. This figure is small compared to the Anglicans' 223,290 and the Methodists' 207,656 (and, indeed, compared to the Maritime Baptists), but progress was evident and growth would soon accelerate. Unity among the increasing numbers of Baptists would be achieved through the formation of yet another Society, one that had a greater will to pledge its advancement than previous societies had had. Before the decade was out, two societies had been formed.

Conventions West and East

The first of the new societies really arose from the ashes of the Regular Baptist Union of Canada, but unlike its predecessor, which had been established by a number of the associations, the Regular Baptist Missionary Society of Canada was formed by a number of individuals who were prominent in the denomination. A. T. McCord, then chamberlain (treasurer) of the city of Toronto, provided the spark that produced the flame. He extended invitations to all the churches to send representatives to a conference to be held in Hamilton in October 1851. The response was good, and from the perspective of later years, it would appear unfortunate that the new body that emerged did not continue its membership on a delegate basis, in order to be truly representative of the churches.

Convention Designation

At the conference, a decision was taken on an important motion. It was proposed "that no church shall be considered a Regular Baptist Church that practices open communion"[2] and that this proviso be written into the constitution. The surprising defeat of the motion by more than a two-to-one ratio[3] certainly indicates that the rigid attitudes prevailing just three years earlier were beginning to soften. At that time restricted communion was one of the major criteria for membership. The new society was certainly still "Regular" and strongly Calvinistic and it would take many years for mutual concessions to be feasible, yet this was a small step towards unity. It is probably significant that John Gilmour, a notable proponent of the open position was also present at the meeting.

By 1854 the "Society" designation had given way to the name Convention, although there was no organizational move to warrant the change. At the annual meeting of 1858, "West" was added,[4] and thus the Regular Baptist Missionary Convention of Canada West came into being.

Although the Convention was constitutionally able to undertake various facets of service, it wisely confined most of its early efforts to home or domestic missions. Later, its scope was widened to include educational interests. During the first years of its life, the new organization also became the major Baptist voice in pressing for a resolution of the long-standing issue of clergy reserves.

The Canada Baptist Missionary Convention East

The bounds of the Convention were confined to Canada West in 1858 because a number of easterly churches had formed their own fellowship that year. Responding to a call issued by the St. Helen's Street church of Montreal, representatives of thirteen churches gathered there that spring "to consider the expediency of forming a Society for Missionary and other purposes, in connection with the Baptist denomination East of Kingston."[5]

As a result, the Canada Baptist Missionary Convention East, was founded for "the promotion of the Gospel in Central and Eastern Canada, by employing Evangelists, aiding feeble churches, circulating religious publications, and by other suitable means."[6] Like the Convention West the new body was more like a home missionary society, again with a one-dollar yearly fee for membership, although provision was made for churches to send a delegate if they paid a subscription fee of ten dollars per year and further delegates for multiples of twenty dollars.

Although the new eastern Convention included a number of churches and pastors who did not subscribe to strict communion, it did require that all officers, members of the board of directors, missionaries and agents should be members "of regular Baptist Churches"[7] — Calvinistic although not requiring close communion.

The Will to Effectiveness

A line running due north from Kingston was the boundary between the two Conventions. Each Convention, in a move which would hardly have been expected in those times, granted its executive board wide latitude in meeting mission demands. That of the East was authorized to employ and fix salaries of agents and generally to "direct and manage the business of Convention."[8]

While at the founding meetings of each Convention the number of churches represented was limited — thirty in the West, thirteen in the East — the will to make them effective was immediately apparent. The secretary's letter, printed and distributed with the first eastern minutes, announced the engagement of an experienced evangelist-colporteur, while, as has been seen, the larger West set out with three employed field staff and had acquired eleven by 1858. The next year Thomas Davidson, the West's long-time secretary, informed the churches that in the first nine months of the current year fourteen missionaries had been employed, nine of them full-time. They had travelled over 10,000 hard miles on their itineraries, serving at 52 stations with 777 members and 566 "Sabbath School" students.[9] The value of the Sunday school was obviously being recognized, the registration approaching seventy-five percent of the total church membership.

An interesting historical footnote of the times also points to Baptists' developing concern for youth. The first YMCA on the North American continent was organized in First Baptist Church of Montreal in November 1851. T. J. Claxton established the association for young men who were members of the church, as well as their Christian companions in the city.[10]

Educational Accomplishments

One of the driving forces behind the formation of the Regular Baptist Missionary Convention of Canada West was the need for theological training for prospective pastors — and, indeed, for the many ill-prepared ministers already in the field. The Regular Baptists, of course, had shunned Canada Baptist College, the only Baptist school in the region, and that school was numbered among the institutions that perished by mid-century. Ironically, the very year the Baldwin Bill was passed by the legislature — providing for a central secular university and opportunity for affiliated denominational colleges, Montreal College was closed. (Baptists and Free Kirkers had been the main supporters of the Bill.)[11] Baptists of Canada West were right back where they were before 1838 when prospective ministers, if they were to have any training, had to go to the United States.

Maclay College

The new western Convention did not take long to face the issue. At its first annual meeting in 1852, appreciation was expressed for the educational opportunities made available through recent legislative action. Then, realizing that such provision "merely embraces a literary education," the Convention proposed steps to secure £10,000 as an endowment for a theological institution.[12]

As has been seen, the man to raise the funds was at hand. Dr. A. Maclay of Toronto agreed to undertake the task, and he quickly achieved a good proportion of the necessary financial backing — at least in total commitments. Plans were formulated to found Maclay College, named in honour of the fund raiser, and Maclay himself was to be professor of theology. By 1855, however, the project had still not moved ahead very quickly, it became apparent that the committee of management was encountering difficulties. A number of major prospective donors withdrew their pledges . . . and there were even some undertones of the communion debate. The end result was that Maclay College never did become more than a dream.[13]

The Baptists of the province of Canada were not yet ready, however, to accept an offer from the new Rochester Seminary of New York state, to have a Canadian professor appointed there.[14] Under R. A. Fyfe, the western Convention's satellite education society renewed its committee in pursuit of an idea that Fyfe had been considering — the founding of a combined secondary school and theological training institution. He had, in fact, made the suggestion as a kind of "trial balloon" in a letter to the Baptist paper, the *Christian Messenger*, late in 1855.[15]

A Hard-to-Match Contribution

Robert Alexander Fyfe, born in La Prairie, a suburb of Montreal, was part of a new breed of Baptist leaders. While appreciating his Scottish heritage, he had already demonstrated something of the incipient nationalism of the times while addressing an 1847 public meeting in Toronto in support of a nonsectarian provincial university. He had said:

> . . . I cannot but lament a state of affairs too prevalent in this country. Men come to this country from Ireland, England or Scotland retaining all their peculiarities, nay even their nationalities. . . . It is natural and right that we should love our native land. But, while this is true, we must remember that when we take up abode in this country, we ought to consider its interests.

We ought to look upon ourselves as Canadians and earnestly enquire by what means we can advance the interests of this country. . . .[16]

This was to be his stance wherever educational matters were discussed.

Fyfe had been on the scene for some time, but only intermittently, as he had spent several periods in the United States. After attending Montreal College for a short period, he took further studies at Madison University (later Colgate), finally graduating in theology from Newton Seminary in 1842. He was ordained the same year in nearby Brookline, Massachusetts. After organizing the church at Perth, Fyfe served briefly as principal of Canada Baptist College, then moved in 1845 to Toronto as pastor of the March Street church (later successively called Bond Street and Jarvis Street). At that time he remained in the pastorate just three years, resigning on a matter of principle, and soon went to the United States again. Responding to a pressing invitation from the (by then) Bond Street church, he was back in Canada once more in 1855.[17]

A Disaster?

Under Fyfe's guidance, planning for the prospective school quickly took shape. Woodstock was chosen as the site, both for its central location and for the strong local support offered. By 1857 the supporters had formed the Canadian Literary Institute, elected their own trustees, and laid the cornerstone. Although plagued at first by financial troubles, the co-educational institute opened on July 4, 1860, with seventy-nine students enrolled that September.[18] Fyfe, who had resisted the offer when first approached, finally accepted the principalship, serving with distinction until his death at age sixty-two in 1878.

With well over a hundred students in prospect for the January 1861 term, an apparent disaster struck the very night before the opening. Fire burned the new building to the ground. "The labor of years is a mass of smoldering rubbish," wrote Fyfe, adding that "God is trying us sorely, but I am persuaded that this is meant for good."[19]

Fyfe's trust was soon vindicated. Although a mountainous debt of some $6,000 remained after the insurance settlements, immediate plans were made to construct a new building somewhat larger than the first. The good citizens of Woodstock rallied to the cause, taking students into their homes, making arrangements for the use of the local Woodstock Hotel for classes and offering to make a substantial grant from civic funds. All were gratefully accepted except the last. The Baptists, writes John A. Moir, "met this catastrophe and rebuilt their college on the voluntary principle of accepting no public money. . . ."[20]

It was at this crucial point that Toronto businessman William McMaster came on the scene. McMaster responded to the situation by offering $4,000 toward the debt and rebuilding, provided that $20,000 could be raised elsewhere. The new building was completed by mid-1862, and by the 1873 and 1874 terms, enrolment had soared to 253.[21]

Theological Department Detached

During the first two decades of the Canadian Literary Institute's life, a typical ministerial student who sought adequate preparation would do secondary school work at Woodstock, move to Toronto and its university for training in Arts and return to Woodstock for theology. Because of this difficult arrangement a good number did not return to Woodstock for the theological studies, and a number of others went to the United States.[22]

Largely through the influence of McMaster and his Toronto pastor, John H. Castle, the theology department was detached and moved to Toronto in 1881, becoming the Toronto Baptist College. Its name changed to Woodstock College two years later, the Institute continued as an academy until 1926. The new Toronto unit was housed in a building named McMaster Hall, after the man whose gift made the building possible.

Toronto Baptist College proved to be a sound bridge to yet greater accomplishments. There were eleven Baptist churches and mission stations in Toronto, then a city of 90,000, when the college was settled there, offering good opportunities for field work by the ministerial students. However, while many of the students had to be satisfied with the basic academic and theological training available at Woodstock and the relocated college, it was not yet possible for any to secure a full-orbed education under denominational auspices. For a full Arts program, a student had to attend the University of Toronto. Over a period of time negotiations were conducted with that university, but these did not prove satisfactory, and thoughts soon turned to the possibility of establishing a full Baptist university that would incorporate Woodstock College and the Toronto Baptist college.

The McMaster Charter

At first the idea met with a lot of opposition from Baptists and from the public, for the concept of a state university with affiliated denominational seminaries had become widely accepted. Within Baptist ranks there was also disagreement as to the best location for the institution—Toronto or Woodstock. The federationists, who were pushing for a Baptist institution affiliated with the University of Toronto, gradually backed down, influenced in some measure by the decision of Presbyterian Queen's University not to become federated with the University of Toronto. In the end, the Baptist university was located in Toronto, although not at U of T.

On November 1, 1887, the Ontario Legislature granted a charter for the establishment of McMaster University. The founders hoped that it might become a national university for the denomination that would offer theological training to graduates of Baptist institutions in the land.[23] So while the two separate but soon-to-be-merged Conventions of Ontario and Quebec would receive the annual reports of the new university and would have the exclusive right to name the board of governors (twelve from the Ontario Convention; four from the smaller Quebec Convention), no fewer than eight places were open to the Maritime Convention (to sit when the senate was dealing with theological education).[24]

Earlier, Principal John H. Castle of Toronto Baptist College had extended a similar invitation and the response was positive. Acadia did drop theological courses and Daniel M. Welton, who headed Acadia's Theological Institute, resigned to accept a faculty position at Toronto Baptist College. However, the Acadia committee first studying Castle's proposal recommended acceptance only as "a present expedient." Because of distance and cost very few students from the Maritimes actually made the journey to Toronto, many going to Newton or even to Rochester, while others simply did not take graduate studies. By 1889, just as McMaster was getting underway, Acadia had been obliged to reinstate some courses in theological studies.[25] From her perspective, the results of the attempted co-operation at the time were disappointing.

A Christian School of Learning

In spearheading the founding of both Toronto Baptist College and McMaster University, McMaster, now a member of the Canadian Senate, and his supporters—together with their fellow Baptists in central Canada —insisted that the institutions have a strong Christian and biblical focus. The trust deed conveyed by the senator to the college trustees, included a forceful Regular Baptist statement, beginning with "the Divine inspiration of the Scriptures of the Old and New Testaments and their absolute supremacy and sufficiency in matters of faith and practice."[26]

The university charter, which projected "a Christian school of learning," precluded any alterations of the trusts in the deed of Toronto Baptist College[27] and specifically required that faculty be members in good standing of "an Evangelical Church" and that theology professors be members "in good standing of a Regular Baptist Church." Respecting theological faculty members, the board of governors also had the right "to require such further or other tests as to religious belief . . . as to the said board of governors may seem proper." There were to be no religious or denominational qualifications for students, "other than in the faculty of theology."[28]

Classes at the new university began in the fall of 1890. John Castle had declined the position of chancellor, so Malcolm MacVicar, a close confidant of the senator, was appointed to the position, and the first faculty included Albert H. Newman, Maritimers Daniel Welton and Theodore H. Rand, Newton Wolverton and Peter S. Campbell.[29]

The Embodiment of the Protestant Ethic

On September 21, 1887, while he was attending a meeting of the charter committee of McMaster University, William McMaster died, but his passing did not for a moment delay those he had inspired in this, his last great project. The bulk of his large estate was left to the board of governors — an amount of some $900,000, the will's final words stipulating that they seek "the best possible facilities for a thoroughly practical Christian course of education."[30]

Described approvingly by the famous Methodist educator, Egerton Ryerson, as the embodiment of the Protestant ethic, William McMaster was one of the giants of the Toronto business establishment in the mid to later nineteenth century. An Irish immigrant of County Tyrone, he had come to Canada in 1833 where at age twenty-two he found work with an established dry goods firm. He was a partner by the following year, and secured full possession of the firm in the next decade after the original proprietor retired. His mercantile interests broadened and, branching into finance, he became one of the founders of the Bank of Commerce and its first president. He went on to become a member of the legislative council of the province of Canada and, with the formation of the Canadian Upper House at Confederation, he was named one of the nation's first senators.[31]

Received by R. A. Fyfe into Bond Street church, Toronto, in the final year of Fyfe's pastorate there, William McMaster became a tower of strength in the church and the burgeoning denomination both through his dynamic leadership and his generous benefactions. In addition to his seemingly boundless interest in education, McMaster was the first president of the Superannuated Ministers' Society, and he provided the endowment that made possible the first and continuing appointment of a home missions superintendent for the western Convention. McMaster also granted the Publication Society $40,000 to bring its journal and book centre under full denominational control. It was he more than any other who made possible the erection of the fine church edifice on Toronto's Jarvis Street to replace the former Bond Street building.

A Step Further

As might be expected, the Toronto entrepreneur was often at the storm centre of events, open to criticism for his part in the removal of the theology department from Woodstock to Toronto and for finally favouring Toronto over that town when the university was established. One disgruntled writer vehemently disapproved of "the marble baptistry . . . the organ . . . [and] a spirit of centralization and aggrandisement"[32] about the new Jarvis Street church. Yet McMaster's was the voice and his the financial backing that stimulated his sometimes reluctant fellow Baptists to joint action and finally union.

Senator McMaster's widow, the former Susan Moulton and the third of that family name[33] to figure prominently in early Canadian Baptist history, was soon to carry her husband's educational goals a step further —again to the chagrin of Woodstock College supporters. A native of New York state, she had long been active in the home missions work of the Northern Baptist Convention (now American Baptist Churches) when she married McMaster, and she continued with the same energy on the Canadian scene.[34]

Within eight months after the senator's death, Susan offered the new university her large mansion on Bloor Street East, Toronto, for use as a training school for women. The governors, who now controlled Woodstock College as well, gratefully accepted and closed the women's department at Woodstock to open Moulton Ladies College in the former McMaster home as a department of the university. It continued as an academy for women until 1954 while, as has been seen, Woodstock College carried on as a preparatory school for men until 1926. From having no training schools whatever in 1850, the province of Canada had three forty years later, linked together under the Convention.

Canadians in Kakinada

No real overseas mission initiative was taken in the Canadas until 1866 when the fifteenth annual meeting of the Regular Baptist Missionary Convention of Canada West took place. ("Missionary" in the Convention name referred primarily to work at home. That year, however, as a result of the visit of an agent of the American Baptist Missionary Union, a Canadian Auxiliary to the ABMU was formed. The following year the first missionaries, Americus V. and Jane (Bates) Timpany, left "to labor in the Presidency of Madras, British India, among the Teloogoos [Telegus],"[35] where the Americans had a struggling mission. The journey from New York lasted eleven days short of six months.[36]

John McLaurin, pastor of the Stratford church, and his wife Mary (also a Bates, sister of Jane Timpany, both daughters of Woodstock pastor John Bates) were the next to volunteer. Americus Timpany wrote to his earlier college friend: "During the week of prayer we prayed for two more missionaries; the next day I got father Bates' letter telling of your step."[37] The McLaurins left late in 1869.

As in the Maritimes, the goal of an independent mission was soon proposed. At the 1870 meeting the Western Convention, now Ontario, reorganized its satellite Foreign Missionary Society, electing John Bates as president.[38] While the Timpanys and McLaurins were having continued success under the aegis of the American Baptist Missionary Union, in 1873 an urgent appeal was received to assume responsibility for a small personally initiated mission in Cocanada (now Kakinada), which neither the American or British Baptists could undertake for lack of financing. After careful consideration, the Ontario Convention's Foreign Mission Society agreed to the proposal and the Canadian Baptist Telegu Mission became a reality, the McLaurins reaching their new field early the following March.[39]

In 1875 the Convention urged "that the sisters connected with our churches form themselves into mission circles."[40] The ladies moved with dispatch. By the following year the Women's Foreign Missionary Society of Ontario was formed, thirty circles being in operation another year later.[41] Almost concurrently, a similar society was organized among the women of the Quebec Convention, and seven circles were formed the first year.[42] As in the Maritimes, the women responded dramatically.

As already noted, the Maritime missionaries who had been serving in Burma and Siam moved over into India in 1875, and four couples reached Kakinada that summer. The two groups worked side by side until the formation of the Canadian Baptist Foreign Mission Board three and a half decades later.

Another Step towards Union

While giant steps had been taken in the areas of education and overseas missions, the Conventions West and East had not neglected what they perceived to be their prime responsibility — growth through home missions. By the end of its first decade the Western Convention was employing twenty-three missionaries at 127 stations,[43] and just three years after its 1858 founding the East sent out seven full- and part-time workers.[44]

The Regular Baptist Missionary Convention of Ontario — as it came to be known at Confederation when the province of Canada was divided in two — reported that in the years from 1856 to 1872, seventy-four chapels were built by mission congregations. While not neglecting the rural areas, the society had begun to focus on the expanding towns. Nor were its efforts confined to the English-speaking population. It was noted in 1864 that the German Baptists in Brant were building a chapel, having been served by missionary John Stumpf,[45] while four missionaries were preaching in German by the year 1870. Three missionaries also ministered that year to Indians of the Six Nations and one served "coloured brethren," while a number preached in Gaelic as well as English.[46] By 1873 John Stumpf was engaged in working among German people in ten places.[47]

A Decade of Progress

As in the Maritimes, widespread revival movements played a major role in the rapid expansion. Revivals were reported among a number of churches in 1870,[48] and by 1875 the wave was high, to remain so for several years. By 1876 the twelve associations of the Ontario Convention reported new membership by baptism of 2,603 and a total church membership of 21,332. Fifty-one missionaries served mission churches in Ontario that year.[49] While over the next seven years the total increment by baptism dropped to an average of just over 1,500,[50] the increase for the decade was a healthy 1,767. Yet this very productive period was at a time of "commercial depression and financial stringency" when, "crippled by the stinted resources at its command, the Board [was] compelled in a measure to curtail its operations."[51]

Progress was also seen in the much smaller Canada Baptist Missionary

Convention East (which was about a fifth the size, with 4,553 members in 65 churches in 1885),[52] but it occurred at a much slower pace during the period, accessions by baptism averaging about 265.[53] On a limited scale, the Eastern Convention was also involved in ethnic outreach, sponsoring a German church at Arnprior.[54] Both Conventions were constantly plagued by insufficient funding to match the needs and opportunities around them. It appears that the churches were not giving as much as they could. A. H. Munro, secretary of the eastern body complained in 1880: "We are compelled to believe that the smallness of our resources has not arisen entirely from necessity."[55]

Denominational Consciousness Develops

The very success of the Conventions established after 1850 provided the impetus for greater consolidation, the board of the Western Convention commenting in 1862 on the "unity in the body . . . which happily exists at the present time, and has existed for the past nine years."[56] Three years later, a five-person delegation from Canada East attending the Western Convention expressed the hope "that the Baptists of East and West, as being one in faith, practice, and name, might be one in heart and feeling."[57] The following year the East, noting a "low state of religion throughout our churches," and calling for "a day of humiliation and prayer for the outpouring of the Spirit," invited the West to participate, which it readily did.[58]

The formation of the Superannuated Ministers' Society and the Church Edifice Society in 1864 and 1868 not only demonstrated concern for pastors with meagre income and churches with limited resources, but signified a developing denominational consciousness and a drawing together of the people. Strong men gave initial leadership. As has been seen, Senator William McMaster was the first and long-time head of the Superannuated Ministers' Society, while the Honourable Alexander Mackenzie, later the nation's second prime minister, was the founding president of the Edifice Society.

Common interests also developed in the publication field. By 1854 first issues of *The Christian Messenger*, published privately in Brantford, were off the press. Five years later, the paper moved to Toronto and became *The Canadian Baptist*. A Book Room was soon opened in Toronto.

In a further move to strengthen and consolidate outreach efforts, a part-time superintendent of missions was appointed in 1872. William Stewart was first named, followed by Thomas L. Davidson and Alexander Grant, the last being full-time in the position.

Union Close at Hand

In yet another stumbling step toward actual union, the short-lived Canada Baptist Union, which had been revived briefly in 1855, was resuscitated once more, in 1880. The two Conventions seemed to agree that its object was "the promotion of missions, education, literature, superannuated ministers' aid, and church edifice funds, and all denominational interests and enterprsies.[59] All too clearly indicating its failure to persuade the various societies to relinquish their prerogatives, the Union had to hold a "reorganization" meeting just two years later to modify its aims. The new objects were much more modest and less specific, including the promotion of "brotherly intercourse" and "discussion of such questions and the transaction of such missionary and educational and other business as belongs to the body as a whole in the Provinces represented."[60]

True unity was close at hand, but the Canada Baptist Union was not to be the medium. The first sure steps were taken with the amalgamation of the two home missionary societies: the Regular Baptist Missionary Convention of Ontario and Canada Baptist Missionary Convention East, together with the satellite societies. The crucial decisions were taken in separate meetings in October 1886. The Eastern Convention met first, on the 6th and 7th, unanimously adopting this motion: "Whereas the Baptists of Ontario and Quebec are now united in the work of Foreign Missions, Christian Education, Church Edifice building, the support of Superannuated Ministers, and Publication, it seems highly desirable that they should also be one in the work of Home Missions."[61]

Resulting from that approved motion, a delegation was appointed to meet with the Ontario Convention.

The following year, 1887, the Eastern Convention met in October. Without dissenting voice, it accepted the simply stated recommendation of its committee on union "that we unite with the Home Missionary society of Ontario in Home Mission Work."[62] A week later the Ontario Convention moved as simply, and decisively. Also carried unanimously was the resolution: "Whereas this question of union has been carefully considered both by the Society in the East and by us, Resolved, that we do now receive the Eastern Society [Convention] into union with us," naming a parallel committee to meet with the East "with reference to the details of the union that has been consummated. . . ."[63]

The Baptist Convention of Ontario and Quebec

As an initial step toward complete consolidation, the Ontario Convention removed the word "Home" from its constitution and, for the first time in a Baptist body in central Canada, a basic membership was established composed of "delegates of Baptist Churches." Officers of the "Society" (as at that point they wrongly termed themselves) were also to be members, as were five representatives from McMaster University.[64]

In 1888, the Regular Baptist Missionary Convention of Ontario merged with the Canada Baptist Missionary Convention East and the Baptist Foreign Missionary Society of Ontario and Quebec. The Church Edifice Society for Ontario and Quebec and the Superannuated Ministers' Society joined as well, to form the Baptist Convention of Ontario and Quebec. On March 22 of the following year, an Act of the Dominion

Parliament legally effected the union and "created for the first time a true convention . . . a true assembly of churches, which acted through their accredited delegates."[65]

The former satellite societies and publication boards became boards of the new Convention—five at the outset: home missions, foreign missions, superannuated ministers, church edifice and publication. The boards were each incorporated as legal entities, while the Convention itself was not, a situation destined to hamper the Convention's essential role at a later date. Yet the achievement was monumental. What had been merely a motley collection of churches in 1850 had become a denomination forty years later. The wilderness wanderings were behind them.

CHAPTER 17

Going West I:
Manitoba and the Northwest

"Our preoccupation with the fruits of our faith
should be balanced with an equally earnest quest
for the roots of our faith."
—*J. K. ZEMAN*

When pioneering Baptist missionary Alex McDonald arrived in Winnipeg in 1873 to find no more than one Baptist in or near the settlement, he made the prophetic statement that he had come "to make Baptists." Brave it may have been but it was in sharp contrast to the views expressed four years earlier by the missionary body that finally dispatched him westward. Using the model of the two spies that Moses sent into Canaan (Number 13:16ff), the Regular Baptist Missionary Convention of Ontario had sent two observers in 1869 to discover opportunities for Baptist missions west of the Great Lakes.

The two, Thomas Baldwin and Thomas L. Davidson, made as exhaustive a survey as their limited resources permitted, reporting on the soil, the climate, the political situation and the state of religion. "We would not recommend to the Convention," they said, "to send a missionary for the sake of the present inhabitants" adding that "the conditional appointment of a missionary, provided a colony of Baptist families would unite, move and settle together, in the great North-West" would be warranted.[1]

These were not men with myopic vision . . . they were being characteristically cautious. The fragile unity of their own Convention, which was actually but an unrepresentative society, had existed for no more than two decades—the 1850s and the 1860s. But they did recognize that they were already late, very late in even attempting such a venture. They wrote: "The labour of the denomination has been increased perhaps ten fold by its tardiness of action in regard to mission work in the beginning of villages, towns, and cities."[2] Other denominations were already well established.

The West Opens Up

The land that Baldwin, Davidson and then McDonald visited was no longer inhabited only by Native peoples and a few hunters and traders. The two scouts recorded a population of 14,000 in the Northwest and found a growing number of communities, large and small. The true West was on the verge of explosive development.

The first Europeans to penetrate as far as the plains were the French. The English fur traders followed afterwards. In 1789 Alexander Mackenzie of the North West Company reached the Arctic Ocean, and four years later, he became the first European to reach the shores of the Pacific by land. On a rock by the edge of the ocean he wrote his now-famous inscription: "Alex Mackenzie from Canada by land 22d July 1793." In the next decade Simon Fraser made the treacherous voyage down the river that now bears his name, looking for a water route to the west coast that could be used by fur traders. Another explorer, David Thompson, spent twenty-seven years surveying the Northwest, leaving a legacy of precise maps, also to be used in fur-trade operations. The northern half of the continent had been spanned. Other explorers, including James Cook and George Vancouver of Britain and Juan Francisco de la Bodegoy Quadra of Spain, had arrived on the Pacific coast earlier by sea.

The Hudson's Bay Company

Traders soon followed the paths of the explorers, and they, in turn, were followed by settlers. One of the first to sense the opportunities was the 5th Earl of Selkirk, a Scottish nobleman with deep concern for his impoverished countrymen. After sending many settlers to Prince Edward Island and Upper Canada, Selkirk secured from the Hudson's Bay Company a huge tract of land lying in the watershed of the Red River at the south end of Lake Winnipeg. The first of his homesteaders arrived at the Red River Colony in 1812.[3]

The Hudson's Bay Company, which eventually incorporated the North West Company, at first assumed almost total control of the area west of the Rockies and as far south as the mouth of the Columbia River before that territory became part of the United States. Soon after that occurred, in 1849, the Company obtained Vancouver Island as a grant from the Crown and moved its far western headquarters from Fort Vancouver on the Columbia to Victoria. With the discovery of gold in the bed of the Fraser River in the early 1850s a deluge of prospectors arrived in the small town, drawn from the mining camps of California and from as far away as Australia. Along with the furs and commodities traders on the mainland, the prospectors increased the population, as well as opportunity for Christian outreach.[4]

In 1866 the British government bought Vancouver Island back from the Hudson's Bay Company and linked it with the mainland as one Crown colony. Victoria was named the capital the following year.[5] The far western colony joined the new Dominion of Canada as the province of British Columbia in 1871. The area around the Red River Settlement had entered Confederation as the Province of Manitoba the previous year, while Alberta and Saskatchewan were not to become distinct Canadian provinces until 1905.

The Religious Vanguard

In their 1869 assessment of the religious life they discovered in what was known at the time as the North West Territories, Baldwin and Davidson estimated that there were some 5,000 to 6,000 Roman Catholics, about an equal number of Anglicans, about 800 Presbyterians and an under-termined number of Wesleyan Methodists. Both the Anglicans and the Roman Catholics had provided most of the spiritual leadership since the area was first settled.[6]

The Anglicans

John West, appointed chaplain of the Red River Settlement in 1820, was the first Anglican to blaze the trail. A missionary of the evangelical Church Missionary Society of Britain, commonly known as the CMS, West took with him schoolmaster G. Harbidge, and soon the two established both a mission church and a boarding school for Native peoples.[7]

In 1840, Henry Budd, "one of John West's Indian boys," who had become a teacher in the school, was sent as teacher and catechist to Cumberland House on the Saskatchewan River to open a mission. Later moving to The Pas, he became the first of his race to be ordained. Soon afterwards another British man, Abraham Cowley, arrived, serving as a missionary for half a century. James Hunter later joined the growing group.[8]

When the Hudson's Bay Company moved its headquarters to Victoria, it also appointed R. J. Staines chaplain and schoolmaster there. Edward Cridge, a strong evangelical, succeeded him six years later. William Duncan, a lay teacher and catechist, was sent out by the CMS in 1857 to work among the Native peoples. Two years later W. W. Kirkby settled in Port Simpson on the mainland coast, building both a school and a mission house. To serve an influx of some 25,000 people in the first year of the Gold Rush, W. B. Crichmer was sent from London. By 1859 a bishopric was established at Victoria under George Hills[9] and growth thereafter was significant.

The Presbyterians

The first Scottish crofters to take advantage of the Earl of Selkirk's generous offer of settlement on the Red River secured a promise that a minister of their church would accompany them. In the early days, it was not possible to fulfill this condition, so an elder, James Sutherland, specially licensed to christen and to perform marriage, was sent with the colonists.

When John Black, the first ordained Prebyterian minister, arrived in 1851, three hundred of the Scottish settlers joined the church at the first service of sacrament. Soon they had erected a substantial stone building, established a school which later became Manitoba College and made plans for "the planting of missions not only near by, but out into the distant Saskatchewan country," including work among the Native peoples.[10]

On the Pacific Coast, the Presbyterian Church in Ireland was responsible for the initial work of that denomination. John Hall was the first Presbyterian minister to arrive in Victoria—in 1861—to be followed by Thomas Somerville of the Church of Scotland and, on the mainland, by Robert Jamieson, sent by the Presbyterian Church in Canada.[11]

The Methodists

It was early in 1840 that the Wesleyan Methodist Church in England accepted an invitation from the Hudson's Bay Company to send missionaries into their territories. Four men were intially chosen: James Evans, already in Canada, Robert T. Rundle, William Mason and George Barnley. Before the year's end Evans was at work at Norway House, Mason at Rainy Lake, Barnley at Moose Factory on James Bay and Rundle at Edmonton.[12] In 1868 George Young opened a Methodist mission at the Red River Settlement.[13]

Among the throng who arrived at Victoria during the Gold Rush was a Cornish Methodist, John T. Pidwell, who gathered a group for fellowship. From this little gathering a plea was sent to the Wesleyan Church both in Canada and in England. Once again four men answered the call: Ephraim Evans (brother of James), Edward White, Arthur Browning and Ebenezer Robson, all reaching Victoria in 1859. Evans remained in Victoria, while White was dispatched to Queensboro (New Westminster), Browning to Nanaimo and Robson to Hope. Four years later Thomas Crosby began working among the Native peoples on the coast.

Why So Late?

It is apparent that by the time Alexander ("Pioneer") McDonald arrived in Winnipeg on May 30, 1873, other major Protestant denominations were already well established and poised to meet the wave of new immigration about to pour into the West. It was a handicap that long restrained the Baptists.

Why were the Baptists so late on the scene? The lack of unity in central Canada was one critical factor. While two missionary societies had developed, their focus was on missions within their own region. With one notable exception, so were their satellite interests. Spurred on perhaps by the Maritime example, they did set up a foreign missionary society, but the needs of the West took a little longer to grip the imagination. It might be suggested that the well-organized Maritime body might have "leap-frogged" the centre to undertake the task, but the distances were just too vast and their natural line of communications remained with the New England states rather than with central or western Canada.

The Pioneer Arrives

The account of the two "spies" sent to Winnipeg was received with equanimity by the Regular Baptist Missionary Convention of Ontario late in October 1869. News of the Riel Rebellion may have slowed the process, but it was two years later before the western call was addressed serously, though not conclusively. That year, while the Manitoba mission committee urged speedy action to send one or more missionaries to Manitoba, the Convention dallied, its minutes concluding dolefully that "the Report or finding of the Committee will be doubtless given to the churches through the Baptist [paper] as it does not come within the sphere of this body as at present constituted."[14]

Behind the scenes, however, the committee (which had been appointed by the Convention) kept doggedly at its task. R. A. Fyfe, whose leadership was once again decisive, reported to the 1872 annual meeting that widower Alexander McDonald, pastor at the Yarmouth and Sparta churches in Elgin county, Ontario, had volunteered and would proceed to the West the next spring. Continuing to stress that the work did not come "within the sphere of the Convention proper," the body nevertheless "cordially approved" the action of the committee.[15] There is no indication in the minutes at that time that they even considered a measure that would have cleared the issue — acting on a notice of motion of the previous year to add "Manitoba and the North-West Territories" to the Convention name alongside Ontario.[16]

Even the funding was undertaken privately. Through the pages of the *Canadian Baptist*, the Committee appealed for one hundred subscribers to pledge an amount of $10.00 each year for three years to provide the necessary support for one missionary. The response was encouraging and McDonald was commissioned.

McDonald and McLaurin

Alexander McDonald was born in the township of Osgoode south of Ottawa, in 1837, one of ten children of godly farming parents who had emigrated from the Perthshire Highlands five years before. Converted as a boy and given a good education for the times, he answered the call to the ministry, completing his formal theological education at the Canadian Literary Institute. In 1872, a year before he left for the West, his wife died. Their three-year-old son was left with his grandparents when McDonald went west in 1873.

McDonald's early life forms an interesting parallel with that of another well-known Canadian Baptist — John McLaurin, a pioneer missionary to India. Both were born in Osgoode township, converted and baptized about the same time under the ministry of Daniel McPhail, "the Elijah of the Ottawa Valley," said by one historian probably to have organized more Baptist churches and to have seen more of his converts enter the ministry than any other minister in Canada.[17] Both graduated from the

Canadian Literary Institute at about the same time. After pastorates in Ontario, each in 1873 opened a new mission field—McLaurin in Kakinada, McDonald in the Canadian West. And, as McDonald himself attested at his commissioning service in London, Ontario, it was McLaurin who first drew his attention to the claims of the Northwest.[18]

After a journey of almost ten days—by steamer from Sarnia on Lake Huron to Duluth at the west end of Lake Superior by rail to Moorehead, Minnesota, and by steamer up the Red River to Winnipeg, McDonald reached his destination on a Friday evening late in May 1873. Winnipeg, the capital of the new province, was rapidly becoming the gateway to the swelling west. Theo. T. Gibson comments on the scene:

> To give temporary shelter to bone-weary and often famished immigrants arriving over the Dawson Route—up to 2,500 in a single season—rough wooden sheds had been thrown up, and Alex noted that they were filled to capacity with over one hundred men, women and children. Most of these would move on within days or weeks, to wrest a livelihood out of the virgin prairie, but Alex had reached his primary destination and found a place in one of the many boarding houses in the town.[19]

A Cool Night

Two days later, on invitation, McDonald preached in the Presbyterian churches of Winnipeg and Kildonan. (Kildonan was the pulpit of John Black, the first ordained Presbyterian minister to the Selkirk Settlers.) The following Tuesday, after walking some twenty kilometres to Springbank, northeast of Winnipeg, he met the only settled Baptists in the district at the time, sawmill owner and soon-to-be MLA, William R. Dick, and his wife. Late the next day he set out for Stony Mountain about twenty-five kilometres to the northwest, but got lost and had to spend the cool spring night under the stars.

Such was Pioneer McDonald's introduction to his new mission field, and by the name "Pioneer" he has subsequently become known, the man who finally blazed a trail for Baptists in Canada's West. The next Sunday morning he again preached for Black, and in the evening for Methodist George Young. The same afternoon, in "one of the poorest specimens of a schoolhouse, as open as a barn, provided with a few miserable backless benches," as he described it, McDonald held the first Baptist service. "A goodly number" were present, but no Baptists were there, as W. R. Dick was away.[20]

The Pioneer did not confine his initial efforts to Winnipeg but for six months, like the Methodist circuit riders, he crossed and recrossed the frontier area, covering all the settlements within a hundred-mile radius: Poplar Point, High Bluff, Portage-la-Prairie, Palestine, Third Crossing, Stony Mountain, Springfield, Gladstone, Westbourne, McIntyre, McArthur, Irvine and McLaurin. Most often he travelled on foot, but sometimes he went by stage, buckboard, horse and buggy or on horseback. Welcomed warmly, he received along the way several offers of land and funds to build chapels. In Portage-la-Prairie and in Winnipeg, W. R. Dick was even ready to donate two valuable town lots!

No Help from Ontario

Writing that October, McDonald was particularly elated that four more Baptists had "turned up" in Winnipeg, and he also expressed the hope that his young mission would not be forgotten during the forthcoming Ontario Convention.[21] It was. No reference is made to the Manitoba Mission in the minutes, no place given to a report on the mission from the Manitoba Mission Committee. Still considered outside the scope and responsibility of the Convention, the work was being supported through the continuing efforts of the committee and through publicity in the *Canadian Baptist.*

In developing his outreach McDonald faced a double deficiency: of manpower and of funds. He decided to face the issues head on, and in December 1873, with plans for chapels at Winnipeg and Portage-la-Prairie in his baggage, undertook the long trek back to Ontario to appeal for helpers and for greater financial aid to support them. He wanted at least one more missionary.

For the next six months his schedule visiting Ontario churches was as heavy as it had been in Manitoba. Travelling from Windsor to Montreal, he spoke almost daily in churches, and several times on Sundays. Limited funds were secured but, to his disappointment no prospective missionary came forward. And yet, McDonald did not return to the West alone. A new bride accompanied him, a woman from Middlesex county in western Ontario.

Lucinda York, a teacher and fellow graduate of the Canadian Literary Institute, whom McDonald married in June 1874, proved to be an invaluable missionary associate as well as a good wife. The story of their long trek to Winnipeg in July and August with two young children — McDonald's son James and his wife's nine-year-old orphaned niece Louisa — is an adventure in itself. "Three weeks of travel by land and water, camping at night when the brave woman cheerily sang 'Tenting Tonight on the Old Camp Ground,' and sixty changes from one means of transportation to another brought them finally to their destination."[22]

The First Winnipeg Congregation

Although McDonald had managed to drum up very little financial support and no missionary help, he returned to a much brighter scene in Winnipeg. Demonstrating the vigour of the new frontier, W. R. Dick had already started the new church building, although there was not yet enough money to cover construction costs. That November, though the building was not nearly completed, the little group began to meet in what was to be the Sunday school room, and on February 7, 1875, the First Baptist Church of Winnipeg was organized, with seven members (and seven adherents, whose letters of dismission from other churches had not been received.

As has so frequently been Baptist practice, the initial congregation used a statement of faith as part of their founding service. On this occasion it was the New Hampshire Confession of Faith, which later became part of the constitution of the new Convention of Manitoba and the North-West.

Reinforcements Come Slowly

Meanwhile, the Manitoba Mission Committee had held a "most success-ful" anniversary meeting in Ontario that fall of 1874, authorizing the treasurer to donate up to $2,700 toward the new Winnipeg building. Funds on hand were some $650 less than this amount, but the treasurer, with backing from R. A. Fyfe and Thomas Davidson, sent the full amount warning McDonald that "he must not expect the churches of these prov-inces to furnish any further amounts toward the Winnipeg Chapel fund."[23] About the same time the Church Edifice Society to which McDonald had also appealed for a grant, declined on the all-too-familiar grounds that their constitution would not permit it. One bit of news was a little more optimistic: the Missionary Committee intimated that word was expected any moment from a man who had been challenged to become the second missionary.

That particular challenge apparently fell on deaf ears, for by 1876 no further help had been sent. However, help arrived in an unexpected way. Daniel McCaul, a former pastor from Wellesley, Ontario, had come to Winnipeg to homestead and to minister part-time. He was present at the organization of the church in Winnipeg, and McCaul spent the winter in the town, taking a number of McDonald's services. This freed the mis-sionary to follow his wide itineraries. The next spring, however, McCaul moved to Emerson, taking up land nearby. This move was hardly in vain, as McDonald discovered when he first visited him at his new homestead. McCaul had already begun Baptist work at Emerson and hoped to add a number of outstations, although he lacked any means of transportation. As no second missionary had yet materialized, the Ontario Committee did vote to give $250 toward McCaul's part-time work, and a church was established at Emerson in 1876—only three years after McDonald's first trip west.

At Least Five Men

The Committee also granted $150 to A. E. de St. Dalmas, a British Baptist who had come to Winnipeg as a druggist in 1875. The funds allowed him to help McDonald serve the many tiny farming settlements around Winnipeg. Within a few months, however, St. Dalmas decided to enter the ministry full-time, enrolled in the Canadian Literary Institute and later attended the Toronto Baptist College, becoming a respected minister in Ontario for many years. He was the first of seven young men to enter the ministry during McDonald's pastorate.

All the while persistent appeals for a second full-time missionary continued, the Ontario Committee quoting McDonald and lamenting in 1877: "The Methodists of Canada have some fifteen or sixteen missionaries in the North West, most of them in Manitoba. . . . The Presbyterians have about the same number or more. . . . Are we as Baptists doing justice to the charge committed to us if we don't have at least five men?"[24]

Finally, in 1878, the second missionary stepped forward. He was Alex Warren of Durham, who arrived in Winnipeg in June of that year, accompanied, unexpectedly, by one John Stewart. Stewart was a veteran pastor who had served at Glengarry near Ottawa and with whom McDonald had been corresponding privately. The Pioneer (as McDonald had come to be known) wasted no time in putting the newcomers to work. Stewart was taken to Rockwood, where he set up the Stonewall church, with aid from the Winnipeg church. McDonald set off with Warren to explore the opportunities among the thousands of Mennonites then settling in the Pembina Mountains. After visting a number of western outstations in Manitoba, they decided Warren would stay for the winter at Palestine, preaching occasionally to the Scots in Gaelic. Alas, such was not to be — the "second missionary" suffered a breakdown in health and was on his way back to Ontario within two months.[25] Stewart did not stay long either, migrating to Dakota in 1880 along with many members of his new congregation as a result of a dispute with the government over land settlement.

McDonald recieved another blow that year when word came that his mentor and friend, Robert Alexander Fyfe had died, that Baptist of great stature who had not spared his manifold talents to serve effectively in nearly every area of denomination work, not least in promoting the Manitoba Mission. In fond memory of his friend, McDonald named his new son, the only child born to his second wife, R. A. Fyfe McDonald.

The West on Its Own

Baptists on the western frontier, though slim in numbers, did not take long to come together. Four churches — Winnipeg, Emerson, Stonewall and High Bluff — formed the Red River Association in 1880, seven years after Pioneer McDonald had arrived in the West. In the intervening years William Murden, pastor at East Williams, Ontario, came to Gladstone, about 160 kilometres northwest of Winnipeg and embarked on missionary work, covering a wide area around that settlement. In 1879 a former Roman Catholic priest, A. C. Turner, who had been baptized in the St. Catherine Street church, Montreal, came on the scene, and in September 1879, he became the first Baptist minister to be ordained in the West. After the ordination at First Church, Winnipeg, he worked as pastor at High Bluff and Portage-la-Prairie with no assurance of support from Ontario's Manitoba Mission Committee. So the field expanded — consistently but slowly. By the mid-1880s it was reported that the Methodists had ninety missionaries in Manitoba and the Northwest, the Anglicans and Presbyterians about eighty each—the Baptists three.[26]

As hundreds of settlements began springing up along the new and forecast railway lines in the 1880s, western leaders decided that they must take significant action themselves. Not surprisingly, McDonald was the pacesetter. This became particularly evident when the would-be Baptist Union of Canada* accepted its Western mandate and then promptly set the work adrift in 1880 by naming a board of the Manitoba Mission composed totally of Manitobans.[27] They hadn't even received the consent of the board members of the western churches.

Such a move certainly pointed to the need for the new Red River Association which in 1881 embraced two more churches: Portage-la-Prairie and Ridgeville. Four more churches were organized in Manitoba that year, but they were not yet linked with the association: Gladstone, Preston, Rapid City and Strathclair.[28] The next year, largely because of the central decision to lay all responsibility for western work on the shoulders of westerners, the group of now ten churches began investigating the possibility of forming a Convention. And in 1882 the Regular Baptist Missionary Convention of Manitoba and the North-West was formed, embracing territories where no Baptist missionaries had even yet set foot — from the Ontario border to the Rockies and to the Far North. The first president was, fittingly, W. R. Dick of Winnipeg, and it is interesting that with one exception the officers and directors—fifteen in all — were laymen. Pastors were in short supply, but laymen were prepared to accept the duties of leadership. This is a mark of the western Baptists which still exists today.

In a major venture, which proved to be beyond their capacity at the time, the little bank of churches that formed the Convention persuaded Pioneer McDonald to leave his Winnipeg pastorate to become superintendent of the total enterprise. Their vision was admirable: they hoped to establish work among the French-speaking people and to set up a French school in conjunction with the newly formed Prairie College, but the lack of funds simply crushed their hopes.

"Ivy-Covered Models"

Even before the Convention began thinking of ways to improve education, an Ontario professor caught a vision of setting up a ministerial training school in the West. His name was John Crawford, and he taught at the Canadian Literary Institute in Woodstock. The project was launched in 1879 in Rapid City, a railway town with much potential for growth. Funds were solicited in central Canada both privately and through the churches.

---

*By this time the old Canada Baptist Union had disbanded completely and in 1880 another attempt was made in Ontario to form an all-Canada connection through a new Baptist Union of Canada. It soon suffered a similar fate.

With G. B. Davis as the assistant principal, the institute was intended to concentrate strictly on training pastors. Students were allowed to work on the buildings and grounds of the institute to cover some of their costs.

The idea was inspired, Crawford gave his all in talent and personal financing and McDonald soon threw his support behind the enterprise. A fair number of students attended, but unfortunately finances were a constant problem, and the Prairie College closed its doors in 1883. Besides its financial difficulties, the college faced two other problems. First, the railway decided to bypass Rapid City. Second, and more serious, the Toronto Baptist College was campaigning to centralize all ministerial education — a step which also harmed Acadia at the time. It is most unfortunate that the Prairie College model was not allowed to succeed. "Built by students and operated on the principle of collective homesteading," as Walter E. Ellis describes it, it suited the frontier needs better than any other 'ivy-covered' models.[29] Yet all was not lost. The positive results were considerable. Student pastors spent their summers serving many churches in the area around the college and beyond, unlike those who were trained elsewhere, most Prairie-trained ministers remained to work where they had studied — in the West.

CHAPTER 18

Going West II: British Columbia

"But yet, thought I, I must venture all with God."
— JOHN BUNYAN

When Pioneer McDonald arrived at the muddy little settlement of Winnipeg in 1873, Victoria, captial of Canada's new province of British Columbia, was already a community of some 4,000 people. Yet First Baptist, Winnipeg, was organized a year before First Baptist, Victoria. If it was daunting—and expensive—to send a missionary to Manitoba, the thought of sending workers to the ends of the country hardly entered the minds of even mission-interested Ontarians of the day. And certainly those in Manitoba and the Northwest, having ventured that far, could hardly be expected to look beyond the impenetrable Rockies. Even after the coming of the railway, Baptists gave little thought to British Columbia until the turn of the century.

So it was that two streams of Baptist life emerged in western Canada and continued to flow widely apart until they finally joined thirty years later. Even their beginnings were very different.

Alexander Clyde

While the work in Manitoba began through (perhaps somewhat reluctant) missionary effort, developments on the Pacific coast arose from an indigenous lay endeavour to meet frontier needs. Alexander Clyde was the key player, although he was not the first Baptist layman to have settled in the Far West. That honour goes to a number of black immigrants and to Yorkshireman John Morton. In 1860, a chief factor of the Hudson's Bay Company made a call for tradesmen and labourers, attracting, among others, some of the first blacks to the colony of Vancouver Island from San Franscisco. They were Fielding Spotts, Augustus Christopher, Madison Fineas Bailey and his wife and Thomas Whitney Pierre and his wife.[1]

Potter John Morton, his cousin Sam Brighouse and friend William Hailstone were first lured to the Pacific coast by the news of gold, arriving in New Westminster in 1862. The trio found no gold but did discover coal and potters' clay. Then "the three Greenhorns" as New Westminster dubbed them, pre-empted, with little knowledge of their future value, "the 550 acres that made up Vancouver's fabled West end—the richest slice of real estate west of Toronto's golden mile." They did not prosper in brickmaking, but sometime later they did strike it rich when the Canadian Pacific Railway chose Vancouver as its western terminus — and land values began to escalate. Now a wealthy man, Morton generously endowed denominational causes, particularly the Ruth Morton Memorial Baptist Church, Vancouver, which bears his wife's name.[2] He was also one of the founding members of the city's First Baptist Church in 1887.

It Pays to Advertise

It was late in 1874 when Alexander Clyde and his spouse ended their long trek from Stratford, Ontario, to take up a new life on the shores of the Pacific in Victoria. Now "the few Baptists in B.C.'s largest town had someone to bring them together,"[3] and Clyde was not long about doing so. Locating four other Baptists, he invited them to meet and soon gained nine further responses through an advertisement in the local paper. The group started a regular prayer meeting and began to look for pastoral leadership. Clyde wrote directly to his Stratford minister, who in turn placed the need before readers of the *Canadian Baptist*. It was William Carnes of Chesley, Ontario, who responded, and within about ten months, he was ensconced in his new position.

On May 3, 1876, fifteen charter members met at the local YMCA to organize western Canada's second Baptist Church: First Baptist, Victoria. The occasion was unique, as the racial composition of the congregation was almost equally divided: eight blacks and seven whites. It was a noble undertaking in times when prejudices were rampant in the surrounding society, but it was other stresses that finally made the attempt something less than successful.

In 1876 the young church approached the Regular Baptist Missionary Convention of Ontario for support. None was forthcoming, so American Baptists came to the rescue of the congregation, which had debts of over $5,200, paid to secure a site and erect a chapel. J. C. Baker, Sunday school missionary and representative of the American Baptist Publication Society, was invited to hold a series of evangelistic services in conjunction with the February 17, 1877, chapel dedication. Fifteen were converted and the initial baptismal service — the first immersion ever in British Columbia — was held during the evening of the dedication. A reporter of the Victoria *Colonist* was present and described the moving service: "The sacred edifice was crowded to its utmost capacity. Rev. J. C. Baker preached an able sermon on God's plan of redemption, and a solemnity such as we have seldom witnessed came over the congregation as the candidates were led into the water. Strong men were seen weeping and a deep impression was made."[4]

The North Star Mission

With any other churches thousands of miles away and communication slow and undependable, the first British Columbia Baptist church

Heare o King], and dispise not ye counsell of ye poore, and let their complaints come before thee.

The King is a mortall man, & not God therefore hath no power over ye immortall soules of his subiects, to make lawes & ordinances for them, and to set spirituall Lords over them.

If the King have authority to make spirituall Lords & lawes, then he is an immortall God, and not a mortall man.

O King, be not seduced by deceivers to sin so against God whome thou oughtest to obey, nor against thy poore subiects who ought and will obey thee in all things with body life and goods, or else let their lives be taken from ye earth.

God Save ye King.

Spittlefield neare London.

Tho: Helwys]

2. The Baptist church at
Cornwallis, about 1850. In 1779,
this church's predecessor — a New
Light congregation — shared with
the Horton Baptist church in the
ordination of itinerant preacher
Henry Alline. *ABHC*

1. An inscription to King James I
in *The Mystery of Iniquity*, thought
to be in the handwriting of British
Separatist Thomas Helwys.
*Reproduced through the kindness
and by authority of the Baptist
Union of Great Britain and Ireland.*

3. Theodore Seth Harding (left)
and Edward Manning, two "fathers"
of the Baptist denomination in
Canada. *ABHC*

CREDIT LEGEND:

ABHC   Atlantic Baptist Historical Collection, Acadia University Archives,
Wolfville, Nova Scotia

CBA   Canadian Baptist Archives, Hamilton, Ontario

EN   *The Enterprisers* by M. L. Orchard and K. S. McLaurin
(Toronto: The Canadian Baptist Foreign Mission Board, 1924).

BMP   *History of the Baptists of the Maritime Provinces* by Edward Manning
Saunders (Halifax: Press of John Burgoyne, Granville Street, 1902).

4

5

6

7

4. The Haldimand (or Wicklaw) Baptist church: the oldest traceable congregation in Ontario and Quebec, organized in 1798. *CBA*

5. The congregation at First Baptist Church, Chatham, Ont., in the mid-twentieth century: one of the black Baptist churches that grew up after former Virginian slave, Elder Washington Christian, established the first Baptist church in Toronto in 1826. *CBA*

6. The church at Alexandra, P.E.I. Its predecessor at Lot 49 was formed by Baptist preacher Benjamin Scott of Yarmouth, N.S., who was shipwrecked near that spot about 1830. *ABHC*

7. The store in Fredericton, N.B., about 1834, where Richard Burpee carried on a thriving business before he left as a missionary to Burma. *From pamphlet "Canada's Pioneer Missionary" by Gordon C. Warren.*

8. Rev. Charles Tupper, Baptist pastor and strong supporter of union in the Maritimes — and father of Sir Charles Tupper, the Father of Confederation. *BMP. Portrait a tribute to Rev. Charles Tupper by the Hon. Charles Tupper, Bart.*

9. John Gilmour, who travelled to Britain in the 1830s to raise funds for missions and education in the Canadas. *CBA*

10. The original mission house where Elder John Miner began work among the Tuscarora Indians in 1841. *CBA. Donated by Mr. J. S. Calvert, Toronto, August 1976. Original glass negatives made by Mr. Calvert from early book, title unknown.*

11. Rev. Joseph Longfish, pastor at Oshweken, the Six Nations Reserve in Tuscarora Township. *CBA*

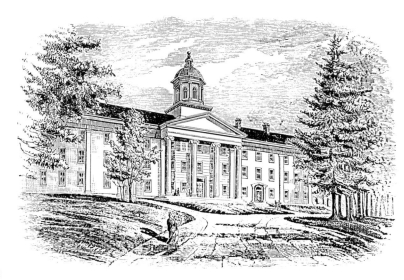

12

13

and property—
and in the inter-
istrate to manage
the Poor to be
s of the Poor.
in the Town, to
terms, for the af-

permanently es-

be filled by per-
is holding simi-
Offices for the
y, with respective
s, Books, &c.
rred, after being
d, by the order
Sessions, on the
same arrangement

their accounts to
er the 30th Sep-

charges of the
with the Fire De-
d other peculiar
e charge for the
.—Each Inhabi-
proportion of both

the above rate; pupils furnishing their own bedding.
Every attention will be given to the comfort and general department of the pupils.
January 3.

THE QUEEN'S COLLEGE, HORTON.

THIS Institution will be opened in due form on Monday, the 21st inst. in the presence of the Committee and Directors of the Education Society, who are hereby notified to attend.

A Preliminary Lecture will be publicly delivered by the respective Professors, to which the friends of the Institution are respectfully invited

The Students will be provided with lodgings in the buildings belonging to the Institution, with the exception of such as will be permitted to reside with their friends in the immediate neighborhood.

The Fees of the Institution are £6 per annum for all the Classes.

Boarding, Lodging and Washing, 8s 6d per week. The Students providing themselves with beds and bedding, and the furniture and fuel of their respective rooms. January 3.

NOTICE.

ALL demands against His Excellency the Lieutenant Governor to December 31, 1838, are requested to be sent in immediately.
January 3, 1839.

12. Acadia College as it looked from 1843 to 1877. It was founded as Queen's College, January 21, 1839. Announcement of the opening of Queen's College, 1839. *ABHC*

13. Preacher-evangelist Rev. Richard Preston, a former slave from Virginia, who organized the African Baptist Association in Nova Scotia in 1853. *ABHC*

14

15

14. Mᵐᵉ Henrietta Feller, the Swiss widow who founded the Grande Ligne Mission in Quebec (left), and her assistant, Louis Roussy. *CBA*

15. The Grande Ligne Mission, Quebec, about 1840. *CBA*

16

17

The Canadian Baptist.

H. LLOYD, EDITOR AND PROPRIETOR.

Toronto, Thursday, July 15, 1869.

LIBERAL CONTRIBUTIONS.

We are gratified to learn that the Hon. Wm. McMaster has given the liberal sum of $2000 towards the $8000 required for the removal of debt, and improvements on the Institute buildings. We learn also, that A. R. McMaster, Esq., of Toronto, and Jas. S. McMaster, Esq., of Liverpool, England, have each contributed $200 towards Ministerial Education.

18

16. Woodstock College, Ontario, first formed by Robert Alexander Fyfe, under the name Canadian Literary Institute, in 1860. *CBA*

17. Notice in the July 15, 1869, issue of the *Canadian Baptist* from the Canadian Literary Institute thanking the Hon. William McMaster for a large contribution. *CBA*

18. The Hon. William McMaster, benefactor of the Baptist church and founder of McMaster University, and his wife, Susan Moulton McMaster. *CBA*

21. John Crawford, who founded the Prairie College in 1879 in Rapid City, Man. *CBA*

22. Alexander Grant, pastor at First Baptist, Winnipeg, in the 1890s. *CBA*

19. Alexander ("Pioneer") McDonald and his wife, Lucinda York McDonald, with their two sons. *CBA*

20. The Strathcona church at Edmonton, Alberta, built while Alexander McDonald was pastor there. *CBA*

23. Brandon College, Winnipeg, opened in 1899. *CBA*

24. First board of the Baptist Union of Western Canada, held November 1907. *CBA*

25

26

28

25. Alexander Clyde, who organized First Baptist Church, Victoria, in 1876. *CBA*

26. Robert Lennie, pastor from Dundas, Ont., who preached at the first Baptist meeting in New Westminster, B.C., held in the town's court house in 1885. *CBA*

27. A meeting of the British Columbia Convention, Summerland, B.C., 1907. *CBA*

28. Okanagan College, Summerland, B.C., closed in 1915. *CBA*

29

30

31

32

29. Russian band at the King Street Mission in Toronto, about 1910. *CBA*

30. Hungarian Canadian pastor Rev. John Monus preaching at Leask, Sask., in the 1920s. *CBA*

31. Black congregation at Pine Creek, Alta., 1917. *CBA*

32. Immigrants from Galicia in the Ukraine established this first Galician Baptist church in the world at Overstone, Man. *CBA*

33

34

THE LIBERAL-FUNDAMENTALIST CONTROVERSY

35

36

33. Four girls at Fort Frances, Ont., who raised money on their own to furnish the Baptist church there. About turn of the century. *CBA*

34. The "home missions" tent at Steelton, Ont., 1902. *CBA*

35. Thomas Todhunter Shields, pastor of Jarvis Street Baptist Church, Toronto, beginning in

1910, and spokesman of the fundamentalist position in the liberal-fundamentalist controversy of the 1920s.

36. McMaster University, the seat of the liberal position in the controversy of the 1920s. (Shown here shortly after its reopening at its new Hamilton location in November 1930.) *CBA*
From the J. J. Cranston Collection.

37

38

39

Vol. XIX. No. 2   February, 1946

The Link and Visitor

A Labor of Love for Britain

Seeking some practical way to express Canadian sympathy for bombed-out British Baptists, the Baptist Women's War Services Auxiliary undertook shipment of Bundles to Britain in April 1942. Since that date, the Packing Committee, convened by Mrs. John F. Kirkland, (first on the left) has met regularly on the fourth Thursday of each month in the big basement room at 223 Church St., to sort and pack the many and varied articles of clothing sent by Baptist women's groups. Collapsible plywood boxes, 27" x 36" by 27" are bought and assembled on packing day. Each filled box weighs approximately 150 lbs. To date 225 such boxes have been sent. Letters from British Baptist headquarters advise that this service, while greatly appreciated, is no longer necessary. Therefore the final shipment will go in the early spring. The last date on which the committee may receive articles will be Feb. 10th. To all who have worked so faithfully for and given so generously to this enterprise, the Committee wishes to say a grateful "Thank you." From Great Britain comes this touching acknowledgment: "God bless you all abundantly and give you the joy within that comes from such a service for a world so sad and broken."

See also page 24

Messages from the Women's Baptist Home and Foreign Missionary Societies of Canada

Authorized as second class mail. Post Office Department, Ottawa.

37. Baptist pastor
Rev. C. J. Smith
and his family in front of
their log home in
Flin Flon, Man., 1938.
CBA

38. A baptism at
Minitonas, Man.,
about 1929. *CBA*

39. Women preparing "Bundles for
Britain" featured on the cover of
the *Link and Visitor*, 1946. *The
Link and Visitor.*

BAPTISTS IN FRENCH CANADA: THE TWENTIETH CENTURY

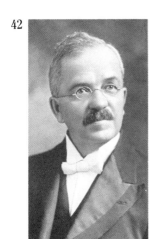

40. William C. Smalley, general secretary of the Baptist Union of Western Canada 1929–1951. *CBA*

41. The first class to enrol at the Baptist Leadership Training School, Calgary, 1949. *CBA*

42. Alphonse de Ligouri Therrien, president of the Ontario-Quebec Convention at the beginning of the century. *CBA*

43. The Bonne Nouvelle Mission tent at Shediac, N.B., near Moncton, in 1935. The mission was based at Henri Lanctin's Moncton bookstore, La Bonne Nouvelle. *CBA*

44. Class in Christian Education at the Centre d'Études Théologiques Évangéliques in Montreal (now the Faculté de Théologie Évangélique). *Union d'Églises Baptistes Françaises au Canada.*

45. Minnie De Wolfe, the first single woman missionary from any Canadian denomination to serve overseas, who began work in Burma in 1868 (*left*), and Hannah Maria Norris, who left as a missionary to Burma in 1870. EN

46. Mid-nineteenth century pioneer missionaries to India. *Top row:* G. F. Currie, R. Sanford, G. Churchill, J. Craig. *Middle row:* Mrs. Currie, Mrs. McLaurin, I. C. Archibald, Mrs. Timpany, Mrs. Churchill, and J. R. Hutchinson. *Lower row:* Miss Frith, J. McLaurin, Mrs. Archibald, A. V. Timpany, and Mrs. Hutchinson. CBA

47. The Telegu Baptist Church in Kakinada built by missionary Americus V. Timpany with funds from the Women's Baptist Foreign Missionary Society of Ontario. EN

48. A group of "Bible women" at work in India. Shown here with Baptist missionary A. E. Baskerville. EN

49. Rev. John Davis, missionary to lepers in Kakinada, India, at the turn of the century. BMP. *Portrait given in memory of the Rev. John Davis, M.A., by the Charlottetown church, of which he was pastor.*

51

50

52

53

54

50. Rev. J. A. and Mrs. Eva Glendinning, who began missionary work among the Oriya traders of India in 1902. *CBA*

51. Industrial schools established at Kakinada in 1925 resulted in operations like this knitting enterprise. *EN*

52. Rev. and Mrs. Archibald B. Reekie and their son. The first

Canadian Baptist missionary to Bolivia, Reekie began work in Oruro in 1898. *CBA*

53. Reverend A. G. Baker in the church at La Paz, Bolivia. *CBA*

54. Missionary to Bolivia Rev. Johnson Turnbull, and his family. Turnbull pressed for devolution of responsibility to indigenous peoples in the 1930s. *CBA*

55

56

57

58

59

60

55. Workers at Peniel Hall Farm, an educational and agricultural centre established by missionaries L. N. Vicherson and Howard Plummer on the site of a former hacienda outside La Paz, Bolivia. *CBA*

56. La Cruz del Sur, the Bolivian Christian radio broadcasting station set up in 1941 by missionaries H. S. Hillyer and Norman Dabbs. *CBA*

57. Norman Dabbs, Canadian Baptist missionary, who was martyred at Melcamaya, Bolivia, in 1949. *CBA*

58. Dr. Orville E. Daniel, general secretary of the Canadian Baptist Overseas Mission Board, with Angolan refugees building a house in Zaire in the early sixties. *CBA*

59. Institut Médical Évangélique (*IME*) at Kimpese, Congo, established in 1949. *CBA*

60. Angolan refugees crowding into Baptist Mission in Kibentele, Lower Congo, in the early sixties. *CBA*

61  62  63

64

61. Rev. Herbert F. Laflamme, who returned from the Indian mission field in 1905 to work towards a union of all Canadian Baptists. *CBA*

62. Watson Kirkconnell, president of Acadia University 1948–1965, who also chaired the All-Canada Committee of the Baptist Union of Western Canada in 1943 and 1944. *Acadia University Archives.*

63. Maud Matthews (Mrs. Albert Matthews), who chaired the Dominion Committee of the Affiliated Baptist Women's Missionary Societies of Canada in 1940. The four existing societies were united in 1953. *CBA.*

65

64. Dr. T. B. McDormand, first full-time executive officer of the Baptist Federation of Canada, and Dr. R. Frederick Bullen, second executive officer of the Federation. *CBA*

65. Crest of the Canadian Baptist Federation. *Canadian Baptist Federation.*

naturally sought fellowship closer at hand. They did not have far to look. The Puget Sound Association in the adjacent Washington Territory immediately welcomed First Church, Victoria, into its ranks and generously changed its own name to the Baptist Association of Puget Sound and British Columbia. The association also recommended that its American churches help Victoria meet its large debt, borrowed at 10 percent interest.[5]

J. C. Baker proved to be an excellent friend. In magazine articles, by direct mail and through addresses made during his wide travels, he supported the cause of the "North Star Mission," as he named it, creating interest as far afield as New York, Boston, Philadelphia, Detroit and St. Louis.[6]

Meanwhile, however, the church was encountering more troubles, although it was growing. William Carnes resigned as pastor in May 1877 over a dispute about finances. J. H. Teal, an Ohio native, accepted a one-year appointment, actually remained seventeen months and was finally succeeded by George Everton of Ontario and J. Spanswich, who had similarly short pastorates. Given the tenor of the times, the racial mix also became a point of irritation. With stresses steadily mounting and funds declining, the black segment of the church finally withdrew, leaving the remaining members unable to handle the debt. The mortgage holder foreclosed, and "after six years of trial and sacrifice"[7] the church was homeless and seemed to have suffered a fatal blow. With assistance, they had managed to reduce their liabilities by half, but it was not enough.

But quit they refused to do. Instead, they began meeting in the Masonic Temple. Apparently at the suggestion of D. G. Pierce, Chairman of the Home Mission Committee of the Puget Sound Association, a decision was made to reorganize the church. To accomplish this they technically disbanded on June 3, 1883, and three days later twenty-three of the members (including seven who had been charter members of the original church) re-formed as the Calvary Baptist Church, their covenant indicating that "no distinction shall ever be made in respect to race, colour or class."[8] Their trials and tribulations had matured them and had indeed provided them with a fine ideal for the future.

Walter Barss, a Maritime Baptist, was secured as pastor. A new three-hundred-seat sanctuary was dedicated in 1885—free of debt, partly as a result of a last-minute appeal from the visiting preacher.[9] Alexander Clyde's vision was very much alive.

The Work Expands

"On the first Lord's day in February," wrote Robert Lennie, "I took my position at the Judge's desk in the Court House, not to pronounce a sentence but to proclaim to every penitent a plenary absolution in the name of the King of Kings."[10] The hall of justice that day was the meeting place of British Columbia's next Baptist Church — First Baptist, New

Westminster, soon to be called Olivet. That was 1885, but the church had been carrying on without a pastor for no less than seven years.

It had been in mid-summer 1878 that a small group of lay Baptists first decided to meet regularly for prayer in New Westminster. After some weeks Victoria pastor J. H. Teal visited, persuading them to form a church and returning a little later with American Baptist missionary J. T. Huff to help them reach that goal. The church was established on August 10, 1878, with seven members, and ten days later a large delegation arrived from Victoria on the old wood-burning side-wheeler *Enterprise* to join them in a service of recognition.[11]

Unable to support a pastor, the small body met regularly in a rented hall with layman J. W. Willen, one of their own members, doing the preaching. It was not until 1883, five years later, that an appeal was made to the Puget Sound Association for aid in securing a regular minister. At about the same time Robert Lennie, a Dundas, Ontario, pastor moved to Washington Territory on the Pacific coast for reasons of ill health. A graduate of Spurgeon's College in England, Lennie did not rest for long. Because of the appeal to the association, an American missionary recommended that he go to New Westminster, and that is how he ended up one Sunday morning in early 1885 behind the court house desk.[12]

From a New Dominion Board A Modest Grant

Determined not to repeat Victoria's mistake of overextending debt, Lennie proceeded cautiously in making building plans. "There is no royal road to success in this city," he wrote, "especially when a Baptist pastor comes in, twenty-five years after the ministers of two other denominations."[13] A new building, like Victoria's seating three hundred, was completed and dedicated on December 12, 1886. J. C. Baker, by then superintendent of missions for the American Baptist Home Mission Society, preached in the morning and Victoria's Walter Barss in the afternoon. The church of thirty-five members had raised $2,400 themselves and the American Baptists gave $500 in addition to paying $750 of Lennie's $1,000 annual salary. A $200 grant was also made by a new Dominion Board of Home Missions, which had been founded the previous year by the missionary Conventions in Ontario and Quebec, the Maritime Convention and the new Convention of Manitoba and the North-West. With the fading of the Manitoba Mission Committee, the Baptist Union of Canada, which in 1880 began another abortive attempt at a national connectional link, did revive some eastern concern for the western work. With the failure of the Baptist Union of Canada, the Dominion Board of Home Missions picked up the reins until the formation of the Baptist Convention of Ontario and Quebec in 1888.[14]

B.C. Baptists and the CPR

Strangely enough, a decision made by executives at the Canadian Pacific Railway affected developments in the Baptist church in Vancouver in the

1880s. The little settlement of Granville on Burrard Inlet was chosen as the western terminus of the railway, rather than Port Moody at the head of the inlet. The decision was critical for John Morton and the other two "Greenhorns" — and later for Vancouver Baptists. Called Vancouver in honour of the captain who had charted the harbour nearly a century before and incorporated as a city on July 4, 1886, the city "had 800 business establishments and a population of 2,000" within weeks of its incorporation. Fire, the bane of sprawling pioneer settlements, almost completely levelled the little city the next June, but by the end of 1887 the population had reached 5,000, a year later it was at 8,000.[15]

Even before Vancouver was incorporated, New Westminster's Robert Lennie had his eye on developments, deciding to initiate a mission there. "There is a fair prospect now that a city of considerable importance will spring up along the shores of Coal Harbour and English Bay," he wrote in the *Canadian Baptist*, "and if so I am very hopeful that I may secure for the denomination a few town lots." He added: "You have no idea of the difficulty of building up a city where the timber is so large."[16] Frequently Lennie travelled the more than twenty-kilometre route to hold services, beginning in the bunk-house of a CPR subcontractor who was one of his New Westminster members.

Early in 1886 Walter Barss was on the mainland for a Sunday pulpit exchange with Robert Lennie, and after conducting the morning service at New Westminster rode a pony to Vancouver for an afternoon meeting there. Barss suggested during the service — held in Blair's Hall at the back of a saloon — that all members of Baptist churches and any others who were interested might remain afterwards. About twenty did, including some from the East whom he knew. When he proposed that a Baptist work be started, the group immediately agreed, setting up a committee to secure a hall and arrange weekly meetings. Barss in turn agreed to approach Ontario Baptists for assistance.[17]

Lennie managed to secure a building site from the CPR, and the congregation erected a small building at the rear of the lot, using volunteer labour and paying $700 for materials. They raised all the money themselves. The Dominion Board of Home Missions promised to send as pastor one of the young men soon to graduate from Toronto Baptist College, and in the meantime, veteran American Baptist pastor J. W. Daniels, originally a Nova Scotian, agreed to undertake the work. So it was that on March 16, 1887, First Baptist Church, Vancouver, was born with Lennie and Daniels participating in the service. A Confession of Faith was read and adopted as part of the historic session.[18]

Eight Churches in Convention

Meanwhile on Vancouver Island another First Baptist was established — in the burgeoning coal-mining city of Nanaimo, which by 1889 boasted a population of 5,000. The Northwest Baptist Convention initially pro-

vided $400 toward the salary of the first pastor, J. A. Banton.[19] Emmanuel
Baptist Church, Victoria, followed in 1890, resulting from a Sunday
school outreach that Calvary Baptist Church had undertaken five years
earlier into the Spring Ridge district of that city. In a fine example of
"hiving off," the mother church dismissed twenty-one of its members to
join with two others to form Emmanuel's charter membership. C. H.
Townsend, an English minister attending the Northwest Convention,
which Emmanuel immediately joined, accepted the call to become the
first pastor. He remained for two years, after which he was succeeded by
P. H. McEwan from Ontario.[20]

Including the church at Chilliwack in the Fraser Valley formed in
1893 (following an abortive attempt to do so two years earlier),[21] eight
British Columbia churches were incorporated within the Northwest Convention by 1894. That Convention, which was formed out of the Baptist
Association of Puget Sound and British Columbia in 1888, intended,
among other things, "to evangelize the population of Washington Territory, British Columbia, and Alaska," such being in co-operation "with
the great American Baptist Home Mission Society."[22]

The Americans were generous to their British Columbia cousins and
neighbours during the first two decades of their frontier development.
Indeed, without their help, it is doubtful that the fledgling churches could
have survived, for as late as 1896 only three of the eight B.C. churches
had become self-supporting.[23] But British Columbia was growing apace
and new opportunities abounded.

While placer mining (panning for gold) had petered out following
several successive spectacular gold rushes, large-scale underground mining soon supplanted it with the discovery of rich veins of ore—gold, silver,
copper, lead and other valuable minerals, as well as coal—in the interior
of the province. This made for the almost instant development of new
settlements. Communities like Rossland, Trail, Kaslo, Grand Forks, Nelson and Fernie mushroomed, as well as many other hamlets which died
almost as quickly as they were born. In the Okanagan J. M. Robinson, a
former president of the Manitoba Convention, saw great possibilities and
persuaded many Manitoba residents to settle with him there, spreading
to communities such as Penticton, Summerland and Peachland.[24]

Coming of Age

So many doors of opportunity were standing ajar that a little group of
British Columbia Baptist pastors meeting in Vancouver in March 1896
concluded that the time for action had come. "They were," writes historian Margaret Thompson, "overwhelmed with a sense of responsibility
for more than forty new towns, with populations ranging from one to five
thousand, which had no Baptist church."[25]

It had become obvious that a new thrust in outreach must come
from an organization of British Columbia Baptists themselves, limited

in strength as they were. Discovering a common concern among the churches, the pastors returned to Vancouver the next month and set up the British Columbia Baptist Extension Society, made up of the minister and two representatives from each of the eight churches.

A Well-Timed Decision

Victoria pastor Ralph Trotter agreed to act as a temporary financial agent, and although previous official aid from the East had been both minimal and spasmodic, Trotter returned from a canvassing visit to the churches of Ontario, Quebec and the Maritimes with more than $4,000 in cash and almost an equal amount in pledges. This provided the new Extension Society with good initial backing, and churches were soon established at Rossland and Trail in the West Kootenay and at Chemainus on Vancouver Island.

The decision to form the Extension Society could not have been made at a better time, for the very next year the American Baptist Home Mission Society informed the province's churches that due to an overwhelming debt it was facing, it could no longer provide any funds for B.C. churches or for expansion. A severe recession in the United States had so affected church receipts that the American Society's liabilities had soared to over half a million dollars, a vast indebtedness for those times. The blow was, of course, sudden and severe to the small British Columbia group and it is little wonder that they immediately telegraphed the less-than-a-decade-old Ontario and Quebec Convention, then in annual session: "American Board discontinues aid to B.C.: we look to you for sympathy and help."[26]

Sympathy and help were rendered by the central Convention—probably not quite as anticipated—through its appointment of a delegation to visit the New York office of the American Baptist Home Mission Society to appeal for a staged withdrawal of support for B.C. rather than an immediate cut-off. Resulting from this plea, maintenance was granted for a further two years, but on a reduced scale. The breathing period was short.

B.C. Convention Formed

Meanwhile, the British Columbia Baptist Extension Society met in 1897 in its first and only annual meeting, its executive having invited the churches to send representatives to consider steps to deal with crisis. After considerable heart searching and debate, the representatives reluctantly decided to form their own Convention, thus severing their trans-border bonds. It was not an easy decision, for the fellowship had been enriching and, as has been seen, the American contribution had been generous.

A different approach from both the Ontario and Quebec and the Maritime Conventions was taken in the instance of women's missionary interests with the formation of an integrated Women's Board of Missions. This "gave British Columbia women full representation without the necessity of a separate convention for women's work."[27]

To Union

So it was that two Conventions developed in adjacent western areas, communication between them being effectively barred by the formidable Rocky Mountains. In due time, however, events were to move them closer.

The Manitoba Convention held a second meeting in the year of its founding, 1882, reporting that it too, had approached the American Baptist Home Mission Society for aid and had been assured of $600. Support for one missionary at least had also been promised by the Maritimes. But Alexander McDonald's visit to central Canada for the same purpose was much less than successful and, thoroughly discouraged, he wrote home in 1882 to submit his resignation from the post of superintendent to which he had been appointed just six months before. The funds were simply insufficient, and with great reluctance the resignation was accepted.

From Association to Convention

The Pioneer's decision was to deprive the Canadian West of his services for a full decade, for although he undertook responsibilities as interim pastor of the new Brandon church, he accepted a call the next year to Grafton, then in Dakota Territory. During the period of his unfortunate absence, McDonald continued to demonstrate his attachment to the churches he had fathered, frequently coming back as fraternal delegate to Conventions. He finally returned in 1893 to become the first Baptist pastor in Edmonton.[28]

Meanwhile, the Manitoba Convention engaged R. H. Yule, formerly of Woodstock, Ontario, as a colporteur, half his salary being underwritten by the American Baptist Publication Society. The Red River Association was then merged into the Convention in 1884, the latter shortening its name to the Baptist Convention of Manitoba and the North-West and framing a new constitution, which included a strong statement of faith.

An Ambivalent Resolution

Support of western development continued to be a fairly contentious issue in central Canada. During the last assembly of the Baptist Home Missionary Society of Ontario the committee report was amended, and a further amendment made to the amendment, but no motion was carried on the issue. Finally, when discussion was resumed at a later session, the Society ended up passing this ambivalent resolution: "to the effect that the Manitoba and North-West brethren conduct their mission work in any manner pleasing to themselves, and collect funds wherever they may please."[29]

Whether this motion reflected a small measure of vexation or simply resignation is difficult to assess from the minutes.[30] In any event, the editor of the *Northwest Baptist* was pleased that "disallowances" had been removed.[31] The death-knell of the Dominion Board of Home Missions had been sounded and, for a time, missionaries were given unfettered access to Ontario churches. By 1895 an Ontario-Quebec Committee of Northwest Missions had been established to assist in making collections,[32] an arrangement continued for many years until a Board of Western Missions of the Convention was formed. The Maritimes continued to give their support separately.

Meanwhile — considerably earlier than for British Columbia where the ties were much stronger—the American Baptist Home Mission Society informed the Manitoba Convention in 1886 that they could give no further assistance.[33] The financial problems came at a most untimely moment, for the period was one of considerable opportunity on the Prairies. Historian and long-time superintendent C. C. McLaurin states that the period ending in 1887 was the most trying period in the history of Baptist Missions in the West — "the evening closing in under dark clouds." Many fields were left without support, he writes, and missionaries lacking sufficient income were leaving Manitoba for the East and South.[34] This upheaval was paralleled by political unrest in the form of the second Riel Rebellion.

Only two missionaries were being supported by the Dominion Board in all Manitoba and the Northwest at the point when it discontinued its work in Western Canada.[35] Left to its own devices the Manitoba Convention appointed a superintendent—the first since Pioneer McDonald had left five years before. The need had become crucial.

"The Most Prominent Personage"

John H. Best, who had been pastor of the church at Brandon, Manitoba, for just two years, agreed to undertake the task on a temporary basis, remaining for fourteen months, at which point he returned to his pastorate. Although his tenure was brief, his efforts were rewarded. He even obtained excellent results from his financial appeals during a widespread visitation to the Manitoba churches, secured McMaster and Woodstock students for summer pastorates and received the promise of regular aid from the Maritime Convention. (That aid actually continued until 1970.)[36] J. H. Doolittle was appointed in 1889 to succeed Best, but dwindling receipts because of successive crop failures forced the Manitoba Board to cancel the appointment after he had undertaken a three months' canvass of Ontario churches.

The next year, however, former Ontario and Quebec Home Mission superintendent Alexander Grant, who had come to Winnipeg's First Baptist Church as pastor, was pressed to become editor of the *Northwest Baptist* and corresponding secretary of the Convention. As secretary he acted virtually as superintendent. He took on all these responsibilities in addition to his regular pastoral duties. "In all our history," avers McLaurin, "Grant stands out as the most prominent personage, unless it can be that of Alex. McDonald, our pioneer."[37] When Alexander Grant died suddenly in a canoeing accident in 1897, western Baptists were deprived of a superb preacher and evangelist, a warm-hearted pastor, an able administrator and a citizen widely recognized in the community. He was a constant advocate of support for Western Missions whenever he made appearances before his former Convention of Ontario and Quebec. A memorial fund was gathered to assist the new Scandanavian church in Winnipeg which still bears his name.

Meanwhile — again in the turnabout year, 1887 — official women's work was inaugurated. That year the Women's Home and Foreign Mission Society of Manitoba and the North West Territories was formed, and within three years the society had a threefold impact. Assistance was provided for pastors F. A. Petereit and C. Phaelmann to carry out mission work among the German-speaking settlers; work was initiated among Native peoples near Portage-la-Prairie; and arrangements were made to send the West's first overseas missionary, Lucy H. Booker, to India.[38]

New churches were also on the increase. Butte, Manitoba, was formed in 1883 and in what was to become the province of Saskatchewan in just over two decades, a church was founded at Moose Jaw in the summer of the same year, with G. G. Davis, formerly of the Rapid City College and Academy, as pastor.[39] Moosomin church followed two years later under John E. Moyle, a graduate of Spurgeon's College in England.

Beyond, in the future Alberta, Winnipeg businessman H. H. Stovel made a trip to Calgary in 1888 and discovered a small group of fellow Baptists there. Vast throngs of immigrants were flooding west on the recently completed Canadian Pacific Railway, and Calgary was becoming a hub of activity. Even while Stovel was there, the little band of Baptists gathered in a home and established with just seven charter members the church that was destined to become the denomination's largest in Canada: First Baptist, Calgary. Until the arrival of the first ordained minister, George Cross, late in 1889, the congregation was served by two of its own laymen and summer student pastor H. E. Wise. This church later became a prolific "mother" of additional Calgary congregations. Members were generously sent to five new locations to set up churches between 1905 and 1909 — Wesbourne, Heath, Olivet, Hillhurst and Crescent Heights.[40]

Churches followed in quick succession in Neepawa (1889), Medicine Hat (1890), Regina (1891), and Edmonton (1893). First Church, Regina, resulted from the church-planting abilities of J. Harry King of Saint John, New Brunswick. Fifteen members formed the church in September; by year's end the number had reached forty-seven.[41] In Edmonton, a town then boasting a population of 1,000, a Mrs. Thomas Bellamy had discovered five fellow Baptists within a month of her arrival to take up residence, and wrote to Alexander Grant of the opportunity. In February

1893, with assistance from new superintendent H. G. Mellick, a church of nineteen members was formed. Reaching high, they issued a call to Pioneer Alexander McDonald, still in Grafton, (by then North) Dakota and he accepted.[42] In just two years, growth was such that members living on the south side of the river were able to withdraw and form a second church, Strathcona. Ever the pathfinder, McDonald, went with the Strathcona group — all nineteen of them.[43]

Nine German-Speaking Churches

Henry G. Mellick, a Prince Edward Island native, had taken over the superintendent's duties from Alexander Grant in 1892, the latter noting with some relief that a full-time missions officer was an absolute necessity. "You must remember that all except three of our churches are Missions — and there are about forty of them!" he wrote, adding that "Baptists in other parts of the country have their Home Missions: in our case, Home Missions have the Convention!"[44]

Unfortunately, the financial situation was destined to become even worse than it already was. The recession that plagued most of North America during the nineties cut mission giving from the central provinces to a trickle. Superintendent Mellick reported in 1894 that only $150 net was received after four months' canvassing in that Convention.[45] Despite the financial handicaps, however, by 1896 the number of Prairie churches had increased to fifty-two: thirty-six in Manitoba, nine in present-day Saskatchewan, and seven in what would later be Alberta. Included were nine German-speaking churches, one Scandinavian and one composed of Native peoples.[46]

A Disappointment

At the turn of the century, thoughts of co-operation and unity were strong in the minds of many Baptists, including those in western Canada. With Pioneer McDonald as moderator, an association of seven churches, including the German-speaking congregations of Leduc field, was founded in 1899 in the future Province of Alberta. Six years later the Assiniboia Association emerged in Saskatchewan, while in Manitoba three associations merged into one in 1907.[47]

The first all-Canada Baptist congress met in Winnipeg in 1900. Andrew J. Vining, an Ontario pastor who had moved to that city to minister in the Logan Avenue Church only to be persuaded to succeed H. G. Mellick as superintendent in 1897, played a key role in arranging the congress, which drew delegates from Halifax to Victoria. Hoping for movement toward a continuing all-Canada Convention, those in the West were disappointed — a disappointment confirmed next year when the central Convention gave no further consideration to the proposal.[48]

For western Canada the chief benefit proved to be the opportunity to show their eastern visitors something of the work first-hand. In "the best session of the Congress"[49] — moved from Winnipeg to Brandon for the occasion—delegates participated in the laying of the cornerstone of Brandon College. After the Congress was over, some of the delegates also continued across the continent to attend the regular annual sessions of the British Columbia Convention.[50]

That recently formed body had also been mobilizing its resources, bringing D. Spencer from Ontario to be its first superintendent. After reviewing the situation, Spencer declined the position and J. E. Coombs of Washington state, a former pastor of Calvary Church, Victoria, was persuaded to take it. Coombs remained less than two years, however, and was replaced by P. A. McEwen.

The Linking

Meanwhile, a close associate of McEwen, Wesley Thomas Stackhouse, former pastor of First Church, Vancouver, and of the mission church at Rossland, B.C., moved to Manitoba to succeed A. J. Vining as superintendent there. When financial stringency forced McEwan from office in British Columbia in 1904, that province with some reluctance agreed to a proposal made earlier by the Ontario and Quebec Convention that Stackhouse assume joint superintendency of the two Conventions, which he did the following year. The next logical step was, of course, to link the two Conventions. This was accomplished in 1907 as the Baptist Convention of Western Canada was formed. Two years later, after some organizational adjustment, its name was changed to the Baptist Union of Western Canada, its current designation.

Although the consolidation of the two Conventions was accomplished in a relatively short time, it did not come without struggle. Separated by a mountain barrier and claiming a distinctive history, British Columbia Baptists did not surrender their provincial prerogatives easily . . . indeed, they did not do so completely for some sixty years.

However, it was the B.C. Convention that made the original proposal to integrate, through notice-of-motion by P. A. McEwen in 1905. The Convention of Manitoba and the North-West agreed to the proposal the following year. Both Conventions approved the idea in 1907, and British Columbia was expected to set up a provincial association parallel to those already operating in Manitoba and the new provinces of Alberta and Saskatchewan. The first meeting of the Baptist Convention of Western Canada—representing 186 churches and 10,196 members[51]—was held in November 1907. Although their progress was made along a rocky bed, the two streams of Baptists in the Canadian West had finally been joined.

PART IV

Visions and
Nightmares

THE STORY IS TOLD OF A CANADIAN Baptist church in a mid-sized town, the centre of a fertile farming region. A special meeting of the church had been convened to consider the calling of a new pastor, one recommended by the pulpit committee.

As they discussed the qualities of the young man being appraised and his suitability to lead the 600-member congregation, one old-timer had some nagging doubts. A man who was always "Mr. Valiant-for-Truth," he got to his feet and asked, "What do we know about this fellow . . . what he believes? Is he liberal or conservative?"

There was a pregnant pause and finally a similarly venerable and equally concerned long-time member arose, drew himself slowly to his full height and remarked: "Oh, I don't think we should trouble about the man's politics" . . . and sat down.

And there ended the discussion. The vote was taken, the minister called.

Unfortunately the important problem of liberal or conservative theology, which was particularly acute during the restive twenties, did not usually lend itself to such a simple solution.

CHAPTER 19

A World View

"Had I a million pounds sterling I would still be a missionary."
—A. V. TIMPANY

One day in May 1792, an undistinguished and unimposing young cobbler-turned-village-pastor spoke these now-celebrated words in a sermon he delivered to the British Northampton Baptist Association: "Expect Great Things from God; Attempt Great Things for God." (based on Isaiah 54:2-3). He so gripped his listeners that a decision was soon made to form a "Baptist Society for propagating the Gospel among the Heathens."[1] The moment was historic. William Carey not only became "the heart and soul of the initial missionary enterprise of the Baptists,"[2] but is more generally recognized as having inaugurated "a wider and grander missionary movement than the world had seen before."[3]

Most Baptists—and not least Canadian Baptists—have continued to be devoted to the cause of missions. In the Maritimes, involvement in this endeavour may be traced back to 1814 when the first such missions project was launched. Writes historian Edward Saunders in the colourful prose of his era: "Carey's descent into the well of heathenism thrilled them and kindled in their hearts a fire of foreign missionary zeal. Every item of intelligence from Carey's mission, eagerly read by them, was fuel to the flame. . . . The missionary zeal flamed up at Chester."[4]

While that zeal found initial expression in financial support for the overseas outreach of others, the Maritimes were to produce a missionary couple of their own by 1845 — Richard and Laleah Burpee, who sailed that year for Burma. The central region of Ontario and Quebec followed in 1867 when Americus and Jane Timpany were commissioned for service in India, while in another twenty-two years the much later organized western Baptists provided their first overseas recruit in the person of Lucy H. Booker, who was sent to India under the Ontario and Quebec Board.

A Canadian Mission

The part of India that has been the scene of Canadian Baptist missionary endeavour for a period now stretching well into its second century is situated on the east coast off the Bay of Bengal. Work began in what is now the state of Andhra Pradesh. The state capital, Hyderabad, is near the two principal harbours Visakhapatnam and Kakinada, which play a large part in the Canadian Baptist overseas story.

Ontario's John McLaurin and his wife had arrived at Kakinada (then spelled Cocanada) early in 1873, and Mary Bates McLaurin herself gives a glimpse of the scene:

> Cocanada! And what did the eager missionaries find? A city of 20,000 inhabitants including 20 or 30 European government officials and business men; a lively export trade in cotton, tobacco, rice, oilseed, and various grains. There were three cigar factories — and every man, most women, and many children smoking . . . . On every hand were towering idol temples and tawdry wayside shrines, and the people . . . were wholly given to idolatry.

The only churches in the area were a Roman Catholic and an Anglican church, she adds, the latter being in charge of a government chaplain "whose last days before leaving on furlough were disturbed by the advent of the 'Anabaptist' missionary, against whom he warned as 'being a wolf in sheep's clothing who had come to rend the flock.' "[5]

A Survey of the Territory

It appears that John McLaurin was the one who first made the proposal to bring the Maritime missionaries from Siam and Burma to the Telegu country.[6] In 1875 W. B. Boggs, Rufus Sanford, W. F. Armstrong, George Churchill and their wives crossed the Bay of Bengal to join the McLaurins at Kakinada. Another couple arrived the following year, George F. Currie and his bride. The latter, the former Maria Armstrong, was the only member of the Maritime contingent who had stayed behind in Burma and there she had married Currie, who was on his way to India. Although the Curries were both Maritimers, they served under the Ontario and Quebec Convention, as the Maritimes had not been able to acquire the funds to send George Currie out.

Soon after their arrival at Kakinada, Boggs and Churchill joined McLaurin in an ox-cart survey of the territory north of the city, their goal being to set up mission stations beyond Visakhapatnam. On the way they preached in many villages, seizing every opportunity. At Vizianagram, a town of 50,000, with the aid of a British army surgeon, they established a Baptist church with eleven charter members. Their travels took them as far north as Palkonda and west to Bobbili.[7]

By 1879, after language study, the Maritime missionaries had become established in a separate adjacent mission in the northern area, the Sanfords at Bheemunipatnam, the Churchills at Bobbili and the Armstrongs at Srikakulam. The Boggs had been forced to return to Canada because of serious illness.[8]

Supreme Devotion

The work of those early years in the Telegu mission areas was difficult and debilitating. Various maladies and fevers such as cholera were a constant threat. Recently arrived Ontario-Quebec missionaries, the John Craigs, buried their first-born infant at Kakinada in 1879 and two years later Craig's wife, Martha, gave her own life soon after the birth of their second child. Also in 1881 the Churchills' little son Willie died in convulsion at Bobbili, aged six and a half. Pioneer missionary A. V. Timpany, just forty-five, died of either cholera or poisoning at Kakinada in 1885 and George Currie, who had cut short his Canadian furlough to take over Timpany's responsibilities there "soon fell at his post" (in 1886), stricken with dysentery and worn from the rigours of his first term, having had insufficient time at home to recover. He was only forty-two.[9] The cost of missionary service in the nineteenth century was high.

Yet with supreme devotion the little group pressed on. A mission school for boys was opened by John McLaurin on the porch of his Kakinada residence in 1875. By the following year, classes had been regularly established and the school was moved to a rented building in town. Soon a missionary compound was purchased and boarding facilities were made available. In the summer of 1876, Mary Bates McLaurin started a similar venture for girls, "but there were objections," she writes: "It was not the custom for girls to study. The gods would be angry. What did girls want with reading, anyhow? It was their business to cut grass for the buffaloes. Teach girls to read? Better go and teach the donkeys to read. Reading? No man would marry a girl that could read. She would read his letters and find out all his affairs. . . . All the same, the Girls' School became a fact, with the pupils attending Sunday school, and sometimes their mothers with them." When the McLaurins left on their first furlough over eighty girls were enrolled.[10]

Reaching the People

"For a long time," writes missionary and administrator Orville E. Daniel, "missionaries found Telegus in the strong grip of traditional Hindu customs and regulations."[11] Many of the people among whom they laboured were on the lowest rung of the caste system, really the outcasts or untouchables, and among these there was a growing response. However, among the Brahmins, the task was considerably more difficult, for a converted Brahmin always encountered severe persecution.

One successful approach was village evangelism. Frequently travelling by ox-cart, missionaries and/or national workers would stop in one of the hundreds of teeming villages, pitch their tent and call the villagers to hear the Word of God. Services would often continue from early morning until dark. Such tours might encompass twenty-five villages or more, and from the outset the missionaries enlisted capable nationals to work along-side them. A good deal of time was spent in training them for such tasks.[12]

High Tribute

The government of the United Kingdom, which claimed India as part of its empire for nearly a century before 1947, brought many benefits to the country, while the British themselves capitalized on the rich trading opportunities of the subcontinent. The warring land knew a great measure of peace, communications were vastly improved and a system of canals provided irrigation and improved crop production. On the other hand, the British Raj so dominated the political scene, in both the government and the civil service, that Indian leadership was frustrated and basic freedoms were denied the general population. In addition, education for the teeming millions seemed to be an impossible task, and when the Canadian Baptist missionaries arrived, little had been done in this area.

High tribute is paid by secular historians to the educational contribution of the missionaries, one notable authority citing the British Baptists who pioneered in the region just north of the Canadians, for particular achievement in this regard.

> [The missionaries] not only devoted themselves with courage to their special work of evangelization but also were the first to study the vernacular dialects spoken by the common people. Just as two centuries earlier the Jesuits at Madura, in the extreme south, composed works in Tamil, so did the Baptist mission at Serampore, near Calcutta, first raise Bengali to the rank of a literary language. The interest of the missionaries in education had two distinct aspects. They studied the vernacular, in order to reach people by their preaching and to translate the Bible; and they taught English as the channel of nonsectarian learning.[13]

In the Telegu area a good number of village schools were instituted by the Canadian Baptists, some of them residential. Often they were primitive, for it was difficult to find qualified teachers. Yet by 1880 there were thirty of these rural schools, some of them up to third grade, and "operating with various degrees of efficiency."[14] A seminary for the training of national workers in preaching and teaching was established by the McLaurins at Samalkot in 1882, the site having been donated by the Rajah of Pithapur.

Baptist Women Heard

The 1881 annual report of the Women's Baptist Foreign Missionary Society West (i.e., Ontario) contained the statement: "We have now a lady missionary appointed to work among the Zenanas" — not a new tribe, but simply "the women's section of the household,"[15] a group that had long suffered from low status. It must have been difficult for them to believe at first that "there is neither Jew nor Greek, . . . bond nor free,

. . . male nor female: for ye are all one in Christ Jesus" (Gal 3: 28). But thanks to the women of Ontario and Quebec, Mary Jane Frith brought the gospel to them, arriving at Kakinada late in 1881 specifically to work among them. Within two years she was able to write: "My hopes and expectations have been far surpassed; and we have no difficulty in getting into the houses; the doors have opened to us as fast as we were able to enter," and she reported that thirty-three zenanas were being visited by the staff—herself, a young Anglo-Indian assistant and a Bible woman— making at total of 635 visits that year.[16] (A Bible woman was a native Christian woman, trained by missionaries, who went into the homes in the villages, teaching scriptures to other women.)

In 1884 the central boards of the woman's aid societies of Nova Scotia, New Brunswick and Prince Edward Island merged to form the Woman's Baptist Missionary Union, forerunner of the current United Baptist Woman's Missionary Union. In the same year the Maritimes sent two single women as missionary reinforcements to India, A. C. Gray and H. H. Wright. Wright, like Mary Jane Frith, was assigned to zenana work—in her case to serve among the women at Chicacole.

To Relieve the Suffering

Nor were the needs of the body forgotten, either by the Foreign Missionary Society or by the women's societies. Aware of the desperate physical needs around him and finding little suitable medical aid, A. V. Timpany spent some of his precious furlough time in Canada attending lectures at the Toronto School of Medicine. On his return to India, he was immediately able to put his minimal medical knowledge to effective use with the aid of a set of instruments given him by women of the Toronto Baptist churches. He wrote: "We have to do no end of work here, besides preaching. I have more cases of sick to attend to than an ordinary doctor"[17]—and he did all his work from his little boat while he was out on evangelistic tour.

One of the three women sent to India in 1888 by the Ontario and Quebec women's missionary societies to do zenana service was Sarah H. Simpson. She had been trained as a nurse, and spent part of each morning in a clinic on her verandah to relieve the suffering around her—the only woman with medical skill in Kakinada, by then a city of 50,000. Five years later Dr. Everett Smith became the pioneer missionary doctor in the city, and he and his wife, Mary Chamberlain Smith, a nurse, served as a medical and evangelistic team. "To Dr. Smith," it was said, "the practice of medicine and the preaching of the Gospel went together."[18]

In 1895 the Smiths took charge of Yellamanchili, a fourth field, which had been opened four years before. There they ministered to both soul and body and also built a small hospital which by 1905 served nearly 3,000 patients annually. In 1904 Dr. Smith was responsible for the erection of the Bethesda Hospital in Pithapuram. Meanwhile, his sister Pearl, also a medical doctor, had come to India to marry missionary Jesse Chute and to serve with him on the Akividu field—he to become deeply involved in rural evangelism, she to serve at the Star of Hope Hospital, which they established.

Just before the turn of the century, missionary John Davis, having secured funding from the Mission to Lepers, began working among a large number of those so stricken at Ramachandrapuram, near Kakinada. By 1900 Davis had constructed a leprosarium that housed forty-one patients. The third year eighteen were converted. Yet Davis paid a high price. He himself contracted the dread and then incurable disease and was forced to return to Canada. He spent some years on a Manitoba farm until the advance of the malady forced him to be hospitalized in a New Brunswick sanitorium, where he died, a martyr to his Master's cause, in 1916. In letters painfully dictated just before his death, Davis wrote, "My mouth, throat and stomach are full of ulcers. . . . I cannot eat solid food . . . and sometimes I almost choke to death." Yet he was to conclude: "I have come to regard my sickness as a sacred trust from God."[19]

The Difficult North

By 1900 the number of churches in the three Telegu areas served by the Canadian missionaries — the south and centre manned by Ontario and Quebec, the north by the Maritimes — had reached forty-three.[20] The response had varied widely from area to area. Thirty-five of those churches were in the centre, around Kakinada, and to the south, where the missionaries from central Canada were working. Although by that time the staff of Maritime missionaries in the northern area totalled twenty, in addition to more than ninety native workers, their numerical results were less spectacular, their eight churches having a membership of 415.[21] Their harvest, while certainly more encouraging than the initial efforts of the celebrated Adoniram Judson in nearby Burma, who laboured for nearly six years before seeing the first convert, hardly matched the far more heartening results granted their next-door neighbours. In the six-and-a-half years from 1894 to mid-1900, the number of baptisms in the south and central areas reached 2,582,[22] the former yielding a large influx of sub-caste Telegus, the latter bearing spiritual fruit among all classes.[23] The northern region proved to be the most difficult of the three areas, although the "Serving Seven" had been reinforced over the years by a whole team of stalwart missionaries.

The Spirit Worshippers

In the years following union among Maritime Baptists, interest in missions overseas increased still further, eighteen new recruits setting out for India between 1905 and 1910. S. C. Freeman set sail in 1902, as did J. A. Glendinning, who, with his wife Eva,[24] was assigned to work among the hill people, settling in Parlakhemundi in 1905. It was a strategic move. Within two years Glendinning reported "a religious movement among the Paidi people which resulted in the baptism of thirty-two persons."

These were Oriya traders; who were much different from the Telegus of the plains among whom the Canadian Baptists had been serving.

There were to be more converts. A primitive tribe of spirit worshippers, the Soras, also lived in the hill villages — and Glendinning made them his chief priority. However, while the gospel had an immediate impact on the Oriyas, its effect on the Soras was to be delayed, though strong. But these were the small beginnings of the Sora and Oriya Missions.

To South America

The age-old debate as to whether people are largely shaped by events or whether events are shaped by people has never been resolved. There is little doubt, however, that the dream of one young man brought South America — and specifically Bolivia — to the attention of the Canadian Baptists. While the first missionary efforts were taking place in India, a student pastor in Pilot Mound, Manitoba, like William Carey before him, was summoned by a region of the world where the pure gospel had not yet penetrated.

The student, Archibald B. Reekie, attended McMaster University, and during the school year of 1895 was profoundly impressed by an article he read in the *Canadian Baptist*. It was about the deplorable state of religion in South America. Bolivia, one of the most deprived countries of the region, became his consuming interest, and the following year he decided to go there to see the situation for himself.

Dream Becomes Reality

After a long voyage from New York, Reekie landed at Lima, Peru, in 1896, where he remained for two months, studying Spanish with some British missionaries who were in the city. Moving on to La Paz, Bolivia, he was to make two discoveries: first that the deplorable spiritual state he had read about was all too pervasive, the country's Catholicism in a state of serious malaise; second that it would be dangerous to the point of death for him to attempt missionary work in that land. The constitution specifically stated that anyone who tried "to establish in Bolivia any other religion than that of the Roman Catholic Apostolic Church shall suffer the penalty of death."[25] Undeterred, Reekie returned to McMaster to complete his studies and then sought support to go back to Bolivia to work. His fearless enthusiasm must have been infectious. Despite the formidable deficit carried by its foreign mission board, the Baptist Convention of Ontario and Quebec responded with zest, and the young bachelor was commissioned as the first Canadian Baptist missionary to the Republic of Bolivia, arriving in Oruro on April 20, 1898.

Historian Orville Daniel describes the people among whom he was to labour:

Matching Bolivia's three-level topographic formation (divided by the towering

Andes — a bleak tableland, 3800 metres above sea level; a series of fertile valleys and a lowland region) her four and one-half million people have emerged in a three-level social structure. At the bottom are the Aymaras and Quechuas, descendants of two South American Indian tribes. These comprise over half the population. The middle class, totalling a third of the people, is composed of mestisos, obviously of mixed Indian and Spanish blood. At the top are the cultured "whites" . . . of predominantly European background . . . [who] control the country politically and commercially.[26]

It was providential that the city Reekie chose for the inception of his work was Oruro. A mining centre, it was also the focal point of a revolutionary liberal political movement which the year after his arrival toppled the entrenched reactionary government, which had been supported by the Roman Catholic Church.[27]

The Changing Religious Climate

After starting a small Sunday school class, Archibald Reekie opened Bolivia's first Evangelical day school in 1899, and on April 20, 1902, four years to the day after his arrival in Oruro, he baptized the first three converts and established the Republic's first Baptist Church. By that time seven reinforcements had arrived: Robert Routledge, A. G. Baker and Charles N. Mitchell, along with their wives and Bertha Gile. The Routledges began work in La Paz; the Bakers followed them to that city and the Mitchells began work in Cochabamba—the three cities of Oruro, La Paz and Cochabamba quickly becoming centres of outreach. Bertha Gile became a teacher first in Oruro and then in La Paz.

The first converts in La Paz included a Roman Catholic priest, and a church was formed there in 1903. As a sign of the changing religious climate, the Routledges had many upper-class students attending the day and night classes of their English school, where the Bible was one of the subjects. Among them were a nephew of the president, two Cabinet ministers and several prominent lawyers. Mrs. Routledge taught private English classes; among her students were two daughters and a niece of the president.[28]

In 1905 the liberal government passed a Bill granting religious liberty in the country. Although the Roman Catholic church remained the state church, a constitutional amendment passed the following year permitted "the public exercise of any faith." Missionary martyr Norman Dabbs was later to write: "It is highly probable that the granting of religious liberty would have been long if not permanently postponed had it not been for the presence of the resolute band of Baptist missionaries.[29]

The Canadian Baptist Foreign Mission Board

With the responsibilities of two widely separated overseas fields weighing heavily upon them, Baptists in the three regions of Canada began to consider seriously the possibility of united action—at least in that phase of their total mission. The India enterprise under the Ontario-Quebec and Maritimes boards was growing. Some eighty missionaries had been sent by the turn of the century: thirty-one men and forty-nine women, twenty-two of the latter being single women supported by the Canadian women's societies. Nearly three hundred native associates were also employed by the boards. The ninety day schools and ten boarding schools served nearly 5,000 pupils with three hundred forty teachers.[30] The demand for medical services was insatiable.

After an almost model beginning in Bolivia, difficulties outside the country put obstacles in the path of the missionaries there. When the home board* denied the Routledges the building funds they needed, they resigned to work for forty years in Cuba under the American Baptist Foreign Missionary Society. Bertha Gile married a La Paz businessman active in the city's small evangelical circle and left her position as a missionary. The Bakers were forced to leave La Paz because he developed an eye disease. Although Charles Mitchell stoutly remained to support Reekie, his wife had to accompany the Bakers home, also because of ill health. No further reinforcements arrived from Canada to support the staff, which was now down to just two men. In the circumstances, it was decided that Reekie, whose time for furlough had come, should return to Canada to seek additional manpower. Mitchell alone remained, moving to Oruro, the strongest of the three centres.[31]

Although union certainly did not come about only as a result of these movements, they undoubtedly hastened its arrival. As early as 1873, when the Telegu Mission was being considered, the secretary of the Ontario and Quebec Society had suggested the possibility of a union of all Canadian Baptists in overseas work. Although the recommendation was obviously ahead of its time, the missionaries themselves soon took up the cry. At the regular joint conference of the two groups in India in 1879 they pledged personal support to such a merger. At home, the Ontario and Quebec Society apparently made no response, and the Maritime board summarily indicated that such discussions should originate in Canada.

Undaunted, the missionaries repeated the exercise in 1887, the Maritime board on that occasion seeking and receiving authority from the Convention to confer with the Ontario-Quebec board concerning the action recommended by the Missionary Conference. The Ontario-Quebec response of the next year was that the time was not ripe for a merger.[32]

Such action and reaction continued until 1907 and the formation of the Baptist Union of Western Canada (for two years called a Convention). Until that time the Conventions of Manitoba and the North-West and British Columbia had provided their overseas support through the Ontario and Quebec board, but union brought obvious questions as to

---

*At the time—just before the formation of the all-Canadian board, Routledge was supported by the Board of Foreign Missions of the Baptist Convention of Ontario and Quebec.

how future support would be administered. Would the new Union of Western Canada launch out on yet another isolated venture or would Canadian Baptists join in a common cause?

After repeated consultations among the three regional bodies, the obvious decision was finally made. The Canadian Baptist Foreign Mission Board was incorporated in May 1911. Later the term "Foreign" was replaced by "Overseas," and with the founding of the Union d'Églises Baptistes Françaises au Canada, that Union became a member of the partnership. Representatives of each of the Conventions/Unions made up the board.

Canadian Baptists had entered a new era in overseas missions — embarking on a co-operative enterprise that was to become eminently successful in both spiritual and human terms. Another thirty-five years would pass, however, before wider collaboration would take place.

CHAPTER 20

Into the Twentieth Century

*"Only a large faith, built on generous, gigantic lines will
win the thoughtful men and women of the future."*
— WALTER RAUSCHENBUSCH

The Canada that entered the twentieth century had changed immeasurably from the motley aggregation of colonies and hinterland that had existed at the beginning of the previous century. Although it was still an integral part of the British Empire, Canada was a nation making its own decisions and looking to its own future. Sir Wilfrid Laurier, whose Liberals were in power at the turn of the century, was the country's first French Canadian prime minister. His title was a signal of the knighthood accorded him during the Jubilee celebrations marking Queen Victoria's sixtieth year on the throne—a recognition of the man and of his country's coming of age.

The Canadian Pacific Railway, completed in 1885, was proving to be a road of dreams for many a newcomer to the land. The influx of immigrants travelling by train to the West was soon to become a flood. In the decade between 1901 and 1911 the population would increase from about five and a half million to just over seven million, over half of the new immigrants going to western Canada.[1] Within five years two new provinces — Alberta and Saskatchewan — would be added to the seven already in Confederation. A nagging recession was turning into prosperity. In Laurier's famous words, this was to be "Canada's Century."

On the Threshold: Ontario and Quebec

Exhibiting a measure of pride, Baptists in Ontario and Quebec published a *Historical Number Year Book* in 1900, outlining their own accomplishments of the previous half-century. But some boasting could be excused, as church numbers had in fact more than doubled—from less than 200 to 464. About eighty of the new churches had been founded during the previous decade alone. The 8 associations had become 18, and membership had more than quadrupled—from under 10,000 to over 44,000. There were more than 20 Canadian Baptist missionaries in India, and a new mission field had been opened up in Bolivia two years before. Early in the nineties a Baptist Young Peoples' Union had been established for the Ontario and Quebec region.[2] As viewed by the Ontario and Quebec Convention president, John Stark, that year the opportunities ahead were unparalleled, with only one dangerous cloud on the horizon of promise:

> This is the growing time in Canada. Our people are waking up to a consciousness of their own national importance. A new spirit of hopefulness pervades the air. . . . But it is also a time of crisis in Canada. All that is choicest and best in our national life is trembling in the balance. Unless this growth in material things is matched by a corresponding growth in spiritual things, our vaunted prosperity will prove a calamity, rather than a blessing.

Noting the growing urbanization and convinced that historically "the decisive battles . . . have been fought, and lost or won, in the cities," the president reasoned: "This, then, must be our policy for the coming century. . . . The rural districts must be retained, and the cities must be gained."[3] A vision and a plan.

Both Sides at the Table

The coming together of the Baptists of Ontario and Quebec in 1888, with an Act of Parliament giving them Convention status and incorporating its boards the next year, was a successful move from the beginning, late though it was. The communion question, which had divided the constituency so rancorously for a large part of the nineteenth century, does not seem to have been considered much by those who fashioned the Convention structure, although there were some on both sides of the polity fence at the table. The question was never settled by vote of the Convention. While it was apparently assumed that the new body would be as "regular" in its communion observance as it continued to be in designation,[4] the whole matter was to become a non-issue. The "open" position of allowing believers other than members to share in the ordinance became the norm—this despite the continuing inclusion of a close-communion clause in many church constitutions. Open communion is today nearly universal.[5] While there are a few who might view this as a retreat or a weakening of spiritual fibre, it might also be seen as a recognition that new light had been drawn from the scriptures themselves, reinforcing the conviction that as the communion table is the Lord's, the invitation is also His.

The most noticeable break with past forms of organization was the new democratic unity in denominational affairs. Before 1889 any co-operative work had been undertaken by separate Societies, each responsible to its own individual subscribers and not to any general body. The new Convention, made up of church-selected delegates, elected boards to direct the various phases of activity. These reported on their stewardship both to the Convention and through the Convention to the churches. Initially, there were five such boards: home missions, foreign missions, ministerial superannuation, publication and church edifice. As the societies were transformed into boards, they were each incorporated, although they reported to an unincorporated Convention. Since incorporation grants status and protection as a legal body, the Convention's lack of such status proved to be a limiting factor later in the new century, when the boards were finally recast into departments. Originally, the churches were likely reluctant to allow the Convention to be incorporated for fear of its becoming too powerful.

A Significant Thrust

The major advance of the last decade of the nineteenth century continued into the first two decades of the twentieth. By 1920 membership had risen to a peak of 61,500 in 507 churches.[6] Between 1900 and 1910 seventy-five new churches were formed and forty-eight home mission congregations became self-supporting.

A significant thrust was made into what was called New Ontario, now the northwestern area of the province, repeating the outreach of some of the nineteenth-century pioneers. The number of churches in that area increased from five (plus two preaching stations) to thirty churches and more than forty preaching stations. Place names like Sudbury, Sault Ste. Marie, Blind River, Haileybury, Cobalt, New Liskeard, Milberta, Port Arthur, Fort William, Dryden, Kenora and Fort Francis appeared on Baptist maps. And in the large urban centres the number of churches increased—in Toronto from twenty-eight to forty-one.[7]

By the end of the decade, Toronto also had two Slavic missions, and Fort William one, while Scandinavian churches had been established at Montreal, Kenora, Port Arthur and Deer Lake, along with a mission in the Rainy River district northwest of Lake Superior. Dating back to 1851, when a church was founded at Bridgeport following a visit by August Rauschenbusch, twelve German Baptist churches were established. A number of them co-operated as members of Ontario and Quebec associations,[8] although they were still members of the Eastern Conference of the United States.

In the field of Christian education dynamic progress was also taking place. Sunday school pupils, who numbered 23,500 in Ontario and Quebec in 1888,[9] virtually doubled to just under 46,000 by 1920.[10] The Baptist Young People's Union of Ontario and Quebec, which had been organized in 1892, hosted the assembly of the BYPU of America in 1894 when more than 5,000 attended, nearly half of them from Canada.[11] By 1912 there were 205 individual Unions claiming 8,739 members and 31 Junior BYPUs with some 1,300 on their rosters.[12] On the academic scene, the total enrolment at McMaster had increased by 1910 to just over 300 students, 50 of whom were studying Theology.[13] Unfortunately, progress in the university and in the BYPU movement was soon to be reversed by the war. Both suffered heavy losses.

Speaking Out

Especially in the first half of the nineteenth century Ontario and Quebec Baptists had made a great impact on public affairs and church-state relations. They had been in the forefront of the anti-establishment ranks, and their voices had been heard loud and clear during the debate on the university question and the clergy reserves. With the forming of the Convention, Baptists in central Canada had acquired an even more powerful single voice to speak out in such areas — powerful enough that at one Convention, when it was "discovered that Sir John A. Macdonald was in the house," the prime minister, upon invitation, addressed the assembly.[14]

In the late nineties the *Canadian Baptist* carried no fewer than three editorials strongly supporting the Manitoba government's position on the school question, deploring the federal government's attempt to override provincial authority and reinstate separate schools. The Convention of Ontario and Quebec itself protested in similar vein.[15] The 1902 Convention passed a resolution objecting to the use of state funds for the "support of the clergy of any denomination or institutions owned and controlled by religious bodies . . . hospitals, or clergy,"[16] and two years later publicly deplored the action of the Ontario government in permitting municipalities to give aid to denominational universities and colleges.[17]

On more than one occasion the Convention resisted attempts to introduce compulsory Bible study in the public school curriculum,[18] holding it to be the responsibility of home and church. Even the concept of tax concessions for churches or their ministers was opposed.[19] These were hardly lukewarm Christians. There was a continual clamour for prison reform, the Convention Assembly in 1895 condemning the practice of sending "destitute poor to the county jails" and petitioning the federal government to establish a reformatory for young men.[20]

The Convention urged the churches to support the campaign for national Prohibition,[21] and on Prohibition Day, 1902, the *Canadian Baptist* carried the country's flag on its front page.[22] The next issue featured the banner headline, "Victorious." The Prohibition forces had won by a resounding two-to-one margin.[23].

A Cloud on the Horizon

During these times discussions concerning the union of different Christian denominations were taking place. As early as 1895 the Methodist General Conference had been making overtures to form a "Federal Interdenominational (church) Court." Convention responded to the proposals sympathetically, but pointed out that Baptist congregational polity "[rendered] its impossible for [them] to centralize power . . . so as to act authoritatively."[24] Later, in reply to an invitation to join with the Methodist, Presbyterian and Congregational churches in discussions of union, a Baptist committee was appointed to do just that. The report of that committee, which was adopted by the 1903 Convention, indicated that while rejoicing "in all the manifestations of mutual love . . . [they would] not admit that the organic union of all Christians is an essential condition of Christian unity, or even necessarily promotive of it." Citing differences which included varying views on such important principles as the nature of the church and baptism, the response concluded that "Baptists find it necessary to maintain a separate organized existence."[25]

Yet there was a cloud on the horizon that threatened that existence. In what one writer has described as "the initial skirmish,"[26] the Baptist Convention of Ontario and Quebec for the first time in 1908 to 1910 came face to face with an issue that had already thrown European and American religious communities into serious ferment — that of higher criticism. The resulting liberal-conservative or, as some choose to term it, modernist-fundamentalist debate finally resulted in schism. The succeeding chapter will consider the dispute in greater measure, but it can be said here that the almost too easy manner of concluding the preliminary encounter just postponed the final, critical decisions.

Dr. Elmore Harris, of the well-known farm implement family and minister emeritus of Walmer Road Baptist Church in Toronto, was the prime mover on the issue. As a member of McMaster's board of governors, in 1908 and 1909 he brought to that board a series of charges of promoting liberal theology against Professor I. G. Matthews, based largely on a course in Old Testament Introduction that Matthews was teaching at the university. A committee of the governors was established to investigate the matter but "failed to find the charges against Matthews proven," and no further action was taken.[27] The issue was raised at the 1910 Convention, however, where after long debate the Convention approved an amended motion accepting a statement made by the members of the theological faculty to the senate asserting that they relied "on the Senate and the Board of Governors to see that the teaching in the Institution is maintained in harmony [with the statement given by the faculty]."[28] In an all too reassuring comment, a writer of the day concluded: "This action was an endorsation of the general position defined by the Faculty and the senate and at the same time asserted the essentially conservative attitude of the denomination."[29]

Meanwhile, another conflict was drawing heavily upon the resources of the whole nation and the central Convention: World War I.

By the Atlantic Shores

Baptists have sometimes been indicted for being prone to division, but the charge certainly cannot be substantiated historically in the case of the Maritime Baptists. The first hints of a comprehensive union appeared when the New Brunswick Baptist Seminary was re-established in 1882.

Just two years after its revival the Free Baptists of New Brunswick volunteered to share in its operation — and it was renamed Union Baptist Seminary. Although the dually sponsored school fared little better than its predecessor, finally closing its doors for financial reasons in 1896, its establishment became the first significant step in a process which resulted in total amalgamation of the two streams of Baptists — Regular and Free, Calvinist and Arminian — in just over two decades.

A Problem within the Ranks

It had indeed seemed possible that the merger might have been completed in the mid-1880s, for in 1884, when the Maritime Baptist Convention proposed to the Free Baptists of New Brunswick that they join forces in promoting overseas missions, the Free Baptist Conference suggested that the broader question of general union be considered instead. Delighted, the Convention sent a delegation to the New Brunswick Conference's annual meeting in 1886, and a joint committee was set up to establish common principles of union. The committee reached agreement and the Basis of Union was adopted by Convention the following year, only to have hopes dashed when the Conference voted to defer action.

The difficulty facing the Conference was not so much the prospective union with the Convention as a theological problem within its own ranks that was impairing harmony. An extreme form of the doctrine of holiness, the concept of "entire sanctification" by way of a "second blessing," had advanced widely among the Free Baptists of both provinces. Those holding this view maintained that, following the first "blessing" of conversion, a believer might seek, and receive, the further instantaneous blessing of entire sanctification. The result would be a life entirely free from sinning. The Nova Scotia Conference spent many hours during the 1886 annual meeting discussing the internal doctrinal dispute, concluding that their churches should be counselled "to employ no minister who holds views of sanctification not in accord with our standards of faith" and to refuse licensing to any prospective pastor who subscribed to the concept of the "second blessing."[30]

As a result of the controversy, two factions did leave the Free Baptists, one taking the name Reformed Baptists, the other Primitive Baptists. The latter, who adopted a very simple form of church government and resisted an educated and salaried ministry, continue as a very small company; the Reformed eventually joined forces with the Wesleyan Methodists who hold congenial views on the holiness issue.

All Hurdles Cleared

The impulse toward unity did not die. The Convention of 1900 received a communication from Joseph McLeod, then corresponding secretary of the Free Baptists' New Brunswick Conference expressing the hope "that a plan of union honourable to both bodies may at the right time be suggested."[31] Three years later the "right time" appeared to be at hand when in response to further overtures from the New Brunswick Conference, the Maritime Convention formed a committee to meet jointly with the Conference to consider union on the basis proposed in 1887.[32] Assembling the same year, the Conference accepted the Basis of Union with slight amendment, the Convention following suit, again with little alteration.[33]

By 1905 all hurdles had been cleared, the churches of both bodies having had opportunity to consider the matter individually. With early favourable response from over 300 Convention churches[34] and the unanimous approval of the New Brunswick Free Baptist churches, arrangements were made for immediate consummation. The United Baptist Convention of the Maritime provinces officially came into being on October 10, 1905, in Saint John, New Brunswick, before capacity congregations—first in Waterloo Street Free Baptist Church and then in the Main Street Church of the Regular Baptists. This is how the sometimes puzzling term "United" was derived. It continues to preface the name of the now Atlantic Convention as well as its local churches—a term still honoured as a century approaches.

Gifted and Prominent

While a number of leaders among the Regular and the Free Baptists were influential in bringing the merger to pass, two names stand out: those of Dr. George O. Gates and Dr. Joseph McLeod. Minister of the First Baptist Church, Moncton, and then of the Germain Street Church, Saint John, and active in denominational missions, education and youth work, Gates was chairman of the Convention's union committee and secretary of the joint committee which discharged their tasks so effectively. Over many years he worked tirelessly toward the goal of union — "perhaps his most outstanding contribution," according to Maritime historian Frank Sinnott.[35]

Son of Ezekiel McLeod, "the towering figure"[36] of earlier New Brunswick Free Baptist life, Joseph McLeod was as gifted and prominent as his father. He succeeded his father as pastor of Fredericton's George Street Free Baptist Church and also followed in his footsteps as editor of the denominational journal. When that paper was merged into the Convention periodical, Joseph McLeod was initially named associate editor of the new *Maritime Baptist*, becoming its sole editor in 1909. It was he more than any other who persuaded the members of his Conference that unity was paramount. Fittingly, he was elected the United Convention's first president.

A Masterly Stroke

The Basis of Union, which laid the foundation for the United Baptist Convention in doctrine and in polity, was a carefully crafted document composed of a succinct eighteen-clause statement of faith and four simple articles concerning polity. Heading the confession was a strong statement declaring the divine inspiration of scripture, followed by a brief focus on each of the issues customarily included in the many Baptist statements of faith.

In a masterly stroke which overcame one of the main differences between the uniting bodies — that of open or close communion — the Basis simply made direct reference to the description of the Last Supper in Matthew 26:26–30 to allow each church to draw its own conclusion. Any allusion to the "perseverence" of believers or to the possibility of their "falling from grace" was omitted. Again the scriptures were cited as the final authority, hardly an arguable point among Baptists.

As the precepts of church government, while noting that "the voluntary principle* underlies the whole church polity of the New Testament," the Basis placed equal weight on "independence" and "interdependence." The more general bodies were to have power "to advise" the less general bodies and the individual churches, "to enforce advice with the strongest moral motives" and to exercise "the right to withdraw fellowship." Churches in difficulty were urged "to appeal to the more general body" and, should they decline to do so, that body had the prerogative to send a delegation to assist.

Regulations were established for the granting of church licences to preach, and alternative procedures for ordination were outlined. Either a council of representatives of nearby churches was to be called or "the more general body [was to] be requested to attend to the matter." At the request of at least one of the associations,[37] the 1922 Convention reassessed the ordination options after a year's committee study and voted to conduct all ordination examinations thereafter through an examining council whose members were to be named by the associations. Consistency and equality were secured by this method, which has continued to be used up to the present. Ordination is still carried out by the local church, which requests the examination. Although a church could ordain without following the accepted procedure, in turn it cannot violate the free choice of the other churches who have approved the process and compel them to accept or register the irregular ordination.[38]

During the first year of union, the Free Baptists of Nova Scotia held sessions at various church levels and finally decided to merge with the United Baptists. On September 3, 1906, delegates of the Nova Scotia Free Baptists met with those of the year-old United Baptists in Zion

---

*Baptists believe that individuals have been created free to choose their own spiritual direction according to their conscience, without coercion of church or state. Thus, any "establishment" in religious affairs is contested and state interference opposed. Ideally (although there have been more exceptions in Canada than in the United States) no state aid is acceptable and church and state are considered to be separate. In church affairs, the local group of believers has the right to choose its own connectional body.

Church, Yarmouth. The United Baptist Convention of the Maritime Provinces was complete — 64,189 members in 569 churches.

An Expectation of Union

As "the largest Protestant Connection in the provinces by the sea,"[39] the expanded Convention began with high hopes, although some external conditions almost immediately militated against rapid growth. As historian George Levy points out, by the time that union occurred, thousands had begun to leave the Maritimes, seeking greater employment opportunities in the New England states and western Canada. This emigration, which at times almost reached flood proportions, lasted until the Depression of the 1930s and deprived the churches of leadership and membership.[40]

Ministerial leadership suffered similar losses. It had been expected that union would eliminate the serious and long-standing shortage of pastors as churches were regrouped, but the problem did not disappear; there were simply not enough trained ministers.

For this, Acadia University must shoulder some of the blame, for though the forefathers had initially yearned for higher education to prepare ministers, Acadia had never developed a full curriculum of theological education. Because of this many men went for training to nearby New England, and a good proportion of them stayed there.

Although the course offerings improved greatly in 1901 when two chairs were established through the generosity of G. P. Payzant,[41] on the eve of union, the *Nova Scotia Free Baptist Banner* urged the university to make ministerial education its top priority,[42] and the same year the United Baptist Convention of the Maritime Provinces instructed the governors to consider the establishment of a full theological seminary "as soon as possible."[43] The board of governors responded positively the next year,[44] but it was not until 1923 that a complete department offering the Bachelor of Divinity degree was formed.[45] The process had taken the better part of a century.

The War Effort Supported

The advent of the First World War seriously affected the Convention, the churches and Acadia. Many pastors resigned to serve as chaplains or in other capacities, and church members enlisted in the forces by the thousands, many of them leaders of the churches. Of those who stayed behind, the pressures of the war effort at home were all-engrossing.

The smaller home mission churches were particularly hard hit, the New Brunswick board reporting many vacant pastorates in 1917 and not a single ministerial student from Acadia available even for summer service.[46] University enrolment dropped from 244 in 1914 to 127 in 1917. Over six hundred graduates, former students and undergraduates from the university and Horton Academy signed up for service in the war. Of these, sixty-three gave their lives and two hundred were wounded. Many earned decorations, Milton F. Gregg, later a federal Cabinet minister, receiving the coveted Victoria Cross.[47]

There is no doubt that Maritime Baptists gave strong support to the war effort. At the outbreak of the conflict, minutes of the Convention Assembly refer to "the righteousness of the cause," calling on Christian citizens "to aid King and country . . . with the loyal sacrifice of wealth and life itself if the issue demands."[48] Similar resolutions were passed by succeeding assemblies.

Work on the Home Front

The work of the churches did not come to a complete standstill during the conflict, however. Right in the midst of the strife in 1916, the United Baptist Convention of the Maritime Provinces launched a Five-Year Program, with five objectives: to add 20,000 to the churches by baptism, to fill every pulpit, to find capable leadership in all phases of church activity, to raise $75,000 in denominational funds that year and an additional $5,000 each successive year and, finally, to make the voice of the Convention heard on moral and social issues.[49]

While the goals were not fully attained, progress was made in some areas. Membership increased by nearly 10,000 and 75 percent of the financial objective was attained. By 1921 there remained some sixty pastorless home mission causes,[50] but there were fifty young men studying at Acadia for the ministry.[51] Maritime Baptists, at least, had prepared themselves for the aftermath of the war — "a decade of rampant materialism in which mankind began reaping to the whirlwind the awful harvests of hatred, suspicion, and unrest."[52]

The Burgeoning West

Two years after all Baptist work in the West had been merged into the Baptist Convention of Western Canada, that body became a Union. As a Convention, the amalgamated body was composed of three associations — one in each of the Prairie provinces — and the British Columbia Convention, which retained that title. Since British Columbia was reluctant to be downgraded to an association, Manitoba, Saskatchewan and Alberta were also given Convention status, and the whole organization was called a Union. No great change in structure was made until 1937 when the Baptists of Western Canada became a union of churches rather than of Conventions.[53]

Population Explosion

With the merger, a considerable denominational staff, nine in all, was put in place: W. T. Stackhouse, the chief architect of union, as general superintendent, D. B. Harkness as assistant, and provincial missionaries C. K. Morse for Manitoba, C. B. Freeman for Saskatchewan, C. C. McLaurin for Alberta and D. E. Hatt for British Columbia, plus three missionary evangelists.[54] Some objected that such an administrative staff was too expensive for a denomination of 186 churches and just over 10,000 members, but Stackhouse responded: "These men are pastors at large, the Province is their parish. They must visit the scattered Baptists in the new communities. . . . The only difference, is the extent of the mission field and the number of preaching stations."[55]

Stackhouse was probably right, for the area was vast—extending over more than half the nation's land mass — the population was exploding and opportunities for growth abounded. Within a year extensive progress had been made. With 1,150 baptisms, the largest total yet achieved in the West, membership rose to over 11,000, and the number of churches to 201. Like the other denominations, Baptists were doing their best to follow the spreading railroads, the homesteaders and the multitude of new settlements. By 1914 the total reached 253 churches and 17,855 members. But it languished at that level for over half a century. There were many reasons for this.

The early years of the twentieth century had seen the greatest ever wave of immigration, nearly a million and a half new citizens arriving in the Canadian West between 1901 and 1913. The urge to plant new churches was therefore all-consuming and, given the tenor of the times, understandable and commendable. Without the strong eastern support enjoyed by the other denominations and with a serious shortage of pastors, however, many of the new causes soon withered. Over sixty—nearly a quarter of the total—had fewer than fifteen members, and of these only five still survived in 1970.[56] Unlike the Maritimes where distances were much shorter and clusters of churches — "fields" under one pastor — became the early rule rather than the exception, the situation in the West of "the horse and buggy days" was not conducive to such arrangements, so each church grew up isolated from the rest and required its own pastor.

A United Representative Democracy

Initially the Convention, as it was then called, was made up of delegates named by the constituent churches, but the amended structure of 1909 required representation of the four provincial Conventions instead, and a total delegation of just over fifty to meet annually. Provision was made for the calling of a Convention Assembly, but travel costs made this impossible until the mid-twenties. So the Convention was at best a limited "representative democracy."

The new Union took on the functions of home missions policy, foreign missions, education and publications, the last involving the continued publication of the two denominational journals, the *Northwest Baptist* and the *Western Baptist*. They became one paper, initially called the *Western Outlook*.

While the Union was given responsibility for preparing the annual budget and raising funds, the provincial Conventions actually directed the home missions work and decided on expenditures. Stresses arose not only over how the few budget surpluses should be spent but also over the extent of the Conventions' obligation in facing large recurring deficits, sparked by a serious recession in 1907. It was also difficult for the Union's executive committee to act effectively with its fifteen members scattered across the region and unable to meet regularly because of the cost and inconvenience of travel. Most of the decision making thus devolved upon the few members who lived near the Winnipeg headquarters.

The College at Brandon

The issue of higher education also caused some tension. When the Prairie College at Rapid City had to close its doors in 1883, only three years after it was launched, some felt that small faculty and financial problems were the cause of its demise. However, Western Baptist historian J. E. Harris feels that the main reason for the breakdown was the movement to centralize theological training at McMaster.[57] That school's requirement that a student have a complete BA before taking theological training proved to be unrealistic for the hinterland. The editor of the *Northwest Baptist* observed in 1893: "There is not a solitary graduate of McMaster throughout this vast new Canada west of the Greak Lakes," adding, "[nor] a professor at McMaster who knows by contact a solitary thing about this country. . . . We want men graduates or no graduates . . . ."[58]

Facing a serious and continuing pastoral shortage, the Manitoba and North-West Convention had resolved in 1898 to open its own college — following an abortive attempt in Winnipeg eight years earlier. In Brandon, a small private academy was already in place, which had initially succeeded Prairie College at Rapid City. Its founder, G. B. Davis, soon turned the school over to his brother-in-law, S. J. McKee, who had been a Woodstock College professor. A few ministerial students began to attend the academy, the number increasing after 1890. When the Convention decided to inaugurate a denominational college at Brandon, McKee readily agreed to merge his school with the new institution and to serve on the staff.

Brandon College opened its doors in 1899 with Dr. Archibald P. McDiarmid, an Ontario pastor, administrator and graduate of the Canadian Literary Institute and University of Toronto, as principal. Of the 110 students enrolled, just thirty-six were Baptist.

Too Academic

In 1910 Brandon College became affiliated with McMaster in order to secure academic status. In spite of this link with the East, it might have been expected that the new Brandon College would aim to provide unique training to meet the needs of the frontier. But this did not happen, writes G. Keith Churchill in an assessment of the educational outlook of that day:

What is curious in the establishment of Brandon College is how all of the comments that had been made to the effect that what was needed in the west were ministers and not scholars, and that the academic standards set by McMaster were irrelevant and unrealistic in the situation on the prairies, were ignored. For what was established at Brandon was an institution that was committed to the same educational standards for ministry as was its sister institution in the east.[59]

The increasing emphasis on academic rather than theological education presented a serious problem from the standpoint of the churches. Brandon never offered a full theological course leading to a degree.[60] Thus the college satisfied neither those whose ambitions included such standing nor those who sought a more biblical and "practical" training for frontier ministry. As Walter Ellis observes, "The training of pastors was a priority for the churches but not the academics and controversy between the two groups erupted sporadically. Institutional autonomy protected the academics and they continued their ruinous policy."[61]

Although Brandon College made a splendid contribution, providing leadership for the churches and for the wider community, it would seem in retrospect that western Baptists would have been wiser to have focused on theological education designed to meet the spiritual needs of an expanding territory and to have left other facets of higher education to the provincial universities and the public purse. It appears that there just was never enough funding for both types of training in the small Baptist constituency.

To compound the difficulties, all the other western provinces—apart from Saskatchewan—also felt the need for their own colleges.

Okanagan College

When the British Columbia Baptist Convention was founded in 1897, a preliminary plan was adopted to offer matriculation subjects and the first two years of Arts by correspondence. The "hitherto untried"[62] program fell short and was soon discontinued. Interest did not fade, however, and in 1905 three Ritchie brothers who lived in the Okanagan Valley offered a site in West Summerland and seed money of $20,000 for the erection of a college.

The delegates to the 1906 B.C. Convention "closed their eyes to the warning that a more populous and central location should be chosen, particularly in light of the probable opening of a provincial university a few years hence,"[63] and proceeded to build Okanagan College. At no time during its brief history did Okanagan College offer formal theological training, although courses in homiletics and pastoral studies did appear in 1911. Once again, ministerial education was given low priority, a fact which undoubtedly affected church support and hastened the financial crisis that brought about its closing in 1915. Enrolment had reached a high of 121 in 1911–12, only to fall precipitously with the advent of World War I.[64]

McArthur College

Alberta's early venture into higher education was even less productive but also less costly. In 1905, A. J. McArthur of Calgary had offered the Manitoba and North-West Convention a choice site overlooking that city's Bow River and an amount of $25,000 toward the establishment of a Baptist college. With Brandon already operating, the Convention declined the generous but impractical offer. In 1912 McArthur's widow renewed the proposal.

Despite a motion passed by the Baptist Union Assembly that very year to inaugurate "new Art institutions or new Departments . . . only in the event of adequate provision having been made for the theological training of our ministry," the Education Board of the Union accepted the offer, and so did the Alberta Convention.[65] McArthur College was formed, a principal appointed. It never advanced beyond the name, however. The recession of 1913 and the war that followed forestalled any development.

As Churchill points out, a straightforward, consistent and comprehensive educational policy was obviously lacking. "From the outset", he says, "the reason for considering education at all was for the training of ministers. But none of these institutions ever adequately filled that purpose." He adds, "There was, as well, no clear rationale as to why Baptists should be in the business of providing courses in Arts when the provincial universities which were being created at the time could do the job far more adequately."[66]

Even more disconcerting, the one western college that still existed at the end of the 1920s was to be a focal point of a debilitating controversy which was to divide the denomination — Centre and West — and long retard its progress.

CHAPTER 21

In the Eye of the Storm

"The Churches . . . ought to hold communion among themselves
for their peace, increase of love, and mutual edification."
— *SECOND LONDON CONFESSION, 1677*

The controversy that shattered the after-war calm in Canadian Baptist circles central and western could hardly have been contained any longer. The "initial skirmish" regarding liberal and conservative interpretations of the scriptures had been restrained in 1910 but the pressure was building. As Canadian writer Douglas J. Wilson notes, Baptists were confronted with "the 'eroding' influences of modern biblical scholarship"[1] later than most other denominations, but for the immediate future the devastation was to be far more traumatic.

Shifting Foundations

Stemming from the rationalist, liberal thinking of the eighteenth century's Age of Enlightenment, the liberal/modernist theological movement spread from Europe to North America later in the following century. In Europe the movement had been dominated by such German scholars as Schleiermacher, Hegel, Ritsch, Harnack, Baur and Wellhausen and the English naturalist Charles Darwin, and its appearance on this continent was destined to affect greatly the outlook and development of almost every church body, particularly in the last years of the nineteenth century and the first half of the twentieth. As Walter Ellis writes: "Modernism placed reason above the Bible, utilized special tools for interpretation of sacred symbols, and adopted an imminent eschatology and an optimistic attitude to the future which enabled mobile evangelicals under pressure from secular peers to accommodate to the 'scientific symbols' of the age."[2]

The Integrity of Scripture

For the first time in history the Bible was subjected to close scientific analysis, and theological presuppositions were seriously questioned. "Lower," or textual, criticism was applied to the content of scripture, while "higher criticism" approached Holy Writ on a literary-historical basis, plumbing its sources, examining its environment, classifying its component parts and challenging its supernatural elements.

It was the approach of the latter that was so disturbing to orthodox Christians, for some of the "assured results" of this modern analysis questioned the very basis of belief, the integrity of scripture. Writing in the *Encyclopedia of Religion* in the mid-1940s, Martin Rist enunciates the extreme liberal position explicitly: "The Bible is now considered to be a human record, not a record of revelation . . . . [It] is being studied by the best methods of historical criticism applied to all the available sources of information. This is far removed from the traditional methods of Bible study."[3]

As might be expected, many universities and seminaries were at the forefront of this new phase of learning. Although the radical viewpoint expressed by Rist was not embraced by all, few were untouched by it. Of the three Baptist institutions of higher learning in Canada, McMaster University and Brandon College were influenced the most and so came under the sharpest scrutiny by their church constituencies.

The preoccupation with war during the 1914–18 years no doubt pushed these considerations into the background, but the *Canadian Baptist* of October 2, 1919, provided a platform for the opening salvo of a debate on the issue that was to rage for a decade. Surprisingly, the first shot did not censure higher criticism, but defended it. In a lead article on the editorial page of that issue, entitled "The Inspiration and Authority of Scripture," the writer clearly upheld what was by then perceived to be the liberal position, and the battle was on.[4]

A Letter to the Editor

An able exponent of the orthodox, conservative cause immediately took up the challenge. Until his comportment finally brought the large majority of his fellow Baptists to the reluctant decision some eight years later to exclude him from their assemblies, Thomas Todhunter Shields — or "T.T." as he came to be known—was at centre stage. T.T.'s letter appeared just two weeks after the first article had been printed. In it he protested that the first article had been printed. In it he protested that the unsigned article should not have been presented on the editorial page without a by-line, since that gave the impression that the opinion was accepted policy.[5] A reasonable point it seems. Unwisely, as it was to turn out, the *Canadian Baptist* replied with a similar and again unsigned editorial in the same issue as the Shields letter.[6]

Shields then appealed to a forum which for Baptists is definitive — the Convention Assembly. He offered an amendment to the report of the publication board in which Convention declared its disapproval of the October 2nd editorial, although it expressed confidence in the editor: ". . . on the ground that in its representative character as the organ of the Convention, *The Canadian Baptist* in the said editorial commends to its readers some new vague view of the Scriptures different from that to which the Convention declared its allegiance in 1910, and upon which the denominational university is declared to be founded."[7]

William W. McMaster, Senator McMaster's grandnephew and pastor of Hamilton's James Street Church, seconded the motion. It was passed by a large majority after considerable debate. The reference to "the denominational university" in Shields's amendment may indicate that someone connected with McMaster University had written the offending editorial.

A Mediating Role

Born in Bristol, England, in 1873, the son of an Anglican clergyman who had become a Baptist by conviction, T. T. Shields received his only formal education in a small private school and was then tutored by his father. He entered the ministry at the age of twenty-one when his family moved to Canada and he became pastor of the Baptist church in Florence, in western Ontario. His father accepted the call to Vittoria in the same province.[8] After working in a number of other pastorates, T.T. became minister of Adelaide Street Church in London, Ontario, in 1904, serving until 1910 when he was called to Jarvis Street, Toronto, the Convention's largest church.

It is interesting to note that Shields had played a mediating role during the first controversy over the liberal/modernist issue back in 1910. At that time he seconded the motion for an amendment by which Convention approved the statement of the McMaster theological faculty, relying on the senate and board of governors to ensure compliance. He afterwards regretted doing so, contending that at the time he "was young and inexperienced."[9]

Shields had apparently accepted the Jarvis Street call with reluctance. The church and McMaster were both in Toronto, and at an early stage he began to mistrust the university's attitude toward him, probably because of his own relatively limited formal training. Later he was to write with some bitterness: "Non-McMaster men were tolerated for the doing of rough work, even as the Chinese coolies were used to do rough work on the Western Front in the Great War . . . . To my personal knowledge certain of the Faculty of McMaster look upon non-McMaster men as useful only for carrying meals to the graduates . . . . "[10]

Having accepted the call, however, Shields wasted no time in putting his many skills to work. During the first four of the forty-five years he was to spend at Jarvis Street, over seven hundred members were added to the roll. But all was not well. The war brought its strains, particularly as Shields spent a lot of time in England during that period, preaching frequently at Spurgeon's Tabernacle. The very fact that he spoke there is high tribute to his striking abilities as a preacher, but it also suggests he may have had an interest in being called to that church, which was pastorless at the time.

Split at Jarvis Street Church

Serious difficulties concerning Shields's absences, his rigid views and autocratic methods came to a head at Jarvis Street in 1921 and Shields asked for a vote of confidence. This he received, but not with the two-thirds' majority he himself had established as necessary. In spite of this he remained, but shortly thereafter a crucial meeting was called and a resolution was passed asking for his resignation. When he declined, the meeting was adjourned pending further consideration. In the ensuing interval a number of new members were added after an evangelistic campaign. Enough of these newcomers supported the pastor on a second vote that the previous ballot was upset 350 to 310. In the resulting contention nearly 350 members left the church to form a congregation, which later became Park Road Baptist Church.[11]

The stresses engendered by this "split" undoubtedly affected Dr. Shields's relationships within the Convention, particularly since a number of leaders in the denomination were among those who left Jarvis Street. Locally, however, the pastor was now assured of a Jarvis Street membership solidly in his camp, a strong sounding board for the call to arms that was soon to follow.

A Rising Fundamentalism

Meanwhile, the surging American Fundamentalist movement found a strong ally north of the border in T. T. Shields. In 1910 the first of a series of small books entitled, *The Fundamentals: A Testimony of the Truth*, rolled off presses in the United States. Their explicit aim was to defend traditional scriptural positions in the face of the rising liberal/modernist tide. "Fundamentals" quickly became a watchword, a rallying call, and the more militant defenders of the orthodox faith came to be called "Fundamentalists." As their opponents used it, the term was unflattering. The Fundamentalists viewed "Five Points of Doctrine" as basic to any summary of faith: (1) the inerrancy of scripture, (2) the deity of Jesus, (3) the substitutionary atonement, (4) the physical resurrection, and (5) the bodily return of Jesus.[12]

Committed to Cleansing

Shields obviously had problems with the movement, particularly with its dominant premillenial eschatology and dispensationalism.[13] In author Leslie K. Tarr's view, Shields held "a modified amillenial view" of last things and "could be as vitriolic in his denunciation of 'Scofieldism' as he was in his denunciation of modernism."[14] Yet from the first he felt that the common cause in opposing liberalism was paramount, and he publicly supported the World Christian Fundamentals Association when it formed in Philadelphia in 1919. Seven years later he presided over its annual conference in Toronto.[15]

Shields also linked up with the Americans' Bible Baptist Union when it became a transborder organization in 1923. This Union had been formed two years earlier by an extreme faction of the U.S. Northern Baptists, who were dissatisfied with the conciliatory approach of the National Federation of Fundamentalists of that Convention. When the Union expanded, Shields, J. Frank Norris of Texas and William B. Riley of Detroit became co-presidents, Shields remaining an active president throughout the life of the Union.[16]

By then fully committed to the task of cleansing the Baptist Convention of Ontario and Quebec of liberal/modernist inroads, in 1922 Shields began publishing the *Gospel Witness*, a weekly magazine which soon became a powerful vehicle in furthering his cause. The same year he used the pages of that paper and other literature to discourage Baptists in Ontario and Quebec from supporting the re-election of three fellow-members of McMaster's board of governors whom he considered suspect.

At the next Convention Assembly, however, the three were re-elected, along with another he had not opposed. Furthermore, the university was given a strong vote of confidence, "the Convention [deprecating] the method and substance of the attacks made by one member of the Board. . . . "[17]

Inharmonious Views

Taking this setback in his stride, T. T. Shields soon found further cause for protest the following year. When Dr. Howard P. Whidden was installed as Chancellor of McMaster in November 1923, replacing the retiring Dr. A. L. McCrimmon, the university chose the occasion to honour the head of Brown University, Rhode Island, the oldest Baptist institution of higher learning on the continent. In doing this the university had not acted too wisely, for Brown's president, Dr. William H. P. Faunce, had "written disparagingly of those who still combated the evolutionary theory in the schools and the higher criticism in the universities."[18] With this new ammunition, Shields was able to renew his attack on McMaster from the pulpit and through the pages of the *Gospel Witness*.

The majority were with him in this protest. Four associations passed resolutions urging care in the granting of honourary degrees, and Convention itself acted, voting at the 1924 Assembly, "that, without implying any reflection upon the Senate, this Convention relies upon the Senate to exercise care that honorary degrees be not conferred upon religious leaders whose theological views are known to be out of harmony with the cardinal principles of evangelical Christianity."[19]

Referring later in the *Gospel Witness* to the 1924 Convention, Shields wrote: "The action clearly announces to the world that the Denomination stands true to the principles of Evangelical Christianity which Baptists historically have represented . . . . Now that the air is clear we sincerely hope that we may be able to go on with our work."[20] "For many in the Baptist Convention, Dr. Shields' stock was never higher," writes W. Gordon Carder, "the bitter critical note disappeared from his editorials. His sermons seemed to strike a new note."[21]

The Final Issue

Sadly, the calm was short-lived. Within a year the university became the focus of further contention, which ultimately led to rupture. After the sudden death of Dr. J. L. Gilmour, professor of Practical Theology, late in 1925, McMaster's board was unexpectedly faced with the task of finding a replacement. It might have been expected that considering the background of recent Convention experiences and the evident theological thinking of most Baptist church members, the governors would have exercised the greatest care in making their choice. However, as McMaster historian Charles M. Johnston has written, "In considering the appointment, the University appeared to be giving notice that they had no intention of permitting the growing controversy with Shields to impair their right to hire qualified people."[22] The man they hired was L. H. Marshall, English theologian, teacher and pastor, then minister of a Baptist Church in Coventry.

Matching Skills

Shields was in the United States when the university senate confirmed the Marshall appointment in July 1925, but that did not stop him from sending a telegram in protest.[23] Having heard from an English correspondent an allegation that Marshall was in the liberal camp, Shields had urged delay and further investigation.

Marshall arrived in time for the Convention Assembly of October 1925, and there he demonstrated debating skills that matched those of Shields. Defending himself ably against the charges levelled against him in the press and from the Jarvis Street pulpit, Marshall obviously convinced the majority that his cause was righteous, for the Marshall appointment was approved in the end.

This defeat on the floor of Convention only served to increase Shields's militancy. Protest rallies were held and through the pages of the *Gospel Witness* and from the pulpit he expounded upon such sensational topics as "How Professor Pontius Pilate Dealt with the First Fundamentalist."[24]

Soon after the 1925 Convention, in a fateful step which practically ensured that a schism would take place, Shields decided to set up a rival educational institution, editorializing in the *Gospel Witness*, "It is useless to expect united action in our educational work . . . . a group of men in the denomination are determined to force upon us a moderate modernism . . . . Who wants a mild attack of smallpox or leprosy? . . . . All these things make us feel that there is nothing to do but go on with the college enterprise." Gifts for such a college were already being received, he reported.[25]

Apology Requested

At the Convention Assembly of 1926 the debates of the previous year were repeated, with increasing intensity and bitterness. After long and sometimes passionate debate, often featuring Marshall and Shields, the annual report of the university was adopted, 708 to 258. The Jarvis Street minister had all but lost his personal battle.

Adding to Shields's discomfort was a motion offering him the opportunity to apologize. Failing this, his resignation from McMaster's board of governors was requested and Jarvis Street Church was to be notified that he would no longer be an acceptable Convention delegate until the apology was made.[26] Shields, of course, refused to apologize. Then, because the federal incorporation of the Ontario and Quebec Convention made no provision for the dismissal of a church from its ranks, an approved resolution also instructed the executive committee to seek authority from Parliament to make such a change in the constitution.

The dénouement came rapidly. Although Shields had stated that he would not leave the Convention but would "stay and play brother to everybody who needs that help,"[27] his immediate moves indicated that he was planning to do something else. Although Jarvis Street was not the first to do so, the initial action being taken by Stanley Avenue Church, Hamilton, the Toronto congregation at its November 7th service passed a resolution to discontinue support of Convention projects.[28]

Moves to organize outside the Convention soon followed. A "new women's missionary society of Regular Baptists of Canada" was established, and the "college," which Shields had planned in 1925 became a reality with the opening of the Toronto Baptist Seminary in January 1927. Shields was its president. The same month the Regular Baptist Missionary and Educational Society was formed, and the *Gospel Witness* was adopted as its official organ. Shields reported that 311 delegates representing 61 churches attended the Missionary and Educational Society's organizational meeting.[29]

Amendment Passed

Although he essentially removed himself and his church from the Convention at the October 1927 Assembly of the Baptist Convention of Ontario and Quebec, Shields continued to protest the impending dismissal of his church. "Nothing more venomous ever opposed the Gospel of Christ in the days of the Spanish Inquisition or the Bloody Queen Mary, than the venom which McMaster breathes forth," he wrote.[30]

Despite the clamour, the crucial Bill was passed by Parliament, thus putting Convention in the position where it could dismiss the Jarvis Street Church from its ranks. Beginning October 12, the Assembly faced the tragic issue. Although Shields had the previous month asked in a sermon topic: "Shall Fundamentalist Baptists Withdraw and Form Another Convention in October?"[31] he surely was aware that he had crossed his

Rubicon. After several tumultuous sessions Convention passed the resolution to amend the Constitution.[32] The next day the right of Jarvis Street Church, Toronto, to send delegates to Convention was withdrawn,[33] and so the Convention Assembly of 1927 concluded. In the words of the editor of the *Canadian Baptist*, it was "the most tragic and sorrowful ever held by the Baptists of Ontario and Quebec."[34]

Had that ended the matter, the result would have been sorry enough. But there was more to come, much more. Before making the motion to exclude Jarvis Street delegates, the Assembly had resolved that "such churches as have . . . . identified themselves with . . . . support of [the Regular Baptist Missionary and Educational Society] should therefore be considered as being not in harmony and co-operation with the work and objects of this Convention."[35] Others were thus excluded from the Convention, as well.

The Union of Regular Baptist Churches

Fully anticipating this action — one which they had in fact invited — the departing group had already made preparations. Within a day Jarvis Street Church resolved to form a new independent Baptist body, somewhat brashly assuming the name that had long marked the Convention Churches — Regular Baptists.[36]

The following week the Union of Regular Baptist Churches of Ontario and Quebec was formed, with Shields as president. About one hundred churches were represented at the founding meeting, although only some thirty agreed to form a new Union. By the middle of November forty more had become associates, and at the initial convention a year later seventy-seven churches were reported, a half dozen of them newly organized. Membership in the Union was about 8,500. One-seventh of the Baptist churches and members in Ontario and Quebec had thus departed from the Convention. But the loss to the original Convention was to be much greater than the numbers implied.

The Dominant Figure

Thomas Todhunter Shields had both won and lost at this stage, although ultimately he was to be left almost alone and undefended. For the time being he had established and headed a movement which seemed likely to carry forward his often repeated principles. Then, without doubt, he had awakened Baptists generally to a movement in their midst which was more substantial than had originally been admitted.

Later assessment of the position of L. H. Marshall with whom Shields clashed and through whom he essentially came to the point of defeat and schism, would appear to indicate that the able professor was something other than a "conservative evangelical." In an article in the *McMaster Monthly* in 1930 Marshall highly praised the German scholarship that had produced the liberal/modernist thrust: "No matter what subject we study, we cannot afford to neglect German Scholarship," he wrote, adding that, "In the department of theology . . . her contribution is unique. Whatever the vagaries of German radicalism and extremism may be, she has done a vast amount of illuminating and constructive work."[37] Another observer felt that Marshall "did stand in the modernist camp and that he saw his role at McMaster [as] one of championing the new theology against a confederacy of prejudice and suspicion."[38]

The tragedy of the situation is that while Shields had demonstrated by earlier supporting votes that the great majority of his fellow Baptists stood with him in defence of the orthodox faith, his personal traits were to destroy much of their trust. Despite his unmatched gifts as preacher, writer, debater, and publicist, Shields' contentiousness and sometimes obscurantism, together with his passion for power and his dictatorial methods, undid much of his work, and finally left him with few advocates. He made himself such a massive target that even his least perceptive detractors could easily "shoot the messenger" rather than having to deal adequately with the message he bore.

Many of the Convention's preponderantly conservative church members were more than a little confused by the high-powered debates between Marshall and Shields. Although they appreciated the issues, they were unwilling to follow the headstrong Jarvis Street pastor to the limit and demolish the structure that had taken more than a century to build up.

Regrettably, this decade of central Baptist History appears to be the story of one dominant figure. It ought to have been otherwise. More moderate means could have been used to face the crucial issues squarely without making a martyr of a man in the eyes of some, a malcontent in the view of others. Furthermore, schism is a nearly irrevocable action, which inevitably leaves a residue of resentment, and denigrates the cause in the eyes of the community. The crisis was apparently one of leadership, as the differences did not run deep enough among the rank-and-file members to justify such a drastic step.

Estrangement in the West

The West faced a similar convulsion during these years, although it was not of the same magnitude. And just one province was affected to any significant degree—British Columbia.

The Baptist Union of Western Canada entered the decade of the 1920s with mixed emotions. C. R. Sayer, their "lay" general secretary of the war years, led the Union in reducing their heavy $24,000 debt to zero by the end of 1918. A five-year program, aimed at growth in membership, bringing mission churches to self-support, recruiting men for the ministry and relieving the debt of Okanagan College, had resulted in the establishment of ten new churches.[39]

On the other hand, the workload was heavy and human resources were scarce. Out of a resident membership of only 15,000, some 2,500 volunteered for war service. By 1917 nearly a third of the churches were without pastors and of the multitude of small congregations that had proliferated in earlier "advances," thirty had closed. "The startling growth of the denomination was stunted," writes Margaret Thompson, "and never fully recovered."[40]

Patterson Named General Secretary

In 1919 the Reverend Frederick W. Patterson, a former Maritimer, was named general secretary of the Baptist Union of Western Canada after serving pastorates which included the First Baptist churches of Calgary, Edmonton and Winnipeg. He had also assumed extra responsibilities in 1916, becoming editor of the denominational journal, *The Western Outlook*, almost immediately changing its name to *The Western Baptist*. He held the position of general secretary until 1923 when he accepted the presidency of Acadia University.

Patterson was not to leave for the East, however, before the struggle already underway in central Canada had spread westward. Indeed, he was only in his second year of service when the first portents of trouble appeared. As in Ontario, the denomination's school of higher learning — in this case, Brandon College — became the centre of the controversy.

The Rhetoric Heightens

In 1920 a young Vancouver pastor, the Reverend W. Arnold Bennett, a Britisher who had studied at Brandon, stood before the Baptist ministerial association of that city and charged that the teaching of Professor Harris MacNeill, head of the theology department of the college, was heretical.[41] Disturbed, the ministerial association asked Brandon's governors to question MacNeill concerning his convictions about certain tenets of scripture.

MacNeill's responses were obviously satisfactory, for the Vancouver ministerial accepted them unanimously and promised to help restore confidence in the school. Bennett did not desist, however, continuing instead to pamphleteer against "unorthodox and faith-wrecking" teaching.[42] The rhetoric heightened as the 1922 annual meeting of the Baptist Union deplored the growing propaganda as "despicable, unchristian and immoral." The Union did appoint a commission, however, to undertake "a thorough review in the curriculum in [Brandon's] theological department."[43]

At about this time there was also growing unease about the somewhat limited democracy of the Baptist Union. Although the Union had originally been designed as a "convention," composed of delegates of the churches, two years after its founding it had become a Union consisting of a restricted number of representatives from the four western provincial Conventions. In practice, without direct input from the churches, the Union was more like a board of directors than a Convention. This became an additional irritant.

"Interested Laymen"

At the 1921 British Columbia Convention some opposed the continuing support of Brandon College, and the Union was also criticized for allegedly spending most of the budget assigned for ethnic work on the Prairies. These issues were settled, however, and the Union received a unanimous vote of confidence. It was decided that the B.C. churches would be urged to give full support to the Union budget.

Apparently in response to this appeal, a group of "interested laymen" published a pamphlet attacking the Union on the same two points: Brandon College and the disposition of funds for foreign-language mission work. The pamphlet was distributed widely but published anonymously, and when the B.C. Convention's board offered to meet with the authors, they were rebuffed, as the originators "did not want their names known."[44] They were keeping the quarrel going but accepting no responsibility for their actions.

The next year the Union took its first two steps to deal with any possible objections from B.C. laymen and ministers. The B.C. Convention was granted the right to control the expenditure of its own budget receipts, except for a fixed amount for overseas missions, and the requirement for any funds from British Columbia for Brandon was dropped. Two years later the Union removed the stipulation that prevented the B.C. Convention from raising monies beyond the budget. Clearly, the Union had bent over backwards to meet the questionable demands.

But before the end of 1921 the Interested Laymen published a second leaflet, entitled "The Dangerous Peril of Religious Education." Quoting from an address by W. B. Riley (soon to be Dr. Shields's co-president of the Bible Baptist Union), the pamphlet took aim at the Religious Education Committee of the B.C. Convention, its director Dr. J. Willard Litch and its interdenominational connections. Once again major steps were taken to meet the criticism. The name of the committee was changed to "Christian" Education and two years later the interchurch links with the Religious Education Council of British Columbia were cut.[45]

Rending the Fabric of Unity

Meanwhile, the commission on Brandon College appointed at the Union's 1922 annual meeting had been investigating Bennett's charges against Professor MacNeill. In 1923 they delivered their report, clearing MacNeill and the college, but urging that a teacher of practical theology be added and a full theology degree be offered. "Except upon a few points," their recommendations were unanimous and were accepted unanimously.[46]

Those "few points" proved to be crucial, for upon them a case was built to rend the fabric of unity in British Columbia. Two of that province's members on the commission had disagreed that Harris MacNeill should remain on the faculty at Brandon. At the next year's assembly of the B.C.

Convention a motion was offered, noting and supporting that dissent, and disapproving of the Baptist Union's acceptance of the commission's report. Finally this motion was tabled for a year and a committee of ten was appointed to consider relationships within the Union.[47]

Staying Conservative

Returning before the 1925 meeting of the British Columbia Convention, its committee of ten presented majority and minority reports. Both sought to ensure the teaching of orthodox theology at Brandon College. While the majority felt that this could be accomplished by adopting a similar position to the one set forth in the McMaster Charter, the minority held out for a strict statement of faith to which all faculty had to subscribe. In the phrase of one historian the Convention was "hopelessly divided,"[48] the vote to accept the majority report being eighty-nine to fifty-four.[49]

The following year the B.C. Convention, still exhibiting its consistently conservative theological stance, passed a motion requesting the Baptist Union to ensure "that Brandon College should be reorganized in the Department of Theology, and this Department equipped with scholarly men as teachers who believe and stand loyally by the Bible and its teachings, as interpreted by regular Baptists, and who are willing to pledge themselves accordingly."[50]

Finally it became apparent that T. T. Shields was involved in the growing discord, the *Gospel Witness* carrying a critical report of the 1924 B.C. Convention. Through the same medium he censured Brandon College and notified the general secretary of the Baptist Union, that Jarvis Street Church would no longer support the work of the Union unless the Brandon's situation was corrected. In 1925 Shields did just that, first rerouting funds directly to the B.C. Convention, then to those dissenting.[51]

Baptist Bible Union Conference in Vancouver

Following the 1925 B.C. Convention, a number of those who were displeased with the slow pace of change at Brandon and disappointed in their own hopes for election to office in the Convention, did as Shields would soon do in Ontario, forming an extra-Convention body, the B.C. Missionary Council. Through the council, which was composed of individuals rather than churches, they resolved to "express our unqualified protest against the British Columbia Convention and of the Baptist Union of Western Canada." They also subscribed to the confession of faith of the Baptist Bible Union of North America.[52]

The association with the Bible Union was hardly an accident. The president, Dr. Shields, had spoken at a conference of the Bible Union held in Vancouver just before the missionary council was inaugurated, and in his speech he had called "Fundamentalists" to action. Thereafter, Shields consistently supported the council through the pages of the *Gospel Witness*.[53]

One of the Missionary Council's objectives was "to receive and administer all missionary offerings in the promotion of Baptist work true to our Historic Faith at home and abroad," and churches were invited to send their denominational gifts through the council. Initially the council sought to continue an overseas relationship through the Canadian Baptist Foreign Mission Board but attempted arrangements soon broke down. Yet all the while, council members stayed within the B.C. Convention — of it but neither with it nor for it.

A New Constitution

The board of the B.C. Convention sought harmony with the dissenters or, if that was not possible, at least an amiable settlement. But as one historian has written, "[The Council] would not cooperate; neither would it separate."[54] Its leaders plainly had hopes of taking control of the Convention.

At the 1926 annual meeting, the Convention instructed its board to draft a new constitution to meet the needs of the changing times. As part of the proposals for the constitution, supporters of the Missionary Council offered a notice of motion to require that a statement of faith be added.[55] Presented the next year, the recommended new constitution introduced a number of further concessions to meet the objections but also included a clause that would make it possible to dismiss a church that refused to co-operate.[56] Following adoption of the constitution, discussion centred on the proposed statement of faith, which was almost identical to that of the Baptist Bible Union. Its proponents insisted that the statement be the "basis of fellowship," thus ruling out any liberty of conscience, and this undoubtedly caused its defeat by a large majority.[57]

Disaffection and Loss

Following this vote, the representatives of the non-co-operating churches moved out of both the Assembly and the Convention, meeting the same day to undertake the formation of the separate Convention of Regular Baptist Churches of British Columbia. The break was complete.

A third of the forty-eight Convention churches were lost, along with a quarter of the 6,244 members, a total not to be regained for nearly fifty years. The attendant losses were equally destructive. The long years of controversy had turned attention from the tasks of ministry and outreach was cramped. Some of the strong British Columbia leadership which had helped to fuel the Union's progress had departed, and finances were affected. As in central Canada the image of the whole denomination in the community suffered and continues to suffer.

The rupture in British Columbia seems to have been even less justified than the break in central Canada. The Baptist Union had gone far beyond the second mile in meeting polity objections from its dissenting members — so far, in fact, that its own structure was weakened for some forty years. Although the Brandon College governors can certainly be faulted for failing to make the Union-prescribed reforms, B.C. churches had been relieved of their responsibility for providing support, as the dissenters had requested. What is more, the B.C. Convention had consistently demonstrated its theological orthodoxy and its willingness to meet its detractors more than halfway, balking only when faced with a credal statement that left no room for liberty of conscience. However, justified or not, the British Columbia withdrawal was perceived by its proponents to be part of the continent-wide movement to repulse the liberal/modernist threat.

The Supply Pastor of Westbourne Church

As has been intimated, the three Prairie provinces were not much affected by the turmoil. Only in Alberta was there a defection: Westbourne Church in Calgary under lay pastor William Aberhart. Destined to become premier of Alberta, Aberhart was Ontario-born and reared a Presbyterian. Apparently rebuffed in his efforts to train for that church's ministry, he moved west to become principal of Alexandra High School in Calgary, where he first joined a Presbyterian church, then a Methodist.

Moving once again in his spiritual quest, in 1915 Aberhart became supply pastor of Westbourne, a mission of First Baptist Church, where he became a popular preacher and teacher, majoring on dispensational and premillenial themes. During the 1920s, Aberhart remained at Westbourne and joined the chorus of criticism of Brandon College, and in 1925 he established what became the Calgary Prophetic Bible Institute and a radio ministry, moving the Westbourne congregation into the new Institute buildings in 1927. Within two years the congregation divided, part returning to their older church building, where, under the Reverend Morely Hall, who was later to become a leader of the Fellowship Baptists, a rival Bible Institute was established.[58]

The post-war years and the twenties were distressing ones for all Baptists. Although leaders of anti-liberal movements represented widespread concern about moving away from fundamentals of the faith, the methods of men like T. T. Shields left wounds that would take generations to heal. The worst controversies appeared in central Canada and British Columbia, the Prairie provinces being affected very little and the Atlantic provinces hardly at all.

Beyond the Storm

T HE DIRTY THIRTIES. A MAN STAND-
ing on the platform of a CPR
station waiting for a west-
bound train watched as a long freight drew into the station and
hundreds of dusty, unkempt men crawled from the rods and jumped
from flat cars.

Some came into the waiting room, among them two who stood
apart, obviously younger, less worldly wise. One of them, holding
two postage stamps in his hand, approached the ticket wicket somewhat sheepishly. He placed one of the stamps on the counter and
asked the agent if he could possibly have a sheet of notepaper and
an envelope in exchange . . . he wanted to write to his mother.

Studying the lad for a long moment, the agent handed him
several sheets of writing paper and two envelopes. Giving the stamp
back to him, the agent said: "Write home twice, son. Good luck."

The observer then approached the two boys. They were from
Montreal, he learned, recently graduated from high school and
travelling west in search of work. Gently the man pointed out that
work opportunities in the West were almost nonexistent. Tens of
thousands were unemployed there. It would be better to return to
Montreal where they were known.

"Are you a priest?" one of the lads asked. "Yes and no," was
the response. "I am not a Roman Catholic priest but I do represent
One who knows exactly how you feel, for He said, 'Foxes have holes,
and the birds of the air have nests, but the Son of Man hath not
where to lay His head.' "

It was just about train time and the minister asked when they
had last eaten. "Yesterday at noon," they replied. It was 3:00 P.M.
He gave them some money, and urged them to return home . . .
and then caught his train.

A few weeks later a letter arrived from a Montreal mother,
expressing sincerest thanks for the kindness shown her son.

William C. Smalley, general secretary of the Baptist Union of Western Canada, had walked in the footsteps of his Master. And the anonymous ticket agent, if not a Christian, was "not far from the Kingdom."

ADAPTED FROM WILLIAM C. SMALLEY, *COME WIND, COME WEATHER.*

CHAPTER 22

The Atlantic Calm

"There is no such thing as a 'social gospel,'
but there is also no such thing as a gospel
without social implications."
— THOMAS B. McDORMAND

While Baptists in Ontario and Quebec were embroiled in bitter strife, those on the Atlantic coast, true to their Maritime tradition, sailed along in relatively calm waters. Division which so disrupted Baptist life and damaged the cause in central Canada and British Columbia, simply did not occur on the eastern seaboard — nor has it to this day.

It was not that the liberal-modernist /conservative-fundamentalist debate left the Maritimes untouched. No quarter escaped that conflict. But the Atlantic Baptists were able to weather the storm. The difference in their reaction was rooted in history, the characteristics of the region and the qualities of its people.

After War

Maritime Baptists were unable to hold their annual meeting in 1918, the final year of World War I. It was in that year that another killer, adding to the massive war casualties, swept through the civilian population of Canada—a deadly epidemic of influenza. The Assembly was to have been held at Woodstock, but the government had closed all New Brunswick churches. Later in the year a "Skeleton Convention," called by the executive with the co-operation of the boards, was held in Amherst, Nova Scotia. Its actions were ratified by the regular Convention the following year.[1]

A Growing Trend

In preparation for the 1920s, the Home Mission Board of New Brunswick, which had retained its identity, agreed in 1918 that the time had arrived for a full merger with the home missions board of the United Baptist Convention of the Maritime Provinces.[2] The New Brunswick Association finally came to the same conclusion[3] and unification was achieved in 1920 when the Reverend Ernest S. Mason, who had been the Convention's home missions superintendent for five years, assumed overall direction.

The Sunday school and young people's board was renamed the board of religious education and, as part of a growing trend of interdenominational co-operation, joined several other Protestant agencies in 1919 to form the Maritime Religious Education Council (MREC)[4] to pilot some of the children's work. Showing greater willingness to reach beyond their borders, the Maritime Convention joined central Canada and the West to form an army and navy board that would care for service personnel returning from overseas and appoint chaplains for the continuing regular forces.[5]

A parallel development occurred in the area of community involvement, the social application of the gospel. The name of the Convention's committee on social and moral reform was changed to the social service committee in 1919 and was made a full board the following year.[6] The board's first report in 1921 was exceptionally progressive for the times, including a call for such "rights" as equality of opportunity, partnership among owners and workers in industry, fit conditions in the workplace, establishment of juvenile courts, pensions for widows with dependents, provision for the aged and the incapacitated and, for women, "equal pay with men for equal work."[7] This last would have been the most startling proposal in 1921.

To Provide a Refuge

The same year the Baptists joined a partnership of Protestant churches in operating the Maritime Home for Girls at Truro, Nova Scotia. Established to meet the needs of girls under sixteen who had run afoul of the law, the Home became a fine alternative to reformatory for a youngster "committed and cared for in accordance with the law and regulations of the province from which she comes."[8]

Through its social service board the Convention also took an intense interest in young women offenders, again uniting with the Presbyterians, Methodists (later United) and Anglican communions in forming the Interprovincial Home for Young Women, located near Moncton, New Brunswick. Founded to provide a refuge "in place of common jail,"[9] this residence and school aimed "to give proper care to young women . . . who, for crimes committed or delinquent habits formed are legally entrusted to its care."[10] Theirs was an enlightened approach and both homes provided such care over several decades.

A strong proponent of women's rights, the Convention named a committee as early as 1919 to interview the premier of New Brunswick to urge him to set a day when every woman in that jurisdiction could enjoy the "opportunity of having her name placed among the electors of this Province."[11] As to the status of women within its own structure, Convention adopted a resolution permitting the granting of a licence to preach "in the case of women who show special qualifications for this work."[12] It was still only 1921.

Shortsightedness Conceded

There was healthy movement, too, in the expansion of theological education. Although Dr. George B. Cutten, president of Acadia University from 1910 to 1922, held that "the primary object of the founding of our institutions was the education of our ministry, and we have never forgotten this trust,"[13] there were those who would have argued the point with him. Few would have disagreed with his premise, many with his conclusion, for Convention had unceasingly sought more adequate training at home for its theological students — if for no other reason than to staunch the flow of ministers southward. Yet again in 1921 the Assembly of the Maritime United Baptist Convention brought to the attention of Acadia's board of governors the importance of buttressing the theology department.[14] Finally, in 1923, the governors reported that this had been accomplished, with three degrees being offered: BA (Theology), BD and MA (Theology). They concluded (with just a little tongue-in-cheek, surely, after more than eighty years) that this "will more completely fulfill the design of the founders."[15]

A few years later the governors themselves conceded that it had been shortsighted not to establish courses leading to a degree before this time. "Prior to 1923," they said, "the great majority went to the United States for their theological training. The majority did not return to Canada. The loss to the Baptist churches of the Maritimes was incalculable."[16]

Tightening Organization

As these progressive changes occurred among the boards, the Convention itself was clearing the decks for action. The five-year program committee, which had made a limited advance during the latter half of the war and beyond, was succeeded by a promotion committee in 1921. That committee continued; emphasizing four areas: evangelism, education, social issues and financial matters. It might have been better had these responsibilities been entrusted to a reinforced executive committee (with which the promotion committee was eventually merged) but Baptists of that era were consistently fearful of "centralization."

The promotion committee did, however, act like an executive and moved to tighten organization and interrelationships. In 1922 a recommendation was placed before the Convention Assembly, and approved, to provide consistency in the examination of candidates for ordination. Thereafter questioning was carried out by a council composed of representatives of the associations and the president and secretary of Convention.[17]

Two years later — and sixteen years before the Baptist Convention of Ontario and Quebec did the same — the United Baptist Convention appointed what was effectively its first general secretary. The Reverend Henry R. Boyer was initially named executive secretary of the promotion committee, with that unit being given board status and charged "to formulate, and promote the financial policy . . . [and] to coordinate the work of existing agencies."[18]

No Merger Fervour

Many of the moves to tighten regulations and steps to create a more ordered denominationalism came from the grassroots. It was one of the districts (part of an association, a Free Baptist legacy) which sent a resolution to Convention disapproving of licentiates (unordained ministers) conducting baptism and also the practice of baptizing people who did not join the church. Convention concurred in their motion, urging "all who have the welfare of our churches at heart to discourage such practices."[19] The New Brunswick Association followed this action, directing their superintendent of home missions to write to any licentiates who were administering the ordinances, noting that the procedure was irregular and requesting them to desist.[20]

Although the United Baptist Convention of the Maritime Provinces was ever ready to co-operate in interdenominational activities and projects, there is little evidence that it became caught up in the merger fervour of the 1920s. The Convention did take note of "various pronouncements on organic church union," but gave immediate notice that no thought would be entertained of any negotiations "that do not recognize the validity and equality of our ordination with that of all other religious bodies."[21]

Discussions concerning "overlapping" churches in small communities were undertaken with the Presbyterians as early as 1921,[22] and following their union with the Congregationalists and Methodists, further consideration was given to the possibility of interdenominational co-operation both in currently overlapping fields and in the establishment of new fields. Linked pastorates were even discussed. A joint committee recommended such co-operation, but the proposal was deferred by the Assembly[23] and finally declined.[24]

Minor Strain . . . No Separation

Although Maritime Baptists did not suffer the wrenching dislocations and schisms of other Canadian Baptists over the theological disputes of the early decades of the twentieth century, they did not escape entirely unscathed. No significant upset occurred, however.

Criticism from the Island

In 1925 John J. Sidey and J. B. Daggett, then both Prince Edward Island pastors, were instrumental in organizing a laymen's conference which was held in Immanuel Baptist Church, Truro, Nova Scotia. The key speaker was T. T. Shields,[25] with whom Sidey enjoyed a long friendship and who obviously hoped for Maritime support in his own crusade. His hopes were not unfounded, as Daggett and Sidey were on the executive of a body called the Maritime Christian Fundamentalist Association at the time.[26]

As in Ontario and the West, the first overt opposition was aimed at the Convention's school of higher learning, in this instance Acadia, which Sidey accused of fostering modernist teaching.[27] In 1919 he and Daggett established Kingston Bible College on the premises of the Kingston church of which Daggett had become pastor. The next year Sidey joined him as his assistant on the Kingston/Aylesford/Melvern Square field, but within a few months Sidey was the senior and principal of the college, partly because of Daggett's ill health.[28]

Daggett saw the founding of the college as parallel to moves among Baptists in the United States, where Northern Seminary had been established as an antidote to Chicago Divinity School and Eastern Seminary as a counterbalance to Crozier. Although still apparently in fellowship with the Convention, Sidey and Daggett published their own paper, which in one issue featured a glowing account of the ordination of a breakaway pastor in Ontario.[29]

Drawn-Out Court Case

In 1931 Sidey linked the Kingston and Melvern Square churches with that of Lower Aylesford under the name Baptist Independent, clearly throwing down the gauntlet to the Convention. Yet it was not until three years later that both Sidey and Daggett resigned from the three-church pastorate — with mixed results. Lower Aylesford accepted the resignations, while Melvern Square did not. Kingston divided, thirty leaving to form an independent church,[30] while the loyalists asked the Bible College to quit the premises.

Sidey was thus obliged to find new quarters for his Bible College, but it wasn't long before he was given a tract of land in Kingston Village. However, a drawn-out court case was required to settle the disposition of the church properties, and the litigation in the Nova Scotia Supreme Court attracted widespread press attention, most of which was unfavourable to the dissidents.[31]

The action to protect the properties was not taken by the Convention, although it provided support, but rather by members of the churches concerned. Sidey, Daggett and the disaffected members tried to show that the Convention had departed from the historic Baptist faith, a rather daunting task in a secular court of law. The judgment was clearly in favour of those who supported a continuing relationship with the United Baptist Convention and its home missions board, which had been granted contingency rights by its Acts of incorporation of 1908 and 1910. All of the church and parsonage properties were retained by the members loyal to the Convention.[32]

In the end, Sidey did form four small independent churches in addition to the Kingston congregation: Cape Sable Island, Louis Head, Lockeport and Coddles Harbour.[33] In 1940 a tiny Maritime Fellowship of

Independent Baptists was established — just four churches at Kingston, Lower Aylesford, Melvern Square and Coddles Harbour. The remaining handful of other scattered independents were invited to join, but they declined.[34] Three years later the name was changed to the Maritime Fellowship of Baptists (Independent) but by 1968 even this had disappeared,[35] leaving a few widely dispersed churches which, for reasons of their own, have kept apart from the Convention.

No Storms in the Maritimes

Many have tried to determine the reasons for the Maritime Baptists' continuing accord during this period when controversy was raging in central and western Canada. Many factors were — and are — undoubtedly involved, and it is hardly possible to pinpoint any one of them as being the prime cause.

Since the founding of the first association in 1800, Baptists by the Atlantic have been a close-knit body, maturing as a denomination many decades before their fellow Baptists in other parts of what is now Canada. They are a more rural and homogeneous community than their compatriots, for massive immigration has passed them by. Their strongest impact has been on the blue collar and small business strata of society, rather than on the professional and entrepreneurial. This tendency has been reinforced by the fact that the British Baptists had much less influence in the Maritimes than in Ontario and Quebec,[36] where, as Mary Hill points out, "By 1850, Scots and English Baptists were numerous and influential in the larger towns and cities, enabling them to gain control over the Baptist 'infant' denomination. These 'Anglicized' urban areas also influenced rural Baptist churches."[37]

The Communion debate was neither as eventful nor as bitter as that in central Canada, which went on there for much of the nineteenth century, undoubtedly resulting in a discordant residue into the twentieth. Right at the beginning of the nineteenth century, the question in the Maritimes was settled in favour of the close position and, together with the factor of time, the transition to the open viewpoint was eased by the merger with the Free Baptists. They had undoubtedly drawn to their ranks many open communionists who would otherwise have been with the Regular Baptists, which would perhaps have become an early contentious factor. By the time they linked up, the question had really become academic.

In the first decade of the twentieth century, the Free and Regular Baptists joined on the basis of a strong statement of faith which effectively covered all the issues raised in the modernist-fundamentalist controversy, and Maritime Baptists have never been hesitant to remind their members of that statement when theological questions have arisen. The conservative nature of their society has also been reflected in their clinging to long-held and cherished values, including theological views. To a large extent cut off economically and socially from central Canada, they would have been dubious of movements there and even a T. T. Shields did not have significant influence.

Acadia No Target

There were similarities, of course, in the way the pressures of the widespread controversy arose. Like McMaster in central Canada and Brandon in the West, Acadia University came under fire. Coincidentally one of the criticisms was over the granting of an honourary degree, in the instance of Acadia to Professor Shirley J. Chase of the University of Chicago, which Daggett described as "the greatest infidel factory in America."[38] That protest apparently did not reach Convention floor.

It was hard to find fault with Acadia, however — a small institution[39] that had been at the forefront of evangelistic efforts in the constituency for nearly a century. Furthermore, no full theological department was in operation at the university until 1923. After the school of Theology was opened, it took some time for criticism to become defined, and by that time the greatest danger had passed.

No really strong leaders — then or later — arose to question the stance of either the Convention or its university. There was no one of the stature of Shields prepared to mount an attack or, indeed, anyone of L. H. Marshall's capabilities to add fuel to the fire. Neither Sidey nor Daggett displayed charismatic qualities, and the spasmodic efforts of a few who followed in their train came to naught because most were "outsiders" whose activities proved to be unacceptable to the rank-and-file membership. Sidey's image was also somewhat marred by one or two unfortunate episodes in his ministry, particularly one in which the charge was made that "he misplaced a handsome sum of denominational funds as a U.B. [United Baptist] minister on the Kingston circuit."[40]

The judgment which followed the litigation over the property at Kingston Village was also to have a restraining effect on those who in succeeding years might have considered a breakaway. The decision obviously carried the implication that even if dissenters made up a majority in an individual church, they could not be sure that they could take the property with them.

The Spiritual and the Physical

The Maritime Baptists' emphasis on the social implications of the gospel may also have neutralized the effect of the liberal/modernist movement in that region. One of the battle cries of the movement was that social issues had been forgotten by traditional Baptists. Obviously, that argument did not hold water in the Maritimes.

While supporting and constantly pressing for legislation to ensure equality of opportunity, provision for widows, the aged and handicapped, fair labour laws and the like, the Maritime Convention and its university always underlined the need for personal salvation and maturation in the

Christian life. Both the spiritual and the physical were in focus, the spiritual first. As the Convention declared in 1919, "Our aim is the development of every church into an evangelistic and social force in its community."[41]

The Convention was for these and other reasons well able to maintain its unity when others were being buffeted. It is perhaps typical of the Convention and the people of the region that the only mention of the Sidey episode in the Assembly minutes of those years appears to have been a statement by Professor Simeon Spidle in 1936 concerning errors in a court stenographer's record of his evidence in the case—nothing to stir up a controversy.[42]

Toward the Convention's Centennial

Like the rest of the nation the Maritime provinces were hard hit by the Great Depression of the thirties. In the period between 1929 and 1933, after the collapse of the stock market in October 1929, the value of the world's export trade, from which Canada acquired over a third of its national income, diminished by nearly 50 percent and the price of those exports that remained declined drastically.[43] A quarter of the labour force became unemployed. Many were forced to apply for relief and, as for the churches, "in all the denominations there had to be serious cuts in budgets, salaries, programmes, foreign missions, and experimentation."[44]

In his report to Convention in 1931 General Secretary Henry Boyer stated that the Depression was taking serous hold and some communities were in "dire financial straits."[45] Despite these trying conditions, he related in 1932 that a spiritual awakening had taken place in the previous twelve months, a total of 2,123 baptisms having taken place that year.[46] For the first time, however, the Convention was having difficulty raising enough money for the denominational budget.[47]

The Depression Takes Its Toll

By 1932 Dr. Boyer had resigned as general secretary and returned to the pastorate. A survey commission appointed by the previous Assembly indicated that economic conditions made it impossible to replace him. Instead, it recommended that his work be divided among the executive of the board of promotion and finance, the superintendent of home missions and the secretary of religious education. In a further move of consolidation, the commission advocated that an enlarged executive of Convention take over the functions of the promotion committee,[48] this being accomplished through constitutional amendment a year later.[49] Salaries of all staff employed by Convention and its boards (except Acadia and the Canadian Baptist Foreign Mission Board) were reduced by 5 to 10 percent in 1932.[50]

But the repercussions of the Depression went far beyond the financial. In his 1935 presidential address, R. B. Wallace said:

> The faith of many has been sorely tried by the vicissitudes through which they have passed in the last few years .... The waves of Communism, Naziism, Fascism and social unrest have been surging against our shores . ... Discontent is rampant .... Thousands of young men, many of them college graduates, have been herded into relief camps, unable to get unemployment, while their ambition was being destroyed and their morale broken.

Yet Wallace was able "to be thankful that our church life has not been disturbed."[51] But it had been disturbed. The home missions board recorded in 1934 that its financial statement had been in red figures "for seven of the last ten years," the deficit at that point being nearly $25,000, and action was being taken to cut both the salaries of pastors and grants to its churches.[52]

Problems of the Rural Church

The Maritimes continued to experience the loss of its old families, many emigrating to the New England states. Even as early as 1924 when economic times were good, a large exodus was recorded—"possibly the greatest in our history" — mostly from the rural farming and fishing areas.[53] Immigration to Canada, which might have been a balancing factor, passed the Maritimes by for the most part. The home missions port worker in 1932 estimated that 95 percent of the Baptist immigrants were going to central or western Canada.[54] Yet despite all the difficulties, Maritime Baptists looked beyond to the needs of others, a letter being read at the 1936 Assembly expressing thanks for aid sent to the farmers suffering from drought in western Canada. Authorization was also given to mount a special appeal for an additional $5,000 to meet critical needs on the overseas mission fields.[55]

The experiences of these years helped to focus concern upon the particular problems of the rural church, Convention urging Acadia's Theological School to establish a special course of study toward that end.[56] Social involvement continued high on the agenda of successive Assemblies, "translating the teachings of Jesus into our social life, into our social institutions."[57]

Co-operative Publications

Also in the thirties, a new hymnary for cross-Canada use, drawing largely on that of the United Church of Canada, was published jointly by the Conventiins in Ontario-Quebec and the Maritimes and the Baptist Union of Western Canada. Further collaboration with the United Church resulted in the publishing of Canadian Baptist-edited Sunday school materials, as well. These materials were supported by many churches across Canada, but were never fully received.

Outpouring for Peace

By the mid-thirties, while the national economy was beginning to turn around, dark clouds were looming on the international horizon. An Austrian-born former army corporal, Adolph Hitler, had become Chancellor of Germany in 1933 and, backed by his fanatically loyal and disciplined Nazi storm troopers, was rapidly becoming a dictator. Within two years the Saar territory, which had been under the suzerainty of the League of Nations, was returned to Germany through a plebescite after a barrage of propaganda. In 1936 Hitler remilitarized the Rhineland, the same year forging the Rome-Berlin axis and an anti-Comintern pact (against the U.S.S.R.'s Eurasian allies) with Japan. In 1938 his troops began to move. Austria was annexed, Czechoslovakia fell next and, with his hand strengthened by a non-aggression pact with the Soviet Union, Hitler attacked Poland. By September 3, 1939, the world was aflame.

As so often happens when hostilities threaten, there was an equally intense outpouring for peace. In this movement Canadian church leaders had a significant role, reflecting the yearning of most people. As did other church bodies the United Baptist Convention of the Maritime provinces lent support to the peace principle, although often with reasoned reticence in the matter of specific action.

Resolutions supporting peace and "unalterable opposition to war" were passed in 1933[58] and 1935,[59] and the denominational journal filled its front page with an article by Lieutenant-Colonel George A. Drew, later Ontario premier, entitled "Munition makers and Disarmament," extracted from the *Canadian Home Journal.*[60] In 1936 the executive was directed to consider the advisability of holding a peace plebescite in the churches. The next year it recommended that the churches give leadership but not by means of a plebescite, the value of which, they said, would not warrant the labour and expense.[61]

When war was declared, the United Kingdom and her allies were commended for "heroic efforts" to prevent it, and prayer was offered that God might extend grace in the face of impending catastrophe.[62] The 1939 Assembly of the United Baptist Convention was in fact in session on that fateful September 3 and one of the key speakers, Acadia President F. W. Patterson, departed from his scheduled subject, to speak of "the Christian attitude to war."[63] That attitude, in the instance of Maritime Baptists, proved to be consistently supportive of Canada's stand throughout the conflict.

Few Occasions More Unfavourable

In spite of war, the Lord's business was not forgotten. At the same 1939 Convention the initial draft of a seven-year program leading up to the 1946 Centennial Convention was introduced and, although the war must obviously have detracted from their efforts, the program was carried out, with its triple emphasis on evangelism, stewardship of the whole of life and finances. The last involved the raising of a special fund of $60,000 — a third each for home and overseas missions and a sixth each for Acadia and the Ministers' Annuity Fund.[64]

"Few occasions could have been more unfavourable," writes Maritime historian, George Levy. Over thirty ordained ministers and licentiates volunteered for the chaplaincy, YMCA war services or combat duty, and with other dislocations, more than fifty pulpits became vacant and nearly all the churches lost some of their most faithful leaders through enlistment and war work.[65] As in World War I, many Acadia students joined the ranks, and the roll of the university's lost and missing, especially airmen, was large even by 1942.[66] It continued to grow.

By that year the need for full-time Convention leadership had become most apparent, for no replacement had been made for H. R. Boyer, who had relinquished the general secretary's position nearly ten years before. Although the 1942 Convention authorized its executive to make the appointment,[67] they failed to act before the 1943 Assembly and that body named a committee to bring in an immediate nomination. At last, the Reverend Waldo C. Machum, a former Christian Education Secretary, was named to the position.[68] Meanwhile, E. S. Mason, the home missions superintendent, retired after twenty-eight years' service with that board and was succeeded by the Reverend Raymond E. Whitney.[69]

Other advances included the 1942 formation of the board of publication, which assumed full responsibility for the denominational paper, *The Maritime Baptist*, naming the Reverend George E. Levy as its editor.[70] A strong movement among laymen the next year generated the Maritime United Baptist Laymen's Association, and Ralph Loomer was elected the first president.[71] Among the churches, the sharp increase in employment brought on by the war began to make up for the lean financial years of the Depression.[72]

A Gleam of Wider Unity

The early forties were also a time of interdenominational and community co-operation. The social service board recorded its links with the Christian Social Council of Canada, the Canadian Welfare Council and the League of Nations Society,[73] while after considerable discussion the Convention reaffirmed its confidence in the co-operative principle in Christian Education through the Maritime Religious Education Council.[74] A strong inter-church Committee on Protestant–Roman Catholic Relations was formed in 1943 to watch for movements infringing on religious liberty, and to promote Protestantism.[75]

The new general secretary was appointed to attend the organizational meeting of a proposed nationwide chamber of religious bodies, the Canadian Council of Churches.[76] By 1946 the Council was functioning, its initial report emphasizing that one of its objects was "to give expression to that fundamental unity of the Christian communions which is the outcome of their faith in Christ Jesus."[77] There was a gleam of the wider unity of Christendom in many an eye. Indeed, as World War II was moving to its end, a committee studying the question of "The Church and the Problem of Peace" suggested the formation of a world church organization analogous to the Federal Council of Churches in the United States "for the sole purpose of coordinating and giving body to our efforts for peace."[78]

The 1945 Assembly had to be cancelled because the government had banned all conferences involving the travel of more than fifty delegates in order to relieve the congestion caused by returning troops.[79] This was disappointing, as that year's gathering was to have been both a prelude to the events planned for the Centennial of the first Maritime Baptist Convention and the observance of the earlier centennial of Richard Burpee's venture overseas as Canada's first protestant missionary.

The 1946 Centennial Assembly was nevertheless a rousing celebration. A Centennial Fund, for which the objective at the beginning of the seven-year program was $60,000 had more than doubled to $130,000 in 1944, and had reached over $128,000 by 1946. Membership was nearly 63,000 in 588 churches throughout the Maritimes. At the end of World War II, an era spanning 183 years of Maritime Baptist history and a hundred years of Convention life had ended on a high note. The past had been celebrated, and great expectations were held for the future.

CHAPTER 23

The Central Aftermath

"You will never disarm, you will never effect disarmanent
until you renounce war, not merely on paper,
but in the hearts of men."
—*DAVID LLOYD GEORGE, 1931*

It was a quieted and saddened Assembly of the Baptist Convention of Ontario and Quebec that convened in the James Street Church, Hamilton, in 1928. Gone was the man who had kept proceedings in an uproar for several years. Gone too were others who for conscience' sake believed they should follow him. Although the evident numerical drop in the number of churches and members totalled under 15 percent, the inherent losses were greater. The fellowship of decades had been marred and the seeds of suspicion widely sown.

What was even more damaging, the Baptist witness had become open to question, even disparagement, as those without wondered about the Baptists' inability to set their own house in order. And as McMaster University president Dr. G. P. Gilmour reflected, "It lost us much good blood, even though it reduced our apoplectic tendencies," referring not only to "those who left with a shout," but others "who could not endure the disrepute into which they felt we had been brought."[1]

In a review of the "state of religion" before the 1928 Assembly, A. N. Frith pondered both the sorry situation and the possibilities for reconciliation. Aware that "an opposing body has been organized claiming and bearing the name of regular Baptists," he commented: "We have an unfortunate conflict between two bodies avowing their loyalty to the same principles and Master. Evidently much of the discord is due to misunderstanding, misrepresentation and personal prejudice. May we not hope that through the spirit of good will and prayer those who are one in faith will become united in their labour of love."[2]

Many decades later that hope has still to be fulfilled and the prayers to be answered, but there is evidence of a considerably better spirit.

Carrying On

Although the liberal/modernist vs. conservative/fundamentalist debate undoubtedly provided the spark for the blaze which brought division to

Baptist ranks in the 1920s, it should not be assumed that the groups who parted company came down on opposite sides of the issue. Indeed, the great majority of the six-sevenths who remained within the Convention were as theologically conservative as those who stepped out. And they remained that way, although they were not unaffected by the break.

Immanuel Church, Toronto, founded as Alexander Street Baptist Church in 1866, is typical of many. Its minutes of November 9, 1927, record the reports of their delegates who were present at the critical 1927 Assembly "at which a division took place and several churches seceded from the Convention." To ensure that no "misunderstanding" existed, the church unanimously went on record "as continuing to stand especially for the Bible as the inspired Word of God, and its infallibility in all points of faith and practice." It was also decided that they would not allow contention to impair their work; rather "Immanuel Church should refrain from participating in any way in the present controversy."[3] Immanuel Church stayed in the Convention.

A Recognition of Reality

However, it was hardly possible to carry on as if the rift had not occurred. The 1927 Assembly had declined to take action respecting any dissenting church other than Jarvis Street. Although the congregations that were allied with the separatist Regular Baptist Missionary and Educational Society were considered to be "not in harmony," the door was held open. "If they desire to maintain their proper status in the Convention, their co-operation will be welcome," the Assembly offered.[4]

But by the next year, the Assembly had to recognize reality and — still reluctantly — the privilege of sending delegates to Convention was withdrawn from twelve churches by the careful and laborious process of passing separate resolutions for each.[5] For the time being at least, the break was complete, as still other church names were to disappear from the roll.

The 1927 Assembly must have derived some solace from the fact that the Amherstburg Association in Western Ontario had applied for membership in the Convention. Sent to the executive for the customary review, the request was approved the following year when the ten black churches formally affiliated:[6] Amherstburg, Sandwich, Windsor, North Buxton, Puce, Shrewsbury, Chatham, Prince Albert, Union and Dresden. First Baptist, Toronto, and Canfield, also black churches, had joined previously.[7]

The Amherstburg Association, formed in 1841 and initially consisting of small churches on both sides of the Canada–U.S. border, had maintained friendly relations with the Convention in the intervening years. Their 1927 application for membership officially sealed the connection and enabled the home missions board to provide grants of assistance.[8]

The Secularizing Process Begins

Meanwhile, other pressing business was at hand. The 1927 Assembly accepted a proposal which had been mooted four years earlier[9] to relocate McMaster University from its crowded Toronto site to Hamilton. The approval was based on four considerations:

1. Financial assistance from churches in Hamilton was to be provided on a voluntary basis.
2. Control of the university was to be preserved, as provided in the charter.
3. The proposal of the Hamilton citizens' committee to provide a suitable site for the university and to raise $500,000 for a science building was approved.
4. Endorsed by Convention, the board of governors was to raise funds to double the endowment and provide the other necessary university buildings.[10]

The sod-turning ceremony took place during the 1928 Convention,[11] and the university was officially opened in its new setting in November 1930.

As it was to turn out, the relocation did provide McMaster with a splendid campus and means to ensure significant development. However, it proved to be the beginning of a secularizing process that was to render the second stipulation impracticable. Like Acadia University in the Maritimes, McMaster, apart from its divinity department, was destined to be removed from denominational direction. The acceptance of public funding in 1927 was the initial step in that direction.

The decision to move to Hamilton also adversely affected another of the Convention's educational institutions, Woodstock College. It had already suffered a serious blow in the 1880s when its theological department was detached and re-formed as Toronto Baptist College. When that college was reincarnated as McMaster University in 1887, Woodstock College became in effect a male preparatory school placed under the direction of McMaster's board of governors.

As McMaster's move to Hamilton became imminent, the governors became more and more preoccupied with the concerns of the university, and Woodstock drifted into difficult financial waters.[12] Finally, in 1926, the board decided to close the college, albeit in face of strong opposition, "chalking one more misadventure in the record of education by the denomination."[13] Three years later the property was sold,[14] the proceeds aiding McMaster's rebuilding program.

Trying Times

One church historian has written that the whole period from 1930 to 1945 in Ontario and Quebec was hardly conducive to vigorous advance.[15]

Following hard on the heels of the schism came the Depression and then World War II.

Although central Canada suffered neither the severe drought of the West nor the Maritimes' loss of key manpower through emigration, the Depression did have a debilitating effect. It was hard to recoup the losses suffered from the exodus of the late twenties. Churches which numbered 504 (plus 54 missions) in 1928 dropped to 429 (and 53 missions) in 1931, while membership over the same period dipped from 63,062 to 54,034 and Sunday school enrolment fell from 48,006 to 45,033. Suprisingly, youth bucked the tide, the Baptist Young Peoples' Union rising slightly from 12,292 to 12,708.[16] By 1935 church membership had climbed a little, to nearly 57,000,[17] and baptisms, while fluctuating, averaged an encouraging 2,322 a year over the 1926–1935 period.[18]

In the Forefront of Giving

Revenues were particularly hard hit. Budget receipts, which had totalled $179,204 in 1929 had fallen to $105,840 by 1934.[19] Delegates to the 1933 Assembly were informed that "about a dozen" married ministers were among the ranks of the unemployed[20] — an unusual phenomenon. Dr. C. H. Schutt, the home missions superintendent, posed questions in an article in the *Canadian Baptist* (with scarcely any tongue-in-cheek): "Close church doors? Sack the preacher? What shall we do?"[21] According to a survey carried out by one association, the salaries of ministers in their jurisdiction ranged from $450 to $1,000, with parsonage. Payments were often slow and some were in arrears. Parsonages were poorly equipped.[22]

Despite the hard times, Baptists of the Ontario and Quebec Convention were in the forefront in per capita giving. Figures of the United Stewardship Council in those years, comparing the donations of eighteen North American denominations on both sides of the border, showed BCOQ churches as eighth in budget benevolences, first in nondenominational charities and third in each of denominational gifts, congregational expenses and contributions for all purposes.[23]

The churches were also deeply concerned about greater hardships being experienced by others. Centres were established throughout the constituency for the collection of relief supplies for the drought areas of Saskatchewan,[24] and a number of churches, notably Beverley Street, Toronto, and Kensington Avenue, Hamilton, opened their premises to provide meals to the needy.[25]

As in the Maritimes, the Convention through its social service board was in the vanguard of those proposing and supporting enlightened social legislation. In a major article written in 1933 the board's chairman called for action to ensure employment as well as to make provision for unemployment insurance, a more equitable distribution of wealth, and national and world planning.[26] Four years later a board-sponsored resolution on labour was approved by the Assembly, holding that labour was a human element, not a commodity, and that the labourer was entitled to a fair living wage. The principle of a minimum wage was also supported, as was the right of both labour and capital to collective bargaining, co-operation being viewed as the path to industrial peace. Further measures to eliminate unemployment were sought and again measures to introduce unemployment insurance were advocated.[27]

"The Church at the Crossroads"

Rapid growth among rural churches was impeded even more by the population drift to the cities. By 1929 the home missions board noted the growing country and village church problem, including both the exodus of rural dwellers to the urban centres and the influx of French Canadian farmers, nearly all Roman Catholic, to the Ottawa Valley.[28] Actually, the movement to urban communities had been building for most of the century. From 1901 to 1931, the percentage of those living in the rural areas of Canada dropped from 62.5 to 46.3.[29] Large-scale immigration to the cities also increased urban populations.

In 1931 the *Canadian Baptist* headlined a front-page editorial: "The Church at the Crossroads," indicating that if the country church disappeared, one of the last remaining ties binding communities together would be broken. "There are few places where a preacher wields a mightier influence than out in the country," the editor added.[30]

Leadership by the home missions board did result in corrective measures. Churches were grouped and regrouped. A real effort was made to pay "the highest possible" salaries to rural ministers, and financial grants were paid to many churches. Pastors were sought who would identify with rural needs, and a lively program of evangelism, Christian education and community service was advocated.[31]

The converse problem, of course, faced the Christian worker in the burgeoning cities. Although the stream of immigration from overseas had diminished from the heady days of the early century, the pattern had changed. No longer were British newcomers in the majority. New Canadians from many countries and mainly Roman Catholic were entering Canada, filling up the downtown quarters of the cities and pressing current occupants to the suburbs,[32] to the detriment of the downtown churches, some of which were closed.

There were many new opportunities, however, among the incoming citizens. In 1933 twenty-six home missionaries were at work in thirty-four missions among the New Canadians: Russo-Ukrainian, Polish, Romanian, Hungarian, Finnish and Scandinavian.[33] Three years later the superintendent of home missions wrote of six missions among the Russians and Ukrainians, eleven stations among the Scandinavians in northern Ontario and one among the Finns in Toronto. Polish centres of outreach numbered five, Hungarian seven and Romanian two. Two "All Peoples'" missions were also set up: one in Windsor and the other in Ottawa, while the Norfolk Association carried out work among the New Canadians at work in the tobacco lands. A Christian Fellowship Mission was also established to serve Ukrainians. Missionaries of the women's societies worked in many of these endeavours, as well as those under the home missions board.[34]

Structural Changes

The severe stress and loss of the late twenties led the Convention to re-examine its denominational structures — in an attempt to "shape up" to prevent possible further erosion. As early as 1928 a notice of motion was presented to revise the constitution and by-laws with a view to stream-lining boards and committees.[35] The following year action was deferred, but in 1930 a new general by-law was accepted, reducing the number of boards to seven and specifying twelve standing committees.[36] However, for undefined reasons, these changes were not carried out completely, and three years later the executive, sensing the need for action, provided a committee to study "denominational adjustments," including board streamlining.[37]

The following year's Assembly was called to deliberate on a recom-mendation which would have reduced the boards to six: foreign missions, Canadian missions and evangelism, religious education, publications, superannuation and McMaster governors. No formal action is recorded. A decision was made, however, to restrict board members to two three-year terms and service was permitted on only one board at a time. These moves offered increased leadership opportunities. At the same time the Convention's executive was enlarged and given expanded functions, while initial steps were also taken to reduce the numbers of associations by increasing their size.[38]

Moving Gingerly

The next year saw still more dallying in the streamlining process, as it was determined that the proposed board co-ordination needed to be reviewed further before being implemented.[39] The study proposed no action, suggesting instead that pending an appropriate time for such board slimming, "we continue the agencies, and urge all . . . to strengthen each other's hands."[40] A hesitant Convention directed that there be "further consideration" — resulting in the blasé summary "that the most harmonious relations exist between the Boards, that the aim of each is approved and actively supported by all."[41] The engine of change in the entrenched board base had stalled.

The executive was able to move in another direction, however — if gingerly. The same year "denominational adjustments" were appraised, the appointment of a general secretary was proposed.[42] The 1934 Convention approved the idea with the understanding that the new officer would be nominated by the executive for Assembly vote.[43] Once again progress was painfully slow. Five years passed before the executive was able to report that a job description had been prepared and one candidate approached — and he had declined the nomination.[44] Finally, in 1940, the Assembly appointed Dr. H. H. Bingham to the position,[45] one which he filled with distinction until his death ten years later.

The Ordination of Women

Introductory steps were taken in 1929 to tighten the ordination process and to upgrade ministerial standards. To replace the rather loosely supervised and uneven custom of using a locally called examining council, it was proposed that a Convention ordination committee be established, made up of a representative from each association and a number from the Convention. The proposal was sent to the associations and boards for consideration,[46] and they revised it, calling for two representatives from each association plus seven from the Convention. That configuration was approved the following year.[47]

Approval of a more contentious but related issue was refused at that time. The previous year a committee had been charged with the responsibility of studying the thorny subject of the ordination of women. Receiving the report, the Assembly recognized the "unspeakably valuable"[48] work being done by women, but did "not think that there is either a demand or need, especially at the present time, for beginning a practice which is so entirely new to us as a people."[49] That view was to change.

In practice, the new committee on ordination became just advisory, "being almost invariably asked for advice before a local council was called."[50] It never did reach the status enjoyed by examining councils in the Atlantic provinces and the West. In Ontario and Quebec current procedure still calls for the local church to summon a council for examination — after the candidate has been cleared on an academic basis by the Convention's ministerial credentials committee. No council on ordination exists anymore.

The Hymnary and Sunday School Publications

Two important inter-Convention developments were high on the agenda of the thirties, presaging a growing spirit of co-operation among Canadian Baptists. As intimated earlier, the first was a new hymnary, the other a jointly produced series of Sunday school supplies.

The original hymn book to bear the Canadian Baptist name was really the 1900 Baptist Church Hymnal of the United Kingdom with a new cover. In the early thirties committees of the three regional entities sought to design a truly Canadian Baptist volume but, likely because of insufficient finances, they were all driven to the conclusion that they would just revise an existing publication. The United Church of Canada generously allowed them to adapt their hymnal, and thus "The Hymnary—for Use in Baptist Churches" was published by the Conventions of central and eastern Canada, and the Baptist Union of Western Canada in 1936.

Again through a link with the United Church, Canadian Baptist Sunday school publications first appeared in 1938. Approved countrywide the previous year, the materials were produced through a Baptist editor —the Reverend Harold W. Lang—working jointly with his counterpart in the sister denomination. Within a year of their publication the board of religious education announced that 65 percent of the Ontario and Quebec Convention's churches were using the new materials, where previously just 35 percent had used supplies with a Baptist label.[51] For the Maritimes and the West the percentages for the new literature were 43 and 51, respectively.[52]

Golden Jubilee

The Convention's fiftieth anniversary was celebrated in 1939 with a special emphasis on evangelism. Regional rallies were held, a devotional booklet prepared for general use and plans made to raise a Jubilee Investment fund of $100,000 to cover current debts and deficits. A mass Jubilee Convention that year drew 5,000 participants.

Disarmament? War!

Even as the Convention was celebrating, the ominous sounds of battle could be clearly heard. World War II was about to begin. Present at the Jubilee Convention was the lieutenant-governor of Ontario, and the opening resolution centred on loyalty to king and country.[53] This demonstrated a perceptible change of mood, for just the year before the Assembly had resolved "that this Convention urge the churches in the event of war neither to bless nor give support to it as organizations."[54]

There had indeed been a building peace sentiment within the Convention for nearly a decade. At first the emphasis was on "reciprocal disarmament" in the face of "ruinous rivalry in armaments among the nations."[55] Editorials and leading articles in the *Canadian Baptist* focused on the need for disarmament[56]—even unilateral—and one year Convention almost passed a resolution urging the British Commonwealth to lead the way "in making an actual voluntary reduction of armaments and armed forces." Only after long debate was the motion finally tabled.[57]

Yet by 1941 the Convention stated that it recognized "the necessity of employing force to restrain the powers of evil that are abroad in the world today" and expressed the hope "that God will grant victory to our arms."[58] Adolph Hitler had changed many minds.

War Service and Dislocations

By that same year, six of the Convention's ministers had become full-time chaplains, several others serving part-time.[59] Two years later, thirty had joined the forces, two of whom died in services.[60] A war services committee was actively keeping in touch with Baptists in the forces, as well as providing hospitality for those in training.[61] Later it was indicated that funds were being sent to chaplains to provide welfare assistance to the men and women in the services and boxes of clothing were being dispatched to Baptists in Great Britain.[62] By mid-war some 70 McMaster students had enlisted and 283 were involved in the Canadian Officers' Training Corps and Auxiliary Corps.[63]

Other dislocations brought about by the war also affected the churches. During the war, more than 800,000 Canadians outside the armed forces changed places of residence.[64] A committee on the state of religion reported in 1943 that, with exceptions, church attendance was declining. Churches in the cities were receiving few of those moving in from the rural areas.[65] Sunday school enrolment dropped 42 percent from 1935 to 1945, and BYPU registration a massive 63 percent, largely because many of its potential members were fighting in Europe. There was a "wide-spread disintegration of family religion," and a close correlation between the rise of juvenile delinquency and the decline of the Sunday school.[66]

The Ecumenical Problem

These difficulties did serve to bring the Christian community closer together, and Convention Baptists became involved, if warily, in the growing ecumenical movement of the times. Yet the road to interdenominational co-operation was never smooth — in Harrop's phrase, "probably the most difficult problem we face." "Some Baptists," he adds, "hold that this movement stems from a tolerance born of indifference, or worse. Others see in it the work of the Holy Spirit in our day."[67]

A number of individual Baptists attended initial meetings of the Canadian Provincial Committee of the World Council of Churches, but Convention deferred any action pending consideration by the Baptist World Alliance.[68] The BWA declined to join but at its 1943 Assembly, the Convention instructed its executive to appoint representatives to "sit in" with the Canadian executive of the World Council and to provide any necessary financial contribution.[69]

Despite strong leadership advocacy, this particular relationship has never been sealed by Baptists in any part of Canada. However, all did become original members of the Canadian Council of Churches, in 1944.[70] The Convention's board of religious education had for some time been co-operating with the Religious Education Council of Canada (and its provincial counterpart) in promoting boys' and girls' work programs.[71] That agency was soon to dissolve into a department of the Canadian Council of Churches. The CCC, certainly more soul-centred then than in more recent years, was vitally interested in evangelistic outreach and in its early months launched through its department of evangelism a number of special missions — in Saskatchewan and Alberta in the West, and at Mount Allison University in the Maritimes.[72]

An Identity Crisis

In 1944 General Secretary Bingham repeated a note which was being heard more and more throughout the constituency: "We must fairly and frankly face the question of Inter-Church co-operation . . . [although] we have no thought of Church Union . . . we do reverence the ministry of other Christian bodies."[73] Both the Anglican and the United Churches were quick to seize the opportunity, making overtures "to confer concerning a closer unity in Christian life and work" — an approach which the executive received positively, "in order," they said, "that our witness might be heard."[74] The following year, a commission on Baptist beliefs and polity, chaired by Dr. G. P. Gilmour, lamented the failure to develop a relationship with other church bodies in order to make an interchange of membership possible. The commission recommended that such a move be considered, along with "zoning" to avoid overlapping in thinly populated areas.[75]

These were among the far-reaching proposals promoted by the eager ecumenists of the day, who were motivated by the devastating experiences of schism, depression and war. The Baptists faced an identity crisis, reflected in the musings of the above commission that in matters of "Faith," denominational lines had become obscure and in matters of "Order" (the "outward organization of religious life") the lines, while strictly drawn, resulted from "excellent expediency" rather than "Divine order."[76] In the midst of that crisis, the Baptist Federation of Canada — later the Canadian Baptist Federation — was born. Its story is reserved for another chapter.

Post-War and Jubilee

With World War II at an end, a Forward Movement was inaugurated in 1945 to examine the "whole programme of local church and denominational activities," beginning with a "fresh statement of our Baptist beliefs in the language of today."[77] The rehabilitation of returning service personnel was made a high priority, each church being urged to form a local committee to give a warm welcome to the homecomers and to help them return to the "natural" life of the church, the home, the workplace and the community.[78]

By the next year the Federation made plans to help with post-war rehabilitation in Europe and to rejuvenate the home front. It set a national financial objective of $400,000, a third each designated for European relief, foreign missions and extension work in Canada.[79] On Labour Day weekend, 1946, churches in Ontario and Quebec sent representatives to meet for prayer, fellowship and the detailed designing of the following year's activities and ministries.[80] There was a real will to recoup the losses and move on.

Secularization Continues

In the postwar years, McMaster University presented the Ontario and Quebec Convention with a blueprint for a far-reaching program of development. The plan, which was passed by the Assembly only after vigorous debate lasting two sessions, essentially divided the university into two parts. The first, McMaster University itself, retained responsibility for Theology, Liberal Arts and fundamental studies in the Junior Division. Its operation continued under the same elected board of governors. The second was to be a separate college on lands adjoining McMaster, an independent corporation but affiliated with McMaster. The new Hamilton College was supported by public funding and was to be responsible for undergraduate senior science studies.[81]

Although the proposals were intended to balance the perceived demands of a secular constituency against responsibility to the denomination to maintain a centre of Christian-oriented education, it soon became apparent that both could not be satisfied. The university's secularization continued apace. Hamilton College, adjacent to McMaster, was chartered in 1948 under a separate board of management and funded by the city of Hamilton, industries of the area and the Ontario government.[82] It took over all instruction in science and mathematics.[83]

Diamond Jubilee Forward Movement

In 1948 the Forward Movement prepared to celebrate the anniversary of the 1889 chartering of the first Convention. The Diamond Jubilee Forward Movement was highlighted by a three-year evangelism thrust carried out in co-operation with the other Conventions. Included in the central provinces were preaching missions, conferences concerning the recovery of inactive members, small group formation for prayer, study and action and a program of consolidation. Both pastoral and lay evangelists were involved in preaching and visitation. Special emphasis was placed on the development of lay leadership through six associational training conferences per year. Financial objectives included a 10 percent annual increase in funds over the period.[84]

While these efforts were underway, the needs of a distressed world were not forgotten. The slogan chosen by the Baptist World Alliance — "Clothing for a million people . . . a million dollars for food" — was fully realized. As part of this universal Baptist effort, those among the Convention of Ontario and Quebec sent over 13,600 kilograms of relief clothing to occupied Germany and more than 3,600 kilograms to the Netherlands in 1948. Their crusade drive and other gifts for Europe realized over $68,000.[85] Support was also given to the BWA's immigration worker, the Reverend A. Klaupiks, who was helping to settle displaced persons, and the Convention participated by forming the Christian Council of Canada for Refugees.[86] It is little wonder that the Convention executive was able to exult at the Diamond Jubilee Convention: "The Jubilee Forward Movement of Evangelism, Stewardship and Lay Leadership has made a definite impact upon the life of our churches."[87]

CHAPTER 24

The Boundless West

"An honest reading of the New Testament
must always lead to the same general conclusions
about vital things."
—HENRY COOK

When William Smalley came to western Canada to succeed M. L. Orchard as general secretary of the Baptist Union of Western Canada, his "mind [was] full of plans for an advance." But that was 1929 and he found instead that he "had not been called to the West to lead a glorious advance in our Kingdom enterprise, but rather to guide a strategic retreat."[1] Division had a bearing on that situation, but other factors, some beyond the churches' control, also militated against growth.

Although the rupture of 1927 had less effect on the Baptist Union of Western Canada than on its counterpart in Ontario and Quebec, the work in one province, British Columbia, was dealt a severe blow. About a quarter of the membership there was lost and outreach blunted, especially during the period of dissension.

To protect its flank as it were, the Union had made significant concessions to the British Columbia Convention. But even these proved not to satisfy the disaffected party. Neither did they make for a continuing strong partnership among the Baptists of the four provinces: British Columbia persisted in enjoying special status within the Union, a situation which was not finally adjusted until 1968.

Demanding Days

Without doubt the western region of Canada was hardest hit by the stock market crash of 1929 and the Great Depression that followed. In British Columbia, the basic industries of lumbering, fishing and mining were on the verge of collapse. Equally serious, because of its relatively mild climate, the province eventually became a haven for a third of the nation's unemployed, with well over two hundred relief camps dotted across its territory.

Around Vancouver large "hobo jungles" sprang up near the railway yards.[2] Breadlines were a common sight. Demonstrations of the unemployed were frequent and the mood sometimes turned ugly. On one occasion a contingent of infantrymen was sent over from Victoria on a naval destroyer in a show of force to keep the peace.

No Moisture at Seven Feet

On the Prairies the situation was even worse, the economic collapse was accompanied by a drought which persisted for the greater part of the decade in many areas, resulting in a steady succession of complete crop failures. One writer tells of travelling 525 kilometres in southern Saskatchewan in the fertile area from Regina to Moose Jaw to Congress without seeing a single field of grain.

The minister at Congress, who had just conducted two funerals, told him that in digging the graves they had found no moisture in the ground even at seven feet.[3] Many people simply had to abandon their family farms in the vast drought-stricken areas and to move elsewhere in the hope of making a fresh start.

The consequences of such dispossessions and dislocations were distressing for many of the churches. In Vancouver alone, just as the crisis broke, two congregations were about to erect new sanctuaries, and a third was to undertake a major renovation.[4] Only one was able to proceed with its plans during the period of decline. By 1930 the B.C. Convention's membership dropped to just under 4,000—from almost 4,600 following the departure of the dissenters. Sunday school enrolment plunged from 4,141 to 2,264. The latter did rise again to almost 3,900 by 1933, only to level off at about 3,400 at the onset of war. Gordon Pousett attributes this slump to the sudden impact of the Depression on families not well established.[5]

Staff Pared

For the Baptist Union as a whole, the conditions resulted in a financial nightmare. Whereas the churches raised $76,000 for the denominational budget in 1929, six years later receipts stood at $49,115. Other sources of income, including bond interest and gifts from the eastern Conventions, fell during that period from $44,295 to $31,725—an overall loss of a third. Added to all this was an accumulated deficit, large for those days, of over $35,000.

Salaries were cut, along with grants to home mission churches. Even the Assembly, which was held only triennially, was postponed for a year in 1932. Denominational staff was pared to the bone. In 1930 there was a general secretary, three provincial superintendents (plus one to be appointed) and two missionary evangelists among the Swedish churches. From that total of six, the number had dwindled to two by 1937—the general secretary and one other.[6]

Yet the stories of sacrificial sharing are many. Margaret Thompson recounts one contribution coming from a Prairie home to the Baptist office, along with a letter containing this poignant statement:

This mite will be all we can give and I assure you it's not of our abundance. This year we had grasshoppers and drought and they are an awful combination. We did not raise a grain of wheat or anything. Forced to sell our cattle lest they starve, we received three-quarters of a cent per pound for young stock and half a cent per pound for old cows. So we are sending one-tenth to you. Everyone here is on relief.[7]

Large Rural Withdrawal

Some losses came about because of the proliferating new "fundamentalist" congregations. In his well-known study, *Sect, Cult and Church in Alberta*, W. E. Mann lists no fewer than thirty-five such bodies, most of which developed during the two world wars and in the intervening Depression — years, he writes, "which were full of strain and difficulty for the churches."[8] According to Mann, at least some of this drift resulted from the Union's alleged accepting "in large measure the modernist approach to Christian doctrine."[9] Many would argue the point, although Baptist historian Walter Ellis holds that the theological views of the Baptist leaders in the West at the time "were more liberal than those of the conservative constituency they served."[10] There is little doubt, too, that the growing kinship among the major denominations meant that people felt freer to move from one denomination to another.

Like the other denominations, the Baptist Union withdrew from many small rural causes during those years. In the very period when the non-denominational and parachurch movements were multiplying and spreading, the Anglicans, Presbyterians, Methodists and later the United Church of Canada abandoned a host of country locations and merged others. Similarly, the Baptists closed more than eighty rural churches between 1914 and 1944 and, lacking both funds and students, discontinued the summer student supply system for a time after 1933.[11]

A severe blow was suffered in 1938 with the closing of First Church Winnipeg, the mother church of western Baptists, which had been the fulfillment of Pioneer McDonald's dream. Its members scattered to other churches, quite a number linking with Broadway, which became Broadway-First, thus continuing the name. Smalley's assessment was all too valid; a retreat was taking place.

A Focal Point of Controversy

Young people — among them many potential leaders of the church — were also drawn away by the rapidly expanding Bible school movement, particularly in the Prairie provinces. Nearly all of them independent and nondenominational, the schools offered a particularly appealing opportunity, with their emphasis on old-fashioned values and "correct" doctrine, as well as their low fees and expenses. Union Baptists, who prized higher education for their ministers, found this a difficult situation to handle, not only because of their own lack of training facilities but because of the strong antidenominational bias of the majority of the schools at that juncture.

It was during these years that Brandon College was also becoming a focal point of controversy in the denomination. At the same time its facilities for ministerial training were gradually being reduced and finally phased out. As Ellis has written with some justification: "Decisions at Brandon College to stress Arts and cultural courses and eliminate the Theology Department meant that the academicians had 'cut out the heart' of the school. Western churches would remain without pastors while an elite establishment from the East continued to pursue their aristocratic academic interests."[12]

Brandon had also become a financial albatross around the neck of the Baptist Union. It was "simply more of an economic strain than the denomination could stand without going into bankruptcy."[13] By 1938 the inevitable decision was forced upon the Union—to pull out from Brandon College. With total budget receipts that year of less than $100,000, the Union's accumulated deficit had reached nearly $60,000. In addition, $20,000 had been secured as a bank loan for the college, the Union paying the interest.

Letting Brandon Go

As they had done before, the citizens of Brandon came to the rescue of the institution that had become such an integral part of their community. A city businessman, A. E. McKenzie, a member of the college's board of governors, provided a generous endowment, and the Manitoba government was persuaded to make an annual grant. Affiliation was arranged with the University of Manitoba and some years later the college was granted university status.

So Brandon College was added to the list of educational institutions founded by western Baptists from which they later had to withdraw or which they had to close. Yet once again the contribution made during the period of operation was quite significant. During its forty years under Baptist control about 165 of its students entered Christian vocations — about four a year. Among them were many who became denominational leaders. Twenty went overseas as missionaries.[14]

In his study of Western Baptist educational policy, Keith Churchill underlines the fact that Brandon's educational standard mirrored that of McMaster, in that it placed more emphasis on academic study than on ministerial training. Since the West always insisted on having "ministers and not scholars," it is strange, notes Churchill, that "these convictions were disregarded."[15] The price of ignoring this need was high, both in lost leadership and in lost opportunities of reaching a freshly settled country—and there was also the costly failure of yet another educational venture.

While the termination of the Baptist administration of Brandon College relieved the Union's most acute financial distress, it did not completely eliminate the problem. The responsibility for Brandon's heavy debt was carried for another five years until it was finally cleared.[16]

Restructuring

From its inception, which was both late and limited, the Baptist movement in Canada's West has been constantly beset by obstacles to growth. These included a vast territory (over half the nation's land mass), scattered population centres and pitifully restricted resources of manpower and money. Constant rearrangement of staff and frequent restructuring of the organization have always been necessary just to try to keep pace with the opportunities that have presented themselves.

Soon after the Union was formed, the employed staff numbered eight, including a general secretary and an assistant, a superintendent for each of the four provinces and two evangelists. There were also two part-time editors of the paper *Western Outlook* and two financial agents, one in Britain, the other in Ontario. Historian and long-time superintendent of the Union, C. C. McLaurin, comments that it was "quite an army of men"[17]—and so it was. The staff was so large partly because the provincial Conventions had almost complete autonomy within the Union, and each was permitted to appoint its own superintendent. A demand for even more self-government back in 1911 prompted D. B. Harkness, general secretary at the time, to remark ruefully that it would then be "a democracy cursed by individual insanity."[18]

Relocation to Edmonton

For many years the Union had been contemplating moving its headquarters from Winnipeg to a more central location. With the appointment of W. C. Smalley as general secretary in 1929, however, the decision was finally made and the Baptist Union office was relocated to Edmonton. At the time, Margaret E. Thompson, who was much later to become the Union's historian, joined the staff as office secretary and served with distinction for nearly four decades.

About a decade after the headquarters was moved, the first significant restructuring of the Baptist Union occurred. In 1938, after three years of planning and constitutional and by-law changes, the three Prairie Conventions were divided into six associations: Red River Valley and Brandon-Swan River in Manitoba, Northern and Southern in Saskatchewan, and Calgary-Lethbridge and Edmonton-Peace in Alberta. Unfortunately, "for definite and pertinent reasons it was decided to leave reorganization in British Columbia for the present."[19] As it turned out, thirty years were to pass before any reorganization was undertaken.

The new structure continued to make provision for the non-Anglo-Saxon Conferences which remained after the German Baptists dropped their dual relationship in 1919 in favour of exclusive affiliation with their American counterparts. There were four of these conferences: the Swedish Baptist Conference of Alberta and the Central Swedish Conference, as well as the Russo-Ukrainian and Hungarian Baptist Conferences. Entitled to name delegates to Union Assemblies, they were also encouraged to send representatives to meetings of the associations in their areas.

A Tribute to Women

Particular tribute is due the organized women's groups in western Canada for their outstanding service during the period of the Depression. As Margaret Thompson describes it: "They scoured attics, cleaned and mended clothing, received the carload shipments from Eastern Canada and forwarded these to be distributed in areas completely without crops . . . . At the same time they kept up the shipment of supplies for hospitals and schools in India, and did their best to maintain their missionary budget . . . .[20]

In 1934 — a year marking a low point in denominational life — they sent the treasury of the Baptist Union $17,275 for mission purposes. These were the gifts of 113 circles, thirty-four young women's auxiliaries and seventy mission bands.[21]

Women's work had also undergone its share of reorganization. Initiated as the Women's Baptist Home and Foreign Mission Society of Manitoba and the North West Territories in 1887, the movement began in British Columbia ten years later through the board of women's work of the provincial Convention. With the formation of the Union, the two linked to form the Baptist Women's Missionary Society, which fell under the jurisdiction of the board of women's work of the Union in 1914. With the 1938 Union restructuring, each of the new associations sponsored a women's missionary society which in 1940 became linked as the Women's Auxiliary of the Baptist Union of Western Canada.[22]

This group operates differently than those in Ontario and Quebec and the Atlantic provinces. The western group is an auxiliary, while the others act as parallel bodies which, though represented on denominational councils, exercise a good deal of self-government.

Again, the Sounds of Battle

Western Baptist leaders who attended the Congress of the Baptist World Alliance in Berlin soon after Adolph Hitler had taken control of Germany returned home with a sense of foreboding.[23] Yet that was only 1934 and full-scale war was five years away. Like other denominations, many Baptists had vocally opposed war during most of the thirties, offering motions in support of the peace movement, condemning the manufacture of armaments and upholding the right of conscientious objection.[24] Yet when it was reluctantly determined that one side alone could not preserve the peace in face of a relentless would-be conqueror, firm support was given to the Allied cause.

A Changed Agenda

Although war clouds were hanging heavy in mid-summer 1939, the leaders of the Baptist Union felt compelled to launch at the Assembly a fourfold Forward Movement, emphasizing personal commitment, evangelism, Sunday school and youth work and stewardship. A $125,000 financial objective was set in an endeavour to meet the Union's heavy debt of $75,000, as well as to provide greater support for home and overseas missions and funds for ministerial education and a new superannuation plan.

The onset of war changed the agenda, but while less than a third of the financial goal was reached, "the Baptist Union moved from ten of the hardest years that the West has yet experienced . . . to a time when money was plentiful."[25] The Union entered the war period as deeply in debt as it had ever been; by the end of the conflict the budget deficit had been completely cleared.[26] The British Columbia Convention received $47,490 from the John Morton estate in 1942, thirty years after the pioneer's death and three after his widow's passing. The delay resulted from long litigation that took place when relatives tried to upset the will.

Apart from the area of finances, however, the war years brought critical dislocations in every sphere of work. As the annual Assembly convened in the summer of 1940, neutral Norway, Denmark and the Low Countries had been overrun, France fell during the sessions and Britain, facing invasion, stood bereft of support. Unemployment disappeared, of course, as young people flocked to the colours or moved into war-related jobs. For many westerners, however, finding employment meant moving to the industrial centres, and this adversely affected many rural churches, particularly on the Prairies. As the *Western Baptist* reported in 1943, "great groups of Western Baptists moved to Eastern Canada." This movement took an especially heavy toll on the non-Anglo-Saxon churches, the journal adding that "the Ukrainian churches in Toronto and Virgil, Ontario; the Hungarian Church at Welland and the Czecho-Slovak Church in Toronto are at present composed largely of people who have gone east from Western Canada."[27] For the first time, too, many women were now absent from the churches, as they were also involved in the armed services.

Bundles for Britain

Despite all the difficulties presented by the war, the Union and its churches carried on a lively program of service to God and the community at home and abroad. Early in the war the Union supported "Orphan Missions" — overseas missions in Germany and Nazi-occupied countries that were cut off from home bases and support. Through the Baptist World Alliance, the West made a major financial contribution from their then limited resources.[28] Support for war-ravaged countries was also rendered during a nationwide appeal for bombed churches in Britain. In that country the Baptists alone had lost 380 churches during air raids.[29]

Western Baptist women, like their eastern sisters, prepared "Bundles for Britain." Parcels that included clothing, blankets and food were dispatched regularly. In Canada the churches sponsored many activities for servicemen and women during their leave periods both in the church buildings and in private homes. Many churches also kept up correspondence with members overseas.

Preoccupation with Organization

Along with other denominations, western Baptists seized the unique opportunity offered by the 1942 construction of the Alaska Highway, which was built from Dawson Creek in British Columbia to Fairbanks, a distance of almost 3,300 kilometres. Baptists accepted responsibility for construction camps over one section of the road, appointing an experienced northern worker, the Reverend Charles J. Smith, as missionary. Smith hitch-hiked some 13,000 kilometres, preaching nearly every night[30] and offering counsel to the men in the construction and maintenance gangs.

Then, as Margaret Thompson writes, "not even the stresses of world war could prevent a considerable preoccupation with Organization and administration of the Baptist Union."[31] The 1938 constitution had been in effect only five years when a new survey committee was named to suggest further adjustments. In that it had been found impractical for one director to handle all the work of home missions and evangelism, the 1944 Union Convention appointed two field missionary evangelists as assistants; each was to cover two provinces. Those changes proved to be just a beginning, for a new survey committee four years later recommended further modifications.

Indeed, over the next two decades the Union became so embroiled in reorganization — no fewer than five different "named" reports being presented in the period between 1957 and 1967 alone — that any other achievements of the period were truly remarkable.

The most significant postwar accomplishment regarding polity was the passage of the Act of Incorporation of 1951 — one of two "final gifts" of William C. Smalley, who was retiring after twenty-two years as general secretary.[32] This Act, passed by the Canadian Parliament superseded previous Acts of Incorporation in the western Provinces and chartered the Union to function in the Yukon and the Northwest Territories as well as in the four western provinces. Work had in fact already begun in Yellowknife in 1947 at the recommendation of Charles Smith, the missionary who had served on the Alaska Highway and had become a kind of "missionary-prospector."[33] The Reverend J. K. Allaby of the well-known Maritime ministerial family became the first missionary there.

Smalley's second and final gift came in the form of a large financial donation. His lifetime friend Judge W. C. Kelley of West Summerland,

B.C., who died in 1949, left a large estate, through which the Baptist Union benefited to the extent of $375,000. While the Union intended to use this apparent windfall for extension work and other special projects, the eastern Conventions decided to reduce their annual grants in view of the new source of funding, so part of the bequested funds had to be used for regular operating expenses.[34]

Displaced Persons

Social concern did not end with the signing of the peace treaties after the war. Through the Baptist World Alliance, western Baptists contributed over $25,000 in aid to churches in war-ravaged Europe—one of the largest per capita contributions in the BWA.

An additional $6,000 was passed on to the Alliance to help fund their immigration program for Displaced Persons. With the Reverend William Sturhahn of Winnipeg acting as immigration officer, the Alliance brought in over 500 families, most of whom were sponsored by the rapidly expanding German Baptist churches in the West.[35] The North American (German) Baptists continued the program and reported that by 1973 over 6,000 immigrants had been assisted.[36]

Another Educational Venture

Happily, the latest undertakings of the Baptist Union of Western Canada in the field of education have been much more successful than those of earlier periods. It is perhaps significant that the first two of these flourishing institutions was established for lay training.

The Baptist Leadership Training School (BLTS) opened its doors in the final year of the decade, 1949, with a small body of students: eighteen full-time and twelve part-time. Pressure for this training came not only because leaders were needed for rural churches, but also because of the proliferation of Bible schools—particularly across the Prairie provinces. As has been mentioned, these schools, initially rigid in both theological approach and disciplines taught, did attract many young people (and more especially their parents) after the war. Most were starkly independent and many were even antidenominational. When young members of Baptist Union churches began to join their friends in enrolling it was soon realized that many prospective leaders for work at home and abroad were being lost. In his initial report, the first principal of BLTS noted that more than eighty Baptist Union young people had attended non-Baptist residential schools in the previous three years, many of them by then in full-time service for other groups.[37]

Three "Volunteer" Schools

Initially, the Union was asked simply to prepare a lay course of study, and the educational policy committee recommended that a number of ten-day Bible training institutes be established, further suggesting that any young people with available time might attend the Alberta Baptist Bible Academy of the Swedish Baptists, who up to that point still retained a tenuous affiliation with the Baptist Union. This latter recommendation was repeated in 1945 with the added suggestion that the Union place an instructor on the academy's staff. But soon it became apparent that the Swedish Baptists were about to withdraw from the Union in favour of continuing a single relationship with their American counterparts, and this plan fell by the wayside.

In its continuing search for a suitable vehicle, the educational policy committee then proposed the formation of no fewer than three "volunteer" schools in the centres of Vancouver, Calgary and Winnipeg. These were to be located in church buildings, operated by local committees, and they were to offer five- to ten-week courses taught by local ministers.

Although the proposal was somewhat reluctantly approved by Convention, it simply proved to be unfeasible. Unfazed, the committee then advocated a single school to hold classes in a Calgary church and with a full-time principal. This plan was accepted eagerly by the delegates at the 1947 Convention and the search for the first principal began. By September of the following year the Reverend Ronald F. Watts had been appointed, beginning a long career of denominational service which much later culminated in service as general secretary of the Baptist Convention of Ontario and Quebec. The Baptist Leadership Training School was opened on the premises of Olivet Church, Calgary, in October 1949.

With its emphasis on lay training, BLTS has provided the churches with many capable local leaders while some graduates, both men and women, have gone on to further education and the ministry. Its contribution to denominational life is singular. The present brick residence, whose cornerstone was laid in 1962 by Prime Minister John G. Diefenbaker, was built largely through a generous contribution from Calgary businessman James Smalley.

The Baptist Union of Western Canada thus came to mid-century with greater prospects than it had had for at least two decades. A lay education centre had just been launched, and extension activities had been resumed, at least in a halting way. Finances had been turned around and membership had edged up slightly — from 16,796 in 1930 to 17,221 in 1949.[38]

CHAPTER 25

L'Union d'Églises Baptistes Françaises au Canada

*"What we in our hands and in our hearts and souls
deposit of the Word of God will never be destroyed.
We are labouring for the future."*
— THÉODORE LAFLEUR

The dawning of the twentieth century found the Grande Ligne Mission at the end of an era. With the death of its founders, Henrietta Feller and Louis Roussy, the Mission's "Golden Age" had faded. Yet, as Théodore Lafleur wrote in 1900, "after these sixty-five years of labourious service . . . if we take the aggregate results, comprising as it has a right to, all the converts of the different missionary efforts from the beginning of the Grande Ligne Mission . . . we may say that [they total] about forty thousand, about equally divided between the two countries . . . ."[1]

While Lafleur does not claim that all of the approximately 20,000 French Canadian converts came to know salvation through the efforts of the Grande Ligne Mission, most undoubtedly did.

As the century turned, 126 students were enrolled at Feller Institute at Grande Ligne. Churches and missions had been organized at many locations in the Montreal-Ottawa area and even as far afield as Manitoba and Nova Scotia.[2] A new work had also begun in the nation's capital. In 1901, the Reverend George McFaul, who was to be long remembered for his tireless missionary efforts in the Ottawa Valley, accepted an offer from First Church, Ottawa, to use their facilities on Sunday afternoons to hold services in the French language. At first, the congregations were small, ranging from seventeen to fifty, but by the next year the location was shifted to a hall in the French quarter. After being forced out of three consecutive rented halls by pressure from the Roman Catholic church, the little group built their own in 1904. Despite continuing persecution, including peltings with rotten eggs and tomatoes, the congregation developed to the point of erecting a fine new church building in 1920, completely debt-free.[3]

A New Century

In many areas the Grande Ligne Mission was undergoing a time of uncertainty, if not crisis. Indeed, General Secretary John Gilmour, writing in the 1980s, has judged that the mission was "holding on in a closed society"[4] during the whole period from 1910 to 1965. Charles Foster echoes this view, saying that, particularly in the early period, the expansion and effectiveness of the Grande Ligne Mission waned after the beginning of this century."[5]

The Flourishing Institute

One of the major exceptions was Feller Institute at Grande Ligne. Even before the old century had faded, plans were afoot to build a new wing, the pressure on admissions being so great that many had been turned away,[6] more than fifty in 1901 alone.[7] By 1902 the new building and renovations were completed and dedicated, and 139 students were enrolled.

Under the leadership of Dr. G. N. Masse and his brother Arthur, the Institute flourished, new courses being offered which led to university matriculation. Through the pastoral care of Dr. M. B. Parent and the teachers and through the evangelistic endeavours of George McFaul, "each year saw scores of pupils giving themselves to Christ." "Some years," adds Léonard A. Therrien, " it has been our humble joy to report that every last pupil in the house was intelligently and sincerely a professing Christian."[8]

The Spirit of Nationalism

While the surrounding society may have remained closed to the Good News of Christ, it was not shut to other currents more secular and sometimes antireligious in nature. In a review issued in 1907, a member of the mission's board of directors forecast "a tidal wave of infidelity" following in the wake of movements in Europe, especially in France where, he said, "hundreds of priests and whole communities . . . are breaking away from the papacy."[9]

The tidal wave did not beat on the Quebec shore in quite the way that the Reverend T. B. Brown had anticipated, however. A report the following year zeroed in on the Canadian scene, emphasizing that "the growing spirit of nationalism is everywhere manifest."[10] This nationalism, which focused on Quebec as a distinct society and presaged the separatism of the mid-century, was developing only slowly in a largely rural community that was then just beginning to urbanize. At this point the Roman Catholic Church was not yet viewed as an adversary, the French Canadians being more prone to blame the English for their difficulties. Rather than turning to Protestant groups, French Canadians just stopped going to church—especially in the cities. But all of this was yet to come. Meanwhile, the Mission still faced a tightly closed community.

In the early years of the century, Alphonse de Ligouri Therrien, one of the mission's great stalwarts, wrote of their plight in language reminiscent of the words the Apostle Paul used in writing his second letter to the Corinthians. He was responding to criticism from an Ontario pastor:

... we are deprived of all racial sympathy.... We are ostracized by our own kith and kin, looked upon as traitors to our nationality, our language and our religion. Day in and day out ... we wear out our bodies and our souls in a work which humanly speaking seems like attempting the impossible. We find ourselves facing constantly tremendous problems ... tempted in an evil day and by the evil one, to let things go to the four winds of heaven. And it comes to pass that ... when the burden seems almost unbearable, when the enemy taunts us with sneers and scoffings, that a voice supposed to be from our friends ... is saying ... you are not meeting the situation![11]

And he went on to invite the critical Ontario brother to "come down here and try your hand at the work."[12]

Therrien was named president of the Baptist Convention of Ontario and Quebec in 1911. In that same year Grande Ligne colporteurs were arrested on two occasions ostensibly for selling books without a licence — though no such licence was required by provincial law for any regular society.[13]

Supporting Union

The Grande Ligne Mission was an early supporter of efforts to establish an all-Canada Baptist body in the first two decades of the twentieth century. In 1908 the Mission board expressed its willingness "to commit the election of its Board to the Dominion Convention," with the reasonable provisos that the name remain, the board be located in Montreal and that it be at least one-third French.[14] Such a relationship would undoubtedly have provided greater and more even funding for Grande Ligne, but it was not yet to be.

The Struggle to Sustain

In 1910 the Grande Ligne Mission board made a change in direction that could have sounded the death-knell of the mission if it had been undertaken in later years. It was reasoned that since many of the converts had found their spiritual, and sometimes cultural, home among the English-speaking and away from the persecution of family, church and erstwhile friends, perhaps the mission itself should follow the same path. Thus it was decided that the mission should embark on "a gradual dilution of the French orientation of the work."[15]

Intermarriage with the English

Although some services had already been held in English in Ottawa and other locations, St. Paul's Church, Montreal, was chosen as the test site for the new approach. In the words of the Grande Ligne report of that year, it became "the first Bilingual Baptist Church in Canada,"[16] with a membership of forty-six. Other churches later followed suit.

The report of the next year guilelessly forecast the danger. "In all our congregations," the reporter wrote, "many of the French are marrying into English families." Comments historian Nelson Thomson:

> Given the ease with which the newly-planted seedling could be transplanted into English soil, the end result was predictable: in the course of a generation the people were no longer French-Canadians, and the collective witness was to that degree weakened.[17]

Yet the strongest of the French Canadian leaders—even the redoubtable Alphonse Therrien — supported the concept at the time. In his Convention address during the term of his Ontario-Quebec presidency Therrien advocated a nationwide system of education, with English as the national language.[18] It is obvious that Therrien was assuming English would eventually be spoken throughout the country. Since a multicultural society prevailed, however, the Baptists of the Grande Ligne Mission were in danger of losing their advantage in their work among Canada's French-speaking people.

Anglicization

By 1914 St. Paul's evening worship was conducted entirely in English, and services in that language had become "the strongest part of the work."[19] At St. Constant services had become bilingual. Articles in the student paper at the Feller Institute were, with few exceptions, published in English.

As late as 1932 a number of bilingual churches were sending their reports to the annual conference of the mission in English. "Anglicization," writes historian W. Nelson Thomson, "came to be an unquestioned fact of life." He points to the 1927 mission report concerning the situation at St. Constant, where the pastor spoke only English. As the report puts it, "the people, though French . . . [are] familiar with the English tongue, most of them having been students at Feller Institute." "With hindsight," Thomson concludes, "one can regret that the progressive slide to anglicization was not recognized and remedied at the time."[20]

Trends in the society of the time only served to support the changed emphasis. As the confessional public school system developed in Quebec, "Catholic French" and "English Protestant" were two accepted norms, with French Canadian Protestants tending to secure their education and make their business and social contacts in the anglo-saxon Protestant milieu.[21] It was to be many years before French Protestant public schooling was to be made available.

The War's Toll

Not everyone within the little group of churches was pleased with the trend towards anglicization. There is good reason to believe in fact that many of those in the pew were not at all pleased with it. The whole congregation of L'Oratoire Baptist Church in Montreal had shown its concern at an early stage in a letter to its pastor. Regarding their young people, they wrote: "We have this dear youth [of the church]. We do not want to see them dispersed among the English churches . . . . We thank you for all you do to interest and encourage them."[22] But anglicization was not the only threat to the young people of the Quebec churches. As in other parts of Canada, war took its toll from the Grande Ligne Mission. According to one of their writers, "the [First] World War disturbed our work, our fields and our school,"[23] Feller enrolment dropping considerably as numbers of military age enlisted.[24]

Just before and during the war the mission made an effort to forge a closer alignment with the three regional Baptist Conventions in an attempt to bolster their faltering outreach. But finally, in 1916, it was decided that any such action should be deferred until peace was restored.[25] In fact, the arrangement was not made for another twenty years, when the century's second war was impending.

The Struggle Continues

The mid-twenties witnessed a brief revival, the mission reporting eighty-three baptisms in 1927, one of the highest numbers in many years.[26] Resident enrolment at Feller Institute bounced back after the war, and in 1930 it was reported that Grande Ligne included fourteen organized French Baptist churches and missions and fifteen other centres where periodic services were held.[27]

In the next decade, further development took place in the Maritimes through the work of the Reverend Henri Lanctin, a native of France. Lanctin had begun working in 1909 at Lac Long, Quebec, and had visited some sixteen lumber camps in the area, little clusters of converts resulting.[28] After doing service in World War I, he took up his mission work again, this time at Connors, New Brunswick. But he had contracted tuberculosis during the war and had to stop work to take treatment at the sanitorium in Saint John. He couldn't be held back entirely, however, and while in the sanitorium mailed thousands of gospels and evangelistic tracts to the French Acadians. After he was discharged three years later, Lanctin moved to Moncton where, supported by the strong Baptist churches of that city, he opened a small bookstore carrying French literature as well as Bibles placed by the British and Foreign Bible Society.[29] He called the store La Bonne Nouvelle — Good News. From this beginning a mission of the same name developed, and operated separately from the Grande Ligne for many years.

Depression Blows

As in Quebec, there was fierce opposition to the mission in Moncton. And at first, it was overt. On one occasion missionaries holding an outdoor tent meeting in a Moncton suburb were attacked by a mob of five hundred people. Two RCMP officers were beaten unconscious while defending the little group, and the tent was pulled down and burned.[30] Despite such resistance, a church was established at Moncton, becoming part of the United Baptist Convention of the Maritime Provinces, and work was begun in other parts of the Maritimes, including mission stations and radio and summer camping ministries. Later, under the influence of the Reverend Maurice Boillat, who had been pastor of the Moncton French Baptist Church, La Bonne Nouvelle Mission was united with Grande Ligne.

With the onset of the Depression the Grande Ligne's operations suffered more blows. Ontario and Quebec's 1922 *Year Book* records that the Mission experienced declining revenues, increasing deficits, reduced salaries and expanded workloads for the tiny staff of missionaries.[31] Fresh persecution had arisen through the implementing of Quebec's nefarious Padlock Law. Supposedly aimed at "communists," the Act not only attempted to muzzle the press but enabled the police to shut down for a year any building where the promotion of communism was suspected. But "according to reports from all the missionaries, Protestants [were] being described as communists in public statements by the priests on many of our fields."[32] Under such oppression the churches over the quarter-century from 1925 to 1950 failed to produce a single pastor or worker from their own ranks, relying increasingly on Swiss missionaries,[33] and later on men and women from the Anglo-Saxon community.

Even in 1936, the year that marked the one hundredth anniversary of the founding of the Grande Ligne Mission, there was not much to celebrate. The past certainly looked better than the future. Charles G. Smith, representative of the Baptist Convention of Ontario and Quebec to the Mission, pleaded with his fellow Convention members: "Will the Baptists of Ontario and Quebec take this noble Grande Ligne Mission seriously?"[34] At the same time, voices were calling for change, but that change could not occur without reversing the unfortunate decision of 1910.

Feller Lost

Nothing changed during the thirties, however, and World War II had the same debilitating effect on Grande Ligne as it had on Baptist organizations in the rest of the country. In 1940 the amount of money entering the French Canadian field was only a quarter of the amount that had been donated in 1900.[35] Yet the mission was most devastated when the Feller Institute had to be closed. In fact, Feller, of all the Baptist residential schools in Canada, had kept its doors open the longest — until 1943. Then in that year Canada's armed forces commandeered the premises for a German prisoner-of-war camp.[36]

Feller was really lost to the mission and the constituency for over five years. This, writes historian Charles M. Foster, "tended to dishearten both the workers and those interested in the Mission from the outside."[37] It was a low point in Grande Ligne history . . . perhaps the low point. Yet the light continued to shine. One year the German prisoners were readily granted the use of the nearby Roussy Memorial Church for Christmas and New Year services. The latter was well attended, the first packed out.[38]

Over the years, the Conventions and the Grande Ligne board also sought seriously to correct the mission's organizational weaknesses and to increase its financial backing. By 1946 a reorganization of the mission was finally underway. Representatives of the two Conventions and the Baptist Union of Western Canada were to be nominated to the Grande Ligne Board, sitting with seven other directors named by the mission.[39] In April 1947 the Canadian government returned the Feller buildings to the mission,[40] together with a sum of money to renovate them. Because of difficulties in assembling a staff, the college reopening was delayed until the fall of 1948 when Feller, "beautifully restored," inaugurated a new term with ninety students and a new principal, the Reverend Émile A. Boisvert, his wife Freda being principal of the women's school.[41] In the same year the Reverend H. C. Wilkinson replaced Aubrey Small, who had served as general secretary of the Grande Ligne Mission since 1931.

Turnaround and Union

By 1949 the Grande Ligne president felt able to affirm that "everywhere one can feel a deep stirring in the workers and churches of our whole Mission that promises great things for the future." Yet total membership at the time was 872, and although there had been additions, the net loss that year was 68.[42] Members were still moving away.

Some shock treatment was required. "By the 1950's," says one writer, Thomson, "the alarm was being sounded." Principal Boisvert commented: "Several young English Canadians are coming to work among us. That is good, but our churches are not giving us missionaries."[43] Reinforcement was soon received, in the form of Swiss-born Dr. Paul Chodat, who in 1952 persuasively argued that "the penury of workers is such that we must call in English-speaking workers. If that continues the Grande Ligne Mission will not endure as a French Mission."[44]

Although, as Thomson holds, Chodat was not yet aware that "the new English-speaking workers were, to a man, committed to the indigenous concept,"[45] he was certainly thinking along the right lines, being sure that indigenization was essential for survival. So names like Foster, Gillespie, Gilmour, Hunt, Thomson and Seburn began to show up on missionary listings.[46] The list of pastors in 1960 was certainly overbalanced. Included were six English-speaking Canadians who had learned French, two Swiss and one French Canadian.[47]

Maître Chez Nous

Meanwhile, French Canadian society was in ferment — agitation which would profoundly affect Baptist and other evangelical work in Quebec. The Quiet Revolution was triggered by a number of forces, including

Vatican II, urbanization and the simmering demand of the grassroots to "catch up" to English Canada and the world. Canadian historian Donald Creighton writes that it was "the overthrow of a semi-medieval system by a new and vigorous social order."[48]

The Québécois were determined to be masters of their own destiny. "Maître chez nous" was the rallying cry[49] that changed a provincial government, as Jean Lesage was elected in 1960 to replace what was perceived to be the autocratic and debilitating rule of the Union Nationale, a party that had enjoyed strong support from the hierarchy of the Roman Catholic Church in Quebec. Powerful voices were heard openly criticizing ecclesiastical obstructionism, one of them being that of Pierre Elliott Trudeau. A Montreal lawyer and editor at the time, Trudeau chided the ecclesiastics for "fearing progress."[50]

As dissent developed rapidly, it seemed for a while that Quebec might actually separate, especially when the more radical Parti Québécois gained power and proposed virtual separation as the solution to the problem. There was a great sigh of national relief when a plebescite confirmed that Quebec wanted to stay in Confederation.

Preparing with Vision

These societal changes opened wide the door of opportunity for evangelicals in general and Grande Ligne in particular. "Today," wrote John Gilmour in 1964, "is a moment of missionary opportunity in French Canada such as has not been known before." And he added, "At this critical moment French Protestant churches and schools find many seekers after spiritual certainty."[51] The old landmarks were disappearing. Not only was there social upheaval, but Vatican II had "shattered the old, nearly monolithic Catholicism . . . [and] created a dramatic new openness to non-Roman Christians, and especially a new appreciation for the Bible."[52] The Grande Ligne had had the vision to prepare for the change. By 1957, with only half the number of churches, missionaries and schools that it had possessed in 1900,[53] the mission had fully accepted that the policy of bilingualism was a failure and that only rapid movement to indigenization would save the work. Over a number of years study sessions were held under the leadership of Charles Foster, with the purpose of training church members in the principles and consequences of indigenization.[54]

By 1964 the mission was seeking the "re-orientation of its work to meet the changing times."[55] Then in 1966 a leading layman, Dr. Albert Lafrançois, moved that the Association of French Baptist churches affiliate with the Ontario and Quebec Convention, be re-formed into a Union of churches. The motion was widely supported.[56]

It was almost a century since the first tentative French Baptist Union had been formed. The Union des Églises Baptistes Françaises au Canada

—the Union of French Baptist Churches of Canada—was granted federal incorporation and the first full-time general secretary was inducted.[57] He was the Swiss-born Dr. Maurice C. Boillat, who was to give ten years' distinguished service to the new Union before returning to the pastorate.

Problems at Feller

Around the time that Feller College celebrated its 125th anniversary in 1961, difficulties were surfacing — among them, serious financial problems. A "disproportionate number of English-language students" were also enrolling, "who for personality or academic reasons [had] not been able to fit into their home schools."[58] The opening of the first French Protestant public school in Montreal in 1956[59] had improved the situation for evangelical French Canadians, so Gilmour saw a new role ahead for Feller — not primarily to train English-speaking youth but to be a secondary school for French-speaking evangelical Protestants. Feller's second objective was to act as the initial training school for potential pastors and missionaries coming out of French Baptist churches.[60]

Neither goal was to be reached. Laden down by mounting deficits and expanding debt, Feller College was closed in September 1967. At the time, the mission faced unpaid accounts of over $35,000 and an outstanding bank loan of $40,000, along with other liabilities that brought the total to nearly $80,000. The property was sold the next year for $250,000 to a corporation operating day-care units, but the mission still had to carry a twenty-five year mortgage.[61] Although Grande Ligne's debit situation was relieved, many felt that the other costs in losing Feller, the mission's eminently successful educational arm, were too high. Yet the closing may have appeared to be the only option to take at the time.

The Union in Operation

With headquarters in Montreal, the Union developed a widespread radio and television ministry, with its own studio. A youth centre was established in Quebec City in 1969, and a Bible college curriculum was offered. Then, at the 1970 Assembly of the Baptist Federation of Canada (now the Canadian Baptist Federation) the Union d'Églises Baptistes Françaises au Canada was received as the fourth constituent Convention/Union, linking with the United Baptist Convention of the Atlantic Provinces, the Baptist Convention of Ontario and Quebec and the Baptist Union of Western Canada. The French Union also entered the same equal partnership responsible for work abroad through the Canadian Baptist Overseas Mission Board.

In 1971 the French Union recorded a total of eight churches.[62] The next year a serious job of pruning church rolls was undertaken, inactive members being taken off the listings. In the end, total membership was found to be 398, dropping from an unpruned high of 1,008 in 1931.[63] The Union was now lean and ready for action.

The Patterns of Growth

A 1986 publication of the French Union records its advance. From 1972 to 1985 the number of churches increased from 8 to 19, members from 398 to 1,040, a number above even the high of the year 1931. In 1972 just one of the churches was self-supporting. In 1986 nine were in that position. Whereas in the watershed year just 4 of the 13 pastors were French Canadians, in 1985 15 out of 22 were in that category. 1972 saw just one student preparing for the ministry; in 1985 there were 11.[64] During this period former Feller Principal John Gilmour took over as the second general secretary of the Union after Maurice Boillat returned to the pastorate.

Two distinct patterns of growth have been observed — described by the Union as pioneer extension and natural church extension. The former refers to new denominationally sponsored outreach in areas "without any visible presence," where a missionary is sent to start a new cause. This was the method used most by the Grande Ligne Mission and is still continued to some extent. But in more recent days the second method has been used more often. With this procedure, a number of members of an established church move out to a new location to begin another congregation. In some Baptist circles this is called "hiving off."

To provide indigenous leadership for the rapidly expanding outreach, the Union of French Baptist Churches established their "shoestring" seminary.[65] The CETE (Centre d'Études Théologiques Évangeliques) opened its doors in Montreal in 1982, and Dr. Nelson Thomson was named its first director. Official recognition of the school's Baccalauréat en Théologie (Bachelor of Theology) program was granted by Acadia University.[66] In December 1986, CETE joined with the French Union staff in moving a headquarters building on Papineau Avenue, Montreal.[67] And so the work in Quebec has been renewed, adapting to radical social change and responding to the Québécois search for spiritual certainty.

CHAPTER 26

Fellow Baptists

"It is the need of the moment that defines the nature of the mission."
— *JOHN MACNEILL*

There is just enough shaded truth in the old saw that the meeting of two Baptists is likely to produce three opinions to give pause for thought. The numbers and variety of those bodies laying claim to the designation are considerable, for the Baptist insistence on freedom and the primacy of the local church tend to discourage organizational conformity. Of course, it may also be argued that other denominations, while retaining a better semblance of unity, often exhibit similarly discordant inclinations. Perfection has yet to be achieved in the Christian pattern.

Just as our national model is perhaps best described as a mosaic, so the Canadian Baptist shape is incomplete without at least a brief mention of Fellowship Baptists, who are not part of the organizational mainline. In addition to the Fellowship Baptists, there are a few other groups, including churches with particular ethnic ties, that have remained apart.

THE FELLOWSHIP OF EVANGELICAL BAPTIST CHURCHES IN CANADA

The largest of the separate groups is the Fellowship of Evangelical Baptist Churches in Canada, which had its origins in the divisions in Ontario, Quebec and western Canada (mainly British Columbia) in 1927. Those unfortunate episodes were described in Chapter 21.

Although it is technically true that the Baptist Convention of Ontario and Quebec initially excluded some thirteen churches with reluctance, those congregations had previously taken actions that made the dismissals almost inevitable. Not only had the support of Convention projects been discontinued, but the dissident churches had banded together in support of a separate Regular Baptist Missionary and Education Society, Women's Missionary Society, college and official publication, the *Gospel Witness*, even while they remained nominally within the Convention.

The Union of Regular Baptist Churches

The week following the Convention's decision not to seat the representatives of Jarvis Street Church, Toronto, thirty churches formed the Union of Regular Baptist Churches of Ontario and Quebec. T. T. Shields was named president, a position which he held until 1931 and again from 1937 to 1949. In the same year two other breakaway bodies were formally founded: the Fundamentalist Baptist Young People's Association and the Women's Missionary Society of Regular Baptists of Canada — the latter, like the Union, appropriating the historic "Regular" designation of the denomination.

Reducing the Union

Within four years the three groups, born out of conflict, were in conflict among themselves. Although the women's and young people's organizations drew their support and membership from the new Union's congregations, they carried on independent programs and, in the words of Fellowship Baptist historian Leslie K. Tarr, the Union leadership felt they had "diverted Regular Baptist energies and resources without effective church control and direction."[1]

Nine pastors were "named and expelled" from the Union over the hotly contested issue. Their churches then withdrew, as did a number of others, reducing the Union from its by then nearly ninety congregations to sixty.[2] Soon there was to be a third grouping in central Canada, the Fellowship of Independent Baptist Churches, but more of that later.

The new Union had suffered a heavy blow and more were to come. An overseas mission to Liberia was inaugurated in 1928 and ten missionaries had been sent under its auspices by 1937. By that time, however, the small group of churches found it impossible to support the enterprise during the Depression period and the annual meeting voted to discontinue it.[3]

Jailed for Preaching in French

Results in French Canada were initially halting but eventually more enduring. Work was begun in the mid-thirties in the mining area of northwestern Quebec: first in Noranda, then in Val d'Or. Services in the French language were carried on in Val d'Or through street meetings in 1939 and regular meetings the following year. In 1939 a bilingual radio broadcast was also begun by Val d'Or pastor W. J. Wellington.

As in the case of the Grande Ligne Mission, persecution was rife. Pastor Murray Heron, who accepted a call to Noranda in 1946, was jailed along with his associates on several occasions for preaching in French on the streets of Rouyn-Noranda. Others suffered similarly. By 1968 the Fellowship of Evangelical Baptist Churches (now the successor of the Union) had churches in Rouyn-Noranda, Malartic, Val d'Or and Lac Castagnier. Churches had also been established in the south of the province near the American border, as well as in Montreal and Drummondville.[4]

A Showdown

Then the clouds of dissension moved in on the Union of Regular Baptist Churches of Ontario and Quebec once more. T. T. Shields, whose Jarvis Street Church had retained total control of Toronto Baptist Seminary, engineered the dismissal of its dean, W. Gordon Brown. Two other teachers and most of the students departed with him. The year was 1948.

Utterly frustrated by Shields's latest action, a number of pastors and others drew up a paper indicating that the signers would no longer accept his domineering leadership, which they felt was dividing Union ranks. Predictably, Shields's reaction was bitter, ensuring a showdown at the next Convention. With "the great majority . . . determined that they could and would no longer put their time and energy and service into a work whose only future seemed to be another division,"[5] the annual meeting voted in the Reverend A. C. Wood as president. Shields did not accept the defeat gracefully and the following year led his Jarvis Street Church and nine or ten others out of the Union.

Fellowship Baptist historian and former general secretary J. A. Watt characterizes T. T. Shields as "a great man, a prince of preachers, a champion of truth and the voice of fundamentalism. But," he adds, "his tendency to fight his friends and divide the ranks of the people whom he led was too much to face by even those who loved and admired him." Even after Shields left the Union he "experienced more battles among his dwindling number of followers"[6] until his death in 1955.

To replace Toronto Baptist Seminary, which remained under Shields and Jarvis Street Church, discharged Dean Brown joined with pastor Jack Scott of the Independent Forward Baptist Church, Toronto, in establishing Central Baptist Seminary. With Scott as president and Brown as dean, the new seminary offered classes on the premises of Forward Church until a new property was purchased in Toronto. The seminary still operates independently, the stipulation remaining that trustees must be members of an "evangelical Baptist Church."[7]

The Fellowship of Independent Baptist Churches

At the time of the 1927 break, not all the churches that departed from the Baptist Convention of Ontario and Quebec associated with the Union of Regular Baptist Churches. Some remained independent. Then the nine pastors and churches that were excluded from the Union in 1931 immediately became the core of another "loosely-knit fellowship."[8] A rally involving twenty-three of these unattached churches was held in the summer of that year and two years later the representatives of twenty-seven churches and six missions formed the Fellowship of Independent Baptist Churches of Canada.

Since this new body emphasized the independence of the local church, its co-operative efforts grew slowly. Indeed, in 1939, the budget showed a grand total of only $2,110.[9] A paper was published, the *Fellowship Evangel*, and five years after the founding of the Independent Fellowship there were forty-eight organized churches on its roster, over sixty ministers and "likely two-thirds . . . as many workers abroad as at home"[10] — the last working with a variety of missionary societies.

By 1943 a "thin line" of churches of this Fellowship, nearly 70 in number, with membership estimated at 6,500 extended from Montreal to Moose Jaw, with "a few congregations in the Maritimes."[11] The scarcity of Fellowship Baptist churches in the Atlantic provinces points once more to unity in the Baptist churches in that region. As Tarr records, "no Baptist group outside the existing Convention has ever been able to claim a significant following"[12] there.

Convention of Regular Baptists of British Columbia

In the far western province of British Columbia another strand of what would eventually become the Fellowship of Independent Baptist Churches was gathering strength. The sixteen churches that left the Convention of Baptist Churches of British Columbia quickly formed another Convention, the Regular Baptists of British Columbia, like their Ontario counterparts taking possession of the historic "Regular" designation.

Division and Consolidation

Within a year the 16 churches of about 1,000 members grew to 22 and 1,850 members and had established a Women's Missionary Society of Regular Baptists. As in the central provinces, the new Convention launched heavily into a home missions program, with a little financial help coming from the Union of Regular Baptists of Ontario and Quebec.[13]

However, divisions plagued the new body. "Now that the modernist foe was no longer in the camp," writes B.C. Regular Baptist historian John B. Richards, "internecine strife began to manifest itself"[14] — first in the Regular Convention's largest church, Mount Pleasant, Vancouver. Two successive British pastors recommended by T. T. Shields remained only a short time, and one of them, W. M. Robertson, split the church and moved out with half the membership to form Vancouver's Independent Metropolitan Tabernacle. The death of a number of key leaders also created a vacuum, and the absence of a ministerial training centre of their persuasion in the West only weakened their position. In many instances the "imported" leaders from overseas and the continent and the graduates of independent schools did not adapt well to local needs.[15]

A serious contention also arose concerning overseas missions. Cut off from the missionaries of the Canadian Baptist Foreign Mission Board which they had been supporting before the 1927 break, the Regular Baptists cast about for alternatives. A plan to co-operate with their counterparts in Ontario and Quebec in their ill-fated Liberian mission did not materialize. Then an independent, personally directed mission in China invited their support and they sent a couple and a single woman as missionaries.

The newcomers discovered that the Chinese opportunity had been misrepresented, causing considerable controversy on the field and even more at home. Although a special convention backed a board decision to continue with the operation, the three missionaries in China found it impossible and had to abandon the project. Without a base and looking about for a place of service in the Orient, in 1936 these missionaries offered to assist the North Manchurian Mission, then in need of support and direction. This resulted in the adoption of that mission by the British Columbia Regular Baptists as their overseas field. This work was continued successfully until the war years and the Communist occupation. Finally, a new mission to Japan was opened in 1952.[16]

The controversy over the mission had done considerable damage, however. As a result of it, a number of churches, including Mount Pleasant, withdrew from the Regular Convention. Even the Reverend Arnold Bennett, who had been one of the chief Fundamentalist spokesmen at the time of the schism, found himself out of fellowship and left to form an undenominational church. From a total membership of nearly 2,000 in 1932 the Regular Convention dropped to about 1,400 by 1939.[17]

Yet progress was still being made. With the support of the small Alberta Fellowship, who had closed their Western Baptist Bible College in Calgary, the British Columbia Regular Baptists opened Northwest Baptist Bible College in 1945. Initially in Port Coquitlam, it was moved to Vancouver in 1958. The next year, receiving a provincial charter and the right to grant theological degrees, the school changed its name to the Northwest Baptist Theological Seminary.[18]

Following the difficult years of the Depression, the Regular Baptists of British Columbia consolidated their efforts, and associations were developed beginning in 1940.[19] Meanwhile, however, another threat to the Regular Convention's well-being was about to appear.

Southern Co-operation

After World War II the massive Southern Baptist Convention had made rapid progress in the American Pacific Northwest and had organized the Baptist General Convention of Oregon, which soon embraced Washington as well. In 1951 the executive secretary-treasurer of that Convention, Dr. R. E. Milam, was invited to speak to a conference of B.C. Regular Baptist pastors, and his presentation met with wide interest.

The next year Milam and Dr. J. D. Grey, Southern Convention President, were speakers at the Regular Convention, again causing considerable excitement over the possibilities of co-operation. A number of pastors pressed for immediate affiliation, while others strongly opposed the idea, especially because of the "Landmark"[20] tendencies of the Oregon-Washington Convention. In 1953 Emmanuel, a church in the lower mainland, joined two smaller churches in associating with the American group and withdrawing from the Regular Convention. There was also a major division over the issue in First Church, Kamloops.[21] Although the large majority of Regular churches drew back, the way had been opened for Southern Baptists to enter Canada, an opportunity which they seized.

Amalgamation

So there grew up three distinct groups of Baptists who had separated from the mainstream: two in central Canada and one in British Columbia, with minor representation on the Prairies. By the middle of the century all the breakaway groups were thinking of amalgamation, particularly in Ontario and Quebec.

With two schools of ministerial training available in Ontario — the Central Baptist and Toronto Baptist seminaries — a constant stream of graduates was available. And they were all needed, especially within the Fellowship of Independent Baptist Churches. Following their slow beginnings, they had thirty building programs in progress during one three-year period in the late forties. J. F. Holliday, writing in the *Fellowship Evangel* of December 1949, reported that "there are more than a hundred churches and organized missions associated with the Fellowship, and about every week brings news of some new cause starting or seeking affiliation with our group of churches."[22]

With the Union of Regular Baptist Churches also broadening its base in the same territory, thoughts of a merger were bound to arise. In 1949 the editor of the Fellowship paper remarked upon the "steadily growing spirit of co-operation between Fellowship and Union churches." Noting that in doctrine and practice there were virtually no differences, he concluded that "the probable outcome of these trends is obvious."[23]

Statement of Faith

Undoubtedly, the departure of Shields and the small group of rebellious churches from the Regular Union hastened the process of amalgamation. A liaison committee was formed and at the annual meeting of the Union in 1952 there was unanimous approval for a resolution recognizing that a merger was desirable. The next year the Independent Fellowship voted in a similar way.[24]

Preparing a statement of faith was not so simple, however, as there were open and close communionists within the ranks of both groups. And while most Union and Fellowship Baptists were premillenialists, others were not. It was finally agreed that these issues would not be considered a test of faith. Now that the decks were cleared, the two came together on October 21, 1953, as the Fellowship of Evangelical Baptist

Churches in Canada. The Fellowship was incorporated and allowed to use the qualifying "Evangelical" label only after assuring a Canadian Senate committee "that it did not intend its name to suggest that it was the only evangelical group of Baptist churches in Canada."[25]

A Rocky Road

Meanwhile, western Baptists claiming the name "Regular" had followed the amalgamation decisions and subsequent progress with interest. When Holliday wrote his first editorial in the *Fellowship Baptist*, he hinted that the West should eventually amalgamate with the eastern group, indicating that the new Fellowship should "commend itself to fundamental Baptist groups both in the East and in the West."[26] The editor of the *Western Regular Baptist* did not hesitate to take up the torch. Reflecting no doubt on the Oregon-Washington situation, he wrote two months after the Ontario-Quebec merger: "We believe the hour has come for a united fundamental Baptist testimony across Canada. We are Canadians. Let us stay Canadian . . . . "[27]

Progress, was slow, however. In 1956 a conference was convened in Calgary to discuss methods of co-operation between the Regular Baptists of British Columbia and Alberta and the new Fellowship. The report of the conference was adopted by all and a liaison committee formed. Then the committee stumbled along a rocky road for nearly a decade until finally in 1965 the concluding ratification was signed by British Columbia. Formal acceptance of the Regular Baptists of British Columbia into the Fellowship of Evangelical Baptist Churches in Canada took place in October of that year.[28] In central Canada there were 220 churches in the Fellowship at the time, in British Columbia there were 47 and there were also a few dotting the prairies. One church in Nova Scotia joined in 1957[29] and a few have linked up subsequently. By 1982 the number of British Columbia churches had reached 71, the membership 6,500.[30]

SEMBEC

Continuing to stress home mission outreach, the Fellowship added nearly seventy churches in the decade of the sixties: some old and some new. A similar pattern developed in the seventies. Some $26,000 budgeted for home mission grants in 1965 climbed to nearly a quarter of a million dollars by 1978, not including sums spent in British Columbia.[31] A number of new churches were built with money received from the unique and well-established "Minute Man" building program — which had begun under the auspices of the Union.[32] Benefiting from twenty-five years of giving by individual participants, about ninety churches received Minute Man loans, which totalled over $500,000.[33]

The work among French Canadians in Quebec also expanded, as indigenous missionary pastors were secured. A seminary was established in that province — SEMBEC (Séminaire Baptiste Évangelique Canadien) and a full-time French Canada Mission Board secretary was appointed.

Like their counterparts in L'Union d'Églises Baptistes Françaises au Canada and the earlier Grande Ligne Mission, the Fellowship discovered that the principle of bilingual churches was unworkable and rejected it.[34]

Under the combined Fellowship, Christian education and youth work developed apace. The Fellowship Baptist Young People's Association, successors of the original Fundamentalist Association, celebrated their fiftieth anniversary in 1977. Under their full-time director, the Reverend Ray Lawson, a number of singular programs were developed, including SWIFT — the Summer Workers in Fellowship Thrust — in which youth served for the summer months both in home missions churches and overseas. During the first year of the program, ten young people gave service overseas in Colombia, South America, and twenty-five others served at home.[35]

The FBYPA was also responsible for inaugurating the Muskoka Baptist Conference, a retreat centre in northern Ontario's Muskoka district. In 1972 the conference grounds became a self-sustaining corporation but continued to have close ties with the Fellowship.[36]

With overseas mission fields already established in Japan and India, the Fellowship sent a single woman to West Pakistan and a couple to work with the Far East Broadcasting Company in Hong Kong in 1967. Soon another couple was dispatched to Hong Kong and yet another to Colombia. By 1970 there were twenty-eight Fellowship missionaries on those fields and in Bangladesh. Further impetus was given to the overseas program in 1977 when the annual meeting voted to enter Africa and Europe.[37]

Vigorous and forward-looking, the Fellowship of Evangelical Baptist Churches in Canada is upholding its prominent place in the Baptist spectrum.

THE NORTH AMERICAN BAPTIST GENERAL CONFERENCE (GERMAN)

The largest body of non-Anglo-Saxon Baptists in Canada is of German origin, embracing about 15,000 members in congregations located in five provinces. They are now partners within the transborder North American Baptist General Conference and, unlike the Fellowship Baptists, are members of the Baptist World Alliance.

The Setting

"A mix of German immigrants arriving in Canada during the last two centuries . . . from Germany . . . Russia and European points,"[38] the North American Baptists trace their first congregation in this land to Bridgeport, Ontario, and the year 1851. Its founder, the Reverend August

Rauschenbusch, was a former Lutheran pastor from Germany who had come to the Baptist position while serving as a travelling overseer of German-language colporteurs for the American Tract Society. The church resulted from special services held among the predominantly Mennonite and Lutheran population of Waterloo County.

By 1870 fourteen churches had been built, but these were the last to be formed in Ontario for over eighty years.[39] In 1911 they reported a membership of 1,153 organized as the Canadian Missionary Society and the Eastern Conference of the United States; some were also members of associations within the Baptist Convention of Ontario and Quebec.[40]

Fifty-Fifty

Meanwhile, German immigration had largely bypassed Ontario for the West, where Baptist work among them was begun in 1885. The Reverend F. A. Petereit of Minneapolis founded the first German Baptist church in the West—at Edenwold near Regina.[41]

Later, funding of the Western Canadian German mission was undertaken on a fifty-fifty basis by the Baptist Union of Western Canada and the German General Conference of America. The churches' missionary contribution was also divided equally between the Union and the Conference. These arrangements continued until 1920.[42]

Working out from Edenwold, F. A. Petereit covered much of what is now Saskatchewan, and in 1888 moved into the area of present-day Alberta, as well. By 1889 a second German missionary, C. Poehlman, had been appointed by the Manitoba Convention Board and churches were organized at Ebenezer, Saskatchewan, and Winnipeg.[43] Through the joint efforts of Canadian Baptists and German Baptists of the United States, eleven churches and two organized mission stations with a total of nearly 500 members dotted the West by the turn of the century, the combined membership in western and central Canada numbering over 1,400.[44]

An Ominous Signal

In 1899 the Manitoba and Northwest Convention appointed the Reverend William Schunke as superintendent of German work in western Canada on the recommendation of the German U.S. Conference. He served for ten years in that position, and was pastor of the Winnipeg German Baptist Church at the same time. Three years after his appointment Schunke led the western German churches in the formation of the Northern Conference of the German Baptist Conference of North America—still retaining links with the Manitoba and North-west Convention.[45]

Superintendent Schunke resigned in 1909 and was replaced by Yorkton pastor Ferdinand A. Bloedaw. It was at that time there was "an ominous signal that the Germans in the West would opt for a single alignment with the Germans in the United States."[46] The occasion arose when Brandon College President A. P. McDiarmid offered to place a German professor on the college faculty. The Northern Conference declined, holding that, "In the past our supply of pastors came from Rochester [Seminary] and we have no reason to turn from that source of supply. Our German pastors must have their training in a German school."[47]

A New Period

A decade later the connection was severed. In 1918 the German Conference of the U.S.A. broke its long-held link with the American Baptist Home Mission Society. The following year the board of the Baptist Union of Western Canada took the initiative to invite the churches of German origin in its region to become full members of the Union. The Northern Conference chose instead to retain single affiliation with its transborder body.[48]

The situation in Ontario was different. There the historic and strong Berlin (now Kitchener) Baptist Church affiliated completely with the Baptist Convention of Ontario and Quebec in 1920. Others followed the trend.[49]

Before and after the events of 1919 and 1920 Canadian German Baptists participated generously in the overseas mission effort of the North American Baptists. Missions centred in the Cameroons and Europe, particularly the Balkans, Poland and pre-communist Russia.[50] In the period between the two wars the North American Baptists supported missionaries in twenty different countries. Although some doors were closed during World War II work continues to this day in many of these lands.[51]

Pressures

After World War I and again after World War II, a flood of German immigration poured into Canada, and particularly into the West. As a result, churches that were becoming anglicized experienced a strong infusion of German culture and language, the German Baptist numbers in the West expanding from 2,000 to 5,000 in the six years after 1926.[52]

The German Baptists who settled on the Prairies were particularly hard hit during the Depression, since they lived largely in rural areas. During World War II the German churches felt the pressure of being associated with a nation with which Canada was at war. German names of churches were dropped in favour of English ones, and the whole denomination adopted the designation North American Baptist General Conference. Despite the war, however, 600 members were added. Five new churches were established in British Columbia, and these linked up with the Pacific Conference of the U.S.A.[53]

To co-ordinate work among postwar immigrants to Canada, and especially Germans, the Baptist World Alliance appointed pastor and later area secretary Dr. William Sturhann in 1950.[54] Three years later sponsorship of the displaced persons' program was taken over by the North American Baptist Immigration and Colonization Society, and a total of 6,335 persons settled in Canada between 1951 and 1973 with assistance from this body.[55] A limited number of these were Hungarian refugees but most were of German extraction.

By 1975 the German Baptist churches of western Canada numbered nearly 90, with almost 12,500 members, and central Canada had 14, with over 1,700 communicants. North American Baptist Seminary in Edmonton offers a full Master of Divinity program and an adjacent College gives Bible and academic training. The churches have gradually moved from their ethnic beginnings out into the mainstream of society. They are growing, particularly in the larger cities and are attracting evangelicals of many stripes of their ranks. Close fraternal relations are maintained both with the Baptist Union of Western Canada and the Baptist Convention of Ontario and Quebec.

BAPTIST GENERAL CONFERENCE (SWEDISH)

When Alexander Grant was pastor of Winnipeg's First Baptist Church and defacto superintendent of the Manitoba Convention in the 1890s, he was found one day watching the host of European immigrants who were swarming around the pioneer community's railway station. Deeply moved, his eyes welling with tears, he asked, "Who is going to tell these people of our Saviour?"[56] Among the newcomers were settlers from the Scandinavian Peninsula . . . and with them Grant did something in answer to his own question.

It was the spring of 1893 when a number of Swedish Baptists put down tentative roots in Winnipeg. Neither of the two Baptist churches there could meet their language needs, one being English, the other German. Some moved away, but the next year the Reverend Martin Bergh of North Dakota visited the city and, after consulting with Grant, began establishing a Scandinavian Baptist Church. Although Bergh was a Norwegian, he was also fluent in Swedish and in his little congregation there were a number of Danes in addition to the new Swedish arrivals. The same year Bergh visited Scandinavian settlements at Rat Portage (Kenora) and Norman across the Ontario border and, according to the pages of the *Northwest Baptist*, he also travelled as far west as Calgary, Red Deer and Wetaskiwin.[57]

Shortly before his tragic death by drowning in 1897, Alexander Grant visited Ontario and made a strong and fruitful appeal for support of the Scandinavian outreach in the West. When a new church building was completed by the congregation the same year, it was fittingly named the

Alexander Grant Scandinavian Memorial Church[58] — today simply the Grant Memorial Baptist Church.

Swedish Conference Interest

A decade after the initial founding, there were eleven Scandinavian Baptist churches in Canada and as many as twenty-five "preaching points." These were served by just seven full-time pastors and a few summer students.[59]

It was not until 1905 that the Swedish General Conference of America became interested in the work north of the border. That year they appointed the Reverend Fred Palmborg as missionary evangelist to their people in the Canadian West and, co-operating closely with Canadian Baptists, Palmborg served effectively for five years, with five more churches being organized.[60] He was followed in turn by the Reverend J. P. Sundstrom and the Reverend J. Paul Erickson.

The Swedish work was soon organized into two Conferences. By 1948 the Alberta Conference comprised seven Alberta churches and their mission stations. The Central Conference contained six congregations in Saskatchewan and four each in Manitoba and northwestern Ontario, together with their preaching points. The limited work in British Columbia came directly under the American Conference. The two Canadian Conferences, whose Prairie membership totalled about 900 were to that date dually aligned with the Baptist Union of Western Canada and the Swedish General Conference in America.[61]

In 1948 the Central Conference withdrew its affiliation with the Union to continue a single connection with the American body. The Alberta Conference followed a year later. Noting that it is difficult to determine the precise reason for the withdrawal, Western Baptist historian Margaret Thompson feels that the growing reluctance of Baptist Union leaders to grant recognition to Swedish pastors who lacked formal training likely had a bearing on the decision.[62]

SOUTHERN BAPTISTS IN CANADA

"Should there be Southern Baptists in Canada?" This headline appears on a page of the respected religious journal, *Christianity Today*, in its issue of March 16, 1984. Writer Lloyd Mackey really does not come down on one side of the question, however. This is partly because the question is fairly academic, since the Southern Baptists — despite having roots in the American South — are firmly settled in Canada and apparently are not disposed to retire.

A relatively recent addition to the Baptist pattern in Canada, the large and powerful Southern Baptist Convention—over fourteen million strong and the largest single Protestant body in the United States in the late 1980s — is adding still another dimension in a nation where Baptists are a distinct minority. Its Canadian beginnings were in the early 1950s.

A Glowing Report

The decision to move into Canada was taken unilaterally by one of the state components of the Southern Convention — the Baptist General Convention of Oregon-Washington. The southerners had been moving inexorably northward, and by the end of World War II they had established themselves in Oregon. Washington was soon added to their ranks. There, poised on the Canadian border, it was not long before they were given the opportunity to cross.

As noted earlier in this chapter, Executive Secretary R. E. Milam of the Oregon-Washington body had accepted an invitation to participate in a ministers' conference of the British Columbia Regular Baptist Executive Council in 1951. Later the same year the Regular Baptist Executive Council appointed three of their pastors, including their president, to attend a Southern Baptist conference in the northwest as observers. It turned out that the president and one other were prevented from making the trip, but the pastor who did go, the Reverend Ross MacPherson, returned with a glowing report of the Southern Baptist program and the possible benefits of close co-operation with the group. This, writes Fellowship Baptist historian John B. Richards, was the beginning of a number of contacts.[63]

Convinced that affiliation with the Oregon-Washington group was in the best interest of the British Columbia Regulars, MacPherson spearheaded a strong effort to bring that about. It was his Emmanuel Church, Vancouver, that linked up with the Americans in 1953. Its name changed to Kingcrest Southern Baptist, the church hoped to maintain dual affiliation,[64] but as the great majority of Regular Baptists drew back, Emmanuel and two other churches became distinctively Southern Baptist.

Upon this foundation, Milam and his Convention began to build. They petitioned the Southern Baptist Convention for assistance through the home missions board and other SBC agencies.[65] The mother Convention spelled out its policy in 1950, enabling the home missions and Sunday school boards "to develop an indigenous denominational program that will win Canada for Christ" but stipulating that no worker of the two boards should "seek to align existing churches or new churches with our Southern Baptist work."[66]

Liaison Officer

This official policy to promote only indigenous work remained in effect for three decades. The Oregon-Washington group, its name changed to the Northwest Baptist Convention, continued to plant more churches in western Canada, and the Ohio Convention moved into Ontario. A Southern Baptist–Canadian Baptist Conference Committee consisting of Southern Baptist leaders and those of the Canadian Baptist Federation met nearly every year from 1957 on to dissolve possible tensions and to enable the Southern Baptists to provide program assistance where practicable.

That year the Southern Baptist Home Mission Board appointed Dr. W. Bertram King as liaison officer in Canada. King's task as he saw it was "the discovery of a true spiritual affinity between Southern Baptists and Canadian Baptists."[67] Reporting on his activities in 1961 after speaking in 140 Canadian churches, the SBC members of the committee felt that King had opened the way "for future opportunities for assistance to be given in such areas as evangelism, stewardship planning and training, and the improvement of church educational ministries."[68]

While continuing to expand in Canada, the Northwest Convention depended largely on its own resources and private foundation sources of funding. By 1984 it was reported that there were sixty-two congregations in Canada with ties to either the Northwest or the Ohio Conventions.[69] Once again that year, as had been attempted several times, an endeavour was made by the Oregon-Washington leaders to seat messengers (delegates) from the Canadian churches at the annual Southern Baptist Convention. The convention declined, as it had before,[70] but by the mid-1980s, a Canadian Southern Baptist Convention was formed with the official blessing of the American Convention.

Many of the Canadian churches affiliated with the Southern Baptists remain small, but the movement is growing. There was obvious resistance at the outset to the imposition of outside methods by outside pastors in a Canadian setting, but this has decreased as more native-born leaders have come on the scene. After forming a training school of limited scope, the Southern Baptists have established a seminary near Calgary—a move that will enhance their growth opportunities.

Two other small clusters of Baptists should be mentioned here. The splinter of the Union of Regular Baptists which left with T. T. Shields in about 1950 remain as the Association of Regular Baptist Churches, organized in 1957 and led by Jarvis Street Church, Toronto. Then in northern New Brunswick there is the Primitive Baptist Conference, founded in 1875 by George W. Orser. This group lists about 1,000 members in 15 churches.[71] There are, of course, others of many ethnic backgrounds who have through the years become part of the mainstream, among them Hungarians, Ukrainians, Czechoslovakians, Koreans, Chinese, Spanish and many other New Canadians—together making up the Canadian Baptist mosaic.

PART VI

New Horizons

"The skyline is a promise, not a bound."
—*JOHN MASEFIELD*

I T WAS THE NIGHT OF MONDAY, August 8, 1949. Hamilton-born missionary Norman Harold Dabbs, serving in Bolivia under the Canadian Baptist Foreign Mission Board, was in the Indian village of Melcamaya doing what he loved best, sharing the gospel.

He had come that night with the pastor of the Llallagua Church, Carlos Meneses, who often travelled to the mining village on Monday evenings, and a number of believers including Francisco Salazar, President of the Bolivian Baptist Union. Luis Guerrero was driving the truck that took them there.

It was already dark when the little party arrived. They had slides to show and the village had no electricity, so Dabbs connected the projector to the truck battery and the service began with the pictures projected onto the white adobe wall of a Christian's simple home. There was a small congregation.

As the service proceeded, a noise was heard first faintly in the distance and then louder as a shouting mob appeared. Drunken, frenzied and priest-incited, as one of the participants later reported, the mob began to hurl rocks at the little company.

The wounded held their ground at first, but finally took refuge in the truck and pulled away from the scene, their attackers following close behind. They had not travelled far over the rugged terrain when the motor stalled and they were at the mercy of the mob.

Eight Christians died at Melcamaya that August night. Others were wounded. Norman Dabbs, Francisco Salazar, Carlos Meneses and their driver, Luis Guerrero, were among the slain.

But their murder was not pointless. From their martyrs' blood churches were born and strengthened. New missionaries arrived from Canada and the gospel was proclaimed with renewed force.

As Dr. C. Howard Bentall wrote in tribute: "We dare to believe that because of his martyrdom, 'the death of such a life,' under God, Norman has hastened 'the dawn over the Bolivian hills,' " the salvation of many in that needy country.

CHAPTER 27

Canadian Baptists Federate

*"The greater inspirations, the heartier impulse,
the irresistable impetus, the encouragement and fervour . . .
will impart a spirit to all the churches . . . . "*
—H. F. LAFLAMME, 1909, ON THE SUBJECT OF A UNION OF CANADIAN BAPTISTS

Union of all the Baptist churches of Canada was discussed at association and Convention meetings and recorded in minutes for years before it actually occurred. One set of records from a Nova Scotia association makes reference to a letter from Montreal in which the writer expressed "the desirableness of a closer union between all the Baptists of British North America being effected and manifested." The date: June 22, 1846.[1]

The communication came from the Canada Baptist Union — an attempted union of Baptist churches in what are now Ontario and Quebec. Although Nova Scotia Baptists were already busily engaged in their own union discussions at the time, an appointed committee responded, recommending that it was "highly desirable to form a closer union between the Baptists of British North America."[2] That eventually did happen . . . but not for ninety-eight years!

The Long Road

There are many reasons why the pilgrimage towards union lasted nearly a century. Among the obvious ones are distance and consequent cost for a limited membership, differences among the country's three basic regions and, of course, the celebrated reluctance of local Baptist churches, their associations and their Conventions/Unions to surrender any of their cherished autonomy. Canadian Baptist historian Jarold K. Zeman has expressed the situation well:

> Commitment to the principles of soul liberty and local church autonomy inevitably lead to pluralism in view and structures. In all countries, Baptists continually face tension between the centrifugal forces of diversity, sometimes developing into outright disunity, and the centripetal aspirations for greater cooperation and unity. When such organizational diversity is reinforced by geographical, ethnic and cultural differences, as in the case of Canada, the goal of Baptist unity becomes even less likely.[3]

The Momentum Increases

Despite the obstacles, "centripetal aspirations" kept surfacing during that century. When Canada's first provinces entered Confederation in 1867, Baptists also began to think of joining forces. Minutes of the Missionary Convention of Ontario record that Robert A. Fyfe had corresponded with "some of the leading Baptists of the Lower Provinces [the Maritimes] who desired to know whether the Baptists of the Dominion of Canada could not be brought into closer cooperation in regard to matters of general denominational interest and importance." A committee was appointed to correspond "with any committee appointed by them."[4]

The same year the Canada Baptist Missionary Convention East (Quebec) discussed "closer intercourse" with the Baptists of the Maritimes and drafted a fraternal address.[5] As the momentum increased, Dr. Fyfe reported to the Ontario society in 1868 that he had attended the annual meeting of the Maritime Convention in Saint John and brought back with him a fraternal address that had already been published in the *Canadian Baptist*.[6] The following year the Ontario body passed a motion supporting the principle of Baptist union and a second motion seeking "more frequent and intimate personal intercourse."[7]

A Tiny Flame

But the discussions were not to be translated into concrete action for many years. In fact, it was not until 1900 that the first all-Canada Baptist conference took place — in Winnipeg. That assembly recommended the creation of a Dominion-wide board of missions, the appointment of a superintendent and the publication of a Canadian Baptist hymnary, but only the last proposal was implemented. Many were disappointed, particularly in the West where the need for such a coalition had been felt most keenly.

Some interest remained, however, and five years later missionary Herbert F. Laflamme returned to Canada after eighteen years of service in India to take up the cause. He arranged for a representative committee from the three regions to be set up, obtained passes for them from the Canadian Pacific Railway and led them "right through to Victoria [where they] saw the entire wide field of the Union with their own eyes."[8]

A joint committee met in Montreal in the summer of 1907 and after nine prolonged sessions recommended that a Baptist Union of Canada be formed. Several boards were proposed: Canadian missions, foreign missions, French work (Grande Ligne), Sunday school promotion and publications. In that same year the Maritime Convention approved the principle of organic union but tabled detailed consideration of the matter for a year.[9]

In October 1908, about 10 representatives from the West, 60 from the Maritime provinces and some 150 from Ontario and Quebec, met in

Ottawa and formed the Baptist Union of Canada. However, its final consummation was put off until its first meeting, slated for the fall of 1909. That meeting was never held, however, Laflamme blaming the delay on "a small clique of McMaster leaders."[10]

The Maritime Convention adopted the proposal but was informed in 1909 that its sister Convention had "declared by resolution that they were not prepared to enter into such a Union until they had further considered the matter."[11] Once more the flame died down to a flicker.

Hope Deferred

All was not lost, however. At least part of Laflamme's dream was realized. The next year the central Convention, while still frowning on full union, supported a lesser merger in the area of missions abroad.[12] Thus, in 1911 the Canadian Baptist Foreign Mission Board was formed to supervise the overseas interests of the central and Maritime Conventions and the Baptist Union of Western Canada. That board's most successful story is related in the next chapter.

As Walter Ellis has said, the war years were hardly favourable to considerations of union, and the vision became a "hope deferred."[13] In 1919, however, the subject was revived. That year the Maritime Convention unwittingly forecast the shape of the structure that would eventually be used, by calling for a design by which the Baptists of Canada could act "as a unit in matters of national or interdenominational character."[14]

Twelve years later even that goal remained elusive, but a communication had been received from the centre requesting a meeting "to survey the Baptist missionary enterprise in the whole Dominion." Such a meeting was arranged and those doughty representatives once more went beyond their terms of reference to ask each Convention and the western Union to appoint yet another joint committee "to devise ways and means of developing a national Baptist consciousness . . . [which] would lead to closer co-operation. . . . "[15]

Goal Finally Achieved

By 1934 the Ontario and Quebec Convention had picked up the torch once again, approving the recommendation of its Convention Aims Commission to support a triennial All-Canada Convention.[16] Progress waned for a number of years yet, but in spite of another world war, significant steps were taken by both Conventions. In 1942 the Maritimes resolved to continue efforts with the others "in the interests of Canadian Baptist Union,"[17] and Ontario and Quebec followed suit the next year.[18] As usual, the West was more than ready, but still waiting.

Then in 1943 and again in 1944 the United Baptist Convention of the Maritime Provinces, the Baptist Convention of Ontario and Quebec and the Baptist Union of Western Canada formed an All-Canada Committee which met under the chairmanship of Watson Kirkconnell to consider the possibility of some form of national organization and to report back with specific proposals in 1944.[19] The report was presented in 1944, was fully approved by the Convention and Union representatives and became the basis for the formation of Canadian Baptists' first national body. The goal had finally been achieved.

The Baptist Federation of Canada

The organizational meeting of the Baptist Federation of Canada, as the new body was named, was held in the Germain Street Baptist Church, Saint John, New Brunswick, on December 7, 1944. Dr. Gordon C. Warren, Acadia's dean of theology, was elected the first president, and Dr. Kirkconnell of McMaster University and Dr. Elbert Paul of Vancouver were elected vice-presidents. Dr. Waldo C. Machum of Saint John undertook the role of general secretary-treasurer, in addition to his duties as general secretary of the Maritime Convention.

It is significant that a "federal" concept of co-operation was chosen. Defined as a "compact to grant control of common affairs to a central authority but retain individual control over internal affairs,"[20] the federal organization provided a good working arrangement for common and national concerns without disturbing existing structures. The new framework prepared by the All-Canada Committee was based on two restrictive principles: (1) "There should be no infringement on the autonomy of the local church. The national organization should . . . act as a cooperative and consultative agency"; and (2) "There should be no disposition to duplicate activities that are now being effectively administered by the Conventions' Boards and Committees."[21]

General Consent

The Committee also insisted that the Federation "involve only moderate expense" and work without "an elaborate and costly system of boards and paid officials." Over the years this has meant that the national body has had little opportunity to become a "super-Convention." A peculiarly Canadian-style achievement, the continuing Canadian Baptist Federation has fulfilled its mandate: "to express the common judgment of the constituent churches and organizations on matters of national, international or interdenominational importance."[22]

The Constitution did allow for "united policy-making and action" when "general consent" was possible, although it was anticipated that "administrative action [would] rest with the regional conventions, the associations or the churches."[23] As a result, the federation has never taken a major policy action without the agreement of all Conventions/ Unions.

The Federation consists of (1) an Assembly that meets triennially, (2) a council and (3) an executive. Delegates to the Assembly have been both elected and representative, the latter basically being ex officio, with full privileges, including voting.

Up to 1988 the elected delegates were named by the churches across Canada within the participating Conventions/Unions according to the size of church membership. Others entitled to delegate status included all pastors, chairmen of all-Canada boards, chairmen of Convention/ Union standing committees, associational and area officers, missionaries, editors and seminary faculty.

In practice, this procedure became unwieldy and church representation was seldom balanced. In that expenses were generally the personal responsibility of those who attended, it was often difficult for those living at a distance to participate.

At the 1988 Assembly overall representation was simplified by forming a Canadian Baptist Federation constituency of all church members within the present Conventions/Unions. The invitation remains open to the members of churches of other national or regional Baptist Conventions, Conferences or Unions which unite with the Federation. Thus, any member of the CBF constituency is entitled to attend and vote at the triennial Assemblies—and to report to their respective churches on returning.

Effective Authority

Because of the nature of its representation and infrequent Assemblies, the CBF has acted largely through its council and executive, although the council has been required to report regularly. Composed of thirty-nine members, the council, meeting annually, has itself been a little top-heavy and also expensive for the limited Federation budget.

The new council has been cut to twenty-six, composed of six officers (president, past president, three vice-presidents and general secretary), five general secretaries/executive ministers of the Conventions/Unions and the Canadian Baptist Overseas Mission Board, three representatives from each Convention/Union (including one nominee in each instance from the regional women's organization) and one each from Baptist Men and Baptist Youth.

The council's executive, which, as the "working heart" of the CBF, meets twice yearly, is made up of the six officers, the five general secretaries/executive ministers and the chairman of the Federation's Relief and Development Committee.

Meetings of the Assembly will continue to focus on inspiration and fellowship, although actions of the council and executive will be reported.

The First Years

The national organization did not take long to define its territory. From the beginning social concerns and public affairs were high on the agenda. At the Federation's first meeting late in 1944, the Council sent a telegram to Prime Minister Mackenzie King condemning a government action that threatened to deprive certain naturalized Canadians of their citizenship.

The Federation also promised to co-operate with the Canadian Council of Churches in sending a delegation to Ottawa to address the question of racial discrimination in Canada.[24]

No Organic Union

On the inter-church front, the new council had to deal immediately with overtures from the Church of England and the United Church of Canada "to enter into conversations with them on the great matter of united worship and action, in the confident hope that thus we shall be led to the reunion of Christendom . . . . "[25] It was a time of testing for the fledgling body. A precipitous move in support of the proposal might have threatened its very existence. Failure to move at all would have denied its mandate and damaged its credibility.

Canadian Baptists were not ready for organic union with other denominations. As it turned out, neither were the United Church nor the Anglicans. The council's response was carefully phrased. After expressing thanks for the overtures, the council stated "that we intimate to them that while any question of organic union is regarded as impracticable at the present time, we shall be happy to engage in friendly discussion as to possible methods of closer co-operation and united action in matters of common interest."[26]

A Catalyst

In what was later to become a significant decision, a special committee on overseas relief was set up[27] — in this instance with a focus on sending relief to European countries devastated by World War II. The move foreshadowed the times when world relief would rank high among Canadian Baptist concerns.

The Federation also became a catalyst in ensuring that a port worker was still employed at Halifax to welcome immigrants.[28] Responsible to the Maritime Convention the worker received financial support from all three Home Mission boards. Later the scope was widened to include the ports of Saint John, Montreal and Quebec City.

Mission in Newfoundland

One of the Federation's earliest achievements was that of co-ordinating the efforts of the many separate Convention agencies that already existed. The most notable developments occurred in the area of home missions. Not only were the three superintendents of home missions pressed into conferring at least annually, but their boards were asked to establish a program of advance.[29]

In 1951 the superintendents took the first major step in this direction, deciding to seek opportunities for mission in Canada's newest province, Newfoundland.[30] As a result, First Baptist Church, St. John's, was formed in 1955 and others were established shortly thereafter.

At the initial council meeting a survey of the operations of the Grande

Ligne Mission was also proposed. By the time the first Assembly met three years later, C. H. Schutt, chairman of the survey committee, reported that the mission's board had been reorganized to give Canadian Conventions a direct, majority representation they had not previously enjoyed.[31] Nearly twenty years later, when the French-speaking churches were contemplating having their own Union within the Federation, the support of the Conventions/Union was assured.

In the area of women's work, the results were mixed. The Federation proposed that the longstanding Women's Dominion Committee become the Women's Department of the Federation, but the suggestion fell on deaf ears.[32] In spite of retaining its own identity, however, the Dominion Committee has co-operated with the Federation, sharing reports regularly and naming a representative to the council.

Seven Candles on the Cake

A singular accomplishment in its initial years, the Federation managed to persuade the Conventions to fashion a nearly consistent set of standards and regulations for ministerial ordinations and credentials. These were approved at the 1950 Assembly,[33] and while individual Conventions retain the right to make changes, their rules have subsequently remained compatible with each other, enabling an easy interchange of ministers.

At the end of seven years, in 1951, Watson Kirkconnell was able to say with justification: "Today there are seven candles on the cake and a greater sense of confidence in the Baptist household."[34] This followed his earlier remark to the 1951 Council that "for some of us who stood beside the cradle of the new Federation in 1944, the chief anxiety was whether it could survive at all."[35] It had not only survived; it had streamlined many administrative functions and moved Canadian Baptists into new areas of service, among other accomplishments.

Federation Interests Expand

The first executive officer of the Federation was Dr. Waldo C. Machum, who became general secretary-treasurer in 1945. A Maritimer, he handled these duties on a part-time basis, in addition to heavy parallel responsibilities in his own Convention.

After an interim part-time stint by Dr. Abner J. Langley, Dr. T. B. McDormand became the first full-time officer in 1955, being succeeded four years later by Dr. R. Frederick Bullen. He, in turn, was followed by the Reverend R. Michael Steeves, Dr. Keith R. Hobson (a year's interim) and Dr. Richard C. Coffin.

Ties Less Binding

The Federation has also made its mark on the international denominational front. Presidents and general secretaries of the Federation have represented Canada on the executive committee of the Baptist World

Alliance, a number becoming vice-presidents. A maritime lawyer, Stephen S. Steeves, served as head of the BWA Men's Department. In 1953 it was the Federation council that picked up the suggestion of the Baptist Union of Western Canada and recommended the formation of the North American Baptist Fellowship of the World Alliance.[36] The NABF has been a strong force in cementing cross-border relationships. Over many years representatives of the council also sat on the Southern Baptist–Canadian Baptist Conference Committee and helped ease the strain caused by the Southern Baptist incursion into Canada.

Interdenominational ties have been less binding. Links with the Canadian Council of Churches were frequently subject to various pressures. Some were financial, as the Federation could not respond to all the CCC's requests for support. Others resulted from differences on matters of principle or polity. Exception was taken to the CCC's method of supporting "U.S. draft age immigrants in Canada" in 1970[37] and two years later to the selective protest of the CCC over an American nuclear test at Amchitka, Alaska, while nothing was said of similar concurrent tests undertaken by the U.S.S.R. and China.[38]

Similarly, the Federation Council declined to take action on a CCC request to send observers to California to assess the Grape Growers' Dispute and to help set up an office for a Canada-China Committee to promote friendly relations with China.[39] While the Federation did participate in many CCC activities and there was considerable and persistent support for the CCC, particularly from the central region, the Atlantic Convention and French Union finally withheld their support for the interdenominational body. The Federation thus withdrew in 1980 from the CCC but a strong Committee on Inter-Church Relations continues to co-operate with other denominations.

Yearning for Relationships

Since the Federation was formed, it has been seen as the ideal vehicle for co-operation with other Canadian Baptists, and within a decade of its founding, a study committee was formed to consider the possible affiliation of what were then known as the Regular, Independent, North American and Southern Baptists in Canada.[40] Another decade later, confessing that "denominational disunity has hurt and continued to hurt our witness," the Assembly called on all the churches "to build bridges between ourselves and other Baptist bodies now working in Canada."[41]

In the nation's Centennial year, during Assembly deliberations "applause greeted the expressed yearning for working relationships with other Baptist bodies in Canada."[42] This yearning was formalized by the Assembly in 1976 when the Constitution was amended by unanimous vote to open the way for affiliation for "other national or regional Baptist conventions, unions or conferences." One of the clauses of the amendment stated that the Federation aimed to encourage other Baptist organizations to become members of the Federation.[43] The way was opened, the invitation tendered.

Human Rights

The Federation has maintained the Baptists' traditionally strong position on religious liberty, and has taken a great interest in public affairs. Core committees have been able to draw together Baptist bodies outside the Federation to work on public issues, making contacts with governments among other things. In the mid-sixties a submission was made in co-operation with the Public Affairs Committee of the Atlantic Convention to Canada's Commission on Bilingualism and Biculturalism. The presenter and chief architect of the well-received brief was Dr. Maurice Boillat. Published later as *Creed in the Canadian Crisis*, it dealt with the fact that since church and state are so intertwined in Quebec, the assumption was made that all francophones were Roman Catholic and all anglophones Protestant. Dr. Boillat's thesis was that Roman Catholic compatriots thus viewed francophone Protestants almost as traitors and were making life difficult for them.

In 1965 the Federation held a series of public affairs seminars in Vancouver, Calgary and Winnipeg. Three years later a Federation-sponsored public meeting was held in Fredericton, New Brunswick, to mark the International Year of Human Rights. Former prime minister and Baptist layman John G. Diefenbaker was the speaker—his subject, Baptists and Human Rights.[44]

Care in Disbursements

Certainly the Federation's accomplishments in world relief and development make up one of the jewels in its crown. Since 1963 there has been enthusiastic participation across Canada in the annual One Great Hour of Sharing (for world relief in general),[45] as well as in special appeals for disaster relief. Until very recently 100 percent of all such gifts were disbursed for their stated objective, all overhead costs being borne by the Federation budget. This appealing feature was continued until the early 1980s when overhead became too great for the budget. Now overhead of no more than 10 percent is deducted from receipts. And, for the first time, a second Federation staff member was added. The Reverend Larry Matthews became associate secretary, with responsibility for relief and development and, later, publications.

Special care has been taken in making disbursements around the world. These have been carried out almost entirely through the Canadian Baptist Overseas Mission Board, the Baptist World Alliance, Church World Service and other church agencies. By 1985 the total raised by churches across Canada during the three-year period between assemblies was $2,553,423.00.

Emergency aid in the 1982–85 period was sent to nineteen countries, including Bolivia, India, the Philippines, Vietnam, Bangladesh, Lebanon,

El Salvador and Nicaragua. Matching grants from the Canadian International Development Agency, the Federation also sent vast shipments of food through the Canadian Foodgrains Bank to seven countries.[46]

In the late 1970s Canadian Baptists also opened their hearts and their homes to the Indo-Chinese Boat People who sought refuge in Canada. The Federation acted as the correlating agency, calling on the churches to engage in the sponsorship program initiated by the Canadian government.[47]

Areas of Ministry

The Baptist Federation also plays a major part in handling concerns relating to the ministry. Retirement pensions provided by the Conventions were usually insufficient and inconsistent, and a council committee struggled many years to devise an acceptable national pension and insurance plan. Finally, in 1962, a Federation Superannuation Plan was put in place for ministers, church staff and missionaries in all regions. The scheme has been improved since then, so that present benefits in pensions and term insurance are now at an adequate level.[48]

In another area of ministry, the chaplaincy, the Federation has accepted responsibility for the nomination of Baptist chaplains to the armed forces. A chaplaincy committee stays in regular contact with military chaplains, as well as with Baptist chaplains in institutions such as prisons and hospitals.

Effective Linking

Program planning and execution are still largely functions of the Conventions/Unions, but the Federation has played a key role in promoting and correlating such activities. The Federation has been especially active in evangelism, spearheading a number of country-wide crusades. Effective leadership was given in the Baptist Jubilee Advance, a five-year Forward Movement beginning in 1959 and concluding with the momentous Jubilee Convention in Atlantic City in 1964. Five Baptist Conventions in the United States and the Federation in Canada also shared in a series of year-long emphases on some phase of Evangelism. During each triennium a special project in missions has also been highlighted.

Once again in 1970 the Federation was called upon to react to overtures from the United and Anglican churches concerning union. In the invitation the two churches requested a response to the Principles of Union, carefully crafted to bring about their merger, which at that time seemed almost assured. Responding on behalf of the Federation, Dr. R. R. Aldwinckle expressed appreciation for the common thread of doctrine and polity but was compelled to note differences in faith, views of the church, the ordinances and the ministry. These differences, he indicated, "explain why we have always been hesitant about entering any discussions which seem to be aiming directly at organic union."[49] Once more, as things turned out, the question became academic as the Church of England and the United Church also pulled back from taking the final step toward amalgamation.

The Federation, renamed the Canadian Baptist Federation in 1982, made remarkable progress in its history of less than fifty years. Because of its structure it remains largely the instrument[50] of the two Conventions and two Unions—L'Union d'Églises Baptistes Françaises au Canada having become the fourth component in 1970. From time to time proposals have been made for an All-Canada Convention,[51] but these have never been implemented. In 1970 the Assembly instructed the council to appoint a task force on Canadian Baptist unity, one of its duties being to explore the basis for a unified national structure. The council appointed a blue ribbon group under past president J. J. Arthurs to undertake the study. Its findings, reported to the next Assembly, indicated that the task force "found little support for the setting up of a national Convention structure" and that "the interests of Canadian Baptists were being well served by the Baptist Federation of Canada."[52]

During the Parade of Flags at the opening ceremonies of the "Festival 88" Assembly in Calgary's well-filled Jubilee Auditorium in July 1988, President Shirley Bentall commented that services of worship were being held in Baptist churches in Canada every Sunday in twenty-two languages. Later to be flanked by some thirty overseas guests from a number of the countries where Canadian Baptist missionaries are serving — including India, Bolivia, Kenya, Zaire, Brazil, Indonesia and Belgium — she added that the multitude of flags, representing these peoples in Canada and abroad, were reminders of the diversity out of which unity in the Lord is found.

The official crest of the Canadian Baptist Federation, designed by the Reverend Ralph Wright, emphasizes the spiritual significance of denominational life. The circle indicates the fellowship of the Canadian Baptists with well over 35 million Baptists in more than 124 countries through the Baptist World Alliance—the world's largest Free Church body.

The shield in heraldry represents "opinion-makers," or the Christian witness in state and politics—an important phase of Baptist witness. The upper third portrays a dove descending from the blue heavens, recalling the descent of the Holy Spirit at our Lord's baptism and pointing to the Christian's source of power. The left section displays an open Bible. Superimposed are the Greek letters Alpha and Omega, signifying the beginning and the end. The right section shows black ermine tails on a white field, which represent royalty, the Lordship of Christ. This section and the silver background of the left section depict the riches in glory which belong to those faithful to Jesus Christ. The open chalice and patten point to the ordinance of the Lord's supper.

But it is the Federation's motto that most clearly communicates the basis of the whole organization. In the oldest known declaration of Christian faith, it says simply, "Jesus is Lord."[53]

CHAPTER 28

The World Vision Widens

" 'Thy Kingdom come' should and could be turned from a mumble into a stirring call for adventure for and with the Creator, working with Him to push back the frontiers of clouded wilderness in the heart, mind and soul of man."
—*BRUCE F. HASKINS*

With the formation of the Canadian Baptist Foreign Mission Board in May 1911, the dream of Baptist missionaries had finally come to pass. There was now only one directing agency instead of two—and a threatened three if the recently founded Baptist Union of Western Canada had established its own overseas arm.

The single board, representing and responsible to the two regional Conventions and one Union, inaugurated a new era for the world efforts of Canadian Baptists. Inheriting a strong work that had been underway in India for nearly half a century and a more fragile outreach that had been taking place in Bolivia for over a decade, the board was to develop a strategy which by the late 1980s would have missionaries serving abroad in eleven countries on four continents. And all these operations developed a great reputation for excellence.

India

Historically Baptists have been well located for their mission task in India. Missionaries from Great Britain, Australia, Canada and the United States have always occupied adjacent terrain on the east coast, extending all the way from Madras to Calcutta, a total distance of about 1,600 kilometres.

By 1912 Canadian Baptists had taken full possession of their sector and had divided it into "fields," which soon numbered twenty-two.[1] A united missionary conference was formed to provide overall field supervision. The next year the Telegu Baptist Convention was born, uniting the three Telegu Associations. Initially the Convention emphasized inspiration and fellowship, administrative responsibilities being left to the missionaries. But this situation was destined to change soon.

Advances

By 1928 the 43 churches established at the turn of the century had swelled to exactly 100, with a total membership of 20,574.[2] Advances

303

had also been made in medical work. Hospitals at Vuyyuru and Srikakulam had been added to those at Pithapuram and Akividu. A clinic was set up at Sompeta, later to become a hospital, and a dispensary opened in 1927 at Gudlavalleru. In 1913 a second leprosarium, funded by the Mission to the Lepers, was built near Vizianagram; the first had been established by the indomitable John Davis at Ramachandrapuram.[3]

Education continued to be the handmaiden of the faith. By 1930 no fewer than 500 rural schools offering courses up to the fifth grade were in operation, all staffed by trained Christian teachers. In larger centres boarding schools provided higher elementary training.

Demonstrating concern for the whole man, missionaries in Kakinada opened an industrial school with courses in carpentry, automobile mechanics and electrical work in 1925. Classes that had been raised to the secondary level in Samalkot in 1912 were transferred to Kakinada as the nucleus of the new McLaurin High School, whose enrolment topped 600 by 1930. A men's teacher-training institute and a theological seminary also developed there out of small beginnings at Samalkot. The Kakinda Central Girls' School was in full operation by 1926.[4] Education flourished.

Oriya and Sora

By 1934 109 missionaries were serving in India under the CBFMB, the largest number ever. The next year the high point in the number of national workers was attained — 1,525. That year was also a summit for baptisms — 2,601 were performed.[5]

Some of the growth was to be found among the Oriya and Sora hill tribes that J.A. Glendinning had first worked with in 1905. He had concentrated his efforts on the Soras, but it was among the Hindu Paides, the Oriya traders, that results were first evident. "Evangelism among the Oriyas," writes Orville Daniel, "began to spread like a bush fire."[6]

In 1922 four Oriya churches formed the Ganjam Malia Association, later becoming the Utkal Baptist Churches Association. Within fifteen years the association had 10 churches, with a membership of 3,290 — 3,667 by 1940.

In the early forties the higher-caste and gospel-resisting Paiks began fierce persecution of the Paidis Christians, the Paiks inciting the neighbouring Soras to violence against the Paidis. Hundreds wilted under the onslaught and left the faith, church membership dropping to 2,705 in 1945.[7]

Developments among the animistic Soras occurred much more slowly, a few converts being made among some who had migrated to the plains. It was not until 1928 that the first convert among them was made in the upland Eastern Ghats. Gradually the momentum increased so that just over a decade later there was a widespread movement among the Soras around missionary headquarters at Serango, where Dr. J. H. West had established a hospital in the mid-twenties.

Opting for their own central church in 1947 after worshipping previously with the Oriyas, the Soras erected a building in Serango with no mission aid — demonstrating a philosophy of self-sufficiency that characterized their work. Three years later the dispersed groups throughout the hill country formed the first small Sora Association, reconstituted as the Ganjam Malia Association of Sora Baptist Churches in 1958. About forty congregations participated.

As the Soras had no written language, Canadian missionaries led by Perry V. Allaby put their speech into writing and by 1962 had completed the whole of the New Testament.[8]

Toward Indigenous Churches

Writing in 1922, missionary and executive Malcolm L. Orchard said that the ultimate aim of Canadian Baptist missionaries in India was "to make themselves useless as soon as possible by establishing there self-propagating, self-supporting and self-governing Christian churches."[9] That was not easy in a land where at the time only one man in ten and one woman in a hundred could read and write, and the average annual income was ten dollars.

Yet the goal of establishing truly indigenous churches was always kept in view. A major problem was that the Telegu Christians were more than satisfied with the initial paternal relationship. "You are my father and mother," they would proudly declare to the missionaries.[10]

Pace Accelerated

The strong nationalist movement under Mohandas K. Gandhi that led to independence from Great Britain had a significant effect upon the loosening of mission ties as well. Asked in 1931 if he favoured the continued presence of missionaries from abroad, Gandhi replied: "If instead of confining themselves to purely humanitarian work and material service to the poor, they do proselytizing . . . then I would certainly ask them to withdraw.[11] Although he was not a devout Hindu, Gandhi viewed Christianity as a Western import.

The significance of his words was not lost either on the missionaries or on the Indian Christians and they began to work even harder to make the Indian churches self-sufficient. Even before Gandhi made his remark, Telegu Convention President M. Theophilus had urged that "we . . . be *partners* for the good growth of the building."[12] Within months the missionaries passed a motion that "we believe that devolution [of control to Indian Christians] is essential to the harmonious carrying on of the work," and urged the Convention to set up with them a joint committee to work to that end. The Telegu-Oriya Council of the Canadian Baptist Mission was established, its ultimate objective being to turn over the whole work to the churches "through their indigenous organizations such as the Convention, the Associations and the Field Councils."[13]

Composed of delegates of the Convention and missionaries, the coun-

cil functioned until 1947—the same year independence came to India—
when a reconstituted Telegu Convention of Baptist Churches of the
Northern Circars (or Districts) assumed the responsibilities of the council.
"The country, as well as Baptist work on the eastern seaboard, entered
a new era," writes historian Daniel.[14]

Plans in Place

Within the next year twelve missionaries were refused visas to enter India,
although more than sixty were still there in active service or on furlough.
However, even they had to renew their permits every year in order to
remain.[15] Hindu-inspired pressures to restrict entry were mushrooming.

Plans to adjust to the unfriendly atmosphere were in place. "With the
development of the national churches overseas, the role of the missionary
has radically changed," the mission board reported to the Conventions/
Union in Canada in 1968. It continued: "No longer does he have administrative authority unless he is appointed by a national church body to a
position involving supervisory responsibility. Along with capable national
leaders, he serves under the general oversight of an indigenous church."[16]
They had not quite made themselves "useless."

The Kantuta Blooms[17]

While these events were transpiring in India, parallel long-term developments were occurring in Bolivia.

In 1905 Charles Mitchell in Oruro was the only Canadian Baptist
missionary left in the whole of Bolivia. Archibald Reekie had returned to
Canada for furlough and to get reinforcements. Even Mitchell's wife had
left for Canada, because of illness.

Halt the Intruders

Reekie came back the next year with a bride but no other reinforcements.
He assumed responsibilities at Cochabamba, one of the cities viewed as
a strategic point in the hoped-for advance. Violent persecution burst out
following their first service, a rowdy mob greeting them with a shower of
stones. Two of the little party, including Reekie's new wife, were injured.

Charles Mitchell suffered similar treatment when he was preaching in
Punata near Cochabamba, but he escaped serious harm. Some minions
of the state church were doing all in their power to halt the "intruders."

An Excellent Foundation

Reinforcements began to arrive by 1910 to help the tiny staff. Johnson
Turnbull and his wife transferred from the Bolivian Indian Mission, and
the A. G. Bakers returned, going to La Paz that year. There was a nucleus
of only six believers there, but by the end of the year seventy people were
attending the services.[18] The Alexander Haddows and nurse Catherine
Mangan joined the group in 1915.

As the century's second decade ended, all the pioneers had left the scene — Mitchell by death while still working, Baker to a professorship in the United States and the Reekies by retirement.[19] Yet an excellent foundation had been laid under hazardous conditions.

At that time Canadian Baptists undertook a project that was to leave a unique mark on their whole Bolivian enterprise. Less than ten years earlier the American Peniel Hall Society had purchased a hacienda of over 400 hectares to serve the impoverished Aymara Indians. This estate at Huataja on the shore of the legendary Lake Titicaca about 100 kilometres from La Paz was renamed Peniel Hall Farm and established as an agricultural and educational centre. Included in the purchase were 250 Aymaras who were serfs, bound to serve the landowner as in European feudal times.

Unable to carry the burden of the project, the society turned to the Canadian Baptist Mission, who took over responsibility in 1920. The serfs were still included in the deal.

The first missionary, L. N. Vicherson, was an ordained minister and had agricultural credentials, but death overtook him while he was still studying the language in preparation for his work. Howard Plummer, who had similar qualifications, arrived to introduce experimental farming. Plummer's service was confined to a single term, because his wife died while they were on their first furlough, and he did not want to return to the field. He had been able to construct a mission house, however, along with a school at nearby Chilaya and a medical clinic. Church services were begun in two centres.[20]

A First in Latin America

When the Reverend Earl C. Merrick became missionary-in-charge at Peniel Hall Farm, he immediately launched a five-year plan to emancipate the serfs and prepare them for independent farming. He began with the redistribution of work plots.

The climax was reached in 1942 when title deeds to portions of the Farm were given to forty-two heads of families, who were then recognized as freed landholders by the Bolivian government. This was a "first" in Latin America. Eleven years later, writes Orville Daniel, "inspired by the Huatajata achievement, the Bolivian Government enacted an Agrarian Reform Bill . . . designed to confer similar benefits on estate-serfs throughout the Republic."[21]

In 1974 the government of Bolivia invested Dr. John F. Keith, then general secretary of the Canadian Baptist Overseas Mission Board, with the country's highest decoration, the Order of the Condor of the Andes, in recognition of seventy-five years of Canadian Baptist service in that country. In an impressive public ceremony, which was carried live throughout the nation, the land reform at Peniel Hall was cited, along with the benefits of education and medicine.[22] Once more, the missionaries had been pathfinders in meeting human need.

Erection of Sanctuary Halted

The first two Protestant church buildings in the Republic of Bolivia were completed in 1923 and 1924. Johnson Turnbull, who had for many years proclaimed the Good News in Cochabamba and three adjacent valleys, supervised the construction of the first in that city, located just over two blocks from the main plaza.

Although the expected hostility did not arise in Cochabamba, it did in La Paz, and the erection of the sanctuary there was halted by the city's mayor when it was half completed. Eventually the missionaries were forced to sell the property — the purchaser being none other than the mayor (at a fair price, it is said).[23]

Undeterred, the Baptists snapped up a piece of far more valuable land on the finest boulevard in the city and started building again. Their old foe, by now the ex-mayor, used his influence to stop construction but this time an appeal to Bolivia's president brought an overruling[24] and the work was completed. In December 1924 the splendid edifice that still graces the Prado in the heart of La Paz was dedicated.

Together with the chapel in Oruro, which was soon enlarged, the Canadian Baptist Mission had centres in Bolivia's three key cities by the mid-1920s.

Barriers of Race and Culture

"From the earliest days," wrote missionary Norman Dabbs, "the missionaries had known that the seed of the indigenous church was as old as the Great Commission."[25] Johnson Turnbull was one of those early missionaries who, while on furlough in Canada in 1933, heard of the growth of the devolution movement in India and urged upon his return that such steps be taken in Bolivia.

There, too, the path was not smooth, for it was not easy for the nationals to assume the financial burden of increased administration. Long-standing barriers of race and culture had to be surmounted. Under the new arrangements, Aymara and Quechua Indians would be rubbing shoulders with Spanish-speaking cholo.[26]

Despite the obstacles, the Bolivian Baptist Union was formed in 1936, even more indigenous than its Indian counterpart at that juncture. The BBU "was exclusively the Convention of Bolivian Christian laymen,"[27] for there were no native pastors at the time and the missionaries daringly declined to hold office.

As in India the final goal was achieved in 1967 when a restructured BBU, which by that time encompassed both Bolivian pastors and missionaries, took over the remaining obligations of the Missionary Conference. Between 1941 and the Golden Jubilee year, 1948, the number of Bolivian churches grew from nine to forty-one. In that latter year a new Bible college, later to be upgraded to seminary, was completed at Cochabamba.

Sounding throughout the Andes

Christian radio broadcasting came to La Paz and Oruro in 1941 through missionaries H. S. Hillyer and Norman Dabbs. Five years afterwards, Hillyer, who was later to become the Canadian Mission board's general secretary, challenged the board to set up a mission-owned radio station.

That was how the renowned Southern Cross Radio was born. "Sounding throughout the Andes [it] produced echoes in distant places"[28] — Peru, Columbia, Argentina, Chile, Brazil, Uruguay and Paraguay, as well as Bolivia and in many other parts of the world by short wave.[29] The broadcasts and their accompanying correspondence courses made a singular impact. In 1967 Christian Bolivians were given control of the station, although major funding was continued by the Mission.

Hillyer was also heavily involved in literature evangelism and began publication of the *Bolivian Sentinel* beginning in 1942. The first evangelical magazine in the land supported by private subscription, its circulation soon topped 1,200. The earlier missionaries had published a number of pamphlets and Hillyer himself edited *Redencion,* a four-page gospel bulletin of which nearly a million free copies had been distributed throughout the land by the Jubilee Year.[30]

Medical Ministry

Because government policy barred foreign medical doctors to protect the interest of Bolivian physicians, it was not possible for the mission to introduce medical services on the same scale as in India. Nurse-operated clinics were soon functioning, however, to meet the desperate needs of the country.

When Mrs. Alex Haddow arrived in 1915, she pioneered with clinics in La Paz and Oruro. Nurse Jean Pyper opened the largest and most permanent facility in Huatjata in 1933, and nurses reaching out from the Farm also staffed nearby village clinics. In addition to this medical ministry around Lake Titicaca, clinics were planted in other parts of the country, a work that still continues today.[31]

The government's medical barrier was lowered a notch in 1966 to permit service in the lowlands, an area shunned by most of the Bolivian doctors. That year the Reverend John and Dr. Margaret Cserepka took up a combined evangelistic/medical summons to the Chapare region. There Dr. Margaret trained two Quechua girls to assist her as nurses and initiated and supervised the erection of a fine medical clinic.

And that was only a beginning. Because of the extreme hazards of land travel though the jungle, a few dreamed of starting a "floating clinic" on the Chapare River. Canadian Hungarian friends of the Cserepkas made the dream a reality, supplying funds for a hospital boat, complete with living quarters.[32] First under Dr. Robert Taylor and his wife, nurse Suzanne Taylor, the floating clinic took medical aid and the gospel to multitudes of isolated sufferers for many years.

It is significant that Bolivian Baptists sent one of the largest Third World delegations to the Baptist World Alliance Congress in Toronto in 1980. After more than eighty years in Bolivia, Canadian Baptist service and co-operation in that nation was bearing fruit.[33]

On to Africa: Angola and Zaire

A century after pioneer Protestant missionaries Richard and Laleah Burpee departed their Maritime shores to venture overseas, Canadian Baptist envoys were at work abroad on two continents and in two nations. Within a decade a third nation on a third continent was to be added.

In 1951, the Canadian Baptist Foreign Mission Board was invited to take over the fifty-year-old enterprise of the independent British-supported Angola Evangelical Mission. Its founder, Matthew Stober, had just died. Three years later the board assumed responsibility for the mission.

By 1958 the new endeavour had attracted nine missionary couples, five single women and a single man—the largest group ever sent abroad in a comparable period.[34] Baptists across Canada had greeted the decision with enthusiasm.

Centres of Operation

The work in Angola, then a Portuguese colony, took place among the Bakongo, a Bantu tribe. Most members of the tribe spoke only Kikongo, although those fortunate enough to attend school studied Portuguese. So the missionaries had more than the usual preparatory work to do, having to learn two new languages.

Four former stations of the AEM were refurbished, Cabinda, M'Boca, Quimpondo and Ambrizete becoming centres of operation. Inherited too was a structure of scattered village congregations that made up area churches under a senior pastor. Seven area churches in 1958 were composed of 226 of those village congregations, with a total membership nearing 5,000.[35]

A number of boys' boarding schools were also inherited from the former mission. These were renovated and upgraded and facilities for girls were added for the first time.

Medical clinics were improved and at Quimpondo a small hospital was built. To provide both agricultural training and food for the boarding school at Cabinda, a farm project was launched using land next to the mission station. Again, Canadian Baptist missionaries were making provision for the whole person.

Days of Ferment

As in India and Bolivia, the missionaries' immediate objective was to train native Christian workers. This was to prove to be a wise decision, for within a decade of taking over the mission, the last Canadian missionary had departed—but not by choice.

Those were the days of ferment in Africa and, unlike the other colonial powers, Portugal sought to retain her grasp of her colony. In March 1961, rebellion broke out and was ruthlessly repressed. By the next year an estimated 50,000 Africans were dead and about 250,000 had fled the country.[36]

Communists and Protestant missionaries both became convenient scapegoats for troubles that derived basically from Portuguese colonialism. Some mission property was seized by the government and the missionaries had to withdraw, the last three leaving Cabinda in 1963.

Among the Refugees

Many Christians were among the native Angolans who fled their country, most crossing over to the bordering Republic of Congo, which had earlier severed its Belgian link. They were welcomed by fellow members of the Bakongo tribe, who also spoke Kikongo. Before long, however, President Mobutu of Zaire—Congo's new name after 1971—diluted the welcome, decreeing that all Zairians must be addressed as "citizen" and all foreigners, including the Angolans, as "mister." This effectively established a second-class category and turned Angolan eyes and hopes homeward.

Canadian Baptist work among the refugees had begun almost immediately. A doctor and nurse who were travelling to Angola when rebellion broke out were redirected to Congo. Working under the Protestant Relief Association, an inter-church agency, they were assigned to a hospital near the border late in 1961. During a four-month period, more than 10,000 refugees passed through the out-patient clinics there.[37]

Over the next five years fourteen former missionaries to Angola and a new recruit were sent to Zaire after adding French, spoken in Zaire, to their list of languages. In a radical departure from traditional missionary strategy, the Canadian Mission Board decided that they would serve under a bold new model of partnership with the emerging native church. There would be no fixed boundaries or settled mission "stations" — even the specific identity of the Canadian mission would be submerged.[38]

IME

Arrangements were made to work initially under the American Baptist Foreign Mission Society and later the Baptist Community of Western Zaire (the CBZO in its French lettering). This was the country-wide body to which the American missionaries had gradually handed over full responsibility after the Belgians left the Congo. In the face of revolution, devolution had come quickly to Africa. Canadian Baptist missionaries also co-operated with the Congo Protestant Council whose Relief Association gave aid to so many refugees. Three major projects of the council captured Canadian concern. Of these, the Institut Médical Évangélique has become renowned. A health centre with over 350 beds and modern medical and dental facilities, IME (eemee) as it is usually called in English, was established at Kimpese in 1949. Many Canadian Baptists have served on the hospital staff.

On just over 400 hectares bordering IME, the Protestant Council began a community project called CEDECO, again for its French initials. Canadian missionaries have also participated in this program of agricultural training and experimentation, poultry raising, motor mechanics, carpentry and tailoring.

The largest Protestant theological school in French-speaking Africa, the École Théologique Évangélique de Kinshasa, is the third co-operative project in which Canadian Baptists have participated. Opened in the capital, Kinshasa, in 1968, ETEK has offered a widespread extension program for pastors in addition to classroom studies.

Official Decrees

In 1972 President Mobutu had ordered that the interdenominational Protestant Council be replaced by a national church structure — the Church of Christ in Zaire. This body, ECZ, was to be composed of "Communities," the name given to national denominations. Foreign-controlled missions were to be shut down.

These official decrees caused no great consternation, as the American Baptists who were working in Zaire before the Canadians arrived had already moved in that direction. The process of devolution was completed when the CBZO — the Baptist Community of Western Zaire — was set up. It is this Convention (Community) under which Canadian and American Baptists have continued to labour.

The People's Republic of Angola

The Angolan Baptists who had entered Zaire worshipped freely with their new countrymen, since they were of the same tribe and spoke the same language. No new churches had to be founded. In Angola itself the work continued under the African leaders, since Portugal would not permit the missionaries to return.

When Angola was finally granted independence in 1975, the situation did not improve. The new government of the People's Republic of Angola also refused missionary entry into the country. The Canadian Mission Board reported in 1976 that "the future of both church and mission work in Angola is still cloudy," although "powerful optimism" was encouraged.[39] As late as 1986 "uncertainty and continued fighting within the country between rival political parties . . . made it difficult to consider sending new missionaries . . . . [40] Yet contacts have been maintained.

The New Concept

Zaire proved to be a watershed experience for the Canadian Baptist Overseas Mission Board and its missionaries. Out of that experience the "task force" was born.

Mission patterns abroad traditionally called for a lot of capital investment in land and buildings, fixed missionary "stations" and direction of the total program by high-profile missionaries, many of whom remained in the area a lifetime. The task force style, which by 1973 had become "the marked direction of CBOMB," featured goal-oriented activities, time of service defined in advance, emphasis on training roles and the redeployment of personnel.[41] In addition, task forces were sent in response to specific requests for assistance.

The appeal for aid in Kenya came from a national church body, the African Christian Church and Schools, which had become independent of the African Inland Mission twenty years earlier because they wanted to have their own village schools. At the time that mission's policy did not permit such an arrangement.

The Missionary Task Force

After two decades the ACC&S included twenty-three village congregations grouped in four parishes and had a membership of more than 1,500. Scattered over the central hills of Kenya, each Kikuyu village had an elementary school, and government grants supported teachers' salaries.

However, ACC&S leaders finally concluded that they needed limited missionary assistance and they petitioned Canadian Baptists for help. By 1973 an eight-person task force was at work in Kenya. When the task force's work was completed in 1981, the ACC&S had been transformed from a receiving church into a sending church, linking with Canadian Baptists in yet another form of mission — Joint Pioneer Outreach — in new territory among the Somali in northeast Kenya.[42]

By 1978 a new task force of four had begun working with the 100,000-member African Brotherhood Church, a rapidly expanding denomination of Kamba-speaking Christians. Their task was to train pastoral leaders.[43] In 1987 a new urban task force was at work with the ACC&S in Kenya's capital, Nairobi. The Canadian Mission Board looked that year to a partnership with Mission Aviation Fellowship to provide air service for the growing work among the Somali in the northeast.[44]

The KGPI

The task force approach was working well in Africa and was soon to be implemented halfway around the world, in Indonesia. Responding to a request from the Kerapatan Protestant Church (KGPI) for assistance in leadership training, the CBOMB agreed in May 1971 to provide at least two theologically trained missionaries. With a baptized membership at the time in excess of 3,000 and a constituency of some 10,000 adherents, the KGPI was seeking to expand in order to evangelize the nearby islands.[45] At the time it was based near the seaport of Menado at the northeast tip of Celebes.

After long delays waiting for visas, two missionary families left Canada the next year and were assigned by the native church to teach in a Bible school. Fortified by this training program, the KGPI sent a missionary force to adjacent Kalimantan (formerly Borneo) where "a multitude of new congregations of converts resulted."[46] By 1987 four missionary families were serving with the Kerapatan Baptist Churches of Indonesia, and the outreach into Kalimantan continued unbated.[47]

The State of Mato Grosso

"The point of the spearhead"—the mobile task force that allows for rapid thrusts in various forms of mission—is the modern missionary approach. So commented missiology writer David Barrett concerning one of the Canadian Baptists' task forces abroad.[48] This new stimulating form of mission found its third expression in the United States of Brazil, a country occupying nearly half the land mass of South America.

In 1973 the CBOMB was investigating the possibility of sending a Brazilian missionary to Angola, since that field had been barred to Canadians. It was then that the Brazilian Baptist Convention, strong in evangelism, expressed its own need for teaching in follow-up methods. Responding to an appeal to share in theological education by extension in the state of Mato Grosso, missionary couple Lynn and Hannah Stairs began work in Dourados two years later. Within another year the task force grew to five couples, including missionaries Karl and Kathleen Janzen and David and Catherine Phillips, who had been reassigned after failing to gain admittance to Angola.[49] They, too, became involved in theological training—at Dourados and Campo Grande.

With the termination of the original Brazilian task force in 1986–87, other projects were undertaken under Brazilian leadership in the Pantanal (swamplands) of western Mato Grosso, a new ministry was initiated with the seminary at Brasilia and outreach began in the interior state of Carolina.[50]

From Sri Lanka to the Middle East

By the late 1980s, four new regions had been added to Canadian Baptists' overseas locations bringing the total at that time to eleven. At the beginning of that decade, missionary Melbourne J. Otis was in Sri Lanka, where he had been sent as a one-man task force in response to a cry for assistance from the Baptists of that land. There he served alongside Australian, British and American Southern Baptists in a ministry of evangelism and outreach.[51] In 1988 Otis was continuing his lone vigil, although a search was underway for a couple to join him.

Early in the decade a veteran missionary couple was also sent to the Middle East on special assignment. They were later joined by a second couple.

From Flanders to Yangi City

The world's most populous country, the People's Republic of China, became another Canadian Baptist mission field in 1987. The previous year general secretaries Dr. Robert Berry and Dr. Richard C. Coffin of the CBOMB and the Canadian Baptist Federation had met with leaders of the China Christian Conference. Their report encouraged the mission board to send an investigation team to the Republic.[52]

Meanwhile it was learned that teachers would be welcome and soon the first volunteer, Elmah G. Baines, a language specialist who had already spent a year and a half in Shanghai under the Canadian Executive Service organization, was sent to serve with the Department of Education of Yangi City in northeast China.[53]

Finally, in the decade of the eighties, Europe was added to the list of continents served. Belgium, which recorded only eleven Baptist churches with 730 members in 1983,[54] was chosen in response to a Macedonian call. With the approval of the Conventions and Union and the active participation of L'Union d'Églises Baptistes Françaises au Canada,[55] the newest task force was underway.

Relief and Development

Partnership in mission, as implemented through task forces, has now superseded the traditional style of mission on nearly all fronts—and relief and development have also become a vital part of the mission thrust around the world. These approaches have met the late twentieth-century needs, captured the imagination of supporting Canadian Baptists and brought praise from a wide range of impartial observers.

In 1987 the number of missionaries working under the CBOMB totalled 116.[56] Among these were several short-term volunteers, whose numbers have been increasing.

To guide the far-flung interests abroad, Dr. John F. Keith became overseas secretary in 1980, and Dr. Robert Berry replaced Keith as general secretary. Board headquarters, which had been adjacent to those of the Baptist Convention of Ontario and Quebec in Toronto, were moved to Mississauga in 1987. The board has also enjoyed the statesmanlike leadership of general secretaries like Dr. John B. McLaurin, Dr. H. S. Hillyer and Dr. O. E. Daniel—all building for an ever greater tomorrow.

"In the Board's office," writes Overseas Secretary Keith, "there hangs a plaque . . . [from] the Telegu Convention in India. Its most dominant script, ivory inlaid in mahogany, proclaims: IN CHRIST THERE IS NO EAST OR WEST. There is significance in this phrase, and its realization is a worthy one, whether on the international scene or within Canada."[57]

Tradition in transition. Such is the account of Canadian Baptists' overseas ventures in the twentieth century. Innovative measures, including the task force and partnership in missions approaches, together with excellent leadership at home and abroad, have gained for Canadian Baptists a significant place in world missions.

CHAPTER 29

Women Working

"There are times in all our lives when we have the opportunity to venture. . . .
If we decline to do so, we miss the highest purpose that
God has for our lives."
—SHIRLEY F. BENTALL

Hannah Maria Norris, one of Nova Scotia's missionaries to Burma, was once described as "the most impossible of them all."[1] When she was blocked from venturing overseas because of lack of funding in 1870, she set out on a whirlwind tour of the Maritimes to raise support from Baptist women. She initiated no fewer than thirty-two woman's missionary aid societies before she sailed for Burma—and all in three months and three days. Such societies and the regional groups of which they are a part remain strong as the twenty-first century nears. They are the jet fuel of the Canadian Baptist missionary enterprise, particularly overseas.

Leading the Way

After Hannah Norris left for Burma, before the end of 1870, a central committee was formed in Halifax loosely linking the Societies that had been set up. It is believed that the committee was "the first women's group in the world organized for the purpose of sending out single lady missionaries."[2] Soon after, a similar linking committee was established in Saint John, and four years later one began functioning in Prince Edward Island. By 1884 the three provincial bodies had instituted the Woman's Baptist Missionary Union of the Maritime Provinces. The next year the Union listed 123 aid societies in the three provinces, had transmitted $2,525 to the foreign mission board of the Baptist Convention of Nova Scotia, New Brunswick and Prince Edward Island, and still possessed a then-healthy balance of $1,698.[3]

Mission at Home and Abroad

Before the end of the 1870s the Woman's Union had started mission bands for children, usually connected with the local Sunday school, and soon provided cradle rolls to register infants.

Not content to restrict their energies to the support of single women overseas, the Union soon responded to the call of home missions. Nor did they confine their activities to the Maritimes. Their very first "home" contribution was made toward the building of a church in the West at Regina. Through the years the women of the Maritimes have continued this tradition of sustaining mission work both abroad and at home, although their first love—overseas outreach—has always been dominant.

The UBWMU

The Free Baptists of the Maritimes, who joined with the Regular, or Calvinist, Baptists in 1905 and 1906 to form the United Baptist Convention, began organizing auxiliary societies for missions as early as 1869. While some men were involved, the predominant leaders were women. The Free Baptist Woman's Missionary Society of New Brunswick was formed six years later, and by 1905 listed seventy-two societies, twenty-four mission bands and eleven cradle rolls.[4]

With the formation of the United Baptist Convention of the Maritime Provinces, all joined in the United Baptist Woman's Missionary Union. At the time there were eight single woman missionaries overseas under the Maritime board.

Woman Power

The women of Ontario and Quebec were not far behind. Unlike the Maritime women, however, the women of central Canada were first motivated by a man, missionary A. V. Timpany. On furlough in 1876 after his first term in India, Timpany suggested to Ontario's foreign mission secretary that there must be women in their region like Hannah Maria Norris. The secretary encouraged Timpany to seek them out, and not long afterwards the Indian missionary was able to persuade the ladies of St. Catherine Street Church in Montreal and Jarvis Street Church in Toronto to organize support work for women missionaries. "Their response," writes historian Alfreda Hall, was "decisive, for the nucleus of the Society [was] formed immediately in each case."[5]

Four Separate Societies

As there was no unified Convention at that juncture, two women's organizations were founded in 1876, soon to become four. The Women's Baptist Foreign Missionary Society of Ontario (West), established that year, embraced 30 local circles within twelve months . . . and 112 circles and 38 mission bands ten years later.[6] Also founded in 1876, the Women's Baptist Foreign Missionary Society of Eastern Canada later changed the place-designation in its name to Eastern Ontario and Quebec. It included within the next year seven circles, growing to forty-seven, and fifteen mission bands by the turn of the century.[7]

Timpany was also able to prevail upon a number of the women's leaders to publish a small paper, the *Canadian Missionary Link*. Its first issue came off the press in 1878, providing Timpany with a means of communicating regularly with his new home constituency. The publication is still produced today, under the name *Link and Visitor*, having amalgamated with the *Home Mission Visitor* in about 1920.

This was just the beginning. As in the Maritimes, home missions captured the attention of women in Ontario and Quebec. In 1884 the Women's Baptist Home Missionary Society of Western Ontario arose, followed five years later by that of Eastern Ontario and Quebec.

Outreach was soon undertaken by the forty circles of the Western Ontario Society in the Muskoka district and a contribution made to Galician (Russo-Ukrainian) work in western Canada.[8] The more easterly society almost immediately assumed support of two home fields and soon took an active interest in the Grande Ligne Mission.[9]

Women's Society for the West

Despite the tardiness of Baptist development in western Canada, the women in that region were right on the heels of their central and eastern sisters in organizing missionary societies. The first mission circle in Manitoba and the Northwest was born in Winnipeg in 1878 through Lucinda McDonald, wife of Pioneer McDonald. The primary mission objective was to relieve the poverty around them in the frontier settlement, especially among families.

Five years later an attempt was made to link the three or four circles by then operating. A Women's Missionary Society formed, but once the McDonalds moved to Dakota, it faded. In December 1887, however, a new Baptist Women's Home and Foreign Missionary Society for Manitoba and the North West Territories appeared. Combining overseas and Canadian objectives, as in the Maritimes, the new society immediately granted $200 for a new church building at Manitou and voted a similar sum toward the salary of the recently appointed missionary to the German-speaking congregations, F. A. Petereit. Within two years the society nominated a single woman missionary, Lucy H. Booker of Emerson, for overseas service. With her salary underwritten in the West, she sailed for India in 1889 under the Baptist Foreign Missionary Society of Ontario and Quebec.[10]

Close Participation

The women of British Columbia organized even earlier than their counterparts in Manitoba and the Northwest. A year before the opening of the Winnipeg group, a similar circle began functioning at First Baptist, Victoria. Following the same pattern as other B.C. Baptist groups, for over twenty years British Columbia women's circles found their fellowship in the Northern (now American) Baptists' Puget Sound Association and later in its North-Western Convention.

When B.C. Baptists reluctantly severed ties with the Americans in 1897 to form their own Convention, the women's circles became the Women's Board of Missions of the provincial Convention[11] and began a close participation with that body which has continued to be characteristic in the West.

In the first decade of the twentieth century a BWMS was organized for each of the Prairie provinces, while women in British Columbia retained their board within the Convention. Finally, the four groups were linked in 1914 as the Board of Women's Work of the Baptist Union of Western Canada, which was made up of representatives of each who were delegates to the Union Assembly.[12]

Their Master's Business

Throughout these reorganizational episodes, Western Baptist Women were about their Master's business. Missionary outreach was initiated among the Native peoples, as well as among various groups of European immigrants.

Overseas, missionaries in India and Bolivia were sustained and full support provided for the Reverend J. E. Davis in his remarkable leprosy work on the subcontinent. For a time they picked up the suspended publication of the denominational journal, the *Northwest Baptist* — and made it profitable.

By 1896 there were twenty-five circles on the Prairies, which had raised $3,600 for the year. Using figures for 1902 in British Columbia, there were mission circles in seventeen of the eighteen churches, raising over $1,000.[13]

War . . . Controversy . . . Depression

In the twelve months after the formation of the Woman's Baptist Missionary Union of the Maritime Provinces, the merged body began to take on more than just overseas responsibilities, supporting mission projects in the West, as well as work with Grande Ligne Mission and Native peoples. In the Jubilee year, 1920, outreach was begun among immigrants in New Brunswick and with the large black population of Nova Scotia,[14] among whom missionary Agnes Waring was to devote over twenty years of selfless service.

When the Canadian Baptist Foreign Mission Board was established in 1912, all women's societies across the country that had been aiding Convention boards, transferred their energies to the united cause. Those in the Maritimes thus had an additional field, Bolivia, to draw their interest and funding.

Fiftieth Anniversary

During World War I Maritime women did not slacken their efforts, and four single women were commissioned as missionaries from the Maritimes in those years: Bertha Myers, Bessie Lockhart and Grace Baker to India, and L. E. Wilson to Bolivia. Soon after the Armistice three more women were sent to India: Florence Matheson, S. E. Machum and Laura Bain.[15]

Neither did war inhibit the development of significant plans for the celebration of the Fiftieth Anniversary. In addition to the goals at home already mentioned, the Union aimed to increase its numbers and scope in all areas including mission boards, baby bands and young women's societies. These last, which were to become the World Wide Guild, were to provide a constant stream of recruits for the parent UBWMU.

By 1920, the Jubilee year of the Canadian Baptist Foreign Mission Board, President Mrs. David Hutchinson recounted the goals that had been reached by that date. More than 400 circles were operating and eighteen single women missionaries were being maintained in India and Bolivia. In Canada, the Maritimes supported home missions, Quebec supported the Grande Ligne and western Canada supported both English and non-English work.[16]

In the mid-twenties the Maritime Woman's Union set themselves a target of $50,000 to be donated to Acadia University as an endowment for young women planning to be missionaries. In 1929 they reached their goal. The next decade, of course, brought financial troubles, and missionary appointments slowed to a trickle.

A Missionary Organization in Every Church

When world war broke out for the second time in the century, the women of the circles did sewing and knitting, produced food parcels and offered homes away from home for countless servicemen and women on leave. When India was in danger of being engulfed in the conflict, they must have followed developments closely, as that country was still their main mission field.

Another significant anniversary approached as hostilities ground on — the seventy-fifth in 1945. Far-reaching goals were set that year — to link every Baptist woman in the Maritimes with a mission group and to have a missionary organization in every church for children and teenagers, an enlarged missionary staff and an increased budget, including an anniversary fund as a memorial to the pioneers.[17]

Ontario and Quebec Societies Buffeted

Baptist Women in the central provinces did not escape the modernist/fundamentalist controversy of the twenties. Indeed, their historian Alfreda Hall writes that "the twenties, thirties and forties were years of trial: first came the Controversy, then the Depression, and then World War II."[18] All four women's societies were affected, as were many of the circles. Hardest hit was the Home Missionary Society of Western Ontario, whose long-time president, Mrs. C. J. Holman, led a breakaway to form and preside over the Women's Missionary Society of the Regular Baptists. Twelve members of her board also withdrew, along with two missionaries.[19]

Buffeted by such blows, the societies seemed to be ill-equipped to face the Great Depression. Yet they not only survived but also recouped their losses. Both home and foreign societies in western Ontario faced severe deficits. As part of their Diamond Jubilee celebration in 1934 the Home Mission Society in western Ontario set a goal of $5,000 "to check the wave of retrogression." By the end of 1935, they had actually exceeded the goal, acquiring $5,828. By the end of the same year the foreign society had a shortage of over $6,000. By the end of 1935 they had also achieved their goal.

The two societies in eastern Ontario and Quebec suffered similarly. They too made extraordinary appeals in 1934 — even to the extent of initiating a "treasure hunt" for gold trinkets that might be sold for funds.[20]

Depression and War Service

Despite their own difficulties during the Depression, Ontario and Quebec women were at the forefront of efforts to assist others even less fortunate. Whether spearheading the collection of relief supplies for the drought-ridden Prairies or opening church quarters to provide meals for the hungry, they were dedicated in their service. Such activities prepared the way for their ministrations in World War II. It was their War Services Committee that provided "Bundles for Britain" and sparked countless endeavours among the circles to reach out to the services personnel and their families at home and overseas.

New Board in Western Canada

At the 1915 inaugural meeting of the recently formed Board of Women's Work of the Baptist Union of Western Canada a budget of nearly $10,000 was pledged by the four provinces. It was divided three ways: non-English work including Grande Ligne, English-speaking home missions and services overseas. Within seven years receipts had doubled and the number of circles totalled 114.[21]

A valuable tool for both information and promotion was introduced in the West in 1926 in the form of a "reading course." Through the years the various study books — centring on missions, denominational work and the devotional life—have been explored by individual circle members and passed along. The same reading plan was taken up by the women in Ontario within two years and by the mid-thirties was being used Canada-wide.[22]

Deepening Depression

As the Depression deepened in 1932, western women, despite their own often desperate economic conditions, managed to raise more than 90 percent of their annual objective for missions and to assist the needy at home. During that year the Manitoba women alone sent almost seven and a quarter metric tonnes of White Cross medical supplies to India.[23] Gifts from the other provinces were also bountiful. Western Baptist executive C. C. McLaurin wrote of the women's untiring generosity: "By their systematic raising of money they have promoted the grace of liberality throughout the church."[24]

This vigorous response to distress was soon to be transferred, as in the other regions, to conditions of war. Under the slightly altered name of Women's Mission Auxiliary (the name changed in 1940), the women also organized Red Cross units to provide "Bundles for Britain" food parcels for the troops overseas and hospitality for servicemen and women in Canada.

Dominion Committee

As the Women's Missionary Societies grew, thoughts turned to a national organization. Maud Matthews, the wife of Albert Matthews, who was later to become chatelaine of the lieutenant-governor's suite at Queen's Park, Ontario, was the catalyst of the movement. Through the Women's Baptist Foreign Mission Board of Western Ontario, she was able to arrange for a 1935 meeting in Toronto which brought together representatives of all six Canadian missionary societies. She was also the first to occupy the chair of the new Dominion Committee of the Affiliated Baptist Women's Missionary Societies of Canada—so named in 1940.

At first the Women's Dominion Committee was to be "largely a consultative body"[25] that would help centralize the women's work. The Dominion Committee has become an increasingly valuable co-ordinating vehicle, not only among the societies, but also in their joint relationships with the Canadian Baptist Overseas Mission Board and the Canadian Baptist Federation.

"Projects Galore"

Historian Alfreda Hall holds that the Dominion Committee played a significant role "in providing a mental climate for the unification of the four central Societies in 1953."[26] As has been seen, the two foreign missionary societies, founded in the 1870s, and the two home societies, formed in the 1880s, long continued on their separate ways in Ontario and Quebec in spite of the establishment of an overall Ontario/Quebec Convention. From time to time there were flutterings of interest in consolidation but it was not until 1941 that a commission was appointed to assess the possibilities of linking the two western Ontario Societies. Merger did not result but an inter-board committee was formed to facilitate co-operation between the societies.

A Combined Society

Gradually the momentum increased, so that by 1951 a Unification Committee, which included representatives from eastern Ontario and Quebec, was ready with a proposal for the amalgamation of all four societies. This occurred in 1953, seventy-seven years after the founding of the first societies. The new Baptist Women's Missionary Society of Ontario and

Quebec, an auxiliary of the Baptist Convention, had the following aims, among others:

- to share in the evangelization of Canada and those areas overseas in which the Canadian Baptist Foreign Mission Board works;
- to keep before children and young women the claims of missionary service as a life work;
- to contribute funds for missionary work at home and abroad and afford opportunity to train workers.[27]

New Ventures

In the two and a half decades leading up to the Centennial of Women's Work in Ontario and Quebec, it became apparent that, as far as India was concerned, the goal of devolution was being rapidly achieved. Native women were taking over positions of management in hospitals and schools.

Bolivia continued to present a challenge to the combined society, although native leaders were beginning to take charge in that country, Canadian missionaries both male and female were still being welcomed with open arms. New ventures in Angola, Zaire, Kenya, Indonesia and Brazil were also arising to fill the Indian gap. In many ways the women were "helping to move whole nations forward," as missionary Katherine S. McLaurin wrote from India in 1931.[28]

In Canada the major focus for the period was on "Christian fellowship" outreach to the tens of thousands of largely European immigrants who had thronged to the country, settling mainly in the cities. In 1954 the society engaged seven home missionaries in this task. A Christian fellowship centre, providing food and clothing for the needy, was opened at Church House, the headquarters of the Baptist Convention of Ontario and Quebec, and in 1969 the whole program was expanded and renamed Christian Fellowship in Action, which included social service projects. Work continued among Native peoples and the new Union of French Baptist Churches.[29]

Obvious Concerns

The honour roll of missionaries in 1976, the Ontario/Quebec Centennial year, bore a total of 139 names of women supported during the period: 76 of these overseas, 63 in Canada. The theme for the Women's Convention in Ontario and Quebec that year expressed the timeless nature of their task: "Jesus Christ, the same yesterday, today and forever."[30]

Yet there were obvious concerns. By 1980 membership had declined to just over 8,000 from the 1955 figure of 11,400, and there was a parallel drop in the number of groups from 535 to 368. Bucking the trend, receipts were up from $140,299 to $439,609—although the latter figure was in inflated dollars.

President Dorothy Neal and Executive Secretary Audrey Manuel identified the problem, one experienced by many volunteer agencies: the vast movement of women into the workforce. The formation of additional groups and groups with a different focus was called for, not only to "provide fellowship and nourishment for women in the church, but [to] be the means of outreach into the community." Various "interest" groups, coffee hours and Bible studies were suggested.[31]

One year in the mid-eighties, the BWMS took as its theme the concept "love builds bridges." That theme, along with the logo for that year, which depicted a heart stretched to span a community, indicates that society's increased emphasis on reaching out to all women in the community.[32]

Two Bicycles to Sweden

"Projects galore," writes Earl Merrick of the seemingly unlimited activities of the circles of the United Baptist Woman's Missionary Union of the Atlantic provinces. He goes on to list over twenty-five of them — all the way from the maintenance of Bible women in India to service to the black community in Canada, from a sanitorium in Ludhiana to daily Vacation Bible Schools at home.

In 1950, Merrick said, the Union paid for two bicycles for missionaries in Sweden and also gave nearly $60,000 to work abroad and $33,000 to work in Canada.[33] In the intervening years the scope has still broadened and deepened, the gifts greatly enlarged.

In 1957 visitors from the Union were employed at four sanitoriums in the Maritime provinces.[34] Six years later an amount of $522 was earmarked for "Operation Eyesight at Dr. Gullison's hospital, Sompeta"[35] — a harbinger of a popular continent-wide movement to aid the cause of the sightless worldwide.

Among its continuing widespread interests the UBWMU makes grants for home mission pastors' salaries and supports work in the African association, Newfoundland and French Canada. In 1987, a chair in missions, in the name of founder Hannah Maria Norris, was endowed at Acadia Divinity College.

Renewal in the West

President Nancye Gavin of the Women's Missionary Auxiliary of the Western Baptist Union, reporting to the 1967 Penticton Convention, remarked, undoubtedly with a sigh of relief, that the year had been "one of preparation for transition"[36] for the auxiliary. Although the Baptist Union had always been noted for its many constitutional changes, the modifications that occurred during the fifties and early sixties were substantial even for that group. But 1967 was to bring the process to an end . . . and a new beginning. When the Baptist Union of Western Canada was restructured that year to form four provincial areas from the previous six associations, two each in Manitoba, Saskatchewan and Alberta, and the Convention of British Columbia, the Women's Missionary Auxiliary followed the Union pattern of subgrouping.

The work continued unabated. In 1975, in addition to regular mission support at home and abroad through the Baptist Union, the circles shipped nearly 550 kg of White Cross medical supplies to the Akividu hospital in India. Food parcels and cash gifts to the value of some $5,000 went to missionaries in India and Bolivia.

Circles Dropping

At home "the main emphasis [was] on person-to-person relationships with children, the elderly, ill, handicapped and disadvantaged . . . in our neighbourhoods. . . . There were literally thousands of visits to individuals, and gifts of cookies, candy, fruit and flowers . . . [and] many days were brightened by a phone call or cheery card."[37] That year the auxiliary became the Baptist Women of the Baptist Union of Western Canada.

As in the East, the number of actual mission circles began to drop after the mid-sixties. Whereas there were 237 groups with 4,159 members in 1967,[38] twenty years later the number of actual circles had slumped to 117, with only 2,130 members.[39] However, President Gavin's implied prophecy in 1967 that "women generally seem ready for a program which would relate them closely to the total work of the church,"[40] was proving to be accurate. In addition to the 117 circles, there were eighteen fellowship/work groups, sixty-four for Bible study and prayer, nineteen "Morning Out for Mothers" groups and fifteen other women's groups—making a grand total of 233, with a membership of 3,161.[41] This was the church at work within and without, in the wide community.

Writing in 1987, the Western president of that year, Evelyn Richardson, told the story of a Bolivia missionary who had lost his way one dark night, and could only find his way along the slippery roads by climbing onto the roof of his truck to glimpse the mountains for guidance. Evelyn Richardson invited her readers to "Climb up on the roof top," to view "where we have been . . . where we are . . . where we are going." After reviewing some past and present accomplishments, she concluded with words that apply to Baptist women across the land: "Our heritage . . . is marked by women whose faith took Jesus' words seriously. 'This is impossible for man, but with God all things are possible.' "[42]

CHAPTER 30

Assigned in a Secular World

"We cannot live in our heritage.
We can only live worthily by fulfilling our heritage."
— *E. C. HERRICK*

In the latter half of the twentieth century, Canadians — and Canadian Baptists — were in an era more challenging than any previously encountered. Two violent global wars and a debilitating economic depression had left their ingrained mark. Things were never to be the same again. A nation that had been at least nominally Christian was becoming rapidly secularized. Indeed, society's values came to be rooted in secular humanism more than in Christianity.

After World War II times of prosperity and recession followed each other in succession, and new threats to the faith arose: the drug culture . . . lottery line-ups . . . easy divorce and broken homes . . . abortion on demand . . . genetic engineering . . . and the New Age movement. The individual came to be the measure of things and, especially in the eighties, material well-being and professional success became national preoccupations. Women flocked into the workforce and many children spent the greater part of their formative years in day-care centres. Changing women's roles left both men and women uncertain of their goals and desires.

Alternate lifestyles (including homosexual practice) were widely accepted, even in avant garde church circles. Sexual promiscuity was to be rampant. The media became increasingly strident and confrontational. Violence was prevalent in the streets and urban guerillas terrified major world centres. Air hijackings and kidnappings became commonplace. And hanging over all would be the threat of nuclear annihilation.

By the Atlantic

The euphoric mood that had characterized the Baptist Centennial celebrations in the Maritime provinces spilled over into the early postwar years. A two-year advance campaign was launched in 1949 to secure nearly a quarter of a million dollars, to be divided equally among foreign missions, home missions and the annuity board — the last to improve meagre ministerial pensions. Inspired by President Abner J. Langley's

Convention address three years later, a five-year program followed, aiming for 18,000 new members, 45,000 on Sunday school rolls, five new families and five single women volunteers for overseas service and an equal number in training, as well as a denominational budget of $200,000 by the final year.[1]

Their reach exceeded their grasp, for by 1957 only about 11,500 had been received by baptism and Sunday school enrolment stood at about 36,800. However, the budget goal was fully attained and eight families and eight single women had offered for service abroad. One family, three single women and two single men were in training.[2]

Emphasis on Planting

In 1949 the Reverend Lawrence R. Atkinson was named to the new position of Field Evangelist, later to be joined by the Reverend Stuart E. Murray. Over many years the two carried on a most effective evangelistic outreach, including numerous "revival" campaigns and deeper life conferences. Thousands of converts resulted.

Emphasis on the planting of new churches was renewed after being given relatively low priority for some time. The home missions board, charged with this task, reported to the 1954 Assembly that five new congregations had been initiated. The board was authorized to seek $250,000 for the initial extension,[3] and by 1975 an overall Churches for New Communities' program resulted in the founding of sixteen mostly urban churches.[4]

Emphasis on Instruction

In a brand new educational development, the United Baptist Bible Training School (UBBTS) was opened in Moncton in 1949, with the Reverend Myron O. Brinton as the first principal. This move followed a report to Convention a year earlier that well over 100 young people of the churches in the Maritimes were either attending or planning to attend Bible schools elsewhere.[5]

Offering a secondary school curriculum that placed strong emphasis on Bible instruction and included secretarial training and music, UBBTS had 128 students ten years later.[6] However, only nine of these were enrolled in the Bible department per se, so the curriculum was reappraised in 1962 and the secondary school offerings were curtailed. Replacing them were post-high-school (but not university level) preparatory courses for people entering lay church vocations, including church secretarial work, musical leadership in the church and Christian education. At the time, Convention stipulated that UBBTS should not provide terminal (pre-ordination) training for the ministry, as theological training for the Convention was being provided at Acadia University at the time.[7]

In 1970 the school became the Atlantic Baptist College[8] and offered the first two years of university courses in Arts. By 1981, however, a four-year Bachelor of Arts program was instituted, with majors in Biblical studies, music and Christian education. Atlantic Baptist College, records the Convention minutes, had "come of age."[9]

President W. Ralph Richardson reported that for the academic year 1986–87, 149 students were enrolled in the regular college program, with a faculty of eleven full-time and eight part-time instructors.[10] Seven faculty members had doctorates.

Closer to Its Roots

The Acadia story is more mixed. Dr. Watson Kirkconnell, outstanding Canadian scholar and one of the founders of the Canadian Baptist Federation, was named president of the university in 1948. He was to preside over a period of storm.

Over the years Convention had tried to bring the university back to its roots as a Christian institution. At the same time others had tried to alter the complexion of the board of governors and so dilute Convention's influence on the university.

After World War II enrolment took a significant leap as many veterans returned to their studies, but by 1952 the numbers were down to 500.[11] Just four years later, the governors announced that "the day of under-capacity in enrollment is over" and declared that massive funding was essential for development—"a minimum of three million dollars."[12] Convention decided to approve the proposed expansion, but this may well have spelled the doom of denominational influence on the university.

At the same time the lifestyle of many of the students on campus was provoking criticism from the community and the board of governors and administration appeared to be taking no corrective action. To resolve the issue the Convention established a blue ribbon higher education committee in 1964 to study the situation.[13] In a well-documented report submitted the following year, the committee recommended that the educational philosophy of the founders be reaffirmed and that all faculty members be Christians. Endorsing the report, Convention instructed the board of governors (whom it regularly elected) and the higher education committee to report on implementation the next year.[14]

To those in the university circles it was "too much too late." The governors balked and were supported strongly by the associated alumni who immediately announced plans to submit a Bill to the Nova Scotia legislature to strip the United Baptist Convention of its right to name all but a quarter of the board of governors.[15]

The government of the day under Premier Robert Stanfield, apparently concluding that public funding over the years outweighed the rights of the many tens of thousands of Baptists who over the same years had staunchly supported and operated "their" university, forced a legislative settlement which a reluctant Convention could hardly dispute.

Ultimately, the legislation permitted Convention to name fourteen of thirty-six governors, effecting majority secular control while allowing Convention to maintain a small degree of influence. Even this number of Convention representatives was later reduced. Had the choice been made earlier to maintain Acadia as a small "Christian" college, the result might have been different. But now the die was cast, and after more than a century and a quarter, the Baptist university was secularized.

Theological education was safeguarded, however, an agreement in 1967 providing for the establishment of Acadia Divinity College, located on the university campus. Operated by a board of trustees directly responsible to the Convention, the College has the right to grant its own degrees, although it does not do so, affiliated as it is with the university.

In the year following its inception, Acadia Divinity College had twenty students working toward the Bachelor of Divinity, six in the Bachelor of Theology program and five special students.[16] In less than twenty years an international body of 188 credit students was attending the College, seventy-five of them taking the Master of Divinity degree.[17] Its first principal was Dr. M. Cherry, who was followed by Dr. A. J. Langley, Dr. Harold L. Mitton and Dr. Andrew D. MacRae. The college is fully accredited by the Association of Theological Schools.

A central Baptist building, accommodating all departments, the eastern office of the Canadian Baptist Overseas Mission Board and a new book room, was opened in Saint John in 1960. Three years later, in recognition of the new outreach into Newfoundland, the denominational name was changed to the United Baptist Convention of the Atlantic Provinces. Dr. J. Murray Armstrong became general secretary in 1954 after Dr. Raymond E. Whitney had served an interim year following Waldo Machum's death. The Reverend Harry A. Renfree assumed the office in 1958.

Atlantic Baptist Senior Citizens Home, Inc.

Prominent among the "caring" projects of the Atlantic Convention has been a veritable proliferation of facilities for senior citizens. Concerns in this area came into focus in 1966 with the appointment of a study group and Assembly authorization two years later to secure a care home site.[18] Aided by major government funding, the Kenneth E. Spencer Memorial Home, named in honour of a former lay Convention president, was opened in Moncton in January 1973.[19]

Within less than a decade, Atlantic Baptist Senior Citizens Home, Inc., a Convention-elected body, announced a joint effort with Hillcrest Church of Saint John to provide accommodation for seniors in that city — a $25 million project.[20] Close on the heels of this development, additional facilities were made ready at Bathurst, a second in Moncton,[21] the P.E.I. Atlantic Baptist Home in Prince Edward Island and the Gladys M. Manning Memorial Home in Windsor, Nova Scotia. The last includes housing units for retired ministers, missionaries and other Christian workers.[22]

Jubilee Journey

In addition, during the period of the 1960s, there was celebration and development in the Atlantic provinces, and in the 1970s restructuring, that perennial preoccupation of Canadian Baptists in the twentieth century. The Middle Sackville and Sackville churches were honoured at the 1963 Convention to mark the two hundredth anniversary of the founding of their mother church under Nathan Mason. A Jubilee Journey over the years 1967 to 1969 commemorated the Diamond Jubilee of union of the Regular and Free Baptists of the Maritimes. During that time a Baptist foundation was incorporated to provide funds for the churches for building and expansion.

In 1973, following the lead of the Baptist Union of Western Canada, the Atlantic Convention made major organizational changes. A council made up of six commissions replaced the executive and the various departments, and the Atlantic region was divided into four areas, each containing several associations, with a resident pastor-at-large assigned to each area. The Reverend Keith R. Hobson was the first to carry the title of executive minister, succeeding Dr. T. B. McDormand who had taken over the reins in 1967. The Reverend Eugene M. Thompson followed in 1984.

Emphasis on Evangelism

Throughout the Convention, the emphasis on evangelism has been strong and unremitting. Mass evangelism remains a potent force, simultaneous crusades being launched in all four provinces in 1986 and 1987. In a 1986–1990 Atlantic Baptists Reaching Out Project, focus was placed on Lifestyle Evangelism, backed by a LETS training syllabus (Lifestyle Evangelism Training School) produced by Dr. Andrew MacRae, principal of Acadia Divinity College. A director of church extension was also named, and a million-dollar "Giving for Growth" financial campaign was launched to underwrite development. Atlantic Baptists were seeking to penetrate the world's spiritual void with vision.

Central Canada

In January 1955, Dr. Dixon A. Burns, then superintendent of home missions for the Baptist Convention of Ontario and Quebec, wrote a guest editorial in the *Canadian Baptist* entitled "Facing Our Future." Citing a declining rural population, the accelerated development of suburban life and immigration from many countries to Canada's major cities, he pleaded for the recovery of social passion while the denomination remained true to its genius — evangelism and missions.

A rural church committee was established in 1956 and continued over several years to address the problems of the country church. A special conference was held in 1956 to acquaint ministerial students with opportunities in rural areas and the same year a number of rural pastors were sponsored to attend the summer school for clergy at Ontario Agricultural College, Guelph. A refresher correspondence course for town and country pastors was also offered.[23]

Convention had already instructed its Executive to study extension needs in view of "the astonishing home-building boom occurring in the suburban areas of every city in the Convention."[24] A financial campaign to provide funds to match this growth was undertaken right at the half-century, with nearly $275,000 of the $300,000 goal being pledged before that year was out.[25] By 1955 at least fifty new churches and Sunday Schools had been launched and over thirty new church buildings erected.[26] To underline the shift in emphasis, the Church Edifice Board became the Church Extension Board.[27]

As J. K. Zeman has pointed out, Baptist outreach to immigrants reached its climax in the years between the end of World War II and 1970 when there was an influx of political refugees from Soviet-controlled lands. Older congregations were strengthened and new ones such as the Latvian and Estonian churches in Toronto were founded — the latter becoming the fastest-growing congregation in the Convention.[28] By the eighties the Gospel was going out in seventeen languages, one of them Chinese, at the Toronto Chinese Baptist Church, by then the Convention's largest.

A Major Restructuring

Scheduled to retire on September 1, 1950, Ontario and Quebec's first general secretary, Dr. H. H. Bingham, died just two weeks before. He was succeeded by Dr. Thomas B. McDormand, who served until he accepted the parallel Baptist Federation position in 1955, when Dr. P. P. W. Ziemann assumed the role. Ziemann also died in office, in 1960, and Dr. Leland A. Gregory took over the next year, serving until he retired in 1971.

A major restructuring of the Convention was undertaken in 1961. The Convention executive committee became the council, responsible for overall co-ordination. The several incorporated boards were replaced by four departments. In addition to those elected to the departments by the Assembly, each association named one — the aim clearly being to strengthen the associations, whose responsibilities were not always well-defined and whose administrative influence was weak.[29]

Convention's headquarters, Church House, in Toronto was moved to renovated quarters at 190 St. George Street in 1952, the adjacent building being added before the end of the decade. In 1969 the Convention and all its departments moved to more spacious premises at 217 St. George which had provision for limited overnight committee accommodation.

Little Protest

In the field of Christian higher education the Baptists of Ontario and Quebec suffered a loss just as serious as the Atlantic Baptists' loss of

Acadia — and in central Canada the loss took place earlier. In 1948 McMaster University was divided into two parts, Hamilton College being established with public funding to be responsible for undergraduate senior science studies. Within a short time the university itself, which had historically refused any public patronage, began to accept the grants made by government to all universities on a per student basis, the governors in 1952 being "confident the Convention appreciate[d] the changed conditions."[30]

Apparently Convention did, for three years later there was apparently little protest when the governors, while claiming to be "committed to a Christian emphasis in curriculum and atmosphere," indicated distinctly that "our educational responsibility is to the Government of Ontario which incorporated the University in 1887 and gave it its powers."[31]

Viewing the expansion needed to meet the community's educational demands, the governors in 1956 indicated that the future they envisaged "would find [Convention] itself involved in financial responsibilities far beyond anything the denomination can or should face," and advocated that Convention confine its subsequent interest to the Divinity College.[32] An amendment from the Assembly floor seeking to postpone this complete secularization of the rest of the university failed. The die was cast. Authority was given to revise the McMaster charter to form a separate Divinity School under a denominationally appointed board and a completely nondenominational corporation to control the university.[33]

The following year Hamilton College was reunited with a secular McMaster, and the Divinity College was constituted as a distinct entity but still affiliated with the university. Given the right to grant its own degrees, the Divinity College was nevertheless expected to forgo the privilege while affiliated with the university. Convention would directly elect ten of the College's eighteen-member board of trustees. A financial settlement was accepted which turned over some trust funds and provided about $1,500,000 for endowment and building.[34] "You were simply moving a burden off your own shoulders," remarked the Assembly delegate who seconded the motion to approve the separation.[35] The ease with which this change was carried out differed drastically from the agitation that occurred in the Atlantic provinces a decade later over Acadia.

No Small Furor

Meanwhile, Moulton College, which had been founded as a ladies' academy by Susan Moulton McMaster, had gone the way of the Woodstock institution. In 1954 McMaster's board of governors, who also bore the responsibility for the College, announced that Moulton, then in its sixty-sixth year, had an enrolment of 184, up from 162, and then announced that they had decided to shut it down. Among the reasons cited were changes in the surrounding district, aging buildings and financial pressures.[36]

As with Woodstock, no small furor was aroused when the Moulton announcement was made. The Alumni Association protested the "undemocratic procedure" followed by the governors,[37] but the Convention Executive reportedly agreed with the action "reluctantly," [38] and the deed was done.

BTI

Christian education for youth was not about to be abandoned, however. encouraged by the success of the Baptist Leadership Training School in Calgary,[39] the Convention opened the Baptist Training Institute with the Reverend A. G. McDowell as principal in late 1955. Lay leadership studies without academic credit were offered in the Institute, which was first located on the premises of Walmer Road Church, Toronto. It moved to Brantford four years later.

BTI did not completely fulfill its promise. With thirteen regular students and twelve to fifteen taking evening courses a decade later,[40] its numbers fluctuated but remained small until the Institute was closed in 1969. Prospective students then attended BLTS in Calgary, about twenty per year until 1984 when a new Baptist Leadership Education Centre was opened in choice new quarters in Whitby, Ontario. With an enrolment capacity of eighty, and seven full-time staff members led by Principal William Chapman, BLEC has attracted a large group of young people to lay courses, such as Bible, Baptist History and Beliefs, Doctrine and a number of practical ministry and personal growth subjects.[41]

The initial review of McMaster Divinity College in 1958 disclosed the appointment of Dr. N. H. Parker as principal but decried a "seriously reduced" enrolment of thirty-six — down ten from the previous year.[42] Growth was to come. A new building which soon became a landmark on the university campus was dedicated two years later. Dr. Ivan C. Morgan assumed the principalship in 1967, serving until 1978 when Dr. Melvyn R. Hillmer accepted the position. That year there were fifty-four full-time and thirty-six part-time students.[43]

Surprised at the Criticism

Sunday school publications have been a continual conundrum to Canadian Baptists. For many years there was considerable support of materials published co-operatively with the United Church of Canada. When that denomination decided on its New Curriculum in the mid-fifties, the Ontario and Quebec Convention agreed to participate in a Baptist edition,[44] while the others were more wary. They did in fact form the Publications Committee of the Atlantic Provinces and Western Canada to deal with Judson Press of the American Baptists.

"Surprised at the strong criticism it had to face" over the issue at the 1964 Ontario and Quebec Assembly, the Department of Christian Education convened a conference of the ministers early in 1965, resulting in the discontinuance of the joint publishing arrangement by that year's Assembly.[45]

Meanwhile, the Atlantic/Western Publications Committee had appointed the Reverend Harry G. Taylor to edit Judson materials for their use. Providing unity once again, the Baptist Publications Committee of Canada, which had been producing the co-operative materials with the United Church, changed its name to All-Canada Baptist Publications, and the Atlantic/Western committee merged with it. Taylor was the continuing editor in the production of Judson materials for cross-country use.[46]

Although soaring costs and lack of greater acceptance obliged All-Canada Baptist Publications to discontinue the preparation of Canadian editions of the Judson Press materials, supplies of that press, supplemented by those of the Southern Baptists (from 1977) were made available through outlets in the Maritimes and Toronto. ACBP also produced for general church use a number of publications, the most notable being *A Manual for Worship and Service*, edited by the Reverend William R. Cram.

In 1984 all three sponsoring bodies agreed to make ACBP the publishing arm of the Canadian Baptist Federation.[47] The plan proved to be unfeasible, and All-Canada Publications was phased out, being replaced on the Federation level by a publication task force.[48] Once again a significant effort to provide Canadian Baptist Churches with Sunday School materials bearing a national and denominational imprint had fallen short and the churches were obliged to secure their supplies on an individual basis.

The Boat People

An evangelistic outreach continued high on the agendas of churches and Convention in Ontario and Quebec in the sixties, seventies and eighties. In 1982 an evangelistic program called Turning the Tide involved thirty-two congregations in a church-to-church campaign with an equal number of Southern Baptist congregations. In this campaign, individual Southern Baptist churches sent their pastors as evangelists to individual Ontario and Quebec churches. This was followed two years later by a Turn to Life program, when over sixty-five churches participated in a week of simultaneous evangelism. Providing a "smorgasbord of options," the Department of Canadian Missions offered materials and assistance in three programs: WIN, One Step Forward and Evangelism Explosion.[49]

Nor were social concerns neglected during these years. The Boat People from Viet Nam were sponsored in large numbers and other refugees aided. Churches were encouraged to develop local social action programs, for which department support was offered.[50]

Youth were also involved in outreach. A Baptist Mission Corps was formed, through which five young people served briefly in Bolivia in 1986, five more volunteering for overseas short service the following year.[51] At home a Baptist Youth Corps reported that during the summer of 1977 seven Corps workers served in twelve churches.[52] In 1983 five teams of young people ministered in twenty areas, including camps, the inner city and extension.[53]

Seven Areas

Dr. Ronald F. Watts, founding principal of the Baptist Leadership Training School, Calgary, assumed the general secretary's mantle in 1971, serving for thirteen years. Department of Canadian Missions Secretary, the Reverend Albert E. Coe followed in 1984, retiring four years later.

Then Kentville, Nova Scotia, pastor and former Atlantic Convention president and staff member Dr. Bryon W. Fenwick took office in June 1988, as the first executive minister in the midst of a major restructuring. The reorganization resulted in the abolition of the departments and regular staff positions and the appointment of three associate executive ministers, an assistant to the executive minister, a treasurer/business manager and seven area ministers.

The new Council, elected by the Assembly and the associations, was composed of three Commissions with whom the associate executive ministers function: congregational life, shared mission and pastoral resources. The development of seven strong regional areas within the Convention, each given on-the-spot service by an area minister, was made a top priority.[54]

Also launched in 1987 was a $2,500,000 financial campaign to provide $1,500,000 for church extension and $1,000,000 to fund a chair of missions and evangelism at McMaster Divinity College. The Baptist Convention of Ontario and Quebec was girding itself for action as it entered its second century.

Facing West

Looking through the eyes of its treasurer, the Baptist Union of Western Canada crossed over into the second half of the twentieth century with significantly improved prospects. After the desperate days of the Depression the financial picture gradually brightened during the war years until in 1946 a slight surplus appeared on the balance sheet — the first for nearly two decades.

A Mid-Century Advance produced nearly $90,000 of which over $20,000 was given to the Foreign Mission Board. The rest went to extension, mission support, youth camping and sponsorship of a radio program. Then Judge W. C. Kelley of West Summerland, a good friend of retiring General Secretary Dr. William Smalley, arranged a legacy, which after his death provided an additional $375,000. Of this, $25,000 was used to improve the meagre pension fund for pastors and $35,000 as a loan fund for extension.[55] To have a small endowment fund and be relieved even slightly of fiscal pressure for a year or two was a new experience for the western Union.

Re-examining Structures

Yet the nearly two decades ahead were to be years of uncertainty. The Baptist Union of Western Canada had yet to assure itself, to uncover its place among the various denominations at work in the West. The pressures of establishing and maintaining identity as a small minority among religious giants were enormous.

To prepare for the task, the Union re-examined its structures, an undertaking which between the years 1957 and 1967 produced no fewer than five distinct reports from an equal number of diligent survey commissions. Four of these were internal studies, but final action was taken on none of them either by the board or the annual Conventions. Comments historian Margaret Thompson: "Whether this was wisdom or sheer irresponsibility, the next generation may decide."[56]

Expressing frustration at the failure of the sundry domestic attempts to bring revision, the Union board in 1964 reached over the international border to secure the expert survey services of the Reverend Lawrence H. Janssen and a team from the American Baptist home mission societies. The ensuing wide-ranging "Janssen Report" of 1965[57] resulted in administrative and program recommendations which ultimately became the basis for radical change in the outlook and operation of the Union and a model for later consideration by the other two regional Conventions.

Decentralization

After the Janssen Report, the six Prairie associations and the British Columbia Convention became four areas, mostly according to provincial boundaries. All areas are "alike in organization and power," with British Columbia retaining at least temporarily its former legal status as a Convention in order to safeguard certain trusts.

Policy making is the function of the Union and its board, the administration of the program that of the area and its executive. An executive minister replaced the general secretary as the senior administrative officer, and area ministers were appointed to act as "pastors to pastors" and liaison officers with the respective areas.

This decentralization initially eliminated the "specialist" staff positions in home missions, evangelism and Christian education as an economy measure, but particular efforts have been made to secure area ministers with skills in these fields and to give them a Union-wide advisory role. The new organization was enthusiastically endorsed by the Union and the B.C. Convention in back-to-back Assemblies in 1968. By supporting the proposed changes British Columbia relinquished its special status within the Union constitution,[58] a factor which had been the cause of some heartburning elsewhere.

Headquarters to Calgary

Dr. W. J. MacDonald, Ontario and Quebec Home Missions Superintendent, had succeeded Smalley as general secretary in 1951, and he was followed by the Reverend J. Frank Patch for two years in 1957. Dr. Smalley then returned for an interim year and was followed by the Reverend Theo T. Gibson, during whose term the American survey team was invited. When Gibson accepted a pastorate in 1964, Dr. Patch was recalled for a second term and gave strong leadership during the survey period.

The first executive minister under the new organization was the Reverend Harry A. Renfree, a westerner then serving as general secretary of the Atlantic Convention. He held office from 1967 to 1981 when the Reverend Douglas N. Moffat, a Montreal-born pastor with wide experience in all three regions of Canada, assumed the responsibilities. Headquarters offices of the Union were moved to Calgary in 1973 — a change which had been recommended in the Janssen Report.

A Good Base Fashioned

Despite the structural uncertainty of the 1980s and 1960s, there was a good deal of activity. Indeed, between the years 1953 and 1963, more new churches were founded than in any similar period since the end of World War I. Thirty-one were established altogether.[59] Included was a chapel fellowship in Beulah Garden Homes, Vancouver, a project undertaken by British Columbia Baptists to provide affordable housing for senior citizens.

Over the twenty years following the mid-century the Baptist Union granted, loaned or guaranteed nearly two million dollars for church expansion and renovation. Yet the number of members in the denomination stayed about the same, the 1950 figure being 17,008, that of 1970, 17,055.[60] But a good base had been fashioned. By 1980 the figure had risen by 18.6 percent to 20,237, six years later to 21,297 — and these in a period of roll-cleansing. The Baptist Union of Western Canada was the only one of the three regional bodies to show an overall membership increase in that period.

Century Two

In 1976, a year after the Centennial of the first western church, the Union launched a capital fund campaign for one million dollars, primarily for extension and outreach.[61] The targeted amount was surpassed, $1,089,000 being attained,[62] and the Assembly accepted a continuing goal of $250,000 a year for extension. This, too, was consistently achieved until the amount for extension was finally included in the regular budget of the Union. That budget has almost always been realized and often surpassed. Even in the economic downturn year of 1982, 99 percent of the projected amount was received.[63] For the first time in 1988 the budget topped two million dollars (by $38,450)[64]—a significant mark for a small denomination.

At the 1980 Assembly, the Baptist Men, stressing men's support of the entire program of the local church, introduced a new extension-support program. Century II Club they called it, members agreeing to donate on call no more than three times a year at least ten dollars. Some $90,000 had been obtained for extension through this program by 1986.[65]

Initial steps toward the formation of a foundation were taken in 1971 —its function being "to create a rotating fund for church building financing, to promote outreach ministries at home and abroad, and to assist in other [approved] projects." By 1980 the foundation had assets in gifts and loans of $500,000 and offered the additional service of estate planning to churches and individuals.[66] Six years later the fund stood at over $2.5 million, with loans out that year to forty churches, six agencies and nineteen pastors.[67]

Carey Hall

After several abortive dips into the sometimes chilling waters of ministerial training, the Baptist Union took a significant plunge in 1980 with the signing of an agreement with Regent College, Vancouver, to conduct "joint theological education."[68] The story had begun fifty-five years earlier when the then new University of British Columbia dedicated property for the use of all the major denominations.

Over a somewhat tortuous path of negotiation between the Baptist Union and the British Columbia Convention, the Convention had in 1958 secured a charter from the B.C. legislature for a full-scale theological school. It was named Carey Hall after the celebrated British Baptist missionary, William Carey. With a major grant from the Union given on the understanding that educational policy should remain a Union prerogative, Carey Hall was opened in 1960, not as a theological school but as a residence on the university campus.

For two decades the Hall offered home-away-from-home facilities to a generation of selected UBC students, about half of them Baptist, plus the ministrations of a residential dean, who doubled as Baptist chaplain to the university. But as G. Keith Churchill has written, "The clear intention was, as well, that in co-operation with the Baptist Union, Carey Hall would one day become a theological college."[69]

Meanwhile, in 1969, the Baptist Union followed up on another recommendation of the Janssen Commission and designated a list of seminaries (including Acadia and McMaster) at which attending Baptist Union students would receive bursaries.[70] A further option was offered the next year through the College of the North American Baptist General Conference in Edmonton.

In 1972 the Union inaugurated an in-service training program through a new Division of Christian Studies, with Dr. Samuel J. Mikolaski, Principal of BLTS, as academic dean and Dr. C. Howard Bentall of the denominational staff as administrative dean. Courses were offered in a variety of subjects by correspondence or group study. By 1975 over 800 had enrolled.[71]

That year, in a further development, a "flexible program of internship [for pastors] and adult education" was instituted, and Dr. J. Ernest Runions became full-time academic dean of the program which was offered at Carey Hall. Internships were arranged and courses in counselling and other aspects of ministry were offered[72] both for students and as "refreshers" for active pastors.

Carey/Regent

Moving toward the provision of full theological education, the Union first tried to plan a common undertaking with the North American Baptist General Conference on their Edmonton campus. When this proved to be unacceptable, the 1979 Assembly authorized the exploring of "a well-defined linkage between Carey Hall and Regent College,"[73] a widely recognized "transdenominational" (Regent's own term), evangelical college adjacent to UBC.

An agreement to provide joint theological education, with Carey Hall supplying nearly half of the required courses for a Master of Divinity degree, was signed at the Assembly the following year.[74] Dr. Roy D. Bell was named the first principal and the Reverend Philip Collins associate professor and director of field education. Later Dr. Samuel Mikolaski completed the initial three-member faculty. Dr. Collins became principal in 1985.

In the academic year 1986–87, Carey Hall enrolled fifteen Baptist Union students in the M. Div. program, with another thirty in the preliminary Diploma program. Thirteen more were in other degree programs and twenty-seven were seeking the Certificate of Ministry. Twenty-three others were undertaking a variety of courses and writing theses — a total of 108 students from Baptist Union churches.[75]

The Carey/Regent partnership, with Regent currently granting the degrees and Carey Hall holding its right in abeyance, has been fully accredited by the Association of Theological Schools. A constant supply of well-trained pastors and other church leaders for western Canada has thus been assured.

Recommendations Accepted

Receiving a mandate to establish clear objectives for future work,[76] the Union board set up a Goal-Setting Task Force in 1986 which reported to the Assembly the following year. It has isolated seven areas of special concern:

- the planting and sustaining of new churches in a multi-cultural society
- evangelism and discipleship
- the Christian education of all believers
- the equipping and use of lay ministries
- the family
- youth
- pastors . . . including continuing education and pastoral needs.

Recommendations of the task force were readily accepted and questionnaires were prepared for local church response. On the 1988 Assembly program three hours were allotted for consideration of the quantitative goals,[77] an indication of the importance the Baptist Union of Western Canada has placed on future plans for demanding days.

Toward the Twenty-First Century

Unity the Goal

Many opportunities exist for still greater co-operation among the four Convention/Unions. The problems of time and distance which plagued the founders have been eased, and instant communication is now possible. Many voices suggest that a national paper, published by the Canadian Baptist Federation, would be invaluable. With regional inserts, it would provide knowledge of the whole and be a strong unifying instrument. Recommended on numerous occasions, such a magazine has been supported in principle at various times by all regions, but has not yet been implemented.

The Federation itself should continue to draw the sundry denominational interests together. With a constitution wide open to the entry of other Baptist groups, it also offers an umbrella for those who felt obliged to part in the twenties. Unity is surely the goal as the differences of the years fade. Common interest is vital in a fractured world.

Canadian Baptists in general have remained uneasy about ecumenism in the second half of the century. Initially the Conventions/Unions were members of the Canadian Council of Churches through the Federation, and at one time the Ontario and Quebec Convention also favoured membership in the World Council. Lacking the support of the others, however, such an alignment never occurred.

The Baptist Convention of Ontario and Quebec alone retained membership in the Canadian Council of Churches when the Canadian Baptist Federation withdrew. The Baptist Union of Western Canada affiliated with the Evangelical Fellowship of Canada in 1986.

As the end of the twentieth century approaches, Canadian Baptists within the Federation remain more loosely structured than many other denominations. A tradition of upholding individual liberty of conscience and the autonomy of the local church has limited the growth of organizational superstructure. However, unity has been achieved to a great degree and common goals achieved through the Conventions, the Unions, the Federation and the Overseas Mission Board.

It would be heartening to be able to conclude that growth has been steady and outreach unremitting. This is not the case, however. It has often been necessary to run in order to stand still. Numerically there has been little advance. Atlantic Baptists recorded 64,180 on their rolls in 1907, the year after their union; 64,043 in 1985.[78] In 1930, following the modernist/fundamentalist schism, Ontario and Quebec Baptists numbered 56,368; in 1983, 44,068.[79] The new Baptist Union of Western Canada in 1907 listed just over 10,000 members; in 1986 there were 21,297.[80]

While it may be protested with some justification that large-scale roll-trimming in latter days has undoubtedly reduced the total, it remains painfully obvious that Canadian Baptists have lagged far behind in percentage as the nation's population multiplied. It is of small comfort to discover that this is also true of the Christian churches in Canada generally except for the Roman Catholic, which benefited earlier from a higher birth rate, as well as from greater immigration.

A Typical Sunday

Reginald W. Bibby, University of Lethbridge sociologist and erstwhile "budding Baptist minister" (his own phrase), upset many a cart of rosy apples in every denomination in the land with the 1987 publication of his well-documented book *Fragmented Gods: The Poverty and Potential of Religion in Canada*.[81] There a listing of census figures indicates all too clearly that the proportion of members in all mainline Protestant churches to total population had plummeted in the century between 1881 and 1981 — the Baptists, including all branches, plunging from 7 percent to 3 percent. If Mennonites are included, as they were in the 1881 census, the 1981 figure would still be only 3.8 percent.[82]

What is even more serious, Dr. Bibby pointed out, using poll data, that whereas two out of three Canadians would have been found in church on a typical Sunday in 1946, forty years later that ratio had dropped to one out of three.[83] While this does not necessarily mean that fewer people were attending church — actual numbers may have on occasion risen a little with the church-building boom of the fifties and sixties — the proportion plunged as the population burgeoned.

One aspect of the losses may be found of course among the "social" membership — those who in earlier years attended services because it provided status and everyone who "counted" was doing it. Those days and most of those people have gone. Yet this failure to reach significantly into the rapidly expanding community poses a special challenge for Canadian Baptists.

Heavy with Destiny

There is also, as Dr. Bibby points out, an even more fateful peril, and it arises from within. "Religion, Canadian-style, is mirroring culture," he writes, adding that "consumer-minded individuals are provided with a smorgasbord of fragment choices."[84] Are Baptists also about to succumb to "the cancer of consumerism," to use Queen's historian George Rawlyk's phrase.[85] Perhaps there is a pointed reminder for all in the expression of British Baptist Henry Cook: "The days are heavy with destiny and God has seen fit to match us against them."[86]

In order to meet the challenge, Baptists will not have to return to the forefathers' Biblical principles — they have not been greatly forsaken — but they will have to reaffirm them. These are precepts such as the inspiration and authority of scripture, the Lordship of Christ, the priesthood of believers, the believers' church, with its twin ordinances of believer's baptism and the Lord's supper, and religious freedom with its corollaries, the separation of church and state and democratic church government. And a life that expresses them.

These have stood the test of time. Borne out in a "non-consuming" lifestyle, they do "tell the world something that the world is not already telling itself."[87]

Heritage and Horizon

It is well into the third century since Ebenezer Moulton first stood on the Bay of Fundy shore watching the ebb and flow of its swelling tides. He could hardly have anticipated as he looked to the western horizon that the movement of the Spirit he represented would one day spread across the whole northern half of the continent — at that time no semblance of a nation even existed. Yet it was men and women like Moulton and John Hebbard, Alexander McDonald and Henrietta Feller, Hannah Maria Norris and Watson Kirkconnell who dreamed the dreams and viewed the visions that brought it about.

Heritage and Horizon — one is past, the other future. Canadian Baptists are between the two, sensing that the tomorrows will not be as numerous as the yesterdays. They are reminded of a familiar call: "Occupy till I come."[88]

Henry Alexander Renfree — Harry to all — is a native of Victoria, British Columbia, where he had early education up to first-year university. Following eight years in business and four with the YMCA War Services in World War II, he entered ministerial training at Acadia University. He holds a B.A., M.Div. and D.D. (honoris causa) from Acadia and the D.Min. from Southern Baptist Theological Seminary, Louisville, Kentucky. After serving in pastorates in Nova Scotia and New Brunswick, he entered nearly a quarter-century of denominational service, first as director of stewardship for the United Baptist Convention of the Maritime (now Atlantic) Provinces. In 1958, Renfree became general secretary of that Convention, serving for nine years. He returned to the West in 1967 to become the first executive minister of the Baptist Union of Western Canada under its renewed structure, an office held for fourteen years. Harry Renfree left office in 1981, returning to Victoria where he and his wife of forty-six years have subsequently been living in active retirement. Much of his time to date has been occupied with the research and writing of this historical volume.

SELECTED BIBLIOGRAPHY

Aldwinckle, R. F. *A Baptist Response to the Principles of Union*. Brantford, 1970.

Alline, Henry. *The Life and Journal of the Rev. Mr. Henry Alline*. Boston, 1806.

Anderson, Elmer G. "The Work of American Baptist Missionaries in Upper Canada to 1820." Unpublished B.D. thesis, McMaster University, 1952.

Backus, Isaac. *A History of New England with Particular Reference to the Denomination of Christians Called Baptists*, 2nd ed. with notes by David Weston, vol. II. Newton, 1871.

Baker, Robert A. *A Baptist Source Book*. Nashville, 1966.

Baptist Advance. Nashville, 1964.

Bell, Inez J., ed. *The Kantuta Blooms in Bolivia*. Toronto, 1971.

Benedict, David. *A General History of the Baptist Denomination in America and Other Parts of the World*. Boston, 1813.

Bentall, Shirley F. *Buckboard to Brotherhood: The Baptist Churches in Calgary*. Calgary, 1975.

Bibby, Reginald W. *Fragmented Gods*. Toronto, 1987.

Bill, I. E. *Fifty Years with the Baptist Ministers and Churches of the Maritime Provinces of Canada*. Saint John, 1880.

Boillat, Maurice C. *The Case for French Evangelism*. Halifax, 1960.

Campbell, George W. "Canada Baptist College, 1838-1849." Unpublished B.D. thesis, Knox College, 1974.

Canadian Baptist Home Missions Digest (Toronto, annually, 1953 to 1966–67).

Carder, W. Gordon. *Hand to the Indian Plow*. Secunderabad, India, 1976.

Churchill, G. Keith. "The Educational Policy of the Baptist Union of Western Canada." Unpublished D.Min. thesis, San Francisco Theological Seminary, 1980.

Clark, Jeremiah S. *Rand and the Micmacs*. Charlottetown, 1899.

Coleman, R. V. *The First Frontier*. New York and London, 1948.

Cox, F. A., and J. Hoby. *The Baptists of America*. New York, 1836.

Crandall, Joseph. *New Brunswick Baptist History*. Acadia University Archives.

Creighton, Donald. *The Story of Canada*. Toronto, 1971.

Culliford, Stanley H. "The History of the Freewill Baptists in Canada." Unpublished B.D. thesis, McMaster University, 1952.

Cuthbertson, Brian C., ed. *The Journal of John Payzant*. Hantsport, 1981.

Dabbs, Norman H. *Dawn over the Bolivian Hills*. Toronto, 1952.

Dakar, Paul R., and Murray J. S. Ford, eds. *Celebrating the Canadian Baptist Heritage*. McMaster Divinity College, 1984.

Daniel, Orville E. *Moving with the Times*. Toronto, 1973.

Dozois, John D. E. "Dr. Thomas Todhunter Shields — In the Stream of Fundamentalism." Unpublished B.D. thesis, McMaster University, 1963.

Eaton, Arthur Wentworth Hamilton. *History of Kings County, Nova Scotia*. Salem, 1910.

Ellis, Walter E. "Modernist Schism in North America, 1895–1934." Unpublished Ph.D. thesis, University of Pittsburgh, 1974.

————————. "Organizational and Educational Policy of Baptists in Western Canada, 1873–1939." Unpublished B.D. thesis, McMaster University, 1962.

Fitch, E. R., ed. *The Baptists of Canada*. Toronto, 1911.

Ford, Murray J. S. ed. *Canadian Baptist History and Polity*, McMaster Divinity College, 1982.

Foster, Charles Melvin. "Protestant Evangelism in French Canada." Unpublished B.D. thesis, McMaster University, 1950.

Gibson, M. Allen. *Along the King's Highway*. Lunenburg, 1964.

Gibson, Theo. T., *Beyond the Granite Curtain*. Ancaster, 1975.

Grant, John Webster. *The Church in the Canadian Era*, vol. 3. Toronto, 1972.

Handy, Robert T. *A History of the Churches in the United States and Canada*. Toronto, 1979.

Hall, Alfreda. *Wheels Begin to Turn*. Toronto, 1976.

Harris, J. E. *The Baptist Union of Western*

Canada: A Centennial History, 1873–1973. Saint John, 1976.

Hill, Mary Bulmer Reid. "From Sect to Denomination in the Baptist Church in Canada." Unpublished Ph.D. thesis, State University of New York, 1971.

Hillyer, H. S. *Bolivian Mission Jubilee.* Toronto, 1948.

Ingraham, Mary Kinley. *Historial Sketch of the United Baptist Woman's Missionary Union in the Maritime Provinces.* Kentville, 1945.

Ivison, Stuart, and Fred Rosser. *The Baptists in Upper and Lower Canada before 1820.* Toronto, 1956.

Johnston, Charles M. *McMaster University,* vol. 1. Toronto, 1976.

Kuhn, William, et al., eds. *These Glorious Years.* Cleveland, 1943.

Levy, George E. *The Baptists of the Maritime Provinces.* Saint John, 1946.

——————, ed. *The Diary of Joseph Dimock.* Hantsport, 1979.

Lewis, James K. "Religious Life of the Fugitive Slaves and Rise of the Coloured Baptist Churches, 1820–1865, in What Is Now Known as Ontario." Unpublished B.D. thesis, McMaster University, 1965.

Longley, Ronald Stewart. *Acadia University, 1838–1938.* Wolfville, 1939.

Lower, Arthur R. M. *Colony to Nation.* Toronto, 1977.

MacIntosh, J. U. "Some of the Labours and Disputes of the Open and Close Communion Baptists in Ontario and Quebec." Unpublished B.D. thesis, McMaster University, 1936.

McDonald, Mrs. J. R. *Baptist Missions in Western Canada, 1873–1948.* Edmonton, 1948.

McLaurin, C. C. *Pioneering in Western Canada.* Calgary, 1939.

Mann, W. E. *Sect, Cult and Church in Alberta.* Toronto, 1955.

Merrick, E. C. *These Impossible Women.* Fredericton, 1970.

Moir, John S. *The Church in the British Era.* Vol. 2 of *A History of the Christian Church in Canada,* ed. John Webster Grant. Toronto, 1972.

——————, ed. *The Cross in Canada.* (Toronto, 1966)

Moody, Barry M., ed. *Repent and Believe: The Baptist Experience in Maritime Canada.* Wolfville, 1980.

Norton, Jacqueline M., ed. *From Sea to Sea.* Toronto, 1940.

Orchard, M. L. *Canadian Baptists at Work in India.* Toronto, 1922.

Palmer, Gertrude A. *The Combatant: Biography of John J. Sidey.* Middleton, 1976.

Pitman, W. G. "The Baptists and Public Affairs in the Province of Canada, 1840–1867." Unpublished M.A. thesis, University of Toronto, 1956.

Pousett, Gordon H. "A History of the Convention of Baptist Churches of British Columbia." Unpublished M.Th. thesis, Vancouver School of Theology, 1982.

Rawlyk, George A., ed. *New Light Letters and Songs.* Hantsport, 1983.

Rice, B. F. "Sketches of Life in Canada West, 1800–1860." Unpublished B.D. thesis, McMaster University, 1942.

Richards, John B. *Baptists in British Columbia: A Struggle to Maintain "Sectarianism."* Vancouver, 1977.

Saunders, Edward Manning. *History of the Baptists of the Maritime Provinces.* Halifax, 1902.

Shields, T. T. *The Plot That Failed.* Toronto, 1937.

Schutt, C. H. and C. J. Cameron. *The Call of Our Own Land.* Toronto, nd.

Sturhahn, William J. H. *They Came from East and West.* Winnipeg, 1976.

Tarr, Leslie K. *This Dominion His Dominion.* Willowdale, 1968.

Therrien, Eugene A., et al. *Baptist Work in French Canada.* Toronto, nd.

Thompson, Margaret E. *The Baptist Story in Western Canada.* Calgary, 1975.

Torbet, Robert G. *A History of the Baptists.* Valley Forge, 1963.

Trinier, Harold U. *A Century of Service.* Toronto, 1954.

Underwood, A. C. *A History of the English Baptists.* London, 1947.

Watt, J. H. *The Fellowship Story: Our First Twenty-Five Years.* Toronto, 1978.

Wilson, Douglas J. *The Church Grows in Canada.* Toronto, 1966.

Zeman, Jarold K. *Baptist Roots and Identity.* Toronto, 1978.

——————, ed. *Baptists in Canada.* Burlington, 1980.

REFERENCES

Chapter 1 Roots

1. As used in this volume, the term Free Church refers to church bodies that are not linked to the state through "establishment" or similar concordat and, generally speaking, have fluid, rather than formal, patterns of worship. The term Believers' Church goes further, to describe denominations whose churches are composed essentially of baptized believers, "gathered" from society, rather than having a "mixed" membership of believers and potential believers or of people from within certain territorial boundaries.

2. A succint sketch of the Anabaptist movement may be found in Kenneth Scott Latourette, *A History of Christianity* (New York, 1953), 778–86. Another excellent study appears in the monograph by Ernest A. Payne, *The Baptist Movement in the Reformation and Onwards* (London: Kingsgate Press, 1947).

3. Watson Kirkconnell, *The Baptists of Canada: A "Pocket-Book" History* (Toronto, 1958) 4.

4. A. C. Underwood, *A History of the English Baptists* (London, 1947), 33.

5. W. T. Whitley, *A History of the British Baptists* (London, 1923), 21.

6. Underwood, *English Baptists*, 47.

7. Ibid., 47, 48.

8. Kenneth Scott Latourette, *A History of the Expansion of Christianity*, vol. 3 (Grand Rapids, 1970), 383.

9. T. B. Howell, *State Trials and Proceedings*, vol. II (London, 1816), 85, 86. Cited in R. V. Coleman, *The First Frontier* (New York and London, 1948), 127.

10. Underwood, *English Baptists*, 35n.

11. Robert T. Handy, *A History of the Churches in the United States and Canada* (Oxford and Toronto, 1979), 18.

12. Alexander Young, ed., *Chronicles of Massachusetts*, 351–52. Cited in Coleman, *Frontier*, 197.

13. Massachusetts Colony Records, vol. 1, 87, 366. Cited in Coleman, *Frontier*, 202.

14. Ibid., 75. Cited in Coleman, *Frontier*, 198.

15. Coleman, *Frontier*, 203.

16. Thomas Armitage, *A History of the Baptists* (New York, 1887), 624.

17. Latourette, *A History of Christianity*, 953.

18. Henry S. Burrage, *A History of the Baptists in New England* (Philadelphia, 1894), 104–5, 108.

19. David Benedict, *A General History of the Baptist Denomination in America and Other Parts of the World* (Boston, 1813), 375. Here Benedict quotes from "a manuscript Governor Joseph Jenks wrote near one hundred years ago."

20. William Warren Sweet, *Religion in Colonial America* (New York, 1942), 133.

21. Ibid.

22. Latourette, *Expansion of Christianity*, vol. 3, 214, 216.

23. Cited in J. M. Cramp, *Baptist History* (London, 1868), 511.

24. Handy, *History of the Churches*, 93.

25. Henry C. Vedder, *A Short History of the Baptists* (Philadelphia, 1954), 309.

26. Robert G. Torbet, *A History of the Baptists* (Valley Forge, 1963), 223–24.

27. Armitage, *History*, 644–45.

28. Torbet, *History*, 234–35, 243.

Chapter 2 An Inviting Climate

1. C. C. Goen, *Revivalism and Separatism in New England*, 1740–1800 (New Haven and London, 1962), 237.

2. Gustave Lanctot, *A History of Canada* (Toronto and Vancouver, 1965), 44.

3. John S. Moir and Robert E. Saunders, *Northern Destiny* (Toronto, 1970), 109.

4. Arthur R. M. Lower, *Colony to Nation* (Toronto, 1977), 106.

5. Ibid., 107.

6. Quoted in George E. Levy, *The Baptists of the Maritime Provinces, 1753-1946* (Saint John, 1946), 19.

7. Maurice W. Armstrong, *The Great Awakening in Nova Scotia* (Hartford, 1948), 20, 21.

8. Lower, *Colony*, 106, 107.

9. Isaac Backus, *A History of New England with Particular Reference to the Denomination of Christians Called Baptists*, 2nd ed. with notes by David Weston, vol. II (Newton, 1871), 31.

10. George E. Levy, *The Baptists of the Maritime Provinces, 1753-1946* (Saint John, 1946), 10, 11.

11. Goen, *Revivalism*, 103.

12. Levy, *Maritime*, 11.

13. Backus, *New England*, vol. II, 468.

14. Edward Manning Saunders, *History of the Baptists of the Maritime Provinces* (Halifax, 1902), iii.

15. Will R. Bird, *Historic Nova Scotia* (Halifax, nd), 47.

16. The letter, signed by Peter Bishop, John Turner and Daniel Harris, is extant, located in the manuscript collection of the Western Reserve Historical Society,

Cleveland, Ohio. In J. M. Bumstead, "Origins of the Maritime Baptists," *Dalhousie Review* (1969): 88–93.

17. Minute Book of Second Baptist Church of Swansea, Mass., 1680–1819, a handwritten transcript (Providence), 5, 6. In Robert G. Gardner, "Early Baptists in Sackville, New Brunswick," unpublished monograph, Acadia University Archives, 1980, 5.

18. Gardner, Ibid., 6, 7.

19. John Asplund, *The Annual Register of the Baptist Denomination in North America to the First of November,* 1790 (Southampton County, Virginia, 1791), 111.

20. W. G. McLoughlin, ed., *The Diary of Isaac Backus,* vol. II, 662. In Gardner, monograph.

21. E. Frame, *Harvard Graduates in Nova Scotia,* unpublished ms, 36. In Armstrong, *Awakening,* 38.

22. Letter signed by Peter Bishop, John Turner and Daniel Harris, in manuscript collection of the Western Reserve Historical Society, Cleveland, Ohio. In J. M. Bumstead, "Origins of the Maritime Baptists," *Dalhousie Review* (1969): 88–93.

23. Gardner, monograph, 12.

24. Joseph Crandall, *New Brunswick Baptist History,* handwritten ms, Acadia University Archives, 10.

25. Watson Kirkconnell, *Bicentennial Essays: The Wolfville United Baptist Church* (Hantsport, 1978), 10.

26. Ibid., 8.

27. Letter in Backus, *New England,* vol. II, 468.

28. R. A. Guild, *Early History of Brown University* (Providence, 1897), 10, 42, 214. In Armstrong, *Awakening,* 38, 39. Armstrong holds that the presence of Manning with John Sutton is the basis of the tradition that James Sutton also visited Nova Scotia, but Payzant's statement would seem to be conclusive that both were present.

29. George E. Levy, ed., *The Diary of Joseph Dimock* (Hantsport, 1979), 8, 9.

30. John Payzant, *An Account of the Commencement of Religion in Nova Scotia, 1760-1763.* In *The Journal of John Payzant,* ed. Brian C. Cuthbertson (Hantsport, 1981), 21.

Chapter 3   The Nova Scotia Awakening and the Awakener

1. John Asplund, *The Annual Register of the Baptist Denomination in North America to the First of November, 1790* (Southampton County, Virginia, 1791), 5.

2. I. E. Bill, *Fifty Years with the Baptist Ministers and Churches of the Maritime Provinces of Canada* (Saint John, 1880), 13.

3. Henry Alline, *The Life and Journal of the Rev. Mr. Henry Alline* (Boston, 1806), 67.

4. Brian C. Cuthbertson, ed., *The Journal of John Payzant* (Hantsport, 1981), 22.

5. Alline, *Journal,* 48.

6. Ibid., 3.

7. Ibid., 6.

8. Ibid., 35.

9. W. B. Bezanson, *The Romance of Religion: A Sketch of the Life of Henry Alline* (Kentville, 1927), 16.

10. Alline, *Journal,* 42.

11. Ibid., 46.

12. Ibid., 179.

13. Robert E. Osborne, "Henry Alline, the Apostle of Nova Scotia," unpublished monograph, McGill University, 1952, 16.

14. Osborne, "Alline," 13, 14.

15. Bezanson, *Romance,* 63.

16. Edward M. Saunders, *History of the Baptists of the Maritime Provinces* (Halifax, 1902), 39, 40.

17. Ibid., 47, 48.

18. Osborne, "Alline," 11, 12.

19. Saunders, *Maritime Provinces,* 14.

20. Alline, *Journal,* 158. In George E. Levy, *The Baptists of the Maritime Provinces, 1753-1946,* (Saint John, 1946), 38.

21. Osborne, "Alline," 14. Quoting John Wesley Letters, VII, 182.

22. Cuthbertson, *Payzant,* 30.

23. Ibid., 24.

24. Robert T. Handy, *A History of the Churches in the United States and Canada* (London and New York, 1979), 137. Quoting Charles H. Metzger, *Catholics and the American Revolution* (Chicago, 1962), 43ff.

25. Wilfred Brenton Kerr, *The Maritime Provinces of British North America and the American Revolution* (New York, 1970), 53, 55, 57.

26. J. Bartlet Brebner, *Canada: A Modern History.* New edition revised and enlarged by Donald C. Masters (Ann Arbor, 1970), 99.

27. George A. Rawlyk, ed., *New Light Letters and Songs* (Hantsport, 1983), 27.

28. Thomas H. Raddall, *The Path of Destiny: Canada from the British Conquest to Home Rule, 1763-1850* (Toronto, 1957), 87.

29. Arnold J. Toynbee, *A Study of History.* Abridgement of volumes I–VI by D. C. Somervell (New York and London, 1947), 286–87.

30. Will R. Bird, *Historic Nova Scotia* (Halifax, nd), 59, 60.
31. George E. Levy, *The Baptists of the Maritime Provinces, 1753-1946* (Saint John, 1946), 19.

Chapter 4 The Days of the Fathers
1. Edward M. Saunders, *History of the Baptists of the Maritime Provinces* (Halifax, 1902), 130.
2. Ibid., 70
3. I. E. Bill, *Fifty Years with the Baptist Ministers and Churches of the Maritime Provinces* (Saint John, 1880), 142.
4. John M. Cramp, *The Baptists in Nova Scotia*. Gathered proofs of pages for *The Christian Messenger*, edited in Cramp's handwriting, 61-62.
5. Bill, *Fifty Years*, 151-52.
6. Ibid., 176.
7. Ibid, 20. Much of the material regarding David George, including quotations, is drawn from his own writings — a report which he gave in person on a visit from Sierra Leone to London and to Dr. Rippon's church there. Contained in *Rippon's Register*, vol. 1, 473-83.
8. Ibid., 22.
9. Ibid.
10. Ibid., 24.
11. Henry Alline, *The Life and Journal of the Rev. Mr. Henry Alline* (Boston, 1806), 153.
12. Bill, *Fifty Years*, 163.
13. Brian C. Cuthbertson, ed., *The Journal of John Payzant* (Hantsport, 1981), 43.
14. Cramp, *Nova Scotia*, 52, 53.
15. Ibid., 55.
16. Ibid., 58.
17. Ibid., 59.
18. Cuthbertson, *Payzant*, 81.
19. Bill, *Fifty Years*, 129.
20. John Davis, compiler, *Life and Times of the Late Rev. Harris Harding* (Charlottetown, 1886), 4.
21. Ibid., 5.
22. Ibid., 15.
23. Maurice W. Armstrong, *The Great Awakening in Nova Scotia* (Hartford, 1948), 55.
24. George E. Levy, *The Diary of Joseph Dimock* (Hantsport, 1979), 100.
25. Cuthbertson, *Payzant*, 59.
26. Levy, *Dimock Diary*, 13.
27. George E. Levy, *The Baptists of the Maritime Provinces 1753-1946* (Saint John, 1946), 19.
28. Rev. Joseph Crandall, "New Brunswick Baptist History" (nd), 1, 2.
29. Ibid., 3-6.
30. Ibid., 10.

31. Ibid., 12.
32. Saunders, *Maritime Provinces*, 75.
33. Bill, *Fifty Years*, 220.
34. Levy, *Maritime*, 48.
35. Bill, *Fifty Years*, 220.

Chapter 5 Origins in the Canadas
1. Anne Merriman Peck, *The Pageant of Canadian History*, 2nd ed. (David McKay Co., 1963), 155.
2. Donald Creighton, *The Story of Canada* (London, 1971), 83.
3. John S. Moir and Robert E. Saunders, *Northern Destiny: A History of Canada* (Toronto, 1970), 129.
4. W. L. Morton, *The Kingdom of Canada* (Toronto, 1963), 163.
5. John S. Moir, ed., *The Cross in Canada* (Toronto, 1966), 68. Citing H. Têtre and C. O. Gagnon, *Mandements, etc.*, vol. II (Quebec, 1877) 264-65.
6. Arthur R. M. Lower, *Colony to Nation: A History of Canada* (Toronto, 1947), 78.
7. Ibid., 117-18.
8. Morton, *Kingdom*, 183.
9. William Thomas Manning and William W. Manross in *Encyclopaedia Britannica*, vol. 18 (London and Chicago, 1961), 612.
10. Robert T. Handy, *A History of the Churches in the United States and Canada* (Oxford, 1979), 133.
11. Moir and Saunders, *Destiny*, 169.
12. Douglas J. Wilson, *The Church Grows in Canada* (Toronto, 1966), 53.
13. Lower, *Colony*, 117.
14. *The Globe*, Toronto, July 1, 1867.
15. Stuart Ivison and Fred Rosser, *The Baptists in Upper and Lower Canada before 1820* (Toronto, 1956), 156. The writer is greatly indebted to the Reverend Stuart Ivison and Dr. Fred Rosser for a good deal of the information drawn for the latter half of this chapter. Their exhaustive work is definitive for the period.
16. David Benedict, *A General History of the Baptist Denomination in America* (New York, 1848), 899.
17. E. A. Owen, *Pioneer Sketches of Long Point Settlement* (Toronto, 1898), 63.
18. Benedict, *General*, 899.
19. Elmer G. Anderson, "The Work of American Baptist Missionaries in Upper Canada to 1820," unpublished B.D. thesis, McMaster University, 1952, 41. Citing *Massachusetts Baptist Missionary Magazine* I (1803): 64-68.
20. *Baptist Year Book*, Historical Number, 1900. Writes historian A. H. Newman: "That there was a Baptist church in the neighbourhood in 1796, with Arthur Gray

as the leading member and William Holmes as pastor, seems well attested." (Toronto, 1900), 73.

21. Ibid., 42. Citing Lemuel Covell, *A Narrative of a Missionary Tour, etc., in the Fall of 1803*. Reprinted in Mrs. D. C. Brown, *Memoir of Lemuel Covell* (Boston, 1835).

22. Anderson, thesis, 41. Citing *Massachusetts Baptist Missionary Magazine* II (1808): 150–54.

23. E. R. Fitch, ed., *The Baptists of Canada* (Toronto, 1911), 103.

24. Anderson, thesis, 13. Citing *Massachusetts Baptist Missionary Magazine* I (1803): 64–68.

25. Ibid., 52. Citing *Western New York Baptist Missionary Magazine* II (1818): 243.

26. Ivison and Rosser, *Before 1820*, 85.

Chapter 6 A Developing Awareness

1. Harry A. Renfree, *What Baptists Believe* (Calgary, 1975), 1.

2. David Benedict, *A General History of the Baptist Denomination in America and Other Parts of the World* (Boston, 1813), 354–55. "The Learned Hooker," to whom Sanderson refers, was the Reverend Thomas Hooker, described as "the most eloquent of the Bay (Mass.) clergy" by William Warren Sweet, *Religion in Colonial America* (New York, 1942), 89.

3. Winthrop H. Hudson, *Baptists: The Pilgrim Fathers and the American Revolution*, in *Baptists and the American Experience*, ed. James E. Wood (Valley Forge, 1981), 25.

4. Edward M. Saunders, *History of the Baptists of the Maritime Provinces* (Halifax, 1902), 77.

5. Arthur Wentworth Hamilton Eaton, *History of Kings County, Nova Scotia* (Salem, 1910), 314.

6. Saunders, *Maritime Provinces*, 84–85.

7. Ibid., 85.

8. Ibid., 86.

9. *Historical Sketch of the Nova Scotia Baptist Association in Jubilee Year, 1850* (report booklet of the Nova Scotia Baptist Association).

10. Ibid., 87.

11. Arthur R. M. Lower, *Canadians in the Making* (Toronto, 1895), 147.

12. From Rules of the Association, 1800. Cited in I. E. Bill, *Fifty Years with the Baptist Ministers and Churches of the Maritime Provinces* (Saint John, 1880), 38.

13. Stuart Ivison and Fred Rosser, *The Baptists in Upper and Lower Canada before 1820* (Toronto, 1956), 85.

14. Elmer G. Anderson, "The Work of American Baptist Missionaries in Upper Canada to 1820," unpublished B.D. thesis, McMaster University, 1952, 12–13. Quoting from *Massachusetts Baptist Missionary Magazine* I (1803): 64–68.

15. Ibid., 24–25, *Magazine*, 76–77.

16. Ibid., 61–62, *Magazine*, 71–72.

17. Ibid., 64–65.

18. Saunders, *Maritime Provinces*, 89.

19. Ibid. Citing Isaiah W. Wilson, *History of Digby County*.

20. Ivison and Rosser, *Before 1820*, 129.

Chapter 7 Frontiers of Faith and Order

1. Cited in Edward M. Saunders, *History of the Baptists of the Maritime Provinces* (Halifax, 1902), 122–23.

2. Saunders, *Maritime Provinces*, 70.

3. From handwritten minutes of the association, June 26–28, 1809, Acadia Archives.

4. Cited by I. E. Bill, *Fifty Years with the Baptist Ministers and Churches of the Maritime Provinces* (Saint John, 1880), 45.

5. G. A. Rawlyk, "From Newlight to Baptist: Harris Harding and the Second Great Awakening in Nova Scotia," in *Repent and Believe: The Baptist Experience in Maritime Canada*, ed. Barry M. Moody (Wolfville, 1980), 1–8.

6. Ibid.

7. Bill, *Fifty Years*, 49.

8. Association minutes, 1815.

9. Stuart Ivison and Fred Rosser, *The Baptists in Upper and Lower Canada before 1820* (Toronto, 1966), 98–117 and 88–93, where Ivison and Rosser sketch the early life of these churches.

10. Minutes of the Shaftsbury Baptist Association, 1804. Cited in Elmer G. Anderson, "The Work of American Baptist Missionaries in Upper Canada to 1820," unpublished B.D. thesis, McMaster University, 1952, 48.

11. Ivison and Rosser, *Before 1820*, 43.

12. Ibid., 40.

13. David Benedict, *A General History of the Baptist Denomination in America and Other Parts of the World* (Boston, 1813), 899.

14. Minutes of the Townsend Church, August 22, 1818. Cited in Ivison and Rosser, *Before 1820*, 105.

15. Minutes of the Home District Assizes, June 1813. Cited in Ivison and Rosser, *Before 1820*, 125.

16. Ivison and Rosser, *Before 1820*, 138–39.

17. Ibid., 114.
18. *Massachusetts Baptist Missionary Magazine* I (1803): 14. Cited in Anderson, "Work," 11.
19. Ibid., 64–68; cited Ibid., 13.
20. Ibid.; cited Ibid., 14.
21. Ibid.
22. Ivison and Rosser, *Before 1820*, 126.
23. Ibid.
24. *Massachusetts Baptist Missionary Magazine* II (1808): 150–54. Cited in Anderson, "Work," 41.
25. Ibid.

Chapter 8   Hiatus and Hope
1. Arthur R. M. Lower, *Canadians in the Making* (Toronto, 1958), 185.
2. Ibid., 175.
3. Minutes of the Nova Scotia and New Brunswick Association, Sheffield, New Brunswick, 1813.
4. Lower, *Canadians*, 185.
5. Ibid., 181.
6. Minutes of the Shaftsbury Baptist Association, 1813, 8. Cited in Elmer G. Anderson, "The Work of American Baptist Missionaries in Upper Canada to 1820," unpublished B.D. thesis, McMaster University, 1952, 45.
7. Romans 8:28 KJV.
8. A report to the president and directors of the Hamilton Baptist Missionary Society, *New York North-Western Christian Magazine* I (1816): 349–52. Cited in Anderson, "Work," 49–50.
9. *New York North-Western Christian Magazine* I (1816): 357, 401; cited Ibid., 53.
10. Stuart Ivison and Fred Rosser, *The Baptists in Upper and Lower Canada before 1820* (Toronto, 1966), 59.
11. Minutes of the Shaftsbury Baptist Association, 1816. Cited in Anderson, "Work," 47.
12. Ivison and Rosser, *Before 1820*, 58.
13. G. Gerald Harrop, "The Baptist Convention of Ontario and Quebec," in *Baptist Advance* (Nashville, 1964), 160.
14. Robert Wilson, "Alexander Crawford," unpublished ms (nd), 2.
15. Albert Henry Newman, "Sketch of the Baptists of Ontario and Quebec to 1851," *Baptist Year Book for Ontario, Quebec, Manitoba and the N.W. Territories and B.C., 1900*, 77.
16. Owen L. Burry, "The Canadian Canaan: A History of Black Baptists in Ontario," unpublished ms, senior seminar, McMaster Divinity College, 1981, 8.
17. Joseph D. Bann, "Canadian Baptists and Renewal," in *Canadian Baptist History and Polity*, ed. Murray J. S. Ford (McMaster Divinity College, 1982), 153.
18. Burry, "Canadian Canaan," 10.
19. John Stark, "Some Conditions of Baptist Progress in Home Missions," *Baptist Year Book for Ontario , etc., 1901*, 45.
20. Mary Bulmer Hill, "From Sect to Denomination in the Baptist Church in Canada," unpublished Ph.D. thesis, State University of New York, 1971, 156.
21. S. D. Clark, *The Canadian Community*, 375–89. Cited in David J. Green, "An Investigation of the Role of the Baptist Church as a Moral Court on the Niagara Frontier," unpublished ms, McMaster University, nd, 24.
22. Newman, "Sketch," BYB, 1900, 74.
23. Ibid.
24. Newman, "Sketch," BYB, 1900, 74.
25. E. R. Fitch, ed., *The Baptists of Canada* (Toronto, 1911), 111.
26. Cited in Anderson, "Work," 52.
27. *New York Gospel Witness*. Cited in Newman, "Sketch," BYB 1900, 78.

Chapter 9   Coming of Age
1. Minutes of the Nova Scotia and New Brunswick Baptist Association, Newport, 1818.
2. Ibid.
3. Ibid., Fredericton, 1817.
4. Ibid., Lower Granville, 1820.
5. Ibid., Onslow, 1821.
6. Ibid.
7. Henry Alline, *The Life and Journal of the Rev. Mr. Henry Alline* (Boston, 1806), 159.
8. George E. Levy, *The Baptists of the Maritime Provinces* (Saint John, 1946), 97.
9. Robert Wilson, "Alexander Crawford," unpublished ms, nd, 4.
10. Alexander McDonald in *The Christian Visitor*, January 12, 1848. Cited in I. E. Bill, *Fifty Years with the Baptist Ministers and Churches of the Maritime Provinces* (Saint John, 1880), 662.
11. Edward M. Saunders, *History of the Baptists of the Maritime Provinces* (Halifax, 1902), 504.
12. *The Baptist Missionary Magazine of Nova Scotia and New Brunswick* I (July 1827).
13. Bill, *Fifty Years*, 59, and Levy, *Maritime*, 109.
14. Minutes of the Nova Scotia Association, Amherst, 1825.
15. *Missionary Magazine* II (January 1828).
16. Minutes N.S. Assn., 1836.
17. Minutes N.B. Assn., 1837.
18. Ibid., 1827.
19. Ibid., 1831.

20. Ibid., 1827.
21. Ibid., 1831.
22. Minutes N.B. Assn., 1822. In Nova Scotia in 1830 the association recommended that when members "commit offenses of public notoriety, except the same be of such nature as to require immediate exclusion, that in order to effect their restoration to the Church, they be required to make public acknowledgment of such offense before the world," Minutes N.S. Assn., 1830.
23. Minutes N.B. Assn., 1834.
24. Minutes N.S. Assn., 1829.
25. John S. Moir, *The Church in the British Era*. Volume 2 of *A History of the Christian Church in Canada*, ed. John Webster Grant (Toronto, 1972), 150.
26. Saunders, *Maritime Provinces*, 227.
27. Minutes N.B. Assn., 1837.
28. Minutes N.S. Assn., 1838.
29. Ibid.
30. Minutes N.B. Assn., 1838.
31. Minutes N.S. Assn., 1839.
32. Ibid.
33. Ronald Stewart Longley, *Acadian University, 1838-1938* (Wolfville, 1939), 41–42.
34. Minutes N.S. Assn., 1844.
35. I. E. Bill, *Fifty Years*, 277.
36. Saunders, *Maritime Provinces*, 221–22.
37. Minutes N.S. Assn., 1834.
38. Minutes N.B. Assn., 1836.
39. Minutes N.S. Assn., 1837.
40. Ibid., 1840.
41. From a letter written by Edward Manning. Cited in Saunders, *Maritime Provinces*, 222.
42. Levy, *Maritime*, 141.
43. Minutes N.S. Assn., 1835.
44. Saunders, *Maritime Provinces*, 222.
45. Minutes N.S. Assn., 1830.
46. Ibid., 1832.
47. Ibid., 1836.
48. Ibid., 1842.
49. Minutes N.S. Assn. 1844.
50. Minutes N.B. Assn., 1844.
51. Minutes N.S. and N.B. Assns., 1845.
52. Cited in I. E. Bill, *Fifty Years*, 352.
53. Minutes N.B. Assn., 1847.
54. Minutes N.S. Assn., 1850.
55. Minutes N.B. Assn., 1840.
56. Minutes N.S. Assn., 1846.
57. E. R. Fitch, ed., *The Baptists of Canada* (Toronto, 1911), 116.
58. Minutes N.S. Assn., 1846.
59. Minutes N.S. Assn., 1846.
60. Minutes of the Convention of Nova Scotia, New Brunswick and Prince Edward Island, 1847.

Chapter 10   Growing Pains

1. Donald Creighton, *The Story of Canada* (London, 1971), 111.
2. Ibid., 117.
3. Ibid., 124.
4. F. A. Cox and J. Hoby, *The Baptists in America* (New York, 1836), Preface.
5. Ibid., 217.
6. Ibid., 207.
7. Ibid.
8. Ibid., 200.
9. Professors Newman and Campbell, eds., *Memorial of Daniel Arthur McGregor* (Alumni Association of Toronto Baptist College, 1891), 17, 18.
10. Minutes of the Johnstown Association, 1828. Cited in W. G. Pitman, "The Association," unpublished ms, nd, 5.
11. Ibid.
12. Cited in Pitman, "Association," 5.
13. Minutes of the Haldimand Baptist Association, 1844.
14. Minutes of the Ottawa Baptist Association, 1836.
15. Minutes of the Western Baptist Association, 1830.
16. Minutes of the Western Regular Baptist Association, Colchester, 1846.
17. Minutes of the Grand River Association of Regular Baptists, Scotland, 1850.
18. From Minute Book of Charlotteville Church, October 3, 1828. Cited in George Gilbert Stainger, "The Charlotteville-Vittoria Church, 1804–1954," unpublished B.D. thesis, McMaster University, 1954, 26.
19. Charlotteville Minutes, June 30, 1832. Ibid., 27.
20. Minutes Ottawa Assn., 1844.
21. Letter to the Eastern Association from Jacob Price, Church Clerk, Canadian Baptist Archives, McMaster Divinity College.
22. Minutes Haldimand Assn., 1845.
23. Minutes Ottawa Assn., 1846.
24. Minutes Haldimand Assn., 1847.
25. W. G. Pitman, "The Baptists and Public Affairs in the Province of Canada, 1840–1867," unpublished M.A. thesis, University of Toronto, 1956, 21.
26. Minutes of the Upper Canada Eastern Association, 1838. Cited in Pitman, "Public Affairs," 39, 40.
27. Minutes Ottawa Assn., 1837.
28. Extract of Minutes of the Ottawa Association, 1841, in *Canada Baptist Magazine and Missionary Register*, April 1, 1841.
29. G. Gerald Harrop, "The Baptist Convention of Ontario and Quebec," in *Baptist Advance* (Nashville, 1964), 161.

30. Minutes Western Assn., 1836.
31. Albert Henry Newman, "Sketch of the Baptists of Ontario and Quebec to 1851," *Baptist Year Book for Ontario, Quebec, Manitoba and the N.W. Territories and B.C., 1900*, 84.
32. E. R. Fitch, ed., *The Baptists of Canada* (Toronto, 1911), 113.
33. *Upper Canada Baptist Missionary Magazine*, vol. I, no. 6 (May 1837). Cited in Robert E. Freeland, "Pioneer Baptist Journalism in Ontario and Quebec," unpublished B.D. thesis, McMaster University, 1951, 52.
34. Minutes Ottawa Assn., 1836.
35. Canada Education and Home Missionary Society, *Second Report, 1831* (Montreal, 1831). Original document.
36. An interesting account of Bosworth's voyage to North America following his decision to leave England because of "increasing difficulty in providing for my family," is found in his original hand-written "Journal of a Voyage in the Ship 'Baltic Merchant' 1834." In Canadian Baptist Archives.
37. Newman, "Sketch," 81.
38. Ibid., 82.
39. *Canada Baptist Magazine and Missionary Register (Montreal Register)*, vol. II., no. 9 (February 1839). In Kenneth Jackson, *Excerpts from Montreal Register* (McMaster Divinity College).
40. Pitman, "Public Affairs," 108.
41. *Montreal Register*, September 7, 1842.
42. Newman, "Sketch," 84.
43. *Montreal Register*, September 1837. Cited in George W. Campbell, "Canada Baptist College, 1838–1849," unpublished Th.M. thesis, Knox College, 1974, 26.
44. *Montreal Register*, January 1840. Cited in Ibid., 39.
45. J. P. Pryse, "Pioneer Baptist Missionaries to Upper Canada Tuscarors," *Canadian Baptist Home Missions Digest*, vol. 6 (1963–64): 276–77. Dr. Pryse's work is a valuable source of information on early Canadian Indian missions.
46. Ibid., 273–82.
47. Ibid., 278.
48. Creighton, *Story*, 128.
49. *Montreal Register*, February 1840. Cited in Pitman, "Public Affairs," 119.

Chapter 11 Discord and Concord
1. G. Gerald Harrop, "The Baptist Convention of Ontario and Quebec," in *Baptist Advance* (Nashville, 1964), 169.
2. J. U. MacIntosh, "Some of the Labours and Disputes of the Open and Close Communion Baptists in Ontario and Quebec," unpublished B.D. thesis, McMaster University, 1936, 2.
3. David Benedict, *A General History of the Baptist Denomination in America and Other Parts of the World* (Boston, 1813), 521–22.
4. MacIntosh, "Labours," 1, 2.
5. A. H. Newman, "Sketch of the Baptists of Ontario and Quebec to 1851," *Baptist Year Book for Ontario, Quebec, Manitoba and the N. W. Territories and B.C., 1900*, 86.
6. Diary of Newton Bosworth 1843–1847. Handwritten original in Canadian Baptist Archives.
7. Minutes and Report of Second Annual Meeting of the Canada Baptist Union, June 1845, Beamsville (Montreal, 1845).
8. Ibid.
9. By what Arthur R. M. Lower terms "his counterfeit 'Ecclesiastical Charts' . . . Strachan had computed the number of Anglicans by the simple process of adding up known adherents of other denominations and subtracting the result from the total population of the province" (*Colony to Nation*, 239, 240). Thus Strachan had tried to give the impression that Anglicans were the largest church body. However, as a committee from the legislature reported, "the members of the Church of England in Canada were found to be but one-tenth of the entire population." The committee added that there were 117 Methodist clergymen, 45 Baptist and 31 Anglican. Of the 162 Methodist and Baptist, 133 had been "born and educated in Her Majesty's dominions", but the same could be said of only 11 of the 31 Anglican. J. E. Wells, *Life and Labours of Robert Alexander Fyfe, D.D.* (Toronto, c 1885), 123–24.
10. Arthur R. M. Lower, *Colony to Nation* (Toronto, 1977), 239.
11. Minutes of the Canada Baptist Union, 1844. Cited in W. G. Pitman, "The Baptists and Public Affairs in the Province of Canada, 1840-1867," unpublished M.A. thesis, University of Toronto, 1956, 18.
12. John S. Moir and Robert E. Saunders, *Northern Destiny* (Toronto, 1970), 221.
13. Lower, *Colony*, 191.
14. W. Stewart Wallace, ed., *The Encyclopedia of Canada*, vol. II (Toronto, 1935), 82.
15. Lower, *Colony*, 191.
16. W. L. Morton, *The Kingdom of Canada* (Toronto, 1969), 228.
17. Ibid., 258.

18. Donald Creighton, *The Story of Canada* (London, 1971), 120.
19. *Montreal Register*, January 16, 1845. Cited in Pitman, "Public Affairs," 65.
20. Minutes of the Canada Baptist Union, 1849. Cited in Pitman, "Public Affairs," 76–77.
21. D. Lawr and R. Gidney, *Educating Canadians* (Toronto, 1975), 95. Cited in Anne Carmelle LeGendre, "The Baptist Contribution to Nineteenth Century Education for Women," unpublished M.A. thesis, McMaster University, 1981, 25.
22. *Montreal Register*, May 11, 1842. Cited in Pitman, "Public Affairs," 108.
23. *Montreal Register*, September 21, 1842. Cited in Pitman, "Public Affairs," 111.
24. Minutes of the Canada Baptist Union, 1844.
25. Morton, *Kingdom*, 286.
26. Pitman, "Public Affairs," 147.
27. *Montreal Register*, January 19, 1843. Cited in A. J. McLachlan, "Canadian Baptists and Public Questions before 1850," unpublished B.D. thesis, McMaster University, 1937, 15, 16.
28. *Montreal Register*, August 1, 1844. Cited in McLachlan, "Questions," 21.
29. Motion of the Canada Baptist Union, 1847. Cited in Pitman, "Public Affairs," 173.
30. *Montreal Register*, April 9, 1846. Cited in McLachlan, "Questions," 23.
31. McLachlan, "Questions," 23–24.
32. Minutes of the Canada Baptist Union, 1848.
33. Pitman, "Public Affairs," 120.
34. *The Evangelical Pioneer*, June 3, 1842. Cited in George W. Campbell, "Canada Baptist College, 1838–1849," unpublished Th.M. thesis, Knox College, 1974, 84.
35. *Montreal Register*, March 9, 1843. Cited in Pitman, "Public Affairs," 23.

Chapter 12 A Yearning for Learning
1. Ronald S. Longley, *Acadia University 1838–1938* (Wolfville, 1939), 15.
2. H. T. DeWolfe, "Acadia History, Traditions, Ideals," *The Maritime Baptist*, September 14, 1932.
3. E. A. Crawley, "The Rise and Progress of Higher Education in Connection with the Baptist Denomination in the Maritime Provinces," in *Memorials of Acadia College and Horton Academy* (Montreal, 1881), 29. In this regard, Crawley refers specifically to Edward Manning, Theodore Harding, T. H. Chipman "and others."

4. Longley, *Acadia*, 15.
5. Letter of March 13, 1828, from Caswell to Manning. Cited in Ibid.
6. Letter of March 18, 1828, from Manning to Tupper. Cited in Ibid.
7. Prospectus of the Nova Scotia Baptist Education Society, and of the Literary and Theological Institution to be Connected Therewith. Cited in I. E. Bill, *Fifty Years with the Baptist Ministers and Churches of the Maritime Provinces* (Saint John, 1880), 67–68.
8. Ibid.
9. Ibid.
10. Edward M. Saunders, *History of the Baptists of the Maritime Provinces* (Halifax, 1902), 199.
11. Minutes of the New Brunswick Baptist Association, 1833.
12. Ibid., 1834.
13. Ibid., 1835 and 1836.
14. Minutes N.S. Assn., 1830. Resolution of the Association and the Board of Directors of the Education Society.
15. Saunders, *Maritime Provinces*, 203.
16. Minutes N.B. Assn., 1835.
17. Ibid., 1840.
18. Saunders, *Maritime Provinces*, 242.
19. Longley, *Acadia*, 27.
20. Ibid., 26.
21. I. E. Bill, *Fifty Years*, 111.
22. Handwritten Minutes Nova Scotia Baptist Education Society, November 15, 1838.
23. From letter of Colonial Secretary Lord Normanby to Lieutenant-Governor Campbell, March 22, 1839. Cited in Longley, *Acadia*, 35. The intimation is, of course, that the established church would not approve of such a name for a "Dissenter's" institution.
24. Longley, *Acadia*, 50.
25. George E. Levy, *The Baptists of the Maritime Provinces, 1753–1946* (Saint John, 1946), 144.
26. Longley, *Acadia*, 52.
27. Saunders, *Maritime Provinces*, 275.
28. *The Christian Messenger*, March 23, 1849. Cited in Longley, *Acadia*, 58.
29. Albert Coldwell, "History of Acadia College," in *Memorials of Acadia*, 79–84.
30. G. Gerald Harrop, "The Baptist Convention of Ontario and Quebec," in *Baptist Advance* (Nashville, 1964), 163.
31. C. H. Schutt and C. J. Cameron, *The Call of Our Own Land* (Toronto, nd), 47.
32. Harrop, "Convention," 163.
33. D. E. Thomson, "Sketch of the Educational Work of the Baptists of Ontario and Quebec during the Last Half Century," *Baptist Year Book of Ontario and Quebec, etc., 1900*, 248.

353

34. Robert Hamilton, "The Founding of McMaster University," unpublished B.D. thesis, McMaster University, 1938, 16.

Chapter 13   The Other Line

1. Arthur R. M. Lower, *Canadians in the Making* (Toronto, 1958), 161.
2. I. D. Stewart, *The History of the Freewill Baptists* (Dover, 1862), 39, 40. Cited in Stanley H. Culliford, "The History of the Freewill Baptists in Canada," unpublished B.D. thesis, McMaster University, 1952, 8.
3. Robert G. Torbet, *A History of the Baptists* (Valley Forge, 1963), 258–61.
4. This was a natural association for the times, as the Methodists were strong Arminians.
5. S. A. Burgess and J. T. Ward, *The Free Baptist Cyclopaedia* (Boston, 1899), 443. Cited in Culliford, "Freewill," 63.
6. R. W. Sawtell, *The History of First Baptist Church, Woodstock, Ontario, for the First Seventy Years: From April 22, 1822, to April 22, 1892* (Woodstock, 1892), 15.
7. Ibid.
8. Ibid., 12.
9. Culliford, "Freewill," 42.
10. Minutes of the General Conference of the Freewill Baptist Connection 1859–1886 (Boston, 1887), II, 10, 11. Cited in Culliford, "Freewill," 55–56.
11. Culliford, "Freewill," 23.
12. Edward M. Saunders, *History of the Baptists of the Maritime Provinces* (Halifax, 1902), 400.
13. Account by J. I. Porter in the Jubilee Service, 1887. Cited in Saunders, *Maritime Provinces*, 400.
14. Ibid., 242
15. Joseph McLeod, "A Sketch of the History of the Free Baptists of New Brunswick," a chapter in Saunders, *Maritime Provinces*, 411.
16. Ibid., 410.
17. Stewart, "History," 357. Cited in Culliford, "Freewill," 31.
18. McLeod, "Sketch," in Saunders, *Maritime Provinces*, 410.
19. Ibid., 419.
20. Ibid., 418.
21. George E. Levy, *The Baptists of the Maritime Provinces* (Saint John, 1946), 245.
22. McLeod, "Sketch," in Saunders, *Maritime Provinces*, 420.
23. Ibid.
24. *Treatise of Faith, Church Covenant and Church Directory of the Free Christian Baptists of New Brunswick* (Saint John, 1889), Chap. IV, Section 3.

25. Ibid., Section 12.
26. Ibid., Section 13.
27. Minutes of the Free Christian Baptist Conference of New Brunswick, 1850. Cited in Levy, *Maritime*, 246.

Chapter 14   Sur la Grande Ligne

1. Stuart Ivison, "The Heritage of Baptists in the Province of Quebec." Printed copy of address given to the Quebec Association of Baptist Churches, Quebec City, October 1, 1965, 4.
2. Douglas J. Wilson, *The Church Grows in Canada* (Toronto, 1966), 16.
3. Paul Villard, *Up to the Light* (Toronto, 1928), 77, quoting the *Methodist Magazine* of 1816. Cited in Charles Melvin Foster, "Protestant Evangelism in French Canada," unpublished B.D. thesis, McMaster University, 1950, 43.
4. Foster, "Evangelism," 45.
5. E. R. Fitch, ed., *The Baptists of Canada* (Toronto, 1911), 198.
6. Léonard A. Therrien, "L'Histoire des Églises Baptistes Françaises du Canada," in Jacqueline M. Norton, ed., in *From Sea to Sea* (Toronto, 1940), 110, 111.
7. Ibid., 113.
8. Ibid., 115.
9. Foster, "Evangelism," 50.
10. Ibid., 52.
11. John S. Moir, ed., *The Cross in Canada* (Toronto, 1966), 138.
12. J. M. Cramp, *A Memoir of Madame Feller* (Toronto, 1876), 111–13. Cited in Moir, *Cross*, 138–39.
13. Ibid.
14. *Montreal Register*, August 1838. Cited in George W. Campbell, "Canada Baptist College, 1838–1849," unpublished B.D. thesis, Knox College, 26.
15. Foster, "Evangelism," 52.
16. H. C. Wilkinson, "Historic Grande Ligne Church," *Canadian Baptist Home Missions Digest* (May 1957): 66.
17. Théodore Lafleur, "A Brief Historical Sketch of the Grande Ligne Mission from Its Beginning in 1835 to 1900," in *Baptist Year Book of Ontario and Quebec, Manitoba and the N.W. Territories and B.C., 1900*, 298.
18. Cramp, *Memoir*, 150–52. Cited in Foster, "Evangelism," 55.
19. Wilkinson, "Grande Ligne," 67.
20. Lafleur, "Sketch," 301.
21. Mrs. Léonard A. Therrien, "The Story," in Eugène A. Therrien et al., *Baptist Work in French Canada* (Toronto, nd), 60–61.
22. Foster, "Evangelism," 57.
23. *The Canadian Baptist*, July 3, 1862. Cited

in J. U. MacIntosh, "Some of the Labours and Disputes of the Open and Close Communion Baptists in Ontario and Quebec," unpublished B.D. thesis, McMaster University, 1936, 13.

24. CB (*The Canadian Baptist*), March 20, 1862. Cited in MacIntosh, "Labours," 14.

25. CB, April, 1862. Cited in MacIntosh, "Labours," 15.

26. CB, July 3, 1862. Cited in MacIntosh, "Labours," 20.

27. CB, July 24, 1862. Cited in MacIntosh, "Labours," 21.

28. CB, August 7, 1862. Cited in MacIntosh, "Labours," 21.

29. MacIntosh, "Labours," 26.

30. E. R. Fitch, ed., *The Baptists of Canada* (Toronto, 1911), 208.

31. Mrs. Therrien, "Story," 62.

32. Léonard Therrien, "L'Histoire," 120. In Norton, ed., *From Sea to Sea*.

33. Fitch, *Baptists*, 223–34.

34. Lafleur, "Sketch," 304.

35. W. Nelson Thomson, "Witness in French Canada," in *Baptists in Canada*, ed. Jarold K. Zeman (Burlington, Ont., 1980), 50.

36. H. C. Wilkinson, "Concerning Things Historical," in *Canadian Baptist Home Missions Digest* (June 1953): 59.

37. Mrs. Therrien, "Story," 62.

38. Lafleur, "Sketch," 305.

39. Thomson, "Witness," 53.

40. Foster, "Evangelism," 61.

41. Ibid., 62.

42. Eugène A. Therrien, "Centres of Labour," in Eugène A. Therrien et al., *Baptist Work in French Canada* (Toronto, nd), 82.

Chapter 15 In Demonstration of Unity I: The Maritimes

1. Norah Story, *The Oxford Companion to Canadian History and Literature* (Toronto, 1967), 183.

2. Ibid., 393–94.

3. Donald Creighton, *The Story of Canada* (London, 1971), 150.

4. Edward M. Saunders, *History of the Baptists of the Maritime Provinces* (Halifax, 1902), 468. These figures include the Free Baptists, who were not listed separately until the 1871 census and were, of course, dropped again, following the mergers of 1905–6 with the Regular Baptists.

5. I. E. Bill, *Fifty Years with the Baptist Ministers and Churches of the Maritime Provinces of Canada* (Saint John, 1880), 571.

6. Ibid., 516.

7. Ibid.

8. Saunders, *Maritime Provinces*, 304, 307, 308.

9. J. Gordon Jones, "Twelve Men: Tried and True," *Canadian Baptist Home Missions Digest*, vol. 7 (1966–67): 9.

10. Constitution, III, 1846, of the Baptist Convention of Nova Scotia, New Brunswick and Prince Edward Island.

11. Constitution, VI, 1846.

12. Convention Minutes N.S., N.B. and P.E.I., 1846.

13. Convention Minutes N.S., N.B. and P.E.I., 1851.

14. Convention Minutes N.S., N.B. and P.E.I., 1849.

15. Convention Minutes N.S., N.B. and P.E.I., 1850.

16. Convention Minutes N.S., N.B. and P.E.I., 1865.

17. R. S. Longley, *Acadia University, 1838–1938* (Wolfville, 1939), 63.

18. Ibid., 66, 68.

19. Ibid., 15, 21, 11.

20. Saunders, *Maritime Provinces*, 339.

21. M. Allen Gibson, *Along the King's Highway* (Lunenburg, 1964), 13. Citing Edward Saunders, *Maritime Provinces*.

22. George E. Levy, *The Baptists of the Maritime Provinces, 1753–1946* (Saint John, 1946), 161.

23. Gibson, *Highway*, 20.

24. Convention Minutes N.S., N.B. and P.E.I., 1849.

25. Gibson, *Highway*, 47.

26. Ibid., 47–48.

27. Saunders, *Maritime Provinces*, 346.

28. Levy, *Maritime*, 165.

29. John S. Moir, *The Cross in Canada* (Toronto, 1966), 160.

30. Jeremiah S. Clark, *Rand and the Micmacs* (Charlottetown, 1899), 5.

31. Ibid.

32. Ibid., June 1850.

33. Clark, *Micmacs*, xii.

34. Ibid., 21.

35. Ibid., vi, citing Robert Murray.

36. Savanah E. Williams, "The Role of the African United Baptist Association in the Development of Indigenous Afro-Canadians in Nova Scotia, 1782–1978," in *Repent and Believe: The Baptist Experience in Maritime Canada*, ed. Barry M. Moody (Hantsport, 1980), 49.

37. George E. Levy, "The United Baptist Convention of the Maritime Provinces," in *Baptist Advance* (Nashville, 1964), 143.

38. W. P. Oliver, "Home Missions and the African Baptist Association of Nova

Scotia," *Canadian Baptist Home Missions Digest* (June 1953): 17.

39. Gibson, *Highway*, 58.
40. Report of Foreign Mission Board, Minutes of Maritime Convention, 1850.
41. Ibid., 1849.
42. Ibid., 1851.
43. Ibid., 1852.
44. Levy, *Maritime*, 157.
45. Minutes of Maritime Convention, 1856.
46. Ibid., 1857.
47. Isaiah Wallace, *Autobiography and Revival Reminiscences* (Halifax, 1903), 27.
48. Clark, *Micmacs*, 12.
49. Minutes of Maritime Convention, 1867.
50. Ibid., 1869.
51. Levy, *Maritime*, 158.
52. Mary Kinley Ingraham, *Historical Sketch of the United Baptist Woman's Missionary Union in the Maritime Provinces* (Kentville, 1945), 8.
53. Ibid., 10, 11.
54. Saunders, *Maritime Provinces*, 299.
55. Levy, *Maritime*, 197.

Chapter 16 In Demonstration of Unity II: Ontario and Quebec

1. Minutes of the Haldimand Association, 1850.
2. Minutes of the Regular Baptist Missionary Society of Canada, 1851.
3. Ibid.
4. Ibid., 1854, 1858.
5. Proceedings of the Canada Baptist Missionary Convention East, April 28, 1858.
6. Ibid.
7. Ibid.
8. Ibid.
9. Thomas L. Davidson, Circular letter of the Baptist Missionary Convention of Canada West, August 1849, to the Regular Baptist Churches of Canada West.
10. A. J. Gordon, *First Baptist Church of Montreal, 1820-1906* (Montreal, 1906), 9, 10.
11. W. G. Pitman, "The Baptists and Public Affairs in the Province of Canada, 1840–1867," unpublished M.A. thesis, University of Toronto, 1956, 148.
12. Minutes of the Regular Baptist Missionary Society, 1852.
13. Melvyn R. Hillmer, "Baptist Theological Education in Ontario and Quebec, 1838–1982," in *Canadian Baptist History and Polity*, ed. Murray J. S. Ford (McMaster Divinity College, 1982), 42.
14. Charles M. Johnston, *McMaster University*, vol. 1 (Toronto, 1976), 13.
15. *The Christian Messenger*, December 13,
16. Charles A. McL. Vining, *Woodstock College Memorial Book* (Toronto, 1951), 22.
17. Vining, *Woodstock*, 23.
18. Robert Hamilton, "The Founding of McMaster University," unpublished B.D. thesis, McMaster University, 1938, 19.
19. J. E. Wells, *Life and Labours of Robert Alexander Fyfe, D.D.* (Toronto, 1879), 319-322. Cited in *The Cross in Canada*, ed. John S. Moir (Toronto, 1966), 149.
20. Moir, Ibid., 149.
21. Vining, *Woodstock*, 27.
22. Hamilton, "Founding," 27.
23. Johnston, *McMaster*, 30.
24. An Act to Unite Toronto Baptist College and Woodstock College under the name of McMaster University, in *Baptist Year Book, 1888*, 136, 137, 139.
25. R. S. Longley, *Acadia University, 1838-1938* (Wolfville, 1939), 90-92.
26. Hon. Wm. McMaster to Trustees of Toronto Baptist College: Conveyance of the College Site in Trust, December 1st, 1880. Cited in Johnston, *McMaster*, 237.
27. Act to Unite Toronto and Woodstock. Cited Ibid., 242.
28. Ibid., 240-41.
29. Johnston, *McMaster*, 60.
30. Will of William McMaster. Cited in Hamilton, "Founding," 77.
31. Johnston, *McMaster*, 18-21.
32. William Davies, *The Baptist Founder of a Packing Firm*. Cited Ibid., 21.
33. The others: Ebenezer Moulton and Avery Moulton — the former the pioneer in the Maritimes, the latter one of the founders of Free Baptist work in Quebec. Any family relationship among the three is not known.
34. Johnston, *McMaster*, 22.
35. "First Annual Report of the Foreign Missionary Society — The Canada Auxiliary to the American Baptist Missionary Union," *The Canadian Baptist Register for 1868*.
36. M. L. Orchard and (Miss) K. S. McLaurin, *The Enterprise* (Toronto, c 1924), 151.
37. Ibid., 162.
38. J. G. Brown, "History of the Foreign Mission Work of the Baptists of Ontario and Quebec, 1866-1900," *Baptist Year Book, 1900*, 157.
39. Ibid., 162-63.
40. Minutes of the Baptist Missionary Convention of Ontario, October 20, 21, 1875, in *Baptist Register, 1876*, 16.

1855. Cited in Robert Hamilton, "The Founding of McMaster University," unpublished B.D. thesis, McMaster University, 1938, 17.

41. Jane Buchan, "Historical Sketch of the Women's Baptist Foreign Missionary Society Of Ontario," *Baptist Year Book, 1900*, 200–201.
42. Nannie E. Green, "Historical sketch of the Baptist Foreign Missionary Society of Eastern Ontario and Quebec," Ibid., 225.
43. Minutes of the Baptist Missionary Convention of Canada West, 1861, *Canadian Baptist Register for 1862*, 12.
44. Minutes of the Baptist Missionary Convention of Canada East, 1861, Ibid., 27.
45. BMC of Canada West, 1864, in Ibid., 1865, 35.
46. BMC of Ontario, 1870, in Ibid., 1871, 43.
47. Ibid., 1873, in Ibid. , 1874, 42.
48. Ibid., 1870, in Ibid., 1871, 13.
49. BMC of Ontario, 1877, *Baptist Year Book, 1878*, 24, 46.
50. Ibid., years 1878, 1879, 1880, 1881, 1882, 1883, 1884.
51. BMC of Ontario, 1878, *Baptist Year Book, 1879*, 18.
52. *Baptist Year Book, 1886*, 186.
53. Ibid., 1878, 1879, 1880, 1881, 1882, 1883, 1884, 1885, 1876.
54. Ibid., 1886, 19.
55. Minutes of the Canadian Baptist Missionary Convention East, 1880, *Baptist Year Book, 1881*, 35.
56. Minutes of the Baptist Missionary Convention of Canada West, 1862, *Canadian Baptist Register for 1863*, 13.
57. Ibid., 1865, in Ibid., 1866, 8.
58. Minutes of Missionary Conventions East, 1866, and West, 1866, *Canadian Baptist Register for 1867*, 4, 44, 12.
59. "The Baptist Union of Canada," *Baptist Year Book, 1881*, 9–10.
60. Constitution of Baptist Union of Canada: Minutes of Meeting for Re-organization, October 20, 1882, *Baptist Year Book, 1883*, 5.
61. Minutes BMC (East), 1886, *Baptist Year Book, 1887*, 32.
62. Minutes BMC (East), 1887, *Baptist Year Book, 1888*, 45.
63. Minutes BMC of Ontario, 1887, Ibid., 10.
64. Ibid., 15, 16.
65. G. Gerald Harrop, "The Baptist Convention of Ontario and Quebec," in *Baptist Advance* (Nashville, 1964), 162.

Chapter 17 Going West I: Manitoba and the Northwest

1. Minutes of the Baptist Missionary Convention of Ontario, 1869, *The Canadian Baptist Register, 1870*, 46–50.
2. Ibid., 51.
3. John S. Moir and Robert E. Saunders, *Northern Destiny* (Toronto, 1970), 188–89.
4. Duncan McArthur, *History of Canada* (Toronto, 1934), 299–302.
5. Ibid., 302, 305.
6. Minutes BMC of Ontario, 1869. Ibid., 49, 50.
7. Philip Carrington, *The Anglican Church in Canada* (Toronto, 1963), 69, 70.
8. Ibid., 97–99.
9. Ibid., 119–23.
10. R. G. MacBeth, *The Burning Bush and Canada* (Toronto, 1926), 84–87.
11. Ibid., 94–98.
12. J. H. Riddell, *Methodism in the Middle West* (Toronto, 1946), 7, 11.
13. Ibid., 70.
14. Minutes BMC of Ontario, 1871, Ibid., 1872, 17.
15. Minutes BMC of Ontario, 1872, Ibid., 1873, 15.
16. Minutes BMC of Ontario, 1871, Ibid., 1872, 17.
17. E. R. Fitch, ed., *The Baptists of Canada* (Toronto, 1911), 125.
18. Theo. T. Gibson, *Beyond the Granite Curtain* (Ancaster, 1975), 58.
19. Ibid., 61.
20. Ibid., 63.
21. C. C. McLaurin, *Pioneering in Western Canada* (Calgary, 1939), 70.
22. Mrs. J. R. McDonald, *Baptist Missions in Western Canada, 1873-1948* (Edmonton, 1948), 25.
23. Gibson, *Curtain*, 87.
24. *The Baptist Year Book for Ontario and Quebec, 1878*, 118.
25. Gibson, *Curtain*, 113–14.
26. Ibid., 87.
27. BYB, O & Q, 1881, 19, 20.
28. Ibid., 1882, 133.
29. Walter E. Ellis, "Baptist Missions Adaptation to the Western Frontier," in *Canadian Baptist History and Polity*, ed. Murray J. S. Ford (McMaster Divinity College, 1982), 173.

Chapter 18 Going West II: British Columbia

1. John B. Richards, *Baptists in British Columbia* (Vancouver, 1977), 28, 31.
2. Bruce A. Woods, "The John Morton Story." Script of broadcast over station CBU of Canadian Broadcasting Corporation, June 27, 1971.
3. Gordon H. Pousett, "A History of the Convention of Baptist Churches of British Columbia," unpublished M.Th. thesis, Vancouver School of Theology, 1982, 11.
4. J. E. Harris, *The Baptist Union of Western Canada: A Centennial History, 1873-1973* (Saint John, 1976), 14.

5. Pousett, *Convention*, 12, 13.
6. Margaret E. Thompson, *The Baptist Story in Western Canada* (Calgary, 1974), 55.
7. C. C. McLaurin, *Pioneering in Western Canada* (Calgary, 1939), 248.
8. Thompson, *Story*, 55–56.
9. Ibid., 56.
10. Ibid., 57, citing *The Canadian Baptist* (CB), April 19, 1885.
11. Ibid., citing CB, November 7, 1878.
12. Ibid., 57.
13. Ibid., 58.
14. The Dominion Board of Home Missions, First Annual Report, 1886, *Baptist Year Book for Ontario and Quebec, 1887*, 97–99.
15. Pousett, *Convention*, 23, citing Margaret A. Ormsby, *British Columbia: A History* (Toronto, 1964), 297, 299–301.
16. Thompson, *Story*, 61, citing CB, October 22, 1885.
17. Ibid., citing CB, May 27, 1886.
18. Ibid., 61.
19. Pousett, *Convention*, 26.
20. Ibid., 27.
21. Ibid., 30.
22. Ibid., 9, 10, citing J. C. Baker, *Baptist History of the North Pacific Coast* (Philadelphia, 1912), 71–72.
23. E. R. Fitch, ed., *The Baptists of Canada* (Toronto, 1911), 247.
24. McLaurin, *Pioneering*, 257.
25. Thompson, *Story*, 109.
26. Thompson, *Story*, 109.
27. Ibid., 110.
28. Ibid., 99.
29. Ibid., 99–101.
30. *Baptist Year Book for Ontario, Quebec, Manitoba and the Northwest Territories, 1888*, 23, 25.
31. Thompson, *Story*, 89.
32. Ibid., 90, citing CB, July 30, 1896.
33. BYB, 1887, 74.
34. McLaurin, *Pioneering*, 118.
35. Thompson, *Story*, 102, citing BYB, 1889, 150.
36. Thompson, *Story*, 102–3.
37. McLaurin, *Pioneering*, 123.
38. Mrs. A. Spankie, in McLaurin, *Pioneering*, 261–65.
39. Thompson, *Story*, 41–42.
40. Shirley F. Bentall, *Buckboard to Brotherhood: The Baptist Churches in Calgary* (Calgary, 1975), 5–9, 17.
41. Wendon U. Pickel, *First Baptist Church, Regina, 90th Anniversary* (Regina, 1981, 4.
42. Thompson, *Story*, 51–52.
43. Theo. T. Gibson, *Beyond the Granite Curtain* (Ancaster, 1975), 151.
44. Thompson, *Story*, 104, citing *North West Baptist*, August 1, 1892.
45. Ibid., 105, citing CB, March 29, 1895.
46. Ibid., 106, citing BYB, 1897, 164ff.
47. Thompson, *Story*, 121.
48. Ibid., 1901. The matter is not mentioned in Convention Minutes.
49. McLaurin, *Pioneering*, 136.
50. Thompson, *Story*, 114.
51. Thompson, *Story*, 137.

Chapter 19 A World View

1. G. Winfred Hervey, *The Story of Baptist Missions in Foreign Lands* (St. Louis, 1885), 5.
2. Robert G. Torbet, *A History of the Baptists* (Valley Forge, 1963), 80.
3. A. H. Burlingham, "Introduction," in Hervey, *Missions*, xiii.
4. Edward M. Saunders, *History of the Baptists of the Maritime Provinces* (Halifax, 1902), 208–9.
5. Mary Bates McLaurin, "On the Field of Battle," a chapter in M. L. Orchard and K. S. McLaurin, *The Enterprise* (Toronto, c 1924), 186–67.
6. Ibid., 193. McLaurin wrote to both the missionaries and the Maritimes' board to suggest the idea. Correspondence between the Maritimes' and Ontario and Quebec boards and action by a special Maritime Convention gave confirmation.
7. W. Gordon Carder, *Hand to the Indian Plow* (Secunderabad, India, 1976), 48–49.
8. Orville E. Daniel, *Moving with the Times* (Toronto, 1973), 22.
9. Carder, *Hand*, 75, 53–54, 101, 116, 118.
10. McLaurin, "Field," in Orchard and McLaurin, *Enterprise*, 189.
11. Daniel, *Moving*, 26.
12. Ibid., 36, 32.
13. Edwin Haward in *Encyclopaedia Britannica*, vol. 12, 199.
14. Daniel, *Moving*, 39.
15. Carder, *Hand*, 84, 89.
16. Ibid., 87–89.
17. Orchard and McLaurin, *Enterprise*, 246.
18. Ibid., 247.
19. J. E. Davis, *Autobiography of John E. Davis* (1917), 275–78.
20. Ibid., 51.
21. George E. Levy, *The Baptists of the Maritime Provinces* (Saint John, 1946), 205.
22. J. G. Brown, "History of the Foreign Mission Work of the Baptist Convention of Ontario and Quebec, 1866–1900," *The Baptist Year Book, 1900*, 183.
23. Daniel, *Moving*, 36.
24. Levy, *Maritime*, 284.

25. Daniel, *Moving*, 60.
26. Ibid., 62.
27. Ibid.
28. Inez J. Bell, ed., *The Kantuta Blooms in Bolivia* (Toronto, 1971), 22–23.
29. Ibid., 26–27.
30. Carder, *Hand*, 142.
31. Bell, *Kantuta*, 28–29.
32. Daniel, *Moving*, 33–34.

Chapter 20   Into the Twentieth Century

1. Donald Creighton, *The Story of Canada* (London, 1971), 194.
2. F. Tracey, "Sketch of the Baptists of Ontario and Quebec," *Baptist Year Book of Ontario and Quebec, 1900*, 110–12.
3. John Stark, "Some Conditions of Baptist Progress in Home Missions," Ibid., 47–49.
4. While the word "Regular" was not included in the name of the "Assembly to be called 'The Baptist Convention of Ontario and Quebec'" in the Act of Parliament that brought the Convention into being, the word "Regular" does appear several times in the document, in such phrases as "the denomination of Regular Baptists" and "Regular Baptist Church." Constitution, BYB, O & Q, 1900, 33–34.
5. G. Gerald Harrop, "The Baptist Convention of Ontario and Quebec," in *Baptist Advance* (Nashville, 1964), 169.
6. BYB, O & Q, 1921. Cited in Harrop, "Seventy-Five Years as a Convention," *Canadian Baptist Home Missions Digest* (1963–64): 85.
7. E. R. Fitch, ed., *The Baptists of Canada* (Toronto, 1911), 175–76.
8. Ibid., 176–77, 194–95.
9. BYB, O & Q, 1888.
10. Harrop, "Convention of Ontario and Quebec," 174.
11. BYB, O & Q, 1894–95, 172.
12. John H. Dickinson, "A History of the Baptist Young People's Union of Ontario and Quebec," unpublished senior seminar ms, McMaster Divinity College, 1978, 6.
13. Fitch, *Baptists*, 179.
14. BYB, O & Q, 1890, np.
15. Ibid., 1895–96, 22–23.
16. Ibid., 1902, 18.
17. Ibid., 1904, np.
18. Ibid., 1889, 19; 1896–97, 21–22.
19. Ibid., 1890, np.
20. Ibid., 1890; 1895–96, 24.
21. Ibid., 1898–99, np.
22. *The Canadian Baptist*, December 4, 1902.
23. Ibid., December 11, 1902.

24. BYB, O & Q, 1895–96, 14, 15.
25. BYB, O & Q, 1907.
26. John D. E. Dozois, "Dr. Thomas Todhunter Shields—In the Stream of Fundamentalism," unpublished B.D. thesis, McMaster University, 1963, 60.
27. Melvyn R. Hillmer, "Baptist Theological Education in Ontario and Quebec, 1838–1982," in *Canadian Baptist History and Polity*, ed. Murray J. S. Ford (McMaster Divinity College, 1982), 51.
28. Dozois, *Shields*, 61–62.
29. Fitch, *Baptists*, 180.
30. Minutes of the Nova Scotia Free Baptist Conference, September 8–12, 1887.
31. *The Baptist Year Book of the Maritime Provinces of Canada, 1900*, 29.
32. BYB, Maritimes, 1903, 21, 27.
33. Ibid., 1904, 22.
34. Ibid., 1905, 130.
35. F. H. Sinnott, "The Union of the Regular and Free Will Baptists of the Maritimes," in *Repent and Believe*, ed. Barry M. Moody (Hantsport, 1980), 150.
36. George E. Levy, *The Baptists of the Maritime Provinces* (Saint John, 1946), 245.
37. Minutes of the Nova Scotia Central Association, *United Baptist Year Book, 1917* (UBYB), 152.
38. Harry A. Renfree, *The Basis of Union: A Statement of Beliefs of Atlantic Baptists* (Saint John, 1964), 23–24.
39. Minutes of the Nova Scotia Free Baptist Conference 1906.
40. George E. Levy, "The United Baptist Convention of the Maritime Provinces," in *Baptist Advance* (Nashville, 1964), 153–54.
41. BYB, Maritimes, 1901, 59.
42. *Free Baptist Banner*, August 1906, 179.
43. Convention Minutes, UBYB, 1906, 16.
44. UBYB, 1907, 58.
45. Ronald Stewart Longley, *Acadia University, 1838-1938* (Wolfville, 1939), 130.
46. UBYB, 1917, 87.
47. Longley, *Acadia*, 119.
48. Convention Minutes, UBYB, 1914, 12.
49. Ibid., 1916, 11.
50. Levy, "United," 154.
51. George E. Levy, *The Baptists of the Maritime Provinces* (Saint John, 1946), 296.
52. Ibid., 293.
53. William C. Smalley, "Baptist Work in Western Canada," in *Baptist Advance*, 180.
54. Margaret E. Thompson, *The Baptist Story in Western Canada* (Calgary, 1974), 122.

55. *Western Outlook*, December 16, 1907. Cited in Thompson, *Story*, 123.
56. Thompson, *Story*, 137.
57. J. E. Harris, *The Baptist Union of Western Canada* (Saint John, 1976), 27.
58. G. Keith Churchill, "The Educational Policy of the Baptist Union of Western Canada," unpublished D. Min. thesis, San Francisco Theological Seminary, 1980, 13.
59. Ibid., 14, 15.
60. Thompson, *Story*, 424.
61. Walter E. Ellis, "Baptist Missions Adaptation to the Western Frontier," in *Canadian Baptist History and Polity*, ed. Murray J. S. Ford (McMaster Divinity College, 1982), 173.
62. Thompson, *Story*, 421–22, quoting the B.C. Education Board.
63. Gordon H. Pousett, "A History of the Convention of Baptist Churches of British Columbia," unpublished M.Th. thesis, Vancouver School of Theology, 1982, 109.
64. Katsumi Imayoshi, "The History of Okanagan Baptist College," unpublished B.D. thesis, McMaster University, 1953, 24.
65. Churchill, "Educational Policy," 21.
66. Ibid., 23.

Chapter 21   In the Eye of the Storm
1. Douglas J. Wilson, *The Church Grows in Canada* (Toronto, 1966), 117.
2. Walter E. Ellis, "Modernist Schism in North America, 1895–1934," unpublished Ph.D. thesis, University of Pittsburgh, 1974, 253.
3. Martin Rist, "History of Biblical Criticism," *An Encyclopedia of Religion*, ed. Virgilius Ferm (New York, 1945), 76.
4. *The Canadian Baptist*, October 2, 1919.
5. *The Canadian Baptist*, October 16, 1919.
6. Ibid.
7. *Baptist Year Book, Ontario and Quebec, 1919*, 24. The view to which the 1910 Convention subscribed was this: "The Convention declares and affirms its unfaltering faith and belief in the Old and New Testaments as the word of God, and in His Son Jesus Christ as the absolutely inerrant and infallible teacher." BYB, O & Q, 1910, 28.
8. John D. E. Dozois, "Dr. T. T. Shields — In the Stream of Fundamentalism," unpublished B.D. thesis, McMaster University, 1963, 43–44.
9. T. T. Shields, *The Plot That Failed* (Toronto, 1937), 39.
10. Dozois, "Shields," 64–65.
11. Ibid., 69, 70.
12. W. Gordon Carder, "Controversy in the Baptist Convention of Ontario and Quebec, 1908–1929," unpublished B.D. thesis, McMaster University, 1950, 18.
13. According to the premillenial view of last things, the second advent of Christ will precede the millenium, the thousand-year reign of Christ on earth. The amillenial does not regard the millenium as a precise period. The classic example of dispensationalism is the *Scofield Reference Bible*, which divides human history into fixed eras, or dispensations, in which God is believed to work out His purposes specific to that age alone.
14. Leslie K. Tarr, "Another Perspective on T. T. Shields," *Baptists in Canada: Search for Identity amidst Diversity*, ed. J. K. Zeman (Burlington, 1980), 220.
15. Charles M. Johnston, *McMaster University*, vol. 1 (Toronto, 1976), 153.
16. Dozois, "Shields," 110–12.
17. BYB, O & Q, 1922, 40.
18. Johnston, *McMaster*, 175.
19. BYB, O & Q, 1924, 43.
20. Ibid., November 20, 1924.
21. Carder, "Controversy," 31.
22. Johnston, *McMaster*, 181.
23. Ibid., 182.
24. *Gospel Witness*, January 21, 1926.
25. Ibid., November 5, 1925.
26. BYB, O & Q, 1926, 37.
27. Carder, "Controversy," 58.
28. Ibid.
29. Ibid., 58–62.
30. ibid., 64.
31. *Gospel Witness*, September 8, 1927.
32. BYB, O & Q, 1927, 29.
33. Ibid., 34.
34. *The Canadian Baptist*, October 20, 1927.
35. BYB, O & Q, 1927, 30.
36. *The Gospel Witness*, October 20, 1927.
37. Johnston, *McMaster*, 202.
38. Clark H. Pinnock, "The Modernist Impulse at McMaster University, 1887–1927," in *Baptists in Canada: Search for Identity amidst Diversity*, ed. J. K. Zeman (Burlington, 1980), 202.
39. Margaret E. Thompson, *The Baptist Story in Western Canada* (Calgary, 1974), 148–49.
40. Ibid.
41. The title of a pamphlet issued by Bennett at that time is reminiscent of some of Shields's blockbusters: "Jesuit Methods Used by Baptist Union of Western Canada." Comments J. B. Richards in "Baptist Leadership: Autocratic or Democratic": "The title tells it all with respect to the feeling of the author. The

contents do not prove the validity of the charge." In Zeman, *Search*, 231.

42. Gordon H. Pousett, "A History of the Convention of Baptist Churches of British Columbia," unpublished M.Th. thesis, Vancouver School of Theology, 1982, 140.
43. *Year Book, Baptist Union of Western Canada, 1921.* Cited in Pousett, "Convention," 141.
44. Pousett, "Convention," 142.
45. Ibid., 144–45.
46. C. C. McLaurin, *Pioneering in Western Canada* (Calgary, 1939), 201.
47. Ibid., 201–2.
48. McLaurin, *Pioneering*, 202.
49. Pousett, "Convention," 151.
50. YB, BUWC, 1926. Cited in Pousett, "Convention," 152.
51. Pousett, "Convention," 156, 176.
52. Ibid., 157–58.
53. Ibid., 177.
54. Ibid., 163.
55. YB, BUWC, 1926. Cited in Pousett, "Convention," 165.
56. Ibid., 1927. Ibid., 168.
57. Ibid. Ibid.
58. Walter E. Ellis, "Politics in Western Canada," in Zeman, *Search*, 169–70.

Chapter 22   The Atlantic Calm

1. Convention Minutes, *Year Book of United Baptist Convention of the Maritime Provinces, 1918*, 6.
2. *YB, UBCMP, 1918*, 93.
3. New Brunswick Association Minutes, YB, UBCMP, 1918, 157.
4. George E. Levy, "The United Baptist Convention of the Maritime Provinces," in *Baptist Advance* (Nashville, 1964), 156.
5. YB, UBCMP, 1918, 138.
6. George E. Levy, *The Baptists of the Maritime Provinces, 1753-1946* (Saint John, 1946), 299.
7. YB, UBCMP, 1921, 112–13.
8. Levy, *Maritime*, 300, quoting from 1920 report of Maritime Home for Girls.
9. YB, UBCMP, 1924, 142.
10. Ibid., 1923, 146.
11. Convention Minutes. Ibid., 1919, 17.
12. Ibid., Ibid., 1921, 16.
13. George B. Cutten, "Acadia's Ministry to the Denomination," in A. C. Chute and W. B. Boggs, *The Religious Life of Acadia* (Wolfville, 1933), 237.
14. Convention Minutes, YB, UBCMP, 1921, 14.
15. Report of Board of Governors, YB, UBCMP, 1923, 64.
16. Ibid., Ibid., 1931, 73.

17. YB, UBCMP, 1922, 129.
18. Ibid., Ibid., 1924, 11.
19. Convention Minutes, YB, UBCMP, 1917, 11.
20. N.B. Association Minutes, YB, UBCMP, 1918, 157.
21. Convention Minutes, YB, UBCMP, 1921, 15.
22. Convention Minutes, YB, UBCMP, 1921, 14.
23. Ibid., Ibid., 1928, 12.
24. Levy, *Maritime*, 302.
25. Gertrude A. Palmer, *The Combatant: Biography of John J. Sidey* (Middleton, 1976), 71.
26. Ibid., 74.
27. Harold L. Mitton, "Theological Education among Maritime Baptists," in *Canadian Baptist History and Polity*, ed. J. S. Ford (McMaster Divinity College, 1982), 61.
28. Palmer, *Combatant, 86, 93*.
29. *The Gospel Light*, November 21, 1931. The ordination was that of H. C. Slade in First Baptist Church, Timmins.
30. Palmer, *Combatant*, 96.
31. Daggett complained of "unfair" press reports in an article in *The Question*, the organ of the International Christian Mission (March 1935).
32. *The Question* (October 1935).
33. Palmer, *Combatant*, 156.
34. Ibid., 60.
35. Ibid., 160.
36. Robert S. Wilson, "British Influences in the Nineteenth Century," in *Baptists in Canada: Search for Identity amidst Diversity*, ed. J. K. Zeman (Burlington, 1980), 36. Wilson, an historian of the Maritimes, traces the British influence in both regions, but indicates that British support of denominational structures was evident "particularly in Central Canada."
37. Mary Bulmer Hill, "From Sect to Denomination in the Baptist Church in Canada," unpublished Ph.D. thesis, State University of New York at Buffalo, 1971, 60–61.
38. *The Gospel Light* (October 1934).
39. Acadia's enrolment in 1931 was 619. YB, UBCMP, 1931, 70.
40. This allegation is referred to in a letter to the editor from Acadia professor Simeon Spidle in the *Middleton Outlook* of September 17, 1934. As a result of the loss of the money, Sidey's name had been removed from the ministerial roll of the denomination. Letter reprinted in Daggett's *Gospel Light* (October 1934).
41. YB, UBCMP, 1919, 131.
42. Convention Minutes, YB, UBCMP, 1936, 16.

43. Donald Creighton, *The Story of Canada* (London, 1971), 230–31.
44. Robert T. Handy, *A History of the Churches in the United States and Canada* (Toronto, 1979), 391.
45. YB, UBCMP, 1931, 150
46. Ibid., 1932, 163.
47. Ibid., 164.
48. Ibid., 1933, 178, 177.
49. Convention Minutes, YB, UBCMP, 1934, 14.
50. Ibid., Ibid., 1932, 28.
51. YB, UBCMP, 1935, 28–29.
52. Ibid., 1934, 130.
53. Ibid., 1925, 146.
54. Ibid., 1932, 131.
58. Convention Minutes, YB, UBCMP, 1936, 13, 20–21.
56. YB, UBCMP, 1933, 179.
57. Ibid., 1936, 150.
58. YB, UBCMP, 1933, 25.
59. Ibid., 1935.
60. *The Maritime Baptist*, February 24, 1932.
61. YB, UBCMP, 1937, 27–28.
62. Ibid., 1939, 169.
63. Convention Minutes, YB, UBCMP, 1939, 20.
64. Levy, *Maritime*, 314.
65. Ibid., 315.
66. YB, UBCMP, 1942, 66.
67. Convention Minutes, YB, UBCMP, 1942, 14.
68. Ibid., Ibid., 1943, 13, 19.
69. YB, UBCMP, 1943, 33.
70. Levy, *Maritime*, 317.
71. YB, UBCMP, 1943, 32.
72. Levy, *Maritime*, 315.
73. YB, UBCMP, 1939, 153–54.
74. Convention Minutes, YB, UBCMP, 1939, 18.
75. YB, UBCMP, 1944, 179–80.
76. Ibid., 44.
77. Ibid., 1946, 211.
78. Ibid., 1944, 185.
79. Minutes of Executive, acting for Convention, YB, UBCMP, 1945.

Chapter 23 The Central Aftermath

1. G. P. Gilmour, "Seventy Years as a Convention." Historical address to the Baptist Convention of Ontario and Quebec Assembly, 1958.
2. *Baptist Year Book of Ontario and Quebec, 1928*, 73.
3. A. C. Simmonds, *Diary of a Century* (Oshawa, 1966), vii, 53–54.
4. Convention Minutes, BYB, O & Q, 1927, 52.
5. Ibid., Ibid., 1928, 28–32.
6. BYB, O & Q, 1928, 59.
7. C. H. Schutt and C. J. Cameron, *The Call of Our Own Land* (Toronto, c 1936), 219.
8. Ibid., 220.
9. BYB, O & Q, 1923, 38, 131.
10. Ibid., 1927, 172–73.
11. Ibid., 1928, 59.
12. Charles A. McL. Vining, "History of Woodstock College, 1857–1926," in *Woodstock College Memorial Book* (Toronto, 1951), 93.
13. Ibid., 102.
14. Ibid., 104. The property was sold to the Redemptorist Fathers, becoming St. Alphonsus Seminary.
15. G. Gerald Harrop, "The Baptist Convention of Ontario and Quebec," in *Baptist Advance* (Nashville, 1964), 173.
16. BYB, O & Q, 1928 and 1931, 286, 296.
17. Harrop, "Convention," 173.
18. BYB, O & Q, 1936, 68.
19. Ibid., 1941.
20. Ibid., 1933, 102.
21. *The Canadian Baptist*, April 21, 1932.
22. BYB, O & Q, 1938.
23. *The Canadian Baptist*, February 19, 1931.
24. Ibid., October 8 and 15, 1931.
25. BYB, O & Q, 1931, 94.
26. *The Canadian Baptist*, April 13, 1933.
27. BYB, O & Q, 1937, 57.
28. Ibid., 1929, 89, 90.
29. Schutt and Cameron, *Land*, 62.
30. *The Canadian Baptist*, September 10, 1931.
31. Schutt and Cameron, *Land*, 78–83.
32. *The Canadian Baptist*, December 11, 1930.
33. BYB, O & Q, 1933, 103.
34. Schutt and Cameron, *Land*, 145–60.
35. Convention Minutes, BYB, O & Q, 1928, 39–43.
36. Ibid., Ibid., 1930, 32.
37. BYB, O & Q, 1933, 62.
38. Ibid., 1934, 63–64, 35, 40, 31.
39. Ibid., 1935, 46.
40. Ibid., 1936, 75, 48.
41. Ibid., 1937, 58.
42. Ibid., 1933, 62.
43. Convention Minutes, BYB, O & Q, 1934, 41.
44. BYB, O & Q, 1939, 61–62.
45. Convention Minutes, BYB, O & Q, 1940, 47.
46. BYB, O & Q, 1929, 56–57.
47. Ibid., 1930, 58.
48. Ibid., 1929, 68–69.
49. Convention Minutes, BYB, O & Q, 1930, 42–43.
50. BYB, O & Q, 1933, 70–71.
51. Ibid., 1939, 158.
52. Ibid., 170.

53. Convention Minutes, BYB, O & Q, 1939, 41.
54. Ibid., Ibid., 1938, 64.
55. BYB, O & Q, 1931, 62.
56. *The Canadian Baptist*, May 5, 1932; October 5, 1933.
57. Convention Minutes, BYB, O & Q, 1933, 43–44.
58. Harrop, "Convention," 168.
59. BYB, O & Q, 1941, 45.
60. Ibid., 1942–43, 64; 1943–44, 57; 1945–46, 66.
61. Ibid., 1941, 45.
62. Ibid., 1942, 68.
63. Ibid., 142.
64. Ibid., 1943–44, 150.
65. Ibid., 1942–43, 173.
66. Ibid., 1944–45, 170–71.
67. G. G. Harrop, "Seventy-Five Years as a Convention," *Canadian Baptist Home Missions Digest* (1963–64): 87.
68. BYB, O & Q, 1940, 73.
69. Convention Minutes, BYB, O & Q, 1942–43, 44.
70. Ibid., Ibid., 1943–44, 34.
71. BYB, O & Q, 1943–44, 168.
72. Ibid., 1944–45, 56.
73. Ibid., 1943–44, 56.
74. Ibid., 1944–45, 55.
75. Ibid., 1945–46, 107–9.
76. Ibid., 103–4.
77. Convention Minutes, BYB, O & Q, 1944–45, 35.
78. BYB, O & Q, 1944–45, 50.
79. Ibid., 1945–46, 61.
80. Ibid., 62.
81. Convention Minutes, BYB, O & Q, 1944–45, 38–40.
82. Melvyn R. Hillmer, "Baptist Theological Education in Ontario and Quebec," in *Canadian Baptist History and Polity*, ed. Murray J. S. Ford (McMaster Divinity College, 1982), 45.
83. BYB, O & Q, 1947–48, 138.
84. Ibid., 1947–48, 56–58.
85. Ibid., 58.
86. Ibid., 1947–48, 59.
87. Ibid., 1948–49, 64.

Chapter 24   The Boundless West

1. William C. Smalley, *Come Wind, Come Weather* (Saint John, 1969), 90–91.
2. Margaret A. Ormsby, *British Columbia: A History* (Toronto, 1964), 442. Cited in Gordon H. Pousett, "A History of the Convention of Baptist Churches of British Columbia," unpublished M.Th. thesis, Vancouver School of Theology, 1982, 201.
3. W. C. Smalley, *Reorganizing for Advance in Western Canada* (Edmonton, c 1938), 4.
4. Pousett, "Convention," 201.
5. Ibid., 202, 204, 218–19.
6. Margaret E. Thompson, *The Baptist Story in Western Canada* (Calgary, 1974), 175.
7. Ibid.
8. W. E. Mann, *Sect, Cult and Church in Alberta* (Toronto, 1955), 33, 31.
9. Ibid., 53.
10. Walter E. Ellis, "Baptist Missions Adaptation to the Western Frontier," in *Canadian Baptist History and Polity*, ed. Murray J. S. Ford (McMaster Divinity College, 1982), 175–76.
11. W. E. Mann, compiler, *Canada: A Sociological Profile* (Toronto, 1968), 358–59. His statistics on the number of Baptist church closures are taken from L. M. Wenham, "The Baptist Home Mission Problem in Western Canada," unpublished B.D. thesis, McMaster University, 1947, 40–41.
12. Walter E. Ellis, "Social and Religious Factors in the Fundamentalist-Modernist Schisms in North America," unpublished Ph.D. thesis, University of Pittsburgh, 1974, 237–38.
13. G. Keith Churchill, "The Educational Policy of the Baptist Union of Western Canada from 1873 to 1975 and Its Implications for the Next Decade," unpublished D.Min. dissertation/project, San Francisco Theological Seminary, 1980, 22.
14. Thompson, *Story*, 430.
15. Churchill, "Educational Policy," 14–15.
16. J. E. Harris, *The Baptist Union of Western Canada, 1873–1973* (Saint John, 1976), 103.
17. C. C. McLaurin, *Pioneering in Western Canada* (Calgary, 1939), 187.
18. Thompson, *Story*, 142.
19. Smalley, *Reorganizing*, 2, 3.
20. Thompson, *Story*, 289.
21. C. H. Schutt and C. J. Cameron, *The Call of Our Own Land* (Toronto, c 1936), 218.
22. Thompson, *Story*, 270.
23. Ibid., 184.
24. Pousett, "Convention," 238.
25. Thompson, *Story*, 184.
26. W. C. Smalley, "Baptist Work in Western Canada," in *Baptist Advance* (Nashville, 1964), 180.
27. *The Western Baptist*, November 1943.
28. Harris, *Baptist Union*, 109.
29. Thompson, *Story*, 187.
30. Ibid., 188.
31. Ibid., 200.
32. Ibid., 204.

33. Mrs. J. R. McDonald, *Baptist Missions in Western Canada, 1873-1948* (Edmonton, 1948), 29.
34. Thompson, *Story*, 205-6.
35. Harris, *Baptist Union*, 117-18.
36. William J. H. Sturhahn, *They Came from East and West* (Winnipeg, 1976), 299. This excellent volume, published by the North American Baptist Immigration and Colonization Society, gives a comprehensive picture of Baptist immigration to Canada from Europe after World War II.
37. Thompson, *Story*, 437.
38. Ibid., 198.

Chapter 25   L'Union d'Églises Baptistes Françaises au Canada
1. Théodore Lafleur, "A Brief Historical Sketch of the Grande Ligne Mission," *Baptist Year Book, Ontario and Quebec, 1900,* 309.
2. Report of the Grande Ligne Mission, BYB, O & Q, 1900, 284-92.
3. H. C. Wilkinson, "Concerning Things Historical," *Canadian Baptist Home Missions Digest* (May 1955): 53-55.
4. Eugene M. Thompson, "The Status of Transcongregational Polity," *Canadian Baptist History and Polity*, ed. Murray J. S. Ford (McMaster Divinity College, 1982), 101.
5. Charles Melvin Foster, "Protestant Evangelism in French Canada," unpublished B.D. thesis, McMaster University, 1950, 63.
6. Report of the Grande Ligne Mission, BYB, O & Q, 1900, 285.
7. BYB, O & Q, 1901, 164.
8. Léonard A. Therrien, "L'histoire des Églises Baptistes Françaises du Canada," in *From Sea to Sea*, ed. Jacqueline M. Norton (Toronto, 1940), 128-29.
9. BYB, O & Q, 1907, 183.
10. Ibid., 1908, 182.
11. Ibid., 1911.
12. W. Nelson Thomson, "Two French-Canadian Baptist pastors, 1821-1920," in *Celebrating the Canadian Baptist Heritage*, eds. Paul R. Dakar and Murray J. S. Ford (Hamilton: McMaster University, 1984), 87-88.
13. BYB, O & Q, 1911, 162.
14. BYB, O & Q, 1908, 180.
15. W. Nelson Thomson, "Witness in French Canada," in *Baptists in Canada: Search for Identity amidst Diversity*, ed. Jarold K. Zeman (Burlington, 1980), 54.
16. Ibid., citing Report of Grande Ligne Mission, 1910, 9.
17. Ibid., 55, citing Mission Report, 1911, 7.
18. Thomson, *Two Pastors*, 86.
19. Thomson, "Witness," 55, citing Mission Report, 1914, 9.
20. Ibid., 55-56.
21. Charles M. Foster, "Quebec: How the Church Grows," *The Canadian Baptist* (June 1980).
22. Thomson, *Two Pastors*, 87.
23. Mrs. Léonard A. Therrien, "The Story." In *Baptist Work in French Canada*, ed. Eugene A. Therrien (Toronto, c 1926), 67.
24. BYB, O & Q, 1917, 195.
25. BYB, O & Q, 1912, 220; 1914, 17; 1915, 19; 1916, 19.
26. BYB, O & Q, 1927, 206.
27. Ibid., 1930, 176.
28. Foster, "Evangelism," 62—63.
29. BYB, O & Q, 1935, 195-96.
30. Maurice C. Boillat, *The Case for French Evangelism* (Halifax, 1960), 2, 3.
31. BYB, O & Q, 1933, np.
32. Thomson, "Witness," 56, citing *Report of the Grande Ligne Mission,* 1937.
33. Foster, "How the Church."
34. BYB, O & Q, 1936, 218.
35. Foster, "Evangelism," 86. Of course, the war can hardly be blamed exclusively for the Mission's setbacks, for many other factors, some described in this chapter, greatly weakened its operations.
36. Ibid., 63.
37. Ibid.
38. BYB, O & Q, 1945-46, 172.
39. Ibid., 1945-46, 179.
40. Ibid., 1946-47, 213.
41. Ibid., 1946-47, 193; 1948-49, 174.
42. Foster, "Evangelism," 64-65.
43. Thomson, "Witness," 56-57.
44. Ibid., 57.
45. Ibid., 64.
46. Foster, "How the Church."
47. Thomson, "Witness," 57.
48. Ibid.
49. Willard Meldrum, "Feller College and the Challenge of the Future," *Canadian Baptist Home Missions Digest* (1963–64): 53.
50. W. Nelson Thomson, "French Canada Today," *Canadian Baptist Home Missions Digest* (1961–62): 78.
51. John S. Gilmour, "Moment of Opportunity," *Baptist Advance*, (Nashville, 1964), 6.
52. Foster, "How the Church."
53. C. M. Foster, "Why an Indigenous French Canadian Church?" *Canadian Baptist Home Missions Digest* (1957): 57.
54. Thomson, "Witness," 58.
55. R. S. Dunn, "A New Day for Grande

Ligne," *Canadian Baptist Home Missions Digest* (1963–64): 44.

56. Thomson, "Witness," 58.
57. Ibid.
58. Dunn, "A New Day," 43.
59. J. S. Gilmour, "Evangelism and Education in French Canada," *Canadian Baptist Home Missions Digest* (1959): 119.
60. J. S. Gilmour, "The Role of Education in Reaching French Canadians for Christ," *Canadian Baptist Home Missions Digest* (1963–64): 49.
61. BYB, O & Q, 1968–69, 88.
62. John Gilmour, "The Harvest Ripens," in *Baptist Canada* (Toronto, 1980), 7.
63. Thomson, "Witness," 59.
64. *French Canada: A Time to Grow* (Montreal, 1986), 4–5.
68. John Gilmour, "Church Planting in Quebec," *The Canadian Baptist* (December 1984).
66. Nelson Thomson, "CETE: The New Influence," *The Canadian Baptist* (November 1984).
67. John Gilmour, "Day One Dawns," *The Canadian Baptist* (February 1987).

Chapter 26   Fellow Baptists

1. Leslie K. Tarr, *This Dominion His Dominion* (Willowdale, 1968), 96.
2. J. H. Watt, *The Fellowship Story: Our First Twenty-Five Years* (Toronto, 1978), 34.
3. Tarr, *Dominion*, 96.
4. Ibid., 156–59.
5. Ibid., 40.
6. Ibid.
7. Ibid., 42.
8. Ibid.
9. Ibid., 107.
10. Ibid., 108.
11. Ibid., 109.
12. Ibid.
13. Ibid., 115–16.
14. John B. Richards, *Baptists in British Columbia: A Struggle to Maintain "Sectarianism"* (Vancouver, 1977), 101.
15. Ibid., 102.
16. Ibid., 104–5, 107.
17. Ibid., 106–7.
18. Ibid., 113.
19. Tarr, *Dominion*, 119.
20. Southern Baptists supporting Landmark principles insist on "strict" (close) communion and re-baptism of those not previously immersed in their churches.
21. Richards, *Baptists in British Columbia*, 114–17.
22. Tarr, *Dominion*, 127.
23. Ibid., 127–28.
24. Watt, *Fellowship Story*, 45–46.

25. Watson Kirkconnell, *The Baptists of Canada: A "Pocket-book" History* (Brantford, nd), 10.
26. Watt, *Fellowship Story*, 88–89.
27. Tarr, *Dominion*, 148.
28. *Western Regular Baptist* (May 1966).
29. Ibid., 150.
30. *Year Book of the Convention of Regular Baptist Churches of British Columbia, 1982.*
31. Watt, *Fellowship Story*, 152–53.
32. Individuals — Minute Men — pledge "on a minute's notice" to give a modest stated amount for a specific church building project, calls being no more frequent than four times a year.
33. Watt, *Fellowship Story*, 55–56.
34. Ibid., 184–87.
35. Ibid., 164.
36. Ibid., 164, 168.
37. Ibid., 172–74, 182.
38. Edward B. Link, "North American (German) Baptists," in *Baptists in Canada: Search for Identity amidst Diversity*, ed. J. K. Zeman (Burlington, 1980), 87.
39. Ibid., 89.
40. E. R. Fitch, ed., *The Baptists of Canada* (Toronto, 1911), 195.
41. Ibid., 329–30.
42. *The Western Baptist* (November 1943).
43. Margaret E. Thompson, *The Baptist Story in Western Canada* (Calgary, 1974), 306–7.
44. Link, "North American," 92.
45. Thompson, *Story*, 312–13.
46. Link, "North American," 95.
47. Ibid.
48. Thompson, *Story*, 321–22.
49. Link, "North American," 96.
50. Martin L. Leuschner, "See His Banners Go!" in *These Glorious Years*, ed. William Kuhn et al. (Cleveland, 1943), 141–52.
51. M. L. Leuschner, "North American Baptist General Conference," in *Baptist Advance* (Nashville, 1964), 239.
52. Link, "North American," 97–98.
53. Ibid., 98–99.
54. William J. H. Sturhahn, *They Came From East and West* (Winnipeg, 1976), 16.
55. Ibid., 65, 299.
56. Mrs. J. R. McDonald, *Baptist Missions in Western Canada 1873–1948* (Edmonton, 1948), 41.
57. Thompson, *Story*, 324.
58. McDonald, *Baptist Missions*, 41.
59. Thompson, *Story*, 326.
60. *The Western Baptist* (November 1943).
61. McDonald, *Baptist Missions*, 42.
62. Thompson, *Story*, 331–32.

63. Richards, *Baptists in British Columbia*, 115.
64. Ibid., 116–17.
65. Annual of the Southern Baptist Convention, 1954, in Robert A. Baker, *A Baptist Source Book* (Nashville, 1966), 191.
66. Ibid., 1958; Ibid., 191–92.
67. Minutes of the Joint Committee, Southern and Canadian Baptists, Edmonton, October 23, 1957.
68. Minutes of the Joint Committee, Southern and Canadian Baptists, Nashville, February 20, 1962.
69. *Christianity Today*, April 6, 1984.
70. Ibid., July 13, 1984.
71. J. K. Zeman, "Baptists in Canada," unpublished monograph, Wolfville, 1981, 10.

Chapter 27 Canadian Baptists Federate

1. Minutes of the Nova Scotia Baptist Association, June 22–24, 1846.
2. Ibid.
3. J. K. Zeman, *Baptist Roots and Identity* (Toronto, 1978), 31.
4. Minutes of the Baptist Missionary Convention of Ontario, 1867, *Canadian Baptist Register for 1868* (Toronto, 1868), 17.
5. Minutes of the Canada Baptist Missionary Convention, East, 1867, *Canadian Baptist Register for 1868*, 49–50.
6. Minutes of Convention of Ontario, 1868. *Register for 1969*, 7–8.
7. Minutes of Convention of Ontario, 1869. *Register for 1870*, 12, 13.
8. Watson Kirkconnell, "Seven Years of Federation: An Evaluation," in Minutes of Council of the Baptist Federation of Canada, October 31–November 2, 1951, 4.
9. *Year Book of the United Baptist Convention of the Maritime Provinces, 1907*, 123–28, 15.
10. Kirkconnell, *Seven Years*, 4.
11. YB, UBCMP, 1909, 113.
12. Ibid., 1910, 135.
13. Walter E. Ellis, "Organizational and Educational Policy of Baptists in Western Canada, 1873–1939," unpublished B.D. thesis, McMaster University, 1962, 29.
14. YB, UBCMP, 1919, 17.
15. Ibid., 1931, 13–14.
16. *Year Book of Baptist Convention of Ontario and Quebec, 1934*, 60, 30.
17. YB, UBCMP, 1942, 164.
18. YB, BCOQ, 1942–43, 165, 36.
19. Report of the All-Canada Committee, 1943–44. YB, BCOQ, 1943–44, 76.
20. *Funk and Wagnalls Standard Dictionary*, 1962.
21. Report of All-Canada Committee, YB, BCOQ, 1943–44, 76.
22. Ibid., 76, 78.
23. Ibid., 78.
24. Minutes of Council of the Baptist Federation of Canada, November 21–23, 1945, 6, 13.
25. Ibid., 9.
26. Ibid.
27. Ibid., 1945, 10.
28. Ibid., 11.
29. Ibid., November 6–8, 1946, 19.
30. Ibid., October 31–November 2, 1951, 19.
31. Minutes of the Assembly of the Baptist Federation of Canada, August 23–26, 1947, 24.
32. Ibid., 25.
33. Minutes of Assembly of BFC, July 15–19, 1950, 13.
34. Minutes of Council of BFC, October 31–November 2, 1951, 7.
35. Ibid.
36. Ibid., July 10–14, 1953, 5, 7.
37. Ibid., December 3–5, 1970, 27–28.
38. Ibid., February 24–26, 1972, 35.
39. Ibid., February 27, 1974, 30.
40. Ibid., November 10–12, 1954, 9–10.
41. Minutes of Assembly of BFC, August 22–25, 1964, 41.
42. Ibid., July 6–9, 1967, 33.
43. Minutes of Council of BFC, February 27, 1974, 24; Assembly, July 8–11, 1976, 17.
44. Report Volume of the BFC, 1967–1970, 29, 30.
45. Minutes of Council of BFC, May 16–17, 1963, 7.
46. Report Volume of Canadian Baptist Federation Assembly, July 25–28, 1985, 44–46.
47. Report Volume of BFC Assembly, July 12–15, 1979, 23.
48. Minutes of the Assembly of BFC, July 5–8, 1962, 41.
49. R. F. Aldwinckle, *A Baptist Response to the Principles of Union* (Brantford, 1970), 7.
50. Minutes of Council of BFC, February 12–14, 1968, 22. Motion passed at that session "that the Council note the role of the Federation as the instrument of the [then] three Conventions."
51. As from the Re-organization Committee of the Baptist Union of Western Canada, 1961. Minutes of BFC Executive, November 22, 1961, 12.
52. Report Volume of BFC Assembly, July 5–8, 1973, 89–95.
53. Ibid., inside front cover.

Chapter 28 The World Vision Widens

1. Mrs. J. R. Mcdonald, *Getting Acquainted with Canadian Baptist Missions in India* (Edmonton, 1946), 10.
2. Orville E. Daniel, *Moving with the Times* (Toronto, 1973), 73.
3. Ibid., 75.
4. Ibid., 73–74.
5. W. Gordon Carder, *Hand to the Indian Plow* (Hyderabad, 1976), 156.
6. Daniel, *Moving*, 59.
7. Ibid., 140.
8. Ibid., 155–56.
9. M. L. Orchard, *Canadian Baptists at Work in India* (Toronto, 1922), 152.
10. Daniel, *Moving*, 48.
11. Ibid., 91.
12. Carder, *Plow*, 158.
13. Ibid., 158–59.
14. Daniel, *Moving*, 107.
15. Report of Canadian Baptist Foreign Mission Board, Year Book of Baptist Union of Western Canada, 1967, 88–89.
16. Ibid., 88.
17. This heading is borrowed from Inez J. Bell, ed., *The Kantuta Blooms in Bolivia* (Toronto, 1971). The Kantuta is the floral emblem of Bolivia. Its three colours of green, gold and red match those of the nation's flag.
18. Norman H. Dabbs, *Dawn over the Bolivian Hills* (Toronto, 1952), 87.
19. Daniel, *Moving*, 76.
20. Bell, *Kantuta*, 87–88.
21. Daniel, *Moving*, 105.
22. Report of CBFMB, YB, BUWC, 1973–74, 128.
23. Daniel, *Moving*, 78.
24. H. S. Hillyer, *Bolivian Mission Jubilee* (Toronto, 1948), 6.
25. Dabbs, *Dawn*, 152.
26. Ibid., 151–53.
27. Ibid., 232.
28. Daniel, *Moving*, 171.
29. Bell, *Kantuta*, 109.
30. Hillyer, *Jubilee*, 8.
31. Bell, *Kantuta*, 98–100.
32. Daniel, *Moving*, 179–80.
33. Report of Canadian Baptist Overseas Mission Board, YB, BUWC, 1980–81, 176.
34. Daniel, *Moving*, 209.
35. Ibid., 211–12.
36. Report CBOMB, *Year Book of United Baptist Convention of the Atlantic Provinces 1963*, 87.
37. Daniel, *Moving*, 264.
38. Ibid., 265.
39. YB of BUWC, 1975–76, 137.
40. Ibid., 1985–86, 153.
41. Ibid., 1972–73, 127.
42. Report of CBOMB, YB, BUWC, 1979–80, 164.
43. Ibid., in Ibid., 1977–78, 164.
44. Ibid., in Ibid., 1986–87, 178.
45. Ibid., in Ibid., 1971–72, 125.
46. Ibid., in Ibid., 1978–79, 174.
47. ibid., in Ibid., 1986–87, 177.
48. Ibid., in Ibid., 1971–72, 120.
49. Ibid., in Ibid., 1977–78, 164.
50. Ibid., in Ibid., 1986–87, 178.
51. Ibid., in Ibid., 1980–81, 177.
52. Ibid., in Ibid., 1986–87, 179.
53. Elmah Baines, "En Route to China — Again," *The Canadian Baptist* (October 1987): 5–6.
54. Report of CBOMB in YB of BUWC, 1984–85, 311.
55. Ibid., in Ibid., 1986–87, 177.
56. Ibid., 304–6.
57. Report of CBOMB, YB, BUWC, 1971–72, 125.

Chapter 29 Women Working

1. E. C. Merrick, *These Impossible Women* (Fredericton, 1970), 13.
2. Jessie Fitch, Ibid.
3. Mary Kinley Ingraham, *Seventy-Five Years* (Kentville, 1946), 17.
4. Ibid., 25–29.
5. Alfreda Hall, *Wheels Begin to Turn* (Toronto, 1976), 3.
6. Mrs. J. T. Booker, "Historical Sketch, Women's Baptist Foreign Missionary Society of Ontario (West)," *Year Book of Baptist Convention of Ontario, 1900*, 201.
7. Nannie E. Green, "Historical Sketch of the Women's Baptist Foreign Missionary Society of Eastern Ontario and Quebec," in YB of BCOQ, 1900, 225.
8. Mrs. H. E. McMaster, "Historical Sketch of the Women's Baptist Home Missionary Society of Western Ontario," in YB of BCOQ, 1900, 126.
9. L. O. Parson, "Historical and Annual Report of the Women's Baptist Home Missionary Society of Eastern Ontario and Quebec," in YB of BCOQ, 1900, 128–29.
10. Margaret E. Thompson, *The Baptist Story in Western Canada* (Calgary, 1974), 271–24.
11. Mrs. C. Spofford, *Sixty Years of Baptist Women's Missionary Activities in British Columbia* (Victoria, 1937), 6–10.
12. Thompson, *Story*, 286–87.
13. J. E. Harris, *The Baptist Union of Western Canada, 1873–1973* (Saint John, 1976), 197–78, 201.
14. M. Allen Gibson, *Along the King's Highway* (Wolfville, 1964), 52–53.

15. Ingraham, *Seventy-Five Years*, 37.
16. Ibid., 40–41.
17. Ibid., 53–54.
18. Hall, *Wheels*, 29.
19. Ibid.
20. Ibid., 30–32.
21. C. C. McLaurin, *Pioneering in Western Canada* (Calgary, 1939), 278, 281–82.
22. Thompson, *Story*, 289.
23. McLaurin, *Pioneering*, 282.
24. Ibid., 285.
25. Hall, *Wheels*, 45–46.
26. Ibid., 47.
27. Ibid., 49–51.
28. Ibid., 83.
29. Ibid., 67–68.
30. Ibid., 90–93, 84.
31. Report of Baptist Women's Missionary Society, YB of BCOQ, 1979–80, 182, 184.
32. Ibid., in Ibid., 1983–84, 166.
33. Merrick, *Impossible*, 73.
34. Minutes of the United Baptist Woman's Missionary Union, *Year Book of the United Baptist Convention of the Maritime Provinces, 1957*, 35.
35. Ibid., *Year Book of the United Baptist Convention of the Atlantic Provinces, 1963*, 36.
36. Report of Women's Missionary Auxiliary, *Year Book of the Baptist Union of Western Canada, 1967*, 143.
37. Report of the Baptist Women of BUWC, YB of BUWC, 1975–76, 181–82.
38. Report of WMA, YB of BUWC, 1967, 144.
39. Report of Baptist Women, YB of BUWC, 1986–87, 212.
40. Report of WMA, YB of BUWC, 1967, 104.
41. YB of BUWC, 1986–87, 212.
42. Ibid., 83–84.

Chapter 30   Assigned in a Secular World

1. Report of Convention Executive, *Year Book of the United Baptist Convention of the Maritime Provinces, 1953*, 202–3.
2. Ibid., in Ibid., 1957, 220–21.
3. Report of Home Mission Board, YB of UBCMP, 1955, 149–50.
4. Ibid., in *Year Book of the United Baptist Convention of the Atlantic Provinces, 1975*, Part 1, 39.
5. Report of Bible School Committee, YB of UBCMP, 1948, 193–94.
6. Report of Directors of United Baptist Bible Training School, YB of UBCMP, 1959, 175.
7. Minutes of Convention Assembly, 1962, YB of UBCMP, 1962, 23.
8. Ibid., 1970, in Ibid., 1970, 26a.
9. Ibid., 1981, in YB of UBCAP, 1981, 90, 131.

10. Report of Atlantic Baptist College, 1986–87, in YB of UBCAP, 1987, 105.
11. Report Board of Governors of Acadia University, YB of UBCMP, 1952, 83.
12. Ibid., in Ibid., 1956, 90.
13. Minutes of Convention Assembly, 1964, in YB of UBCAP, 1964, 16.
14. Ibid., 1965, in Ibid., 1965, 19.
15. *Acadia Bulletin* (September 1965): 4.
16. Report of Acadia Divinity College, 1969, in YB of UBCAP, 1969, 210.
17. Ibid., 1986, in Ibid., 1986, 138.
18. Minutes of Convention Assembly, 1968, in YB of UBCAP, 1968, 19.
19. Report of Atlantic Baptist Senior Citizens Home, Inc., in YB of UBCAP, 1973, Part II, 105.
20. Minutes of Convention Assembly, 1982, in YB of UBCAP, 1983, 132.
21. Ibid., 1984, in Ibid., 1985, 121.
22. Report of Senior Citizens Home, YB of UBCAP, 1987, 121, 123.
23. Report of Convention Executive, in *Year Book of the Baptist Convention of Ontario and Quebec, 1956–57*, 68.
24. *The Canadian Baptist*, July 1, 1949.
25. Report of Convention executive, in YB of BCOQ, 1949–50, 77.
26. Ibid., in Ibid., 1954–85, 73.
27. Minutes of Convention Assembly, YB of BCOQ, 1955–86, 59.
28. J. K. Zeman, "Witness among Immigrants," in *Baptists in Canada: Search for Identity amidst Diversity*, ed. J. K. Zeman (Burlington, 1980), 71.
29. G. Gerald Harrop, "The Baptist Convention of Ontario and Quebec," in *Baptist Advance* (Nashville, 1964), 163.
30. Report of Board of Governors of McMaster University, in YB of BCOQ, 1951–52, 176.
31. Ibid., in Ibid., 1954–55, 186, 195.
32. Ibid., in Ibid., 1955–56, 238, 240.
33. Minutes of Convention Assembly, in YB of BCOQ, 1955–56, 58.
34. Report of Board of Governors, YB of BCOQ, 1956–57, 94, 96.
35. Minutes of Convention Assembly, YB of BCOQ, 1956–57, 40.
36. Report of Board of Governors, YB of BCOQ, 1953–54, 144–46.
37. Minutes of Convention Assembly, YB of BCOQ, 1954–55, 49–50.
38. Ibid., in Ibid., 1953–54, 42.
39. Ibid., 34.
40. Report of Department of Christian Education, YB of BCOQ, 1965–66, 43.
41. Report of Baptist Leadership Education Centre Management Committee, YB of BCOQ, 1983–84, 73.

42. Report of McMaster Divinity College, YB of BCOQ, 1957–58, 131.
43. Ibid., in Ibid., 1977–78, 109.
44. Convention accepted recommendation of its Board of Religious Education to "continue joint enterprise of twenty-one years," in YB of BCOQ, 1957–58, 107.
45. Minutes of Convention Assembly, YB of BCOQ, 1964–65, C1, CX1.
46. All-Canada Baptist Publications Annual Report, 1966, in YB of BCOQ, 1966–67, 44–45.
47. Ibid., in Ibid., 1983–84, 121.
48. Report of Canadian Baptist Federation, YB of UBCAP, 1987, 90.
49. Report of Department of Canadian Missions, in YB of BCOQ, 1983–84, 107.
50. Ibid., 108.
51. Report of Dept. of Christian Education, in YB of BCOQ, 1968–69, 54.
52. Ibid., in Ibid., 1977–78, 77.
53. Ibid., in Ibid., 1983–84, 106.
54. *Atlantic Baptist* (August 1987): 62.
55. J. E. Harris, *The Baptist Union of Western Canada* (Saint John, 1976), 123.
56. Margaret E. Thompson, *The Baptist Story in Western Canada* (Calgary, 1974), 232.
57. New Occasions . . . New Duties for Convention Baptists in Western Canada. Part 1: Organization for Mission; Part 2: Program Implications (Valley Forge, 1965).
58. Minutes of the Assembly, *Year Book of the Baptist Union of Western Canada, 1967*, 36–37.
59. Harris, *Union*, 140–41.
60. Thompson, *Story*, 221.
61. Minutes of the Assembly, 1976, in YB of BUWC, 1975–76, 46.
62. Report of the board, YB of BUWC, 1979–80, 55.
63. Ibid., in Ibid., 1982–83, 75.
64. Ibid., in Ibid., 1986–87, 166.
65. Report of Board of Baptist Men, in YB of BUWC, 1986–87, 83.
66. Report of Board, YB of BUWC, 1980–81, 86–87.
67. Ibid., in Ibid., 1986–87, 92.
68. Minutes of Assembly, YB of BUWC, 1979–80, 36.
69. G. Keith Churchill, "The Educational Policy of the Baptist Union of Western Canada," in *Canadian Baptist History and Polity*, ed. Murray J. S. Ford (McMaster Divinity College, 1982), 81.
70. Report of the Board, YB of BUWC, 1968–69, 46.
71. Minutes of Assembly, YB of BUWC, 1974–75, 37.
72. Report of the board, YB of BUWC, 1975–76, 91.
73. Minutes of Assembly, YB of BUWC, 1978–79, 41–42, 133.
74. Ibid., in Ibid., 1979–80, 36–37.
75. Report of the Principal of Carey Hall, YB of BUWC, 1986–87, 125.
76. Minutes of Assembly, YB of BUWC, 1985–86, 33.
77. Minutes of Assembly and Task Force, in YB of BUWC, 1986–87, 41 and 108–9.
78. YB of UBCAP, 1987, S156–57.
79. *Baptist Advance*, 162; YB of BCOQ, 1986–87, 279.
80. Thompson, *Story*, 119; YB of BUWC, 1986–87, 243.
81. Reginald W. Bibby, *Fragmented Gods* (Toronto, 1987).
82. Ibid., 47.
83. Ibid., 11.
84. Ibid., 233.
85. George A. Rawlyk, "McMaster University: A Search for Christian Higher Education," Hayward Lecture, Acadia University, 1987.
86. Henry Cook, *Speak That They Go Forward* (London, 1946).
87. William Hordern, *New Directions in Theology Today*, vol. 1 (Philadelphia, 1966). Cited in Bibby, *Fragmented Gods*, 165.
88. Luke 19:13 KJV.

INDEX

Nova Scotia Baptist Education Society, 112, 113, 114, 116, 118, 146
Nova Scotia, Colony of, 25, 26, 27
Nutt, Samuel, 128
Nutting, J. W., 111, 112, 113, 117

O
Okanagan College, 214, 224
Old Light, 10, 14, 19, 24
Oliver, William P., 151
Olivier, Henri, 133
Olmstead, Stephen, 72, 76, 77
Onslow, 36
Open communion, 60, 203, 209
Operation Eyesight, 324
(L')Oratoire, 141, 270
Orchard, M. L., 257
Ordination, 61, 62, 209, 252
Oriyas, 197, 198, 304, 305
Oruro, 198, 199, 306, 308
Osgood, 99
Ottawa, 74, 249
Ottawa Association, 94, 95, 96, 97, 100, 102, 119, 136, 138
Ottawa Valley, 72, 77, 93, 99, 101, 132, 142, 267
Overseas Missions (earlier "Foreign"), 62, 85, 86, 151ff, 163ff, 188, 192ff, 303ff
Oxford, 64, 66, 72, 76, 124, 125

P
Padlock Law, 271
Painter, Thomas, 8
Papineau, Louis Joseph, 92, 137
Parent, M. B., 268
Paris, Treaty of, 12, 25, 132
Parker, N. H., 333
Parrsboro. See Saint John
Particular Baptists, 5, 16, 122
Patch, J. Frank, 337
Patterson, F. W., 225, 242
Paul, Elbert, 295
Payzant, G. P., 210
Payzant, John, 18, 21, 27, 34, 35, 36, 37, 51, 52, 53, 54
Peace movements, 242, 244, 253, 262
Peniel Hall Farm, 307
Pennington, W. E., 128
People's Republic of China, 314
Percy, 64, 67
Perkins, Barnabas, 71
Perth, 128
Perthshire, 72, 80
Petereit, F. A., 188, 285, 318
Phaelmann, C., 188
Philadelphia Baptist Association, 9
Philipsville. See Oxford
Phillips, David and Catherine, 314
Pictou Academy, 110, 115
Pictou County, 24
Pierson, Nicholas, 21, 31, 34, 37

Pilgrim Fathers, 6
Pithapuram, 196, 304
Planters, 14, 15, 19, 21, 28
Plymouth Colony, 6
Poehlmann, C., 285
Polish. See New Canadians
Portage-la-Prairie, 173, 174, 176
Port Rowan, 94
Port Royal. See Annapolis
Port Work, 297
Pousett, Gordon H., 258
Prairie associations, 261
Prairie College, 177, 178, 213
Pre-Loyalists. See Planters
Presbyterians, 23, 24, 43, 44, 83, 104, 105, 110, 170, 176, 177, 205, 236, 259
Preston, 79, 151
Preston, Richard, 151
Priesthood of belivers, 341
Primitive Baptists, 207, 290
Prince Edward Island, 13, 24, 28, 80, 316, 329
Prohibition. See Temperance
Providence, Rhode Island, 7, 8
Pryor, John, 115, 116
Public education, 107, 108, 118, 205
Publications, 162
Pubnico, 126
Puget Sound Association, 181, 182
Puritanism, 4, 5, 6, 7, 50

Q
Quarterly meetings/District meetings, 124, 127
Quebec Act, 41
Quebec City, 142, 143, 297
Queen's College. See Acadia College
Queenston. See Niagara
Quiet Revolution, Quebec, 142, 273

R
Radio, 308, 309
Ragged Island, 33, 60, 61
Rand, Silas Tertius, 149, 153
Rand, Theodore Harding, 119, 161
Randall, Benjamin, 122, 123, 130
Rapid City, 177, 178, 213
Ratcliffe, Philip, 7
Rauschenbusch, August, 204, 285
Rawdon, 64, 67
Rawlyk, George A., 27, 61, 341
Rebellion of 1837, 92, 104, 135, 137
Red River Association, 176, 177, 186
Reed, Joseph, 16, 17
Reekie, Archibald, B., 198, 199, 200, 306, 307
Rees, William, 96, 97, 98, 119
Reformed Baptists. See Wesleyans
Reformers, 2, 4
Reform Party, 95, 116, 117
Regent College, 338, 339